MANAG

MANAGING URBAN AMERICA

SEVENTH EDITION

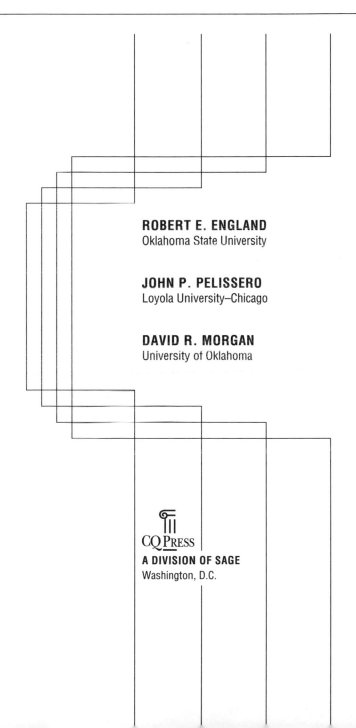

ROBERT E. ENGLAND
Oklahoma State University

JOHN P. PELISSERO
Loyola University–Chicago

DAVID R. MORGAN
University of Oklahoma

CQ PRESS
A DIVISION OF SAGE
Washington, D.C.

CQ Press
2300 N Street, NW, Suite 800
Washington, DC 20037

Phone: 202-729-1900; toll-free, 1-866-4CQ-PRESS (1-866-427-7737)

Web: www.cqpress.com

Cover design: McGaughy Design
Cover photo: Photos.com
Composition: Hurix Systems

⊗ The paper used in this publication exceeds the requirements of the American National Standard for Information Sciences--Permanence of Paper for Printed Library Materials, ANSI Z39.48-1992.

Printed and bound in the United States of America

15   14   13   12   11   1   2   3   4   5

LIBRARY OF CONGRESS CATALOGING-IN-PUBLICATION DATA

England, Robert E.
   Managing urban America / Robert E. England, John P. Pelissero,
   David R. Morgan. —7th ed.
      p. cm.
   David R. Morgan listed first on 6th ed.
   Includes bibliographical references and index.
   ISBN 978-1-60871-672-2 (pbk. : alk. paper)
   1. Municipal government—United States. I. Pelissero, John P. II.
   Morgan, David R. III. Morgan, David R. Managing urban America.
   IV. Title.

JS331.M668 2012
352.140973—dc22

                                            2010052879

To DIAN R. ENGLAND, *my spouse, who has devoted her life to helping others,* ERIC R. ENGLAND, *my son, who also has chosen to be a professor as his career path, and to my five adopted brothers (in chronological descending order by age),* LAWNIE PORTER, BILLY CLEARY, BILL PESSEMIER, CHRIS NEAL, *and* VINCENT BURKE.—R.E.E.

To my wife, PAULA PELISSERO *and my children,* CAROLYN PELISSERO *and* STEVEN PELISSERO—*all are successful managers in their own careers and my best supporters. They make me very proud.*—J.P.P.

To PROFESSOR CAROLYN STOUT MORGAN, *my wife, whose humor, thoughtfulness, and support have sustained me throughout my academic career. I can never thank her enough.*—D.R.M.

CONTENTS

TABLES, FIGURES, AND BOXES

POLICY AND PRACTICE BOXES ─────────────────────────────

PREFACE

Wow, where has the time gone? Three decades have passed since publication of the first edition of *Managing Urban America* in 1979. David R. Morgan was the sole author of the first three editions of this text. Dave asked me to be a coauthor beginning with the fourth edition. We were fortunate when John P. Pelissero agreed to join the team with the sixth edition. David is now professor emeritus of the Department of Political Science, University of Oklahoma. John and I were *privileged* to be Dave's students. He mentored us, and many other young men and women during his long tenure at OU, with an eye toward *our* future. He instilled in us his work ethic, his sense of moral responsibility, and his compassion for urban politics and management. In every respect this book remains Dave's; John and I are honored to update it occasionally.

The seventh edition builds on previous versions; new literature is added, statistics (where possible) are updated, and many of the case studies are new. With the seventh edition we begin a new tradition of adding a global or international flavor to the text. We include several case studies that examine cities around the world. Finally, in this edition we argue that administrative reforms of the past two decades were just that, reforms. The discipline of public administration is better for Reinventing Government and the New Public Management perspectives, but it is certainly time to move beyond discussions about which *model* is the best and carry on with the work of Dwight Waldo, Mary Parker Follett, Frederick Mosher, Peter Drucker, and the many other men and women who built our discipline on a firm foundation. As Janet V. Denhardt and Robert B. Denhardt remind us, *"Public servants do not deliver customer service; they deliver democracy."* [1]

This book is intended to provide a reasonably comprehensive overview of urban management, including the environmental context, political structures, service delivery, organization theory, and management processes. To our knowledge, no other urban politics/administration text grounds students in management literature as this one does, although a number of excellent urban politics texts are available. The thesis of our book remains unchanged: that one can be an excellent administrator and still fail in urban management.

---

[1] Janet V. Denhardt and Robert B. Denhardt, *The New Public Service: Serving, Not Steering,* expanded edition (Armonk, N.Y.: M. E. Sharpe, 2007).

Without a thorough understanding of the "politics" of city administration, city leaders are destined to bail water with a broken bucket.

Beyond the obvious applications of this text in undergraduate and graduate courses, we suggest that it could also be used as the primary text for an introduction to public administration course, with the emphasis and examples shifted from the federal level to the local arena, where most government takes place. Indeed, the title of this book could just as easily be *Public Administration at the Local Level*.

As in all previous versions, this edition makes ample use of case studies—now called "Policy and Practice" boxes—to illustrate the nexus of theory and practice. We have found that students, particularly undergraduates, find case studies useful in providing a bridge to the "real world" of city government. In-service students often provide "me too" experiences after reading various cases.

A large number of people deserve special thanks for their assistance in this and previous versions. Since the list has grown long over seven editions, we say "thank you" to all who have given so generously of your time. You know who you are and how much we appreciate your help. We were late in delivering the seventh edition to our editor Charisse Kiino. She displayed her usual calm and poise, but firmly asked that we get busy. We thank Charisse for not giving up on us. Anna Socrates did an outstanding job as copyeditor; the narrative is much improved after her careful review. At CQ Press, Nancy Loh helped us with permissions, and Belinda Josey served admirably as our production editor. We are grateful that Barbara Johnson and Julia Petrakis provided their expertise in proofreading and indexing, respectively. Finally, we would like to thank the professors who reviewed the manuscript and provided invaluable feedback: Hyunsun Choi, University of North Florida; Michael S. Givel, University of Oklahoma; Marcia L. Godwin, University of La Verne; Myron A. Levine, Wright State University; and Steve Modlin, East Carolina University.

In the final analysis, we wish we could blame someone else for any omissions or commissions of error, but we cannot. The buck stops here. Therefore, please send your e-mails with any questions or comments to me at (bob.england@okstate.edu).

Robert E. England
September 2010

ABOUT THE AUTHORS

Robert E. England is professor of political science at Oklahoma State University. He most enjoys the time he spends with his family and friends.

John P. Pelissero is professor of political science and provost at Loyola University–Chicago. He is the editor of *Cities, Politics, and Policy: A Comparative Analysis* (CQ Press, 2003). His most recent research on cities has appeared in *Public Administration Review* and *Urban Affairs Review*.

David R. Morgan is professor emeritus at the University of Oklahoma, where he was the Henry Bellmon Chair of Public Service and professor of political science. He spent five years in local government, including service as the first city manager of Yukon, Oklahoma.

MANAGING URBAN AMERICA

CHAPTER 1

MANAGING AMERICAN CITIES
IN THE TWENTY-FIRST CENTURY

INTRODUCTION: AMERICAN CITIES CONTINUE TO CHANGE AND EVOLVE

The seventh edition of *Managing Urban America* finds city governments changing and evolving, just as they have been doing since the first edition of this textbook appeared over three decades ago. A decade into the twenty-first century, cities face many of the same challenges they have confronted since the so-called urban crisis of the 1960s: *managing* conflict through politics; *adapting* to environmental influences such as population shifts and changing citizen tastes and preferences; *incorporating* new groups into governing structures; *balancing* own-source funds with intergovernmental revenues; *responding* to federal and state mandates; *negotiating* with other local governments; *delivering* a myriad of local goods and services to the populace; and *seeking* approaches to managing cities that are efficient, effective, equitable, and responsive.

But urban managers at the dawn of the new century are also confronting new issues and challenges. Unlike the situation in the 1960s, cities now operate largely in an intergovernmental milieu best described as "fend for yourself" federalism.[1] Outside of current government economic stimulus programs, the federal government today is less likely to offer financial help to local governments to balance budgets or deliver goods and services. Increasingly, city executives must be innovative and entrepreneurial to find ways to do more with less. Such productivity enhancement requires broad new approaches to running urban America that emphasize *results, performance*, and *accountability* in the day-to-day management of human and fiscal resources, information and technology (IT), and services. Among the new phrases added to the vernacular of urban management in the past two decades, "reinventing government" (REGO) and the "New Public Management" (NPM) have been used as managerial strategies by municipal officials to augment traditional administrative processes to enhance municipal productivity.

Changes in technology have brought other new challenges to twenty-first-century cities. Major transformations have occurred since the 1960s in management information systems (MIS) and geographic information systems (GIS). In many American cities, these two systems—operating either individually or in an integrated framework—result in more efficient payroll and bill processing, dispatching of emergency personnel, and/or infrastructure repair. Personal computers have changed forever the nature of day-to-day work at the local level. Computer hardware and software, for example, allow for more efficient and effective financial administration, computer-based testing in human resources (HR) departments, reliable and efficient storage and transfer of data, and communication with the public.

The technology of the Internet has transformed the modern city into a global community. In addition to the official web pages that most cities maintain, a wealth of governmental, social, economic, business, demographic, and cultural information about almost any city can be retrieved from other Internet sources. This information is available not only to a city's own residents but also to anyone in the world, twenty-four hours a day. Indeed, today technology links every city to every other city on the globe; all that is needed to secure or exchange information is access to the World Wide Web. The Internet also allows for e-government—electronic government. The "electronic village"[2] allows city employees to communicate with each other and citizens to contact their city's political and administrative officials via e-mail. The impact of the Internet on city management is still in its infancy. Local officials are expending much effort to harness and *manage* the power of this technology!

This opening chapter, which is divided into five parts, provides a context for understanding the remaining chapters in *Managing Urban America*. First, we discuss how and why American cities have changed since the 1960s, focusing primarily on financial, social, and demographic changes. Second, we offer an analysis of how cities have responded to these changes by improving their management capacity. The third section of the chapter, in essence, places the entire topic of urban management within the framework of systems analysis: after introducing and explaining the basic concepts of systems theory—which suggests that city officials make public policies in response to environmental stimuli—we focus on the impact of citizen participation and e-government as examples of significant environmental factors that impinge on the management of modern cities. In the next section, we argue that "good management" skills alone are simply not enough to equip the contemporary city executive with the know-how to be successful; an effective city executive also needs to understand the nature of community values, bureaucratic inertia, politics, and leadership. The chapter concludes with an overview of the book's organization.

HOW AND WHY AMERICAN CITIES HAVE CHANGED

City governments today grapple with a host of pressures and conflicts. Even in smaller communities, urban managers must constantly respond to the demands of the groups, institutions, and governmental entities that constitute the external world of the urban polity. These political pressures do not materialize out of thin air: competing and conflicting demands on urban government emerge from the racial, ethnic, social, economic, and governmental diversity that is so characteristic of urban America. To perform effectively, an urban manager must comprehend and come to terms with the often turbulent environment created by these outside forces. Learning to negotiate, to bargain, to persuade, and to compromise may thus be as crucial to a manager's success as is the exercise of traditional administrative skills. In this section, we study the economic and social milieu in which urban managers must operate.

THE STATE OF AMERICAN CITIES: FISCAL AFFAIRS

In the midst of President John F. Kennedy's "New Frontier" and President Lyndon B. Johnson's "War on Poverty" in the 1960s, practitioners and students of urban politics alike assumed that city governments would continue to grow, if not prosper. After all, state and local government payrolls were expanding enormously during the 1960s—and they continued to do so during the 1970s—much faster than those at the federal level. Cities were doing more than ever, responding to new needs and demands. Keith Mulrooney, a former city manager of Claremont, California, describes his activities in the late 1960s:

> Confronting antiwar demonstrators, holding council meetings in Chicano houses, sitting with hippies in a park discussing last week's narcotics bust, bargaining against a labor pro, or contracting with the Black Students Union to conduct reading improvement programs for low achieving black school children.[3]

These challenges of city management in the 1960s represented a significant departure from the issues faced in previous eras, such as building city infrastructures and developing a science of administration that would allow government employees to manage cities efficiently. "The shift in . . . priorities . . . [was] from the physically oriented to the human oriented."[4]

Along with these new problems came lots of federal dollars and a sharp increase in municipal employment and programs. Between 1960 and 1980, for example, the number of federal grant-in-aid programs grew from 132 to well over 500, and there was a corresponding growth in funding, from $7 billion to $91.5 billion.[5] In some communities, local officials developed new programs solely to draw federal dollars; further expansion seemed inevitable. A 1979 report from the International City/County Management Association (ICMA), for instance, suggested that the inevitability of growth was so widely accepted that it functioned as fact.[6] This pervasive view of local government called for growth in every imaginable area: urban populations would grow, budgets would expand, federal grants would increase, municipal jobs would multiply, and benefits would rise as cities were forced to undertake an ever-longer list of responsibilities.

But things do change. Due to an ailing economy in the late 1970s, federal aid to cities began to shrink under the Jimmy Carter administration. Then came the "Reagan Revolution," which brought major reductions in federal domestic spending, including additional cuts in financial assistance to state and local governments (see chapter 2). In 1978 cities had received almost 16 percent of their revenue from federal sources; by FY 1990–1991 the figure was 3.6 percent.[7] Today, the nation's thirty-five largest cities—arguably the cities with the greatest need—receive slightly more than 10 percent of their total general revenue from the federal government.[8]

As holding the line—and, yes, retrenchment—became the order of the day in the 1970s, cities showed more resilience than pessimists thought they would. Cuts were made, budgets were balanced, and taxes were raised in a number of communities. Cities learned to manage with less and emerged from this period of fiscal crisis stronger and more independent than ever. To the extent that they did so, a great deal of credit must go to the tough-minded city officials who made hard choices. Also, state governments proved to be thoughtful parents of their legal offspring, providing much-needed relief, both programmatically and fiscally.

Fiscal conditions improved for many cities in the 1990s, thanks in large part to record growth in the nation's economy under the Bill Clinton administration. By the late 1990s, some cities had escaped the fiscal morass they had experienced just a decade or so previously. For example, in a report, entitled *The State of America's Cities, 1998*, the U.S. Department of Housing and Urban Development (HUD) noted, "Driven by a robust national economy, cities are fiscally and economically the strongest they've been in a decade."[9] The report went on to note that the number of jobs was growing and unemployment was falling in central cities. Cities were improving as places to live; many downtowns experienced a renaissance as centers of tourism, sports, entertainment, and the arts. Crime continued to decline, and home ownership in central cities was on the rise. Similar good news was reported in 1997 in the National League of Cities' *The State of America's Cities: The Thirteenth Annual Opinion Survey of Municipal Elected Officials*.[10] America's elected municipal officials reported steady improvements in city finances and local economies. The overall assessment of the state of American cities was "more positive and optimistic than it has been in quite some time." Then the prosperity bubble burst.

After the new millennium brought the Al-Qaeda backed terrorist attacks in New York City on September 11, 2001, the George W. Bush administration's War on Terrorism resulted in significant American involvement in protracted wars in Afghanistan and Iraq, and a global financial meltdown starting in 2007. As newly elected Barack Obama assumed the presidency in January 2009, he inherited a deeply troubled national economy. Before leaving office, President George W. Bush had asked Congress to pass the Emergency Economic Stabilization Act; in October 2008 lawmakers provided up to 700 billion dollars to bolster the U.S. financial system. Quickly after entering office, President Obama asked Congress to pass a similar bill to stimulate the national economy. Once again, Congress responded quickly. In February 2009, The American Recovery and Reinvestment Act provided almost 800 billion dollars to expand unemployment benefits; fund federal tax cuts; and provide additional money for social, education, health care, and infrastructure programs. Eighteen months into the Obama administration, albeit improved, the U.S. economy has not recovered.

Today, more than ever, cities exist in an era of "fend for yourself" federalism, and this time state governments are not able to help cities to the extent they did in previous decades.

State governments, simply put, are also struggling to balance their budgets. Writing in December 2009, Christopher Hoene, director of the Center for Research and Innovation at the National League of Cities, notes that experts estimate "state government gaps of $190 billion for 2010, $180 billion for 2011 and $118 billion for 2012. The 2010 gap, alone, comprises 28 percent of state budgets for that year."[11] State governments will surely respond to their own budget shortfalls, as they have in the past, by making cuts in money transfers to local governments. As Hoene explains, a conservative 10 percent cut per year from 2010–2012 equals a $21 billion cut in state funds to municipal governments. A 15 percent cut, which is the more likely scenario, represents a loss of 30 billion state dollars to city governments.

In the same article, Hoene provides the following projections about the impact of the current recession on municipal budgets.

- The municipal sector will likely face a fiscal shortfall of between $56 and $83 billion from 2010–2012, driven by declining tax revenues, ongoing service demands, and cuts in state revenues;
- The low point for city fiscal conditions typically follows the low point of an economic downturn by at least two years, indicating that the low point for cities will come sometime in 2011; and
- City leaders are responding with layoffs, furloughs, and payroll reductions; delaying and canceling capital infrastructure projects; and cutting city services.[12]

Examples of local responses to fiscal stress include: Baltimore's $127 million shortfall will result in more layoffs after the elimination of approximately 500 positions; a $130 million decline in Boston has resulted in the loss of 500 municipal employees; Cleveland officials estimate a $23 million shortfall, and that for every $1 million in lost revenue, 20 general city employees or 12 police and firefighters will need to be laid off; and the City of Seattle met its $72 million budget shortfall by eliminating 310 positions and using most of its "rainy day" fund—$25.4 million of $30.6 million.[13]

Cities cannot expect to return anytime soon to the good old days of growth and revenue expansion of the 1960s, early 1970s, and most of the 1990s. Given the current state of the national and global economy most cities, like the federal and state governments, face hard budgetary choices. Until the worst economic downturn since the Great Depression improves, as it surely will, municipal officials must do more with less. Now more than ever, improved municipal management is a necessity. Managing with less demands more dedicated, competent, and politically astute municipal managers. In the broadest sense, that is what this book is all about—improving the management of city governments, from both a technical and a political perspective. In addition to their fiscal concerns, municipal executives must be sensitive to demographic and social changes in local populations. As the urban place changes, so do values, expectations, demands, and economic bases.

THE STATE OF AMERICAN CITIES: SOCIAL AND DEMOGRAPHIC CONDITIONS

In many of America's big cities, the outward movement of people and jobs continued throughout the 1990s.[14] These cities not only lost productive citizens and desirable employers, but also saw their tax bases shrink. Many of the residents who remain need special services. Poverty remains high in many inner-city neighborhoods, where employment opportunities are limited for low-skilled workers. Dependency persists, as welfare rolls remain concentrated in large central cities. So the service needs endure, but resources are often scarce.

Social and Demographic Changes

One of the major demographic trends affecting American cities is the deconcentration of the central city. U.S. cities, in fact, have been decentralizing for many years. The year 1970 marked the first time that more people lived in the suburban rings of metropolitan areas than anywhere else in the country. Suburbia, despite some valid criticisms, does offer open space, cleaner air, better schools, and, above all, a chance for home ownership. Polls show that all groups, regardless of age, class, race, or geographic location, prefer either suburban or small-town living. And the positive pull of suburbia is not the only factor involved, for, in many places, the central city exerts a negative push. As former mayor Michael R. White of Cleveland once noted, people leave to escape crime, congestion, deteriorating housing, poor services, inferior schools, and, in some cases, minority neighborhoods.[15] Of course, not everyone can escape: essentially, the white and the well-to-do have dominated the outward flow, while racial minorities, the poor, the unskilled, the uneducated, and the elderly are left behind.

What are conditions like today in large cities? Two recent studies by the Brookings Institution highlight some of the social and demographic changes taking place in big cities and suburbs. The first study, focusing on racial change in the nation's one hundred largest cities between 1990 and 2000, finds that America's big cities continue to grow more diverse.[16] Between 1990 and 2000, for example, the one hundred largest U.S. cities lost 8.5 percent of their white residents, or 2.3 million people. In these big cities, whites now represent a minority, 44 percent of the total population; the comparable figure in 1990 was 52 percent. In eighteen cities—Anaheim, Riverside, (Calif.) Milwaukee, Rochester, Sacramento, Ft. Worth, Augusta/Richmond (Va.), Philadelphia, Boston, San Diego, Mobile, Montgomery, Columbus, Norfolk (Va.), Albuquerque, Baton Rouge, Shreveport, and St. Louis—whites dropped from a majority to a minority of the population. Seventy-one of the one hundred cities lost at least 2 percent of their white population during the decade; in twenty cities, the decline of the white population was greater than 20 percent. Detroit lost the greatest number of white residents (53 percent), followed by Birmingham (40 percent), and Santa Ana, California (38 percent).

Among minority groups, the Hispanic population grew the most during the 1990s. The nation's one hundred largest cities gained 3.8 million new Hispanics (a 43 percent increase). Slightly over a million Asians (a 38 percent growth rate) moved into these cities between

1990 and 2000, while the black population grew by only 6 percent, or about 816,000 new residents. Over that decade, the Hispanic share of the population increased from 17 to 23 percent, as the black and Asian populations remained fairly stable, at 24.1 percent and 6.6 percent, respectively.

This first Brookings Institution study concludes that changes in the racial composition of big cities have social, economic, and political implications. For example, big cities experience overall population growth when all their racial and ethnic groups grow in size. In the twenty cities that grew the fastest, the white population grew by 5 percent, blacks increased by 23 percent, the Asian population enlarged by 69 percent, and the number of Hispanics rose by 72 percent. Thus, the study says, "Cities hoping to achieve real growth need to provide a living environment that is attractive to families of varying race and ethnicity."[17] Another of the study's implications concerns the service needs of particular groups: "Cities must consider how the structure and delivery of health care, public education and general city services should be adapted to the needs of the changing populations."[18] In Aurora, Colorado, for example, the Hispanic population increased by 271 percent during the 1990s—at the beginning of the decade, one of every fifteen residents was Hispanic; by its end, one in five was Hispanic.

Changing demographics also influence the wealth of the city. The Brookings Institution report notes that census estimates suggest that in 1999 the median household income for Hispanics was $14,000 lower than that for non-Hispanic white households. A growing Hispanic population coupled with a declining white population may, therefore, create real fiscal impacts on cities. On the other hand, an overall increase in a city's population "could increase the total amount of income in cities."[19] Public policymakers must understand, analyze, and manage these competing effects.

Finally, a growing minority presence in big cities means that the electoral base for minority candidates is growing: these increasing numbers may result in the election of more minority mayors, city council members, and school board members. We discuss the implications of minority representation on local policy in chapter 3.

Bruce Katz, director of the Brookings Institution's Metropolitan Policy Program, prepared a second study that focuses on demographic changes in American cities. In a 2005 speech, he highlighted these recent trends in metropolitan areas:

- Suburbs grew faster than cities. Between 1990 and 2000, the one hundred largest U.S. cities grew by 8.8 percent, while their suburban populations increased by 17 percent. The faster growth in the suburbs occurred in all types of households— married with no children, married with children, other family—no children, nonfamily.
- Racial and ethnic group shares of suburban populations increased. Between 1990 and 2000, the African American share of the suburban population rose from 33 to 39 percent; the Asian population living in the suburbs increased from 51 to 55 percent; and the Hispanic population grew from 46 percent to 50 percent. The rate of change for all these minority groups was much greater in the suburbs than

in the cities. Over this same decade, the black population in central cities rose by 5 percent; but the increase in the suburbs was 36.1 percent. The growth rates for Hispanics were 46.2 percent in central cities and 71.9 percent in suburbs. Finally, the Asian population grew by 37.3 percent in central cities, compared to 63.4 percent in the suburbs. Today, 27 percent (about one in four) of all suburban households are minority.

- Educational attainment varies widely across U.S. cities and by race within the cities. In the nation's one hundred largest cities, 10 percent of Hispanics, 14 percent of blacks, 37 percent of whites, and 39 percent of Asians hold bachelor's degrees.

- The *absolute number* of people living in poverty in U.S. metropolitan areas increased from 19.3 million in 1980 to 23.1 million in 1990 to 25.8 million in 2000. The poverty rate in central cities fell from 19 percent to 17 percent between 1990 and 2002, while the poverty rate in suburbs increased slightly, from 9 percent to about 9.1 percent. In fact, the number of suburban residents living in poor suburbs—measured as suburbs in which the per capita income is less than 75 percent of that for its metropolitan area—increased from 8.4 percent in 1980 to 18.1 percent in 2000.[20]

How are cities coping with problems associated with social, economic, and demographic changes? In particular, how is all this affecting their management practices?

Social Change and City Management

Municipalities always have provided extensive local services. Since the turmoil of the 1960s, however, city governments have found it necessary to pay special attention to human problems. This concern for the disadvantaged undoubtedly has contributed to the fiscal squeeze faced by so many large cities. As cities took on new commitments, their spending increased at unprecedented rates. Much of this new money came from the federal government, as an outgrowth of the War on Poverty, Model Cities, Head Start, the Comprehensive Employment and Training Act (CETA), Urban Development Action Grants, Community Development Block Grants, and other programs. In many large cities whose changing demographic and social complexion had created an unprecedented need for social services to aid the elderly, the poor, and the disadvantaged, these programs were lifesavers. But, as we explain in more detail in the next chapter, as the federal government cut domestic spending in the 1980s, many of these urban programs were eliminated, reduced substantially, or delivered in new ways. Cities had to search for less traditional methods of handling urban problems. Recent literature is full of discussions about ways to hold down costs by turning to alternative sources of urban services. Many see *contracting out* to the private sector as an especially promising option. Others urge greater cooperation between the public and private sectors. As a community struggles with serious financial difficulties, the private sector may be able to provide assistance and resources that normally would not be available to local government. Managing the politics of scarcity is no easy task.

As cities hold the line and try to get by on less, they face new political pressures. As long as the municipal treasury is expanding, everyone has hopes of getting more. But as the pie shrinks, the competition among groups to keep their share grows intense. Over time, it becomes difficult to obscure who is winning and who is losing: without growth it is harder to buy off the losers.[21] Fiscal stress produces dissatisfaction among interest groups, service recipients, and, not least, public employees. And this means disenchantment with elected officials and their appointees that voters do not forget at the polls.[22] Perhaps it is the fear of adverse public reaction (if not the loss of their jobs) that leads many local officials to embrace short-term solutions to their problems. For example, cutting the capital budget has been a favorite strategy—one that is now beginning to hurt. Evidence is mounting that the public infrastructure of our older cities and counties is deteriorating at an alarming rate because of deferred maintenance—inadequate expenditures for capital improvements. Another strategy, holding down personnel costs, has led many of the best-qualified and most highly motivated municipal employees to seek work elsewhere. This exodus may result in a long-term decline in management capacity.

Faced with financial constraints, urban public leadership must choose among several options: raise revenue by increasing taxes or fees, cut costs and services, and/or improve operating productivity. There is little popular support for tax-based revenue schemes, however, and although popular pressure is likely to keep costs down, the public does not want services cut. In fact, most people want more and better services. Obviously, urban administrators have little choice, and they must increase productivity.

Beginning in the early 1990s some observers argued that productivity enhancement was not enough to "fix" the problems that plagued governments at all levels—federal, state, and local. Instead, the tough and critical problems facing modern governments require *fundamental* changes in the way cities are governed and managed. One prescription for change was offered by journalist David Osborne and former city manager Ted Gaebler. The two used the label "reinventing government" to describe their pragmatic approach to "curing" the problems of government. As the following section details, reinventing government and its academic counterpart, the New Public Management (NPM), stimulated an intense debate within political science about the proper role of government in contemporary society. Nearly two decades later this controversy has been largely resolved, with a resulting model of modern public management[23] that integrates in a productive way the strengths of traditional administrative processes and the calls for reform.

HOW CITIES HAVE IMPROVED THEIR MANAGEMENT CAPACITY

REINVENTING GOVERNMENT: A PRAGMATIC RESPONSE TO FISCAL CRISIS

Osborne and Gaebler's book, *Reinventing Government: How the Entrepreneurial Spirit Is Transforming the Public Sector*, made a big splash when it was released in 1992.[24] The success of the book was somewhat surprising, since the volume offered very little new in the way of management theory or practice. But, as the authors note in the preface,

"We . . . are not inventing new ideas so much as *synthesizing the ideas and experiences of others*" (emphasis added).[25] And therein lay the success of the book. *Reinventing Government* is a classic example of being "in the right place at the right time," as Osborne and Gaebler were able to integrate the work of numerous academic theories (ideas) in a format that was easy to read, easy to understand, and easy to believe in (who among us likes big wasteful government?).

Moreover, the underlying theme of the book—that government should "steer more and row less"—fit the post-Keynesian, neoconservative mood of the nation. REGO offered federal, state, and local officials a managerial strategy for addressing in a practical fashion fiscal stress, retrenchment, and/or productivity enhancement. President Bill Clinton and Vice President Al Gore, for example, rode the reinventing government bandwagon for eight years and, with the help of Congress, produced in 1998 the first balanced federal budget since 1969 (including a $69 billion surplus, which was followed by a $124 billion surplus in 1999).[26] Similarly, state and local officials used Osborne and Gaebler's principles of REGO to help address their fiscal woes. REGO offers a "prescription" to frontline public officials (elected, appointed, and administrative) on how to manage public resources more efficiently, effectively, and responsively in an environment defined by high citizen expectations and declining resources. It is little wonder, given the "do more with less" environment that has defined public administration at all levels since the late 1970s, that REGO found committed followers who were willing to call for the adoption of all or some of the ten REGO principles.[27]

What started as a cottage industry in 1992 with *Reinventing Government* quickly turned into a franchise. In 1997 Osborne and Peter Plastrik published *Banishing Bureaucracy: The Five Strategies for Reinventing Government*.[28] Instead of ten principles, this work offers five strategies for reinvention: (1) the core strategy, which helps create clarity of purpose; (2) the consequences strategy, which focuses on creating consequences for performance; (3) the customer strategy, which puts the customer first; (4) the control strategy, which shifts control from the top and center; and (5) the culture strategy, which helps to create an entrepreneurial culture. The following year, Osborne and Victor Colón Rivera published *The Reinventing Government Workbook: Introducing Frontline Employees to Reinvention*.[29] This prepackaged, "canned," workbook serves as the basis for others to deliver workshops on reinventing government. Divided into four modules within which individual chapters focus on each of the ten REGO principles as presented in the original Osborne and Gaebler text, this workbook emphasizes problem-solving activities, brainteasers, and overhead material to illustrate and teach the reinventing government principles.

In our opinion, the best of the reinventing government books may be Osborne and Plastrik's 2000 publication, *The Reinventor's Fieldbook: Tools for Transforming Your Government*.[30] Finally, after two prescriptive texts and one workbook, they got it right. In nearly 700 pages, this book provides the "nuts-and-bolts," "lessons learned," "do's and don'ts" that government officials need to implement the broad strategies outlined in *Reinventing Government* and *Banishing Bureaucracy*. In the words of the authors, it "explains in detail the terrain you will encounter, the obstacles you will face, and the equipment and know-how (tools and competencies) you will need along the way."[31] The book provides real-world lessons of what has worked and what did not work, and why. The authors offer over seventy different "tools"—from activity-based costing to performance management to community empowerment. Finally, in 2004, Osborne, writing with Peter Hutchinson, published *The Price of Government: Getting the Results We Need in an Age of Permanent Fiscal Crisis*.[32] The title of the text delivers its thesis very well.

What, then, should we make of the reinventing government movement? Certainly, and rightly so, REGO had its detractors. For example, we agree with the many state and local officials who considered both *Reinventing Government* and *Banishing Bureaucracy* to be "long on suggestions and short on steps for actual implementation."[33] But to Osborne and Plastrik's credit, publication of *The Reinventor's Fieldbook* helped to address this criticism. *Reinventing Government* and subsequent related publications drew so much attention, stimulated so many ideas, and generated so much response that any discussion of managing modern local government would be deficient without acknowledging its influence.

For now, let us offer two general outcomes of the REGO movement. First, to assess the degree to which federal, state, and local governments have implemented its principles, the movement has stimulated significant academic research conducted in the behavioral tradition. This research is theoretically well grounded, empirical, and representative of the best research tradition in urban politics. The case study presented in box 1.1 reviews some of this research at the local level.

The second major outcome of REGO has been its transition from the "field"—primarily the province of the practitioner—to the academy, where it was renamed and studied thoroughly and conscientiously. In other words, as public administration scholar Michael Spicer reminds us, "Reinventors do not appear to attach much importance to broad political and social ideas."[34] Why should they? Given the day-to-day rush to manage the modern city, time for reflection is scarce. Instead, once again, according to Spicer, practitioners implementing REGO strategies in the field seem to follow a narrow "instrumental rationality" perspective, which suggests that the job of the urban manager is to achieve efficiently and effectively whatever ends or objectives he or she is called upon to pursue. Who, then, is to explore the relationship—the "fit," if you will—between the reinventing government movement and the "idea of the state as a purposive association"?[35] The academy is where ideas, concepts, and paradigms are discussed—where, in Spicer's words, the "history of political and social ideas" is debated. University professors are paid to ponder and write about broad political and social ideas. And this is exactly what has happened to the concept of reinventing government: it was moved to the academy and acquired a new name.

BOX 1.1   Policy and Practice

INCIDENCE, PREDICTORS, AND CONSEQUENCES OF REINVENTING GOVERNMENT

To what extent did local governments embrace the concept of "reinventing government"? The only way to really answer this question is through extensive analysis. Two studies published in the late 1990s provide a review of reinventing government efforts based on large samples of U.S. cities and suburbs.

The first study, by Professors Ruhil, Schneider, Teske, and Ji, is based on survey data from 805 suburban communities located in twenty different states. These authors related that a "substantial number" of communities report little or no effort toward reinvention (436). They create four reform indexes on reinvention: total reform (based on a summary of all sixteen REGO policy innovations used in the study); civil service reform (ten REGO activities); employee-empowerment reform (two innovations); and private-sector reform (four policy reforms). On the total reform index, they find that the average number of reforms implemented is 3.9 out of the possible score of 16. Among civil service reforms, the average adoption rate is 2.2 out of 10, for employee empowerment, the average is .84 out of 2; and for "emulating the private sector reforms," the average adoption rate is .96 out of a possible score of 4. Based on these index scores, the authors conclude that the reinventing government effort at the local level in the late 1990s was "muted" (438).

In terms of predictors of reinvention efforts, Ruhil and his associates find that the presence of a city manager is the most important variable favoring the adoption of REGO policy innovations. They conclude: "Our evidence shows that in today's reform movement, the city manager is most likely to play the role of 'modernizer.' And cities with managers are significantly more likely to have signed on to current reforms designed to increase efficiency" (450). The council-manager form of government was associated with a 7 percent increase in overall REGO reform activity, 11 percent increase in civil service reforms and private-sector reforms, and a 9 percent increase in employee-empowerment reforms (444). Finally, their analysis shows that neighborhood groups, public-sector unions, and the use of district elections in a suburban community significantly (statistically speaking) increase the probability of adopting REGO innovations.

The second study is by political science professors Richard Kearney and Carmine Scavo and city manager Barry Feldman. Examining reinventing government attitudes and actions among 912 city managers in cities with populations of 10,000 or greater, they conclude: "Survey data indicate that city managers are highly supportive of reinvention principles" (544). These authors employ three dependent variables in the study. The first is an additive scale that measures city managers' support for reinvention. Sixteen questions are used, with four response categories, the lowest score would be 16, the highest 64, with a mid-point of 40. The average score for all city managers was 48.4, showing strong support for the concept of reinvention. The second dependent variable measures the extent to which managers recommend reinventing government actions—he or she must design and recommend specific programs and actions that implement REGO. Twelve specific reinvention government actions were identified. Analyses of the data show that 3 percent of the managers recommended all twelve actions; 7.6 percent recommend eleven actions. More than one in five managers (22 percent) recommended ten or more REGO actions. Less than 7 percent of the urban managers recommended three or fewer actions. The average score of 7.4 REGO actions recommended once again shows city managers' support for these initiatives. The third dependent variable is the same as the "recommended REGO action scale" just discussed, but here the twelve actions are weighted based on the degree of difficulty

(continued)

BOX 1.1   Policy and Practice (continued)

that city managers attach to each activity (determined through personal and telephone interviews with the managers). In total, the twelve recommended actions were weighted so that the total possible score is 20 instead of 12. Twenty percent of the managers scored 15 or higher on this weighted scale, with fewer than one in ten (9.6 percent) scoring 4 or lower; the average score for all managers is 10.6.

Finally, Kearney and his colleagues determine the predictors of managers' support for reinvention principles. Not surprisingly, the best predictor of whether a manager will recommend REGO actions is his or her attitude about reinvention as a concept—positive attitudes translate into action. Another important variable that predicts REGO action recommendations is the city manager's length of government service—the longer the government service tenure, the more likely it is that the manager will recommend reform policy initiatives. Finally, city managers located in the Sunbelt (southern and western cities) and those who serve in cities with many full-time employees are more likely to adopt REGO reforms.

SOURCES: Anirudh V. S. Ruhil, Mark Schneider, Paul Teske, and Byung-Moon Ji, "Institutions and Reform: Reinventing Local Government," *Urban Affairs Review* 34 (January 1999): 433–455; and Richard C. Kearney, Barry M. Feldman, and Carmine P. F. Scavo, "Reinventing Government: City Manager Attitudes and Actions," *Public Administration Review* 60 (November–December 1999): 535–547.

THE NEW PUBLIC MANAGEMENT MODEL: AN ACADEMIC RESPONSE TO REGO

Osborne and Gaebler's original groundbreaking work was published in 1992. But the *processes* associated with reinventing government—such as load shedding and/or contracting out public services (generally called "privatization"); an increased focus on organizational and individual performance and accountability; performance and expenditure-control budgeting; devolution of authority to the line level; and greater involvement of the community, neighborhood, and citizen in service delivery decisions— have been under way in earnest in the United States, Great Britain, Canada, Australia, New Zealand, Germany, and other Western nations since the late 1970s. For example, Margaret Thatcher (first elected in 1978) and Ronald Reagan (elected in 1980) brought a post-Keynesian approach to public administration[36] and helped to introduce what has alternatively been called "civic-regarding entrepreneurship,"[37] "the post-bureaucratic paradigm,"[38] "managerialism,"[39] "neo-managerialism,"[40] "market-based public administration,"[41] and "entrepreneurial government."[42] But it was University of London professor Christopher Hood who in 1991 coined the term, the "New Public Management" or NPM model to capture the *academic* response to reinventing government, and it is Hood's label that the literature seems to have adopted.[43]

Perhaps the best single text to explain the rise, institutionalization, and nature of NPM from an academic perspective is the third edition of Owen E. Hughes' *Public Management and Administration*.[44] While Professor Hughes, who is director and professor of management at the Graduate School of Business at Monash University in Australia, places the New Public Management model in an international context—that of the Organization for Economic Cooperation and Development (OECD)—his book reads like any other traditional American public administration text and cites all of the relevant U.S.–based literature.

As Hughes explains, the NPM model is based on market-based economic and public choice theory—or what Jeff Gill and Kenneth J. Meier label "neoconservative economics."[45] The argument goes something like this: to make more efficient use of scarce resources, the rational person will maximize benefits and minimize costs. But market-based economic models do not always hold in governmental (generally called "bureaucratic") settings. Rather, given the lack of a well-defined tool (such as profits) to measure organizational success, bureaucrats tend to maximize their own utility by increasing agency power, prestige, and/or budgets. As public choice theorists argue, then, better public policy outcomes derive from "a maximum role for market forces and a minimal role for government."[46] NPM involves "a major cultural shift as the old management paradigm, which was largely process- and rules-driven, is replaced by a new paradigm, which attempts to combine modern management practices with the logic of economics, while retaining the core public service values."[47] The New Public Management emphasizes "results, a focus on clients [citizens], outputs and outcomes; it would use management by objectives and performance management, the use of markets and market-type mechanisms instead of command-and-control style regulation, competition and choice, and devolution with a better matching of authority, responsibility, and accountability."[48]

As the NPM model came to the academy, primarily in the mid- to late 1990s, sides were taken. In fact, one could argue that three distinct camps emerged: (1) those who liked NPM, (2) those who didn't, and (3) those who studied it empirically. Most of the discourse on the New Public Management model was normative and ideological in nature—camps 1 and 2 above.[49] As shown in the case study in box 1.1, during the past two decades, a number of empirical studies (produced by camp 3) focus on the incidence, correlates, and consequences of REGO/NPM at the local level. Jeff Brudney, Deil Wright, and F. Ted Hebert offer additional studies focusing on state government reinvention efforts.[50]

Open and free dialogue is a cornerstone of democracy; the right to disagree is essential. That "camps" emerged to debate the nature of government and its administration is a testament to the professionalism and love of country possessed by those who study, maintain, and preserve the state. That public administration scholars would find a resolution to the debate was never in question; American administrative theory has made room for previous administrative reforms. As we entered the new millennium, modern public administration and management theory incorporated the positive features of the New Public Management model while also recognizing the importance of traditional management processes and rediscovering the importance of governance. As Janet and Robert Denhardt remind us, the purpose of government is to serve the people, not to steer the state.[51] Their 2003 book *The New Public Service: Serving, Not Steering* played a pivotal role in offering a synthesis of the traditional public administration model and the NPM model. As such, we examine the Denhardt book in detail in chapter 8.

SYSTEMS ANALYSIS AND LOCAL POLICYMAKING

SYSTEMS THEORY

Systems theory is based on the belief that policy can be considered a response by a political system to various forces and pressures produced from its environment. Known as the "open systems" framework, this conceptualization of how local policy is made is important for at least two reasons.

First, while not terribly sophisticated, it is an intuitive, instructive, and useful paradigm (model) for understanding what, in reality, is often an extremely complex process. That is, in the case of some public policies, it would take great effort and time to reconstruct the path from "idea, demand, issue, or concern" to actual passage and implementation.[52] In fact, it might be impossible to capture the full dynamics of the process, since the participation of some individuals or groups in the deliberations might not be known, by omission or by choice. In order to understand complex phenomena, therefore, models or abstractions of reality are required. And these models need to be straightforward and understandable if they are to help at all in penetrating the central mysteries of the policymaking process.

Second, systems analysis is important because it requires us to see the big picture and understand how parts of the system are interrelated. It is not enough to know, for example, that a university town has passed a new ordinance prohibiting "block parties" (gatherings of hundreds of students, at which alcoholic beverages are often consumed until the wee hours of the morning). Such a policy was probably adopted in response to pressures from a number of local groups, including nonpartying neighborhood residents and the local police department. In short, the policies that a city government passes, as well as those that its officials choose not to pass, are responses to a host of supports and demands placed on the local political system. A change in one system component usually triggers a change in another part of the system.

Political scientist David Easton, in a series of influential books published in the 1950s and 1960s, applied systems theory—which was originally developed in the natural sciences—to politics.[53] His open (or natural) systems framework demonstrated how local environments shape the policy process and how authoritative decision makers such as city council members, mayors, city managers, and local bureaucrats respond to these environmental inputs by making local policies.

As the systems model presented in figure 1-1 shows, the urban political system is comprised of several key features.[54] Underpinning all these features, of course, is the *environment* that surrounds the city government. Environmental factors such as the economy, technology, interest groups, intergovernmental relations, natural and man-made disasters, neighborhood groups, the media, and others can impact the policy process at any

Figure 1-1   **Urban Political Systems Model**

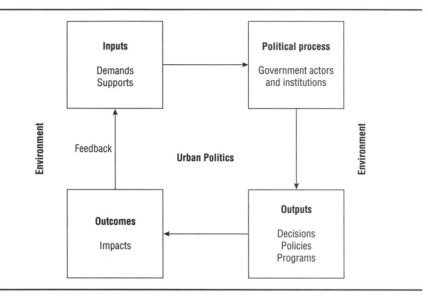

SOURCE: Reprinted with permission from John P. Pelissero, "The Political Environment of Cities in the Twenty-first Century," in John P. Pelissero, ed., *Cities, Politics, and Policy: A Comparative Analysis* (Washington, D.C.: CQ Press, 2003), p. 4.

place in the system. Most often, these environmental stimuli serve as inputs to the system, usually as supports and demands. But it is important to remember that environmental factors such as representatives of neighborhood associations can be sitting in the city council chambers as the council formulates and votes on municipal policies. Also, citizens may carry signs of protest or support outside of city hall, or local builders may lobby council members for changes in a policy immediately after a new ordinance has been passed (the outputs box in the model) or after the policy has been in place for several months (the outcomes box in the model). In short, environmental factors play a pivotal role in shaping the policy process.

Inputs from the environment are transmitted to the political system, where authoritative action takes place. In this stage of the policy process, official policymakers such as the city manager and council members interact to formulate policy. If there is sufficient support for a policy, the council passes an ordinance. This output, in the words of David Easton, represents the "authoritative allocation of values."[55] In terms of the example cited above, the college town's new policy states that block parties will no longer be allowed, under penalty of law. Since such policies have impacts, individuals and the community then have the opportunity to "consume" the outputs and offer assessments of the outcomes of governmental policies. This feedback loop is critical, since it produces vital information that permits the political system to modify, correct, and/or do away with defective policies.

Just as the thermostat in your house allows for changes in temperature, the feedback loop allows policymakers to change policies to fit the political climate of the community. In a democracy, we expect, and demand that political systems will be open and responsive.

As noted by Easton, political inputs drawn from the environment are fed into the political system. These inputs come in two forms: *demands*, which emanate from individuals and groups, and *supports*, which arise out of city conditions and resources. The individuals and groups making demands on city government might include the following examples:

- Individual local citizens or visitors may write letters to or contact city officials to express their concern about an issue or to ask for some type of government action.
- Various organized interest groups, which are not uncommon in cities—especially in medium to large cities—will often represent the business or corporate sector (such as real estate developers, the local Chamber of Commerce, the Downtown Business Association), neighborhoods, labor groups, environmentalists, racial and ethnic groups, and so on. In the United States, interest groups are recognized as powerful participants in the policy process, and public policy is often viewed as the output of bargaining and compromising among interest groups and government officials.
- Political parties represent another group that may make demands on city government. As we learn in chapter 3, the urban reform movement diminished the impact of political parties in many cities in America by prohibiting local candidates from running under party labels, requiring, instead, the practice of nonpartisan elections. Nevertheless, in most large cities, political parties are flourishing, and even in those cities that use nonpartisan ballots, political parties remain active, playing the role of "informal" brokers.
- Finally, the media—the so-called Fourth Estate—is another powerful player in local politics. Many a politician and/or city regime has suffered or prospered at the hands of the mighty media. In a democracy, a free and open press is considered essential, for the print and electronic media serve as watchdogs of the public interest. Newspapers, political talk shows, and evening newscasts reach and influence millions of citizens in urban America.

Supports, according to Easton, represent the second broad type of input into the political system. Supports come from the environment in two varieties, as *active* and *latent* components. Active support—such as voting in city elections, obeying local laws, paying taxes and utility fees—is critical to the functioning of local government. The withdrawal of active support for city government decision makers and institutions can erode the stability of a local political system.

The second type of supports from the environment is latent in nature. Four types of latent environmental subsystems are present in cities: physical, political culture, socioeconomic, and intergovernmental.

- The latent physical support subsystem includes the local climate, geography, and the built environment. Climate and geography affect the types and range of services a city must offer; for example, Oklahoma City, unlike Chicago, has little use for snow removal equipment but must have alarm systems in place to warn of approaching tornadoes. Roads, bridges, subways, public buildings, wastewater treatment facilities, and so on are all part of the built environment, which defines the city infrastructure. Since the early part of the twentieth century, cities have used zoning to regulate land use and thus have significantly affected what the built environment in a city can and will look like.

- As we note later in this chapter, it is important that urban executives understand the political culture of the cities they manage. This concept, while slippery and hard to measure, captures the attitudes and expectations of a citizenry about the proper role and scope of government in a community. James Q. Wilson and Edward C. Banfield gave us the often-maligned "ethos theory," arguing that cities had two fundamental political value systems—public-regarding and private-regarding—each associated with different ethnic and income groups in cities. One ethos could dominate politics in a city, or the two value systems could be competing for dominance.[56] Although research on this theory was subjected to much criticism and found little empirical verification, it still presents a useful dichotomy of competing cultures in cities. For example, a number of large cities in the United States assess a local income tax that is often used to supplement welfare benefits to city residents, but the political cultures of some other cities in America would not support such a tax.

- Of the four latent subsystems, the socioeconomic situation is probably the most recognizable. Common sense tells us, for example, that if a city's economic base is declining, tax revenues will also probably decline. Cities with dependent and elderly populations have a different economic base and very different service needs than do cities with thriving business districts, sports arenas, fully utilized convention facilities, and populations of young, highly educated professionals living in posh apartments and townhouses in the central city. Clearly, the demographic, social, and economic features of a city have a profound impact on local policies, politics, and management.

- The final latent subsystem is defined by the relationships among and between governmental units. As we see in chapter 2, cities operate within a complex system of intergovernmental relations. Not only must they rely on the federal and state governments for financial support, but they must also bargain, negotiate, and compromise with other local governments within large metropolitan areas.

This focus on the environmental inputs to a political system is characteristic of systems theory, which provides the context for this entire book. In the remainder of this section, we

use the examples of citizen participation and e-government to further illustrate the importance of environmental influences on city politics and management.

CITIZEN PARTICIPATION IN CITY GOVERNMENT

Simply put, citizens own city government. In keeping with the concept of political
culture discussed earlier, the citizenry of a city or town set the expectations for and define
the proper role and scope of government in their community. The failure to meet such
expectations, based on fact or fiction, may well mean the loss of community support.
It is the job of the urban executive (1) to understand the nature of community values,
(2) to determine the means and under what conditions to foster citizen participation, and
(3) to strengthen community through civic engagement. The importance of understanding
community values as one key to enlarging management capacity is discussed later in this
chapter. For now, let's focus on the matter of when and how to foster citizen participation
in the decision-making process.

To some analysts, even the suggestion that citizens should not be included in the
decision-making process is heresy. However—although few speak louder or more vocally
than we do for citizen involvement and participation—the real world of city management
shows that decisions should sometimes be made by means of a top-down process. Renée
Irvin and John Stansbury ask the following question as the title of their provocative article:
"Citizen Participation in Decision Making: Is It Worth the Effort?"[57] Using environmental
policymaking as a context, they report some environmentalists' concern that locally based
citizen-participation processes may lead to a relaxation of previously successful environmental regulation, suggesting that the process is potentially wasteful if it is employed in
a "less-than-ideal community." Funds used for citizen participation, these critics argue,
might be more productively applied to "achieve better on-the-ground results."[58] In exploring this policy context, Irvin and Stansbury devote considerable attention to educating the
reader about the advantages and disadvantages of citizen participation and to identifying
the "ideal" and "non-ideal" conditions for citizen participation (see box 1.2).

The lesson to take away from Irvin and Stansbury's research is that citizen participation may not always be appropriate. In chapter 8, we discuss the concept of situational
leadership and the fact that "master managers" must be able to draw on various theoretical
models. One size does not fit all; one model does not work in all situations. If the possible
advantages are great and the ideal conditions for citizen participation are present—and it
is the manager's responsibility to know the advantages and the conditions—certainly she
or he should engage and interact. Research by Kathleen Halvorsen suggests that citizen
participation leads to greater public perception of government responsiveness and greater
tolerance for those who have opposing viewpoints[59]—both of which are laudable outcomes. On the other hand, if the conditions are not right and the potential disadvantages
of citizen participation outweigh the advantages, then the top-down approach to decision
making may be entirely appropriate.

CITIZEN PARTICIPATION IN GOVERNMENT DECISION MAKING

According to Professors Renée A. Irvin and John Stansbury, the disadvantages of citizen participation in the decision-making process accrue to both citizens and government, and they occur at both the decision-process and outcomes levels, creating a 2 X 2 matrix. For citizens involved in the decision process, the disadvantages of participation are that the process is time-consuming and that it is pointless if their concerns are not considered; at the outcomes level, the policy decision may be worse for those citizens if it is "heavily influenced by opposing interest groups" (58). For government officials, the disadvantages of citizen participation may include time, cost, and the creation of ill-will or even hostility toward government if citizen input is ignored. At the governmental outcomes level, three disadvantages seem most pressing: (1) the loss of decision-making control by local officials; (2) the chance that a "bad" decision thus made cannot be ignored, for political reasons; and (3) the use of funds to facilitate citizen participation rather than to actually implement the project.

In terms of non-ideal conditions for citizen participation, these authors offer two sets of factors to consider: low-benefit and high-cost indicators. In general, low-benefit indicators include such considerations as a lack of public hostility toward government, previous government success in decision making without citizen participation, the probability that decisions reached by the participative process will be ignored, and the sense that the same decision is as likely to be chosen by government as by the citizens. Given these conditions, the payoff of citizen participation is low. On the other hand, high-cost indicators of non-ideal conditions include the following possibilities: (1) that citizens are reluctant to participate; (2) that geographic size makes it difficult for citizens to meet and discuss issues; (3) that there are many competing factions and groups, which necessitates a large deliberative body; (4) that the problem to be decided is technical and complex; and (5) that the public does not perceive the issue as a problem.

Within a similar 2 X 2 matrix, the advantages of citizen participation in the decision-making process include these considerations: (1) that citizens can be educated by government officials and in turn can educate government officials; (2) that citizens may be able to persuade and teach government officials; and (3) that the citizen may improve as an activist. The potential favorable outcomes of participation for citizens are these: (1) that gridlock can be broken; (2) that citizens become involved and have some control in the process; and (3) that better policy is made and better policy implementation occurs. For government, the decision process is enhanced because officials can both learn from and teach citizens, build trust and allay citizen fears and anxieties, and develop alliances and gain legitimacy among the citizenry. At the outcomes level, the government can achieve positive results by breaking gridlock, avoiding litigation costs, and producing better public policy and policy implementation.

Finally, in terms of ideal conditions for citizen participation, two types of indicators are important—low-cost and high-benefit indicators. Low-cost indicators include these considerations: (1) that citizens are ready to volunteer and participate; (2) that stakeholders are not too geographically dispersed and can easily attend meetings; (3) that citizen volunteers earn enough income so that participation does not impact their livelihood; (4) that the community is homogeneous, so the group can be smaller; and (5) that the issues at hand are not too technical or complex. With respect to high-benefit indicators, the ideal conditions are these: (1) that gridlock must be broken and a citizen mandate is required; (2) that hostility toward government is high and government policymakers need the validation offered by citizen groups; (3) that community leaders who

(continued)

BOX 1.2   Policy and Practice (continued)

have strong influence and status are willing to serve; (4) that the group facilitator is respected by all group members; and (5) that the issue at hand is of high interest to citizen participants and is at the critical or crisis stage at which it must be resolved.

Clearly, the decision to engage citizens as participants requires the same thoughtful analysis as the decision to make policy with fewer participants. No one said managing urban America was going to be easy!

SOURCE: Renée A. Irvin and John Stansbury, "Citizen Participation in Decision Making: Is It Worth the Effort?" *Public Administration Review* 64 (January–February 2004): 55–65.

To be sure, American cities and towns historically have been and will continue to be the bedrocks of democracy, the locus where civic engagement must take place. One of the critical roles of the urban executive is to facilitate the process of citizen participation. In chapter 4, we examine closely other ways in which citizens influence city government—by voting; by joining organizations such as political parties, interest groups, and neighborhood associations; and by contacting city officials with complaints or requests for services.

IT'S CHILD—E-GOVERNMENT

Information technology (IT) is the engine that drives the modern city, promising increases in productivity, reduced costs, and better access to government by citizens.[60] And while, to date, cities and towns do not universally enjoy these benefits, the IT future seems boundless in possibilities and opportunities. IT's child at the dawn of the twenty-first century is e-government, or, the "electronic village."

As explained by public administration and IT expert M. Jae Moon, e-government can be narrowly defined "as the production and delivery of government services through IT applications" and broadly defined "as any way IT is used to simplify and improve transactions between governments and other actors, such as constituents, businesses, and other governmental agencies."[61] Moon explains further that e-government includes four major internal and external components:

1. The establishment of a secure government intranet and central database for more efficient and cooperative interaction among governmental agencies
2. Web-based service delivery
3. The application of e-commerce for more efficient government transaction activities, such as procurement and contracts
4. Digital democracy for more transparent accountability of government[62]

The extent to which city governments have adopted these internal and external e-government components is well documented in a recent series of articles in the 2001, 2002, 2003, and 2005 editions of the *Municipal Year Book*. In 2001 John O'Looney reported on the use of the Internet for service delivery and citizen participation in a group of about 145 cities and counties with 50,000 or more residents.[63] In general, most cities (96 percent) report providing basic, static web pages for city and county departments. But only 54 percent allow users to search or query databases, and only 9 percent allow for e-commerce activities online. In terms of citizen participation opportunities, 68 percent of the responding cities and counties publish the e-mail addresses of all elected officials, 60 percent post e-mail addresses for professional staff, 58 percent route e-mail to the appropriate departmental staff, and two-thirds (66 percent) of the cities and counties post meeting minutes online. In contrast, less than 10 percent of the jurisdictions offer web audio or video presentations of decision-making deliberations (7 percent), allow citizens to engage with decision makers during deliberations (5 percent), or facilitate citizen-to-citizen discussions (4 percent).

The *2002 Municipal Year Book* report on e-government was based on *The Electronic Government Survey 2000*, with a much larger sample size—about 1,500 cities and counties of the approximately 3,000 surveyed.[64] Findings show that most local governments have websites—86 percent of responding cities and 75 percent of counties. In 1997 the corresponding figure for cities was 40 percent; there was a 115 percent increase between 1997 and 2000. In 1997, when queried if their city had an intranet, only 12 percent of the cities responded affirmatively. In the 2000 survey, over half of the cities and counties (59 percent) reported the existence of an intranet.

Fifty-six percent of the local governments report the employment of a web manager or administrator. This position is full-time in about 25 percent of the cities and counties and is part of another position in about another 68 percent of the jurisdictions; the remaining 7 percent are contract, part-time, or volunteer personnel. Only one in ten local government officials report that they have an overall e-government strategy or master plan.

When asked about citizen satisfaction with local websites, city and county officials report satisfaction ratings among the citizenry of 65 percent stating that the website "meets expectations," 17 percent saying that it "exceeds expectations," and 18 percent noting that the website is "below expectations." Few cities (11 percent) offer financial web-based transactions, but 31 percent said that they post requests for bids and/or proposals on their website.

Respondents noted that barriers to implementation of e-government include lack of expertise, insufficient financial resources, and security issues. Major impacts of e-government activities include (1) increased demands on staff, (2) reengineering processes, (3) changed staff roles, and (4) processes becoming more efficient.

In the 2003 edition of the *Municipal Year Book*, Evelina R. Moulder offers a summary of findings on "E-government: Trends, Opportunities, and Challenges" that is based on a survey of nearly 8,000 cities and counties.[65] The response rate was about 53 percent, from 4,123 cities and counties. As in previous surveys, a supermajority of cities, 74 percent, offer websites in this larger survey. The percentage rises to 88 percent of local governments that have populations in excess of 10,000 (the threshold used in the 2000 survey outlined above), for a 4 percent increase since 2002. Also as in previous reports, topics such as barriers to e-government, changes introduced by e-government, and e-government services offered are discussed and analyzed. In our opinion, one impact of e-government is particularly noteworthy: 48 percent of the cities and counties report that the use of e-government has increased citizen contact with elected and appointed officials.

Two years later in the *2005 Municipal Year Book*, Florida State University Professor David Coursey notes that the percentage of local governments reporting that they have a website had increased from 74 percent in 2002 to 91 percent in 2004.[66] Of the reporting 3,410 cities and counties (a 43 percent response rate) that do have a website, in 51 percent of the cases an Information Technology (IT) department (31 percent) or the city/county manager's office (20 percent) is responsible for the day-to-day management of the site. Survey respondents cite three major barriers to e-government activities in their cities—lack of financial resources (64 percent), lack of technology/web staff (63 percent), and lack of technology/web expertise (43 percent). Between the 2003 and 2005 ICMA e-government surveys, not much occurred at the local level in terms of expanding services offered online. Of the nineteen services reported, with one notable exception, the percentage of services offered in the two years were "nearly, if not exactly, the same."[67] The one exception noted above was that the percentage of cities/counties that offer citizens downloadable forms via the Internet increased from 3 percent in 2002 to 58 percent in 2004. As in previous years, the most widely offered web services were informational in nature, posting the council agenda and minutes (76 percent), listing codes and ordinances (66 percent), online communication with elected and appointed officials (66 percent), and providing employment information and applications (60 percent).

Finally, we note that current research is trying to determine the impact of various structural, demographic, socioeconomic, and organizational factors that influence the use and development of e-government technologies. Based on an analysis of websites among the fifty-five most populous U.S. cities, and a subsequent survey of web masters in these cities, Alfred Tat-Kei Ho, for example, offers a typology of websites according to their design.[68] Two types of website approaches emerge: administrative and nonadministrative. In turn, the nonadministrative category contained two website orientations: informational and user. Based on analysis of survey responses, the cities whose websites are in the nonadministrative category are judged to be more open to external input and collaboration. These cities "emphasized the importance of citizen inputs and collaboration with nongovernmental organizations. Officials in these cities were also more user-oriented and believed more strongly that the web is a tool to enhance customer service for citizens."[69]

Efforts to explain differences in website orientations suggest that population (size of city) and per capita income did not vary across the website orientations. But cities with larger minority populations and cities with lower average years of having a city website are less likely to have the more innovative, nonadministrative type of website. Professor

Ho suggests that these findings support the "digital divide literature," which suggests that differences in socioeconomic background affect the use of the Internet and computers. And, in the case of this study, a lower socioeconomic profile leads to a more administrative-oriented city website. The "learning curve literature" is also supported by this study—that is, with time and experience, cities tend to move their websites from a more administrative orientation to a more informational and user orientation. Ho also reports that internal organizational characteristics of cities impact the decision to create websites that are more administrative or more nonadministrative in character. Cities that adopted more progressive informational and user-oriented websites were cities where non-IT departmental staff supported using the web to deliver public information and services and where sufficient funding and staffing for web development were available. Finally, research by M. Jae Moon finds that council-manager governments are more likely than mayor-council governments to have websites and to be early adopters of web technologies.[70]

As the case study presented in box 1.3 shows, e-government activities can be fun as well as useful.

BETTER MANAGEMENT IS NOT ENOUGH

Today's city executive must be both politician and administrator. Few, for example, would quarrel with the basic proposition that America's cities must improve their management capacity. But improving managerial skills alone will not solve all the city's problems. As the preceding discussion of systems theory suggests, we also *must* recognize the context or environment in which urban management functions. In particular, we need to be sensitive to the limits imposed on administration by such factors as the culture and values of the community, organizational inertia, the political environment, and the personal qualities of those in top leadership positions.

COMMUNITY VALUES

The technical expertise and the managerial tools for urban problem solving are available, both from the private sector and from other levels of government. Why are they not used routinely in city governments? In their early work on city politics, political scientists Edward Banfield and James Q. Wilson offered the following answer:

> To the extent that social evils like crime, racial hatred, and poverty are problems susceptible to solution, the obstacles in the way of their solution are mostly *political*. It is not for lack of information that the problems remain unsolved. Nor is it because organizational arrangements are defective. Rather it is because people have differing opinions and interests, and therefore opposing ideas about what should be done.[71] (emphasis added)

Obviously, urban managers do not grapple continuously with "big" issues such as crime, race, and poverty. Administration, planning, budgets, day-to-day service delivery—all are time-consuming aspects of urban management life. But even in these less-critical areas, urban managers often face obstacles that are essentially unrelated to their technical

---

BOX 1.3   Policy and Practice

POWER TO THE PEOPLE

"Citizens, do you want a red bridge or green bridge?" This is the decision that then-mayor Martin O'Malley asked Baltimore citizens to make concerning the restoration of a seventy-year-old steel bridge in their city. During one week in October, citizens could go to the city's website to vote for a rusty red or a kelly green bridge. And while the mayor was hoping for green, more than 5,000 votes came back with the decision to paint the bridge red. O'Malley had also been attaching surveys about issues to the weekly newsletters that he e-mailed to business and community leaders.

According to law professor Beth Simone Noveck, "We're moving from e-government to e-democracy. . . . The first generation of technology delivered revenue-generating services such as licensing and permitting. Now we are talking about tools that give citizens greater voice in the process" (40). For example, since 1999 the State of Virginia has been trying to get people more involved in the regulatory, rules-making process of state government. In essence, state officials are trying to "turn the comment process into something that almost resembles an Internet chat room" (42).

In another example of government-by-Internet, Maine governor John Baldacci asked citizens to help him to address a $1 billion budget deficit by going to the state's website and "balancing the budget." On one side of the screen, the budget simulation shows the programs for which Maine spends money; on the other side are taxes and other sources of revenue. In the middle of the screen is the budget deficit—$1,078,556,945. As the individual cuts programs or raises taxes, the budget deficit moves toward zero. When the player hits the "send" button, the proposed budget is sent to the governor's office. More than 10,000 people played the simulation, and 1,200 hit the send button. Christopher Swope notes that according to one survey, ten large cities—Seattle, San Francisco, Indianapolis, Charlotte, Denver, Portland (Oregon), Phoenix, San Jose, Boston, and New York City—are leading the way in the use of participatory interactive technologies, such as online surveys and conversation forums. More cities are following everyday.

SOURCE: Christopher Swope, "E-Gov's New Gear: Governors and Mayors Learn to Love the Give and Take of Governing Interactively," Governing, March 2004, 40–42.

---

knowledge of the problem. Municipal budgeting is an example.[72] Practical analysis can show where a city needs to spend more money on infrastructure repairs to meet more severe needs and where spending is less critical, but budgeting more money to one neighborhood over another for such capital projects can lead to protracted political battles. The response of urban managers is often to allocate their budgets equally across a city's political units (districts, wards), knowing that city council support is easier to find when every area is treated in a similar fashion.

In short, the values that the community holds dear often dictate the nature of policy, both for big (nonroutine) and small (routine) issues. This is not to suggest that community values cannot be changed, if need be—one of the many jobs of the urban executive is to adapt and institutionalize community values through his or her leadership. These core values, once articulated, adopted, and acculturated, serve to define and shape the local political culture.

INSTITUTIONAL INERTIA

As we discuss in much greater detail in chapter 4, city workers (bureaucrats) are comfortable with routines. This fact should come as no surprise, since most of us prefer an environment in which we are not constantly forced to adapt to the vagaries of change. Rules, regulations, and established procedures accumulate as organizations mature. Organizational inertia, bureaucratic infighting, agency imperialism, goal displacement, and other forces complicate the task of enlarging the management capacity of city government. A successful city manager *must* be a student of bureaucratic politics and *must* understand organizations both as structures and as webs of human activity. (Chapter 8 discusses both organizational theory and behavior.)

THE POLITICAL ENVIRONMENT

Read any public management textbook or ask any person who has worked in both the world of government and that of corporate America—either will tell you straight out that one of the big differences between public and private management is the degree to which public managers must operate within a political environment: No matter how good the management techniques and no matter how much money is available, the solutions to most complex urban problems require political judgment.[73] Priorities must be assigned, levels and types of taxes must be determined, and resources must be allocated. In the final analysis, these decisions involve judgments about what is best for the people. Under our form of government, these are political decisions, and no amount of improvement in management capacity can change that fact.

Conflict is anything but unusual in city government. After all, one of the two basic purposes of government at all levels is to *manage conflict*. Urban administrators must be prepared to manage pressures and demands emanating from a variety of sources, some of which are internal to the municipal organization, others external to it. To survive, much less be effective, urban managers must be politically sensitive and skillful. No matter how good their administrative abilities, successful managers must learn the art of the possible—how to bargain, how to compromise, and how to negotiate what may appear to be irreconcilable conflicts among competing interests. In the broadest sense, that is what this book is all about: improving the management of city government from both a technical and a political perspective.

LEADERSHIP QUALITIES

Finally, we must consider managers' personal characteristics. No amount of managerial knowledge can take the place of basic leadership resources such as intelligence, perseverance, adaptability, desire to excel, and humor.[74] And we might throw in intuition and luck for good measure. If this list gives the impression that good urban managers must be some sort of superpeople, that is not far wrong. Our cities have enormous problems. Although improving managerial skills may help to solve them, we need very special people as well. Fortunately, for us and for you, we have them.

THE PLAN OF THE BOOK

This book is organized in four parts. The first part, *The Environment of Urban Management*, begins, of course, with the chapter you have just read. This first chapter provides a context for all that follows, establishing the importance of financial and demographic changes, management practices and theories, and the impact of environmental influences, such as citizen participation and technology, on urban political management. Here also, the entire study is placed within the context of systems analysis and politics. Prospective managers must know what seasoned pros know—that they can be excellent administrators, but they must also understand politics and systems. Prominent among the external forces that impinge on local systems are various governmental entities—the federal, state, and other local governments. Chapter 2 places the management of American cities within the system of intergovernmental relations. In chapter 3, we consider the political world of managers from the vantage point of local governmental structures. Research suggests that the supports received by and the demands placed on local political systems vary according to governmental structures, including forms of government, ballot types, electoral systems, home rule, and direct democracy. In order for elected and appointed local officials to gain a proper perspective on how they can manage local political systems, they must understand these governmental structures.

The four chapters of Part Two, *Managing Conflict and Delivering Goods and Services in the Modern City*, provide detail about the two major functions that city governments perform: managing conflict and delivering goods and services. Both functions are managed through the formulation and implementation of public policies. In chapters 4 and 5, we examine local policymaking from a macro perspective. Chapter 4 explores how local policies are made and who makes them. We generally discuss policymaking from a systems perspective and as a rational, orderly process, although alternative models are also offered. The roles and functions of official policymakers—city executives (including city managers and mayors), city council members, and local bureaucrats—are analyzed, and, since all that city officials do is ultimately for the citizenry, we build upon our discussion, presented earlier in this chapter, of citizen participation. In chapter 5, the focus is not on policymaking in general but specifically on the developmental policies of urban planning and economic policymaking. More and more, communities have begun to realize how much their progress depends on strategic urban planning and the vitality of the local economy.

Policymaking is closely tied to another basic management function, decision making; managers, above all, are decision makers. While policymaking is usually broad in scope, decision making is more operational—more micro in nature. In order to implement a specific policy, a number of decisions may need to be made and executed. In chapter 6, we first discuss well-known and established decision-making approaches; then we identify "tools" or decision-making aids, both simple and sophisticated, to make the decision process as systematic as possible; and, finally, we introduce the use of such analytic tools as management information systems and geographic information systems to make more effective decisions. Next, we have to ask: What does the policy process and all the decision making produce? At the local level the answer is services. Citizens demand and deserve excellence in service delivery. Chapter 7 explores the range of service functions provided at the local level and key features of urban service delivery. Services must be delivered efficiently, effectively, responsively, and equitably.

Part Three, *Internal Management Processes*, consists of three chapters devoted to the primary functions of urban appointed and elected officials: managing programs, human resources, and finances. In chapter 8, we discuss general program management by examining four topics. First, we cover the basics required to understand the nature and meaning of modern organizational theory and behavior. In order to understand modern open systems theory, we introduce readers to the classical and behavioral schools of organization thought. Next, we focus on the concept of leadership. Above all, urban managers must be leaders. In the third section, we discuss management strategies, old and new, that emphasize the importance of managing for results. Finally, we offer caveats about the introduction of management techniques new to a city.

Nothing gets done without people, of course. In chapter 9 we address the issue of organizing for human resource administration and consider the common personnel functions in cities. In addition, we discuss a number of personnel issues, such as equal employment opportunity and affirmative action, employee selection and the law, comparable worth, sexual harassment, managing diversity, and accommodations for disabilities. The chapter concludes with a section devoted to labor-management relations. Next, in chapter 10, we consider the vital areas of urban finance and budgeting (operational and capital). Among the questions addressed in this context are these: Where do the funds come from to operate city programs? What are the prospects for expanding the revenue base? All managers worry about how revenue is raised and spent, and the process by which funds are allocated—the budget—looms large as well.

The last part of the book is *The Urban Future*. In chapter 11, we assess what is good, what is problematic, and what is uncertain in the twenty-first-century city. We look closely at the job of the urban manager today and the ways in which education may help. And, once more, we consider the pervasiveness of politics in urban management. How can managers enhance their capacity to operate effectively in a thoroughly political environment? Surely, management skills are crucial, but learning the political ropes may be just as important to a manager's ultimate success. Next, we examine concerns about prescriptive management reforms. Managers must be wary of any management strategy that offers a "one best way." Managing urban America is just plain hard work. Also in this final chapter, we address the issue of administrative ethics. Urban managers absolutely must understand both the consequences of their own behavior and their responsibility to foster the values of honesty and integrity in city government. Regardless of the job they perform, city workers operate in a fish-bowl environment, where they must take care not to lose the confidence of the people they serve. Finally, we place the twenty-first-century city in the post–September 11 environment. Cities have always been vulnerable, but they have also always been resilient as well.

Given the consequences of the 9/11 terrorist attacks, the devastation of New Orleans as a result of Hurricane Katrina, and the BP Gulf of Mexico oil spill, we conclude the book with a discussion of managing man-made and natural disasters.

SUGGESTED FOR FURTHER READING

Brookings Institution three-volume series:

—Katz, Bruce J., and Robert E. Lang, eds. *Redefining Urban and Suburban America: Evidence from Census 2000*. Vol. 1. Washington, D.C.: Brookings Institution, 2003.

—Katz, Bruce J., and Robert E. Lang, eds. *Redefining Urban and Suburban America: Evidence from Census 2000*. Vol. 2. Washington, D.C.: Brookings Institution, 2005.

—Berube, Alan, Bruce J. Katz, and Robert E. Lang, eds. *Redefining Urban and Suburban America: Evidence from Census 2000*. Vol. 3. Washington, D.C.: Brookings Institution, 2005.

Dalton, Russell. *Citizen Politics: Public Opinion and Political Parties in Advanced Industrial Democracies*. Washington, D.C.: CQ Press, 2006.

Denhardt, Janet V., and Robert B. Denhardt. *The New Public Service: Serving, Not Steering*. Expanded edition. Armonk, N.Y.: M. E. Sharpe, 2007.

Easton, David. *A Systems Analysis of Political Life*. New York: Wiley, 1965.

Garson, G. David. *Public Information Technology and E-Governance: Managing the Virtual State*. Sudbury, Mass.: Jones and Bartlett, 2006.

Governing: The Magazine of States and Localities, a magazine devoted to examining public management at the state and local government levels. Available at www.governing.com.

Harrigan, John J., and Ronald K. Vogel. *Political Change in the Metropolis*. 7th ed. New York: Longman, 2003.

Pelissero, John P., ed. *Cities, Politics, and Policy: A Comparative Analysis*. Washington, D.C.: CQ Press, 2003.

Public Administration Review, an academic journal devoted to the study of public administration.

Urban Issues: Selections from The CQ Researcher. 2nd ed. Washington, D.C.: CQ Press, 2005.

NOTES

1. The phrase "fend-for-yourself" federalism comes from John Shannon, "The Return to Fend-for-Yourself Federalism: The Reagan Mark," *Intergovernmental Perspective*, summer–fall 1987. Also see David B. Walker, *The Rebirth of Federalism*, 2nd ed. (New York: Chatham House, 2000), 30 and 152; and Jonathan Walters, "Cities on Their Own," *Governing*, April 1991, 27.

2. See Russell L. Smith, "The 'Electronic Village': Local Governments and E-Government at the Dawn of a New Millennium," *2002 Municipal Year Book* (Washington, D.C.: ICMA, 2002), 25–41.

3. Keith F. Mulrooney, "Prologue: Can City Managers Deal Effectively with Major Social Problems?" *Public Administration Review* 31 (January–February 1971): 6.

4. Thomas W. Fletcher, "What Is the Future for Our Cities and the City Manager?" *Public Administration Review* 31 (January–February 1971): 5.

5. George J. Gordon, *Public Administration in America*, 4th ed. (New York: St. Martin's, 1992), 88–89.

6. Elizabeth K. Kellar, "Get By with Less," in *Managing with Less*, ed. Elizabeth K. Kellar (Washington, D.C.: ICMA, 1979), 2.

7. For 1978, see David R. Morgan and Michael W. Hirlinger, "The Dependent City and Intergovernmental Aid: The Impact of Recent Changes," *Urban Affairs Quarterly* 29 (December 1993): 256–275; for 1990–1991, see Virginia Gray and Peter Eisinger, *American States and Cities*, 2nd ed. (New York: Longman, 1997), 338.

8. Calculated from data provided in table 445, "City Governments—Revenue for Largest Cities: 2006," in U.S. Census Bureau, *Statistical Abstract of the United States: 2010* (Washington, D.C., 2009): 291.

9. See U.S. Department of Housing and Urban Development, *The State of America's Cities, 1998*, at www.huduser.org/publications/polleg/tsoc98/summary.html.

10. Jamie Woodwell, *The State of America's Cities: The Thirteenth Annual Opinion Survey of Municipal Elected Officials* (Washington, D.C.: National League of Cities, 1997), 1–2.

11. Christopher W. Hoene, "City Budget Shortfalls and Responses: Projections for 2010–2012," December 2009, at www.nlc.org/ASSETS/5A4EFB8CF1FE43AB8815B63F/BudgetShortFalls_10.pdf

12. Ibid.; the bullets are direct quotes.

13. Ibid.

14. For a review of current population changes and a discussion of the impact of local economies on residents in metropolitan areas, see "The City as a Place of Opportunity: The Changing Urban Political Economy," chapter 6 in *Political Change in the Metropolis*, 7th ed., ed. John J. Harrigan and Ronald K. Vogel (New York: Longman, 2003).

15. Many years ago, Thomas M. Guterbock presented evidence to refute the view that suburbanization is primarily the result of people fleeing central-city minority presence and crime. See "The Push Hypothesis: Minority Presence, Crime, and Urban Deconcentration," in *The Changing Face of the Suburbs*, ed. Barry Schwartz (Chicago: University of Chicago Press, 1976), 137–161.

16. Brookings Institution, *Racial Change in the Nation's Largest Cities: Evidence from the 2000 Census*, April 2001, at www.brook.edu/dybdocroot/es/urban/census/citygrowth.htm.

17. Ibid., 2.

18. Ibid.

19. Ibid., 2–3.

20. Bruce Katz, *State of the World's Cities: The American Experience*, Brookings Institution, February 2005, at www.brook.edu/metro/speeches/20050201_worldcities.pdf.

21. Kellar, "Get By with Less," 3.

22. Charles Levine, Irene Rubin, and George Wolohojian, *The Politics of Retrenchment* (Beverly Hills, Calif.: Sage, 1981), 211.

23. In *Public Management: A Three-Dimensional Approach* (Washington, D.C.: CQ Press, 2009), p. 32, public administration scholars Carolyn J. Hill and Laurence E. Lynn Jr. pose the question: "Public Management and Public Administration: A Distinction Without a Difference? " Traditionalists, of course, prefer the field be called *public administration*, while recent reformers offer a clear distinction between the two concepts and advance the term *public management* as the appropriate moniker for the discipline. We agree with Hill and Lynn that this distinction is generally not important and, like them, use the terms public administration and public management interchangeably or combine the two concepts together—public administration and management.

24. David Osborne and Ted Gaebler, *Reinventing Government: How the Entrepreneurial Spirit Is Transforming the Public Sector* (Reading, Mass.: Addison-Wesley, 1992).

25. Ibid., xvii.

26. Executive Office of the President of the United States, "Citizen's Guide to the Federal Budget: Fiscal Year 2001," last updated March 30, 2004, at www.gpoaccess.gov/usbudget/fy01/guide04.html.

27. Osborne and Gaebler outline the ten REGO principles in the first ten chapters of *Reinventing Government*.

28. David Osborne and Peter Plastrik, *Banishing Bureaucracy: The Five Strategies for Reinventing Government* (New York: Plume, 1997).

29. David Osborne and Victor Colón Rivera, *The Reinventing Government Workbook: Introducing Frontline Employees to Reinvention* (San Francisco: Jossey-Bass, 1998).

30. David Osborne and Peter Plastrik, *The Reinventor's Fieldbook: Tools for Transforming Your Government* (San Francisco: Jossey-Bass, 2000).

31. Ibid., 2.

32. David Osborne and Peter Hutchinson, *The Price of Government: Getting the Results We Need in an Age of Permanent Fiscal Crisis* (New York: Basic Books, 2004).

33. Jonathan Walters, "Managing the Politics of Change," *Governing*, December 1992, 40.

34. Michael Spicer, "Public Administration, the History of Ideas, and the Reinventing Government Movement," *Public Administration Review* 64 (May–June 2004): 357.

35. Ibid., 353.

36. Amita Singh, "Questioning the New Public Management," *Public Administration Review* (January–February 2003): 116.

37. Carl J. Bellone and George Frederick Goerl, "Reconciling Entrepreneurship and Democracy," *Public Administration Review* 52 (March–April 1992): 130–134.

38. Michael Barzelay and Babak Aramajani, *Breaking through Bureaucracy: A New Vision for Managing Government* (Berkeley: University of California Press, 1992).

39. Christopher Pollitt, *Managerialism and the Public Services: Cuts or Cultural Change in the 1990s*, 2nd ed. (Oxford: Basil Blackwell, 1993).

40. Larry D. Terry, "Administrative Leadership, Neo-Managerialism, and the Public Management Movement," *Public Administration Review* 58 (May–June 1998): 194–200.

41. Zhiyong Lan and David H. Rosenbloom, "Editorial: Public Administration in Transition?" *Public Administration Review* 52 (November–December 1992): 535–537.

42. Osborne and Gaebler, *Reinventing Government.*

43. Christopher Hood, "A Public Management for All Seasons," *Public Administration* 69 (spring 1991): 3–19.

44. Owen E. Hughes, *Public Management and Administration*, 3rd ed. (New York: Palgrave Macmillan, 2003).

45. Jeff Gill and Kenneth J. Meier, "Ralph's Pretty-Good Grocery versus Ralph's Super Market: Separating Excellent Agencies from the Good Ones," *Public Administration Review* 61 (January–February 2001): 9–17.

46. Hughes, *Public Management and Administration*, 11. This discussion draws heavily from Robert E. England, "City Managers and the Urban Bureaucracy," in *Cities, Politics, and Policy: A Comparative Analysis*, ed. John P. Pelissero (Washington, D.C.: CQ Press, 2003), 196–216.

47. Organization for Economic Cooperation and Development (OECD), as quoted in Hughes, *Public Management and Administration*, 5.

48. Ibid.

49. In *Public Management and Administration*, 257, Hughes identifies and provides numerous citations to the work of those who belong to both camps.

50. Jeffrey L. Brudney, F. Ted Hebert, and Deil S. Wright, "Reinventing Government in the American States: Measuring and Explaining Administrative Reform," *Public Administration Review* 59 (January–February 1999): 19–30; Jeffrey L. Brudney and Deil S. Wright, "Revisiting Administrative Reform in the American States: The Status of Reinventing Government during the 1990s," *Public Administration Review* 62 (May–June 2002): 353–361.

51. Janet V. Denhardt and Robert B. Denhardt, *The New Public Service: Serving, Not Steering* (Armonk, N.Y.: M. E. Sharpe, 2003). An expanded version was published in 2007.

52. See, for example, Beryl Radin and Willis D. Hawley, *The Politics of Federal Reorganization: Creating the U.S. Department of Education* (New York: Pergamon, 1988); Marc Reisner, *Cadillac Desert: The American West and Its Disappearing Water* (New York: Penguin Books, 1993); Elaine B. Sharp, *The Dilemma of Drug Policy in the United States* (New York: HarperCollins, 1994).

53. David Easton, *The Political System* (New York: Knopf, 1953); David Easton, *A Framework for Political Analysis* (Englewood Cliffs, N.J.: Prentice-Hall, 1965); David Easton, *A Systems Analysis of Political Life* (New York: Wiley, 1965).

54. This discussion draws heavily from John P. Pelissero, "The Political Environment of Cities in the Twenty-first Century," in Pelissero, *Cities, Politics, and Policy*, 3–13.

55. Easton, *Systems Analysis*, 348.

56. James Q. Wilson and Edward C. Banfield, "Public-Regardingness as a Value Premise in Voting Behavior," *American Political Science Review* 58 (December 1964): 876–887; James Q. Wilson and Edward C. Banfield, "Political Ethos Revisited," *American Political Science Review* 65 (December 1971): 1048–1062.

57. Renée A. Irvin and John Stansbury, "Citizen Participation in Decision Making: Is It Worth the Effort?" *Public Administration Review* 64 (January–February 2004): 55–65.

58. Ibid., 63.

59. Kathleen Halvorsen, "Assessing the Effects of Public Participation," *Public Administration Review* 63 (September–October 2003): 535–543.

60. M. Jae Moon, "The Evolution of E-Government among Municipalities: Rhetoric or Reality?" *Public Administration Review* 62 (July–August 2002): 424–433.

61. Ibid., 425.

62. Ibid. The four points are quoted directly from the article.

63. John O'Looney, "Use of the Internet for Citizen Participation and Service Delivery," *2001 Municipal Year Book* (Washington, D.C.: ICMA, 2001), 28–46.

64. Smith, "Electronic Village," 34–41.

65. Evelina R. Moulder, "E-Government: Trends, Opportunities, and Challenges," *2003 Municipal Year Book* (Washington, D.C.: ICMA, 2003), 39–45.

66. David Coursey, "E-Government: Trends, Opportunities, and Challenges," *2005 Municipal Year Book* (Washington, D.C.: ICMA, 2005), 14–21.

67. Ibid., 17.

68. Alfred Tat-Kei Ho, "Reinventing Local Governments and the E-Government Initiative," *Public Administration Review* 62 (July–August 2002): 434–444.

69. Ibid., 439.

70. Moon, "Evolution of E-Government," 430.

71. Edward Banfield and James Q. Wilson, *City Politics* (New York: Vintage, 1963), 2.

72. Taken from Matthias E. Lukens, "Emerging Executive and Organizational Responses to Scientific and Technological Developments," in *Governing Urban Society: New Scientific Approaches,* ed. Stephen Sweeney and James Charlesworth (Philadelphia: American Academy of Political and Social Science, 1967), 120.

73. Ibid., 121.

74. See Harold F. Gortner, Julianne Mahler, and Jeanne Bell Nicholson, *Organization Theory: A Public Perspective,* 2nd ed. (New York: Harcourt Brace, 1997), chap. 9.

CHAPTER 2

CITIES AND THE SYSTEM OF

INTERGOVERNMENTAL RELATIONS

M ANAGING the modern city is no easy task. As noted in chapter 1, city officials are required to respond to a host of factors when making local policies. In fact, the assumption underlying systems theory is that government policies are a response to forces generated in the environment. Prominent among these environmental factors is *federalism*.

Federalism is as old as the Republic itself. The Framers were intent on creating a system of government in which the national government shared powers with state governments. Many at the Constitutional Convention would have it no other way (see box 2.1 for more of this story). A strong federal government threatened the very rights and liberties the revolutionary Continental Army had just won from a monarch, King George III. At the founding of the Republic, many Americans viewed state governments as "laboratories of democracy;"[1] and they still do.[2]

What about cities? Where do they fit in the U.S. constitutional system? Cities as we know them today developed later in American history. For example, our large industrial cities were born, for the most part, between 1860 and 1920. In the past, as well as today, cities have no standing under the U.S. Constitution—they are wards of state governments. Nevertheless, the modern city is dependent *both* on a state government, from which its powers are derived, and on the federal government, from which much money is received. This chapter outlines the role of the city in the federal system, placing a special emphasis on intergovernmental relations. First, a brief discussion of federalism as a concept is required.

FEDERALISM

Any introductory American Government textbook will provide a standard definition of the term "federalism" based on the concept of *shared power* between units of government. In the United States, the units of government defined in the Constitution are, of course, the national or federal government and the fifty state governments. In a world comprised of about two hundred nations, the United States is only one of about two dozen nations that use a federal system; others include Germany, Canada, Russia, India, and Australia. Most nations rely instead on a unitary system, wherein the national government is supreme (e.g., United Kingdom, Israel, Peru, and South Africa).

BOX 2.1   Policy and Practice

NATION BUILDING, "INFRASTRUCTURAL CAPACITY," AND FEDERALISM: YOU DON'T ALWAYS GET WHAT YOU WANT

As David B. Walker reminds us in *The Rebirth of Federalism*, the decision to create the first American Republic as a confederacy of thirteen states under the Articles of Confederation was "viewed not as an end in itself but as a mechanism for advancing the battle against Britain" (43). After the long war for independence (1776–1783) ended, the process of nation building took place in earnest as the delegates who drafted the U.S. Constitution set forth the framework for the Second Republic. Before the fifty-five men arrived in Philadelphia to deliberate during the hot summer of 1787, James Madison, the Father of the Constitution, framed the essential task of the group: "to construct a polity that was neither a wholly centralized regime nor merely a confederation or league." (45). The Founders, in essence, created a *centralized federalism*, a system that Robyn Hollander and Haig Patapan describe as similar to the one that evolved in Australia. In a centralized federalism system, the vying centripetal and centrifugal forces associated with federation resulted in the pull of the center (national government) overcoming the tug of the periphery (state governments).

Although the American Founders desired to *re*create the confederacy into a federal system to address the weaknesses of the states operating under the Articles of Confederation, a recent article (and subsequent book) by Daniel Ziblatt suggests that just because nation builders desire to create a federal system, their efforts may not come to fruition. He uses the case studies of state formation in nineteenth-century Germany and Italy as examples of how the desire to create federal systems is contingent upon the *infrastructural capacity* of governmental subunits. Ziblatt explains:

> [F]ederalism is possible only if state building is carried out in a context in which the preexisting units of a potential federation are highly institutionalized and are deeply embedded in their societies—and hence are capable of governance. Why? Only subunits with high levels of infrastructural capacity can deliver to both the core and the subunits the gains that were sought from state formation in the first place. . . . It is only via high-infrastructural subunits that the basic paradox of federalism's origins can be resolved. (2004, 71)

In the case of Germany, the condition of infrastructural capacity was met; in Italy, it was not. As a result:

> [I]n Germany in 1867 and 1871 Prussian state builders adopted a *federal* political model in which the formerly independent states became regional states that maintained wide areas of discretion and jurisdiction in policy, administration, and public finance. [I]n Italy in 1861 Piedmontese state builders fused together the long-independent Italian states under a *unitary* political model that erased the formerly independent states from the political map (74).

The hopes of nation builders to create an Italian federal system were thwarted.

The authors' theory certainly helps explain the success of the American experience in federalism. As Walker notes, "The more than a century and a half of British rule had produced a strong pattern of local self-government . . . and a high degree of partial autonomy and authentic assertiveness on the part of the colonial assemblies. . . . In short, there was a distance between and among the colonies, as well as between each of them and London" (40). This colonial separateness began to converge into an American nationalism and "common historical experience" (41) beginning in the 1680s that helped prepare the colonies for an eventual war

(continued)

BOX 2.1   Policy and Practice (continued)

for independence from Great Britain. Moreover, after declaring their independence in 1776, the new state governments drafted constitutions and bills of rights that would serve as models for those at the Constitutional Convention in 1787 to draw upon. Ziblatt's federalism precondition of *infrastructural capacity* was present in the new American states, which facilitated the Founders' desire to create a centralized federal state.

SOURCES: David B. Walker, *The Rebirth of Federalism: Slouching toward Washington*, 2nd ed. (New York: Chatham House, 2000); Robyn Hollander and Haig Patapan, "Pragmatic Federalism: Australian Federalism from Hawke to Howard," *The Australian Journal of Public Administration* 66, (no. 3), (2007): 280–297; Daniel Ziblatt, "Rethinking the Origins of Federalism: Puzzle, Theory, and Evidence from Nineteenth-Century Europe," *World Politics* 57 (October 2004): 70–98; and Daniel Ziblatt, *Structuring the State: The Formation of Italy and Germany and the Puzzle of Federalism* (Princeton, N.J.: Princeton University Press, 2008).

In the U.S. federal system, state governments are theoretically unitary governments. That is, all local governments (municipalities, towns, special districts, counties, and school districts) are creatures of the state governments. In the year 2007, the United States was made up of 89,527 governmental jurisdictions—and more governments are being created every day. There is, of course, one federal government, fifty state governments, the District of Columbia, and a handful of U.S. territories. Local governments define the remaining tens of thousands of governmental jurisdictions, including counties (3,033), municipalities (19,492), towns and townships (16,519), school districts (13,051), and special districts (37,381).[3] As noted above, local governments are the responsibility of state governments.

The nature of the relationships among units of government at the federal, state, and local levels has changed over time. Political scientists and public administration scholars have attempted to capture some of the complexity of changing relations among governments by using "cake" metaphors.[4] For example, based on his review of the literature, long-time public administration expert Nicholas Henry serves up four types of federalism cake.[5] First, we have "layer cake" or "dual federalism," which dominated American politics from the founding of the Republic in 1789 to the Great Depression in 1930. The layers in this model represent the two levels of government, the federal government and state governments, as defined in the U.S. Constitution. For the most part, during this 140-year period the national and state governments, based on delegated and prohibited powers specified in the Constitution, operated independently within their own spheres of authority. If a dispute arose, the U.S. Supreme Court or a lower federal court acted as an umpire. The Civil War enhanced the position of the national government vis-à-vis state governments, but "dual federalism" worked well, as governments at all levels found themselves in an economic environment defined by Adam Smith's laissez-faire philosophy. Then came the stock market crash of 1929.

Spurred by the ensuing depression and by the fiscal policies designed by President Franklin Delano Roosevelt (FDR) to address the economic crisis facing the nation (and the world), the second slice of federalism cake was served. FDR offered the nation "marble cake" or "cooperative federalism," in which the layers between levels of government became much less distinct as the cake "sagged and whorled"[6] into activities between federal, state, and local governments. This period marks the birth of intergovernmental relations (IGR), which William Anderson defines as "an important body of activities or interactions occurring between governmental units of all types and levels within the [United States] federal system."[7] The advent of IGR elevated local governments to full-time, active partnership in federalism, since some of the programs FDR supported and Congress passed attempted to address unemployment at the local level. The federal government returned some of the money collected from the national government's personal income tax to state and local governments via government programs. Similarly, state governments took a more active role in providing resources for their legal offspring—local governments. A spirit of cooperation among all levels of government marked the federalism environment.

The third era of federalism, which has been labeled "pound cake" or "co-optive federalism," is bounded by the election to the presidency of John F. Kennedy in 1960 and of Ronald Reagan in 1980. During this two-decade period, the number of specialized grant programs (generally called "categorical" grants) aimed at state and local governments grew exponentially, as did the dollar amounts flowing from the federal government to state and local governments. However, along with the money "cake" came the "pound"— programmatic rules, conditions-on-aid, and federal mandates that "pounded" state and local governments. Moreover, during this period, local problems became nationalized. The federal government took the lead in creating various grant programs to address such issues as legal aid for the poor, health care, urban redevelopment, environmental policy, employment programs, education, and so on. The weight of the national government (the top layer) of the cake seemed to crush the bottom layers (state and local governments) with rules and regulations. Many subnational governments screamed for regulatory relief and for greater control in the intergovernmental process. They believed that they were being co-opted, with money (grants-in-aid) serving as the tail that wagged the dog.

Under the banner of the "New Federalism," in his second term President Richard Nixon offered some relief from this allegedly oppressive regulatory environment by offering grants to state and local governments with fewer strings attached. First came General Revenue Sharing (1972–1986) and then came special revenue sharing in the form of new block grants. To state and local officials, General Revenue Sharing (GRS) seemed like manna from heaven, for under this policy, the federal government returned to state governments (until 1980) and to local governments (until 1986) a portion of tax receipts based on a formula prescribed by Congress. Until GRS fell under the budget axe in the mid-1980s, this popular program allowed the subnational governments more say in how federal funds would be spent. The new block grants, called "special revenue sharing" under the New Federalism banner, also provided regulatory relief since they offered local governments more decision-making power than the previous categorical project grants had allowed.

Two of the most prominent of the new block grants were the Comprehensive Employment and Training Act of 1973 (CETA) and the Community Development Block Grant Act (CDBG) of 1974. And then along came President Ronald Reagan, to serve up his "crumble cake" federalism.

Under federalism Reagan-style, intergovernmental relations changed dramatically. Transfer payments (grants-in-aid) from the national to the state and local levels began to decline, or "crumble." Driven by the "stagflation" of the late 1970s and by his own promise to get government "off the backs" of the people, President Reagan offered a New New Federalism, in which the block grant became the centerpiece of his approach to federalism. For the most part, block grants took categorical project grants in a particular policy area (such as employment or education) and "blocked" them together. Instead of federal agencies deciding which state and local governments received which grants, as had occurred with project categorical grants, federal dollars were now allocated to eligible subnational governments by means of formulas defined by Congress or by an administrative agency. In addition, with block grants, state and local governments had more decision-making power in determining how to spend federal largesse. In the first two years of his administration, Reagan combined seventy-seven categorical grants to create nine new or revised block grants and eliminated another sixty categorical grants altogether.[8]

In short, under Presidents Reagan and George H. W. Bush (1980–1992) cities found themselves in an IGR environment marked by "crumbling" support in terms of federal dollars, particularly in comparison to the boom years of the 1960s up until the late 1970s. This diminishing support also gave rise to the practice of "competitive" or "fend-for-yourself" federalism.[9] Today, local governments must scramble for federal dollars in a very competitive intergovernmental environment. The rise in the number of block grants did enhance, however, state and local government officials' power in deciding what projects to fund with federal dollars. This *devolution* of power to state and local governments continued during President Clinton's second term, with the passage of a number of new block grants in the areas of health, education, and welfare.

What about federalism in the post-9/11 city during the George W. Bush administration? Because they are the first on the scene and all acts of terrorism are local (see box 2.2), "first responders" to emergencies—fire, police, and emergency medical service workers—benefited from the increasing number of federal dollars and programs to plan for and mitigate possible terrorist attacks. As the case study in box 2.2 suggests, this intergovernmental partnership for homeland security has experienced significant problems in operation. Federal grants-in-aid in other programmatic areas—such as loans and grants to small businesses and other industries that were damaged by the 9/11 terrorist attacks—also increased after 9/11. More specifically, in the three year period 2001–2003, grants-in-aid to state and local governments increased by double-digit amounts, by 11.4 percent, 10.8 percent, and 10.1 percent (8.7 percent, 8.9 percent, and 7.4 percent increases when measured in constant 2000 dollars). In contrast, in the last three years of the

BOX 2.2   Policy and Practice

"ALL ACTS OF TERRORISM ARE LOCAL ..."

The title of this case study is a quote by Rep. John Tierney (D-Mass.) who completed his statement by say-ing, "so each of our communities must be fully prepared in crisis response and consequence management" (538). Since the terrorist attacks on September 11, 2001, the federal government, the level of government responsible for national security, has offered local governments, the locus of America's "first responders" to crisis events, a bevy of intergovernmental programs in the functional area of homeland security. In his article entitled "Imperfect Federalism: The Intergovernmental Partnership for Homeland Security," urban politics expert Peter Eisinger argues that while the "war on terror requires a close, cooperative intergovernmental partnership," since 9/11 this partnership has been lacking in several ways (537).

First, according to Professor Eisinger, at the moment of the tragedy in 2001 the national government was "no longer predisposed or well-positioned to lead and support a close intergovernmental partnership" with state and local governments (537). Since the Reagan administration, the federal government had been "deaf to the fiscal crisis taking hold in the states and diffident toward the cities and their problems" (537). State and local government officials' fears were confirmed when shortly after the attacks in New York City and Washington D.C., President George W. Bush established a Homeland Security Council in the Executive Office of the President without any representatives from the 50 states or over 35,000-plus cities and towns in America being invited to join the council. Moreover, as cities immediately began to develop security plans, Congress did not provide any financial assistance to help defray the development of emergency response plans until March of 2003, one and one-half years after the 9/11 attacks.

Second, once federal funds began to flow through various programs to state and local governments, a number of administrative, technical, and political issues plagued the intergovernmental partnership. For example, after 9/11, funds distributed to first-responders through the Firefighter Investment and Response Enhancement (FIRE) Act were doubled, but "critics complained that the administration of the program was plagued by bottle-necks and inflexibility and the funding was distributed inequitably" (539). Authorized funds were slow to be released, funding caps meant that the "money available to any fire department was not primarily a function of the city's size or the level of threat the city faced," and some evidence points to par-tisanship in the distribution of grant funds (539). An example of a technical administrative constraint on local governments was the requirement under the federal Cash Management Act of 1990 that "required cities that received federal funds to spend their own money for homeland security purposes and wait for federal reimbursement" (540). Some cities simply did not have the cash to spend, while others had to wait months to be reimbursed for their homeland security fiscal outlay.

After passage of the PATRIOT Act in October 2001, new grant programs were passed to help cities pre-pare for and respond to acts of terrorism. Like the FIRE Act grants before them, "the new homeland security funds were allocated without reference to a national security plan" (540). Also, like the previous FIRE Act grants, the PATRIOT Act required that the new grant monies should be broadly distributed and not neces-sarily targeted to those places most at risk or vulnerable to acts of terrorism. For instance, under the early State Homeland Security Grant Program (SHSGP) created by the PATRIOT Act, no state could receive less than 0.75 percent of the total funds appropriated in a fiscal year. The result was that low-population states like Wyoming, Vermont, Alaska, and North Dakota in 2005 received, respectively, $18.23, $15.28, $14.99, and

(continued)

BOX 2.2   Policy and Practice (continued)

$14.48 per capita, while the states of Texas, Florida, California, New York, Ohio, Pennsylvania, and Illinois all received less than $3 per capita.

Finally, according to Eisinger, the federal government showed diffidence in its reluctance to advise local governments on how to prepare for a terrorist attack or what steps to take when the Department of Homeland Security raises the national alert level. The color-code system, introduced in March 2002, was raised from yellow to orange five times in the first two years without providing local government leaders specific information about triggering events. Some city officials even claim that they learn that the alert status has been raised not from the federal government, but from watching CNN or other news media (541).

In conclusion, Eisinger points to subsequent changes in practices, processes, and fund allocation formula that have improved the intergovernmental partnership for homeland security. Nevertheless, he also notes, "Despite some progress toward a more rational public administration of homeland security, the partnership still reflects the deficiencies of imperfect federalism" (537).

SOURCE: Peter Eisinger, "Imperfect Federalism: The Intergovernmental Partnership for Homeland Security," *Public Administration Review* 66 (July/August 2006). 537–545.

Bush administration (2006–2008), grants-in-aid to state and local governments increased by 1.4 percent, 2.2 percent, and 3.9 percent. Measured in constant 2000 dollars, these figures translate to -2.6 percent, -0.7 percent, and -1.1 percent. These latter percentages are similar in size to annual increases in federal grants-in-aid (measured in constant 2000 dollars) to state and local governments for the years 1996 (-1.0) and 1997 (0.9) during the Clinton administration.[10] In short, prior to the election of President Barack Obama in 2008, except for the years immediately following 9/11, federal grant support for state and local governments reflected the general mood of federalism that began under the Reagan administration—small yearly increases (or the loss of funds when controlling for inflation) in transfer payments and the devolution of power to the subnational level.

Although it is too early to assess the long-term impact of the Obama administration on intergovernmental relations, it is estimated that for the year 2009, federal grants-in-aid to state and local governments will increase by over $100 billion (from about $461 billion to $567 billion). This dollar amount represents an increase of 23 percent from 2008's allocations (23.3 percent in constant 2000 dollars).[11] As noted previously, state and local governments have also received significant federal largess in a variety of areas (e.g., bridges and roads, health, energy, education, social programs, and small business loans) through the 2009 American Recovery and Reinvestment Act (ARRA). This national economic stimulus spending effort totaling $787 billion ($288 billion in tax benefits; $275 billion in contracts, grants, and loans; and $224 billion in entitlements) was passed by Congress on February 13, 2009, and signed into law on February 17 by President Obama in Denver, Colorado, at the Museum of Nature and Science.[12] Most of the tax cuts accrue to individuals (about $240 billion) and the rest to companies (about $50 billion). Much of the health care funds goe to help states defray the rising costs of Medicaid ($87 billion dollars) and to help the unemployed pay COBRA health insurance premiums ($25 billion). About $30 billion is allocated for infrastructure repairs to roads and bridges. Another $40 billion goes to U.S. school districts to be distributed through state funding formulas to help restore state education costs, including preventing teacher layoffs. In addition, the law provides funding to stimulate "green" energy initiatives, to extend unemployment benefits, to improve veterans benefits and facilities, to assist rural development programs, and to expand the nation's information and technology infrastructure.[13] Finally, on June, 10, 2010, President Obama urged national lawmakers to approve a $50-billion state and local government aid package to avoid "massive layoffs of teachers, police and firefighters."[14] The president's call for aid did not find enthusiastic support in Congress, however. As House Majority Leader Steny H. Hoyer (D-Md.) explains, "I think there is spending fatigue [in Congress]."[15]

Having established a context for understanding the nature of federalism and identified the various eras through which federalism has evolved, let us turn our attention to a more complete understanding of the broad issues associated with intergovernmental relations in the modern city: fiscal federalism; state-local relations; mandates; and interlocal relations.

INTERGOVERNMENTAL RELATIONS

As longtime federalism expert Deil Wright so aptly reminded us in 1990: "The concept of federalism has two centuries of U.S. history, tradition, law, and practice behind it. The concept of IGR [intergovernmental relations] has a comparatively short half century [or so] of application to the American context."[16] IGR is a process that involves interaction among the various levels of government—federal, state, and local. As suggested earlier, this interaction may take the form of cooperation or co-optation. State and/or local government officials may believe that they are getting "pounded" with rules, regulations, and mandates even as they are left to "fend for themselves" in an environment of, up until only recently (2009–2010), declining or "crumbling" federal largess. Perceptions may vary. The reality is that intergovernmental relations—the day-to-day process of city officials working *vertically* with state and federal officials and *horizontally* with local officials in other local government entities—represents a significant part of the modern city executive's job. Similarly, the number of grants-in-aid programs and the dollars associated with the grants are substantial. In fact, IGR is sometimes called "fiscal federalism."

FISCAL FEDERALISM

As we noted earlier, beginning in the late 1970s, federal aid to cities began to dwindle. During the 1980s and early 1990s, that decline accelerated, as state and local governments suffered cuts of unprecedented size under Ronald Reagan's New New Federalism, later supported by President George H. W. Bush. Beginning in 1992 the decline attenuated as modest relief was granted under the Clinton administration and as a result of President

George W. Bush's response to 9/11. Current stimulus dollars under the Obama administration have been a godsend as cities attempt to balance budgets in these tough economic times, but the long-term ability of the national government to provide stimulus funds to state and local governments is in question, given the current $13 trillion national debt. The bottom line is that compared to the "fat years" of the 1960s and 1970s, the intergovernmental environment since 1980 has been marked by the slogan "do more for less." Not only have the dollars going directly to cities dried up, but many programs have also been cut. In fact, although some critics claim that government programs never die, in the 1980s cities lost two popular and visible urban aid programs, General Revenue Sharing and Urban Development Action Grants. On September 30, 1996, even the thirty-seven-year-old Advisory Commission on Intergovernmental Relations (ACIR) closed its doors and was consigned to the so-called CyberCemetery (see box 2.3).

Some observers, who thought cities had become overly dependent on federal funds, viewed this profound change in the relationship between the national government and the cities as overdue and basically healthy. Yet the cities' newly found independence came at a price. Most cities did cut services—a step that often fell hardest on low- and moderate-income families. And to make up for lost revenue, cities tended to turn to more regressive measures, such as increased fees and charges, that again have adversely affected the economically disadvantaged. Despite all these changes, important federal urban aid programs remain, and both the number of grant programs and the dollars appropriated for various grants have increased during the Obama presidency. We next review the nature and characteristics of key federal programs designed explicitly to assist municipalities.

Federal Grant Programs

Federal grants are a mixed blessing. All cities can use outside funding, but the federal government rarely provides money without attaching guidelines for its spending. In fact, local officials frequently object to what they feel are excessive restrictions accompanying federal grants. About thirty years ago, a member of the Oakland, California, city manager's staff complained:

> The strings attached to most federal programs cause all kinds of trouble. For instance, there was a big build-up last year on a new jobs program, with a lot of publicity which raised a lot of hopes. But there were so many restrictions attached the program couldn't do what we had hoped it would. Sometimes there are so many strings that it's hard even to spend the money.[17]

Some things never change—just when they are noticed and who notices them. In April 2004, for example, James A. Garner, mayor of Hempstead, New York, and president of the U.S. Conference of Mayors, lamented the lack of homeland security funds reaching the local level to help defray the cost borne by local governments to implement the color-coded federal alert system.[18] When the alert is raised from yellow to orange, local governments must stiffen protection of key infrastructure sites. Local officials view this federal alert

THE CYBERCEMETERY

Created in 1959, the Advisory Commission on Intergovernmental Relations (ACIR) performed a number of tasks, including offering Congress and the president recommendations that addressed common problems affecting federal, state, and local governments and explained how to coordinate federal grants programs. Congress specified that the Commission be comprised of twenty-six members: three from each house of Congress, four mayors and four governors, and three from each of the following groups: state legislators, elected county officials, a president's cabinet members, and private citizens. In total, the agency published 130 policy reports that contained recommendations, 194 information reports without such recommendations, 23 public opinion polls on IGR issues, 22 staff reports, and *Intergovernmental Perspective* (a quarterly magazine).

In preparing the first five editions of this text, we relied heavily on various publications provided by the ACIR. In particular, the serial collection entitled *Significant Features of Fiscal Federalism*, published yearly between 1976 and 1995, proved indispensable in allowing us to track information about federal grants-in-aid over time. And although the ACIR no longer exists as a functioning agency, all of the documents published under the auspices of the agency remain just a few mouse clicks away.

The U.S. Government Printing Office (GPO) and the University of North Texas (UNT) have formed a partnership to provide electronic access to publications of former federal government commissions, boards, agencies, etc. These publications can be found at the CyberCemetery at http://govinfo.library.unt.edu. Information pertaining to and produced by about three dozen former government entities is archived at the site, where documents can be downloaded free of charge. Among the now defunct agencies in the CyberCemetery are the Amtrak Reform Council, the Columbia Accident Investigation Board, the National Commission on Terrorist Attacks upon the United States, the Office of Consumer Affairs, and the United States Information Agency.

As time passes, and the documents and reports associated with these agencies, boards, and commissions become harder to find or become worn or lost in government depository libraries, the importance—and the wisdom—of creating the CyberCemetery will become even more evident. As we note later in this text, sometimes government initiatives simply are not successful, while at other times, government gets it right. As a result of the CyberCemetery, historians and social scientists are assured of quick and easy access to important documents relating to both the failures and the successes of government.

SOURCES: Information about the ACIR comes from Bruce D. McDowell, "Advisory Commission on Intergovernmental Relations in 1996: The End of an Era," *Publius* 27 (spring 1997): 111–127. Information about the CyberCemetery comes from http://govinfo.library.unt.edu and www.gpoaccess.gov/cybercemetery.html.

system as an unfunded mandate that costs American cities hundreds of millions of dollars to implement. Cities are not getting the homeland security funds promised them by the federal government, because the dollars are "stuck" at the state level as funding allocation "strings" are untangled. Or, as Mayor Garner notes: "Homeland security money went to the states by Federal Express, but came to the cities by Pony Express."

Why do local officials play the intergovernmental game? The answer is that they simply cannot afford not to—the stakes are too high. When John F. Kennedy was inaugurated as president in 1961, about 45 separate grant programs existed. When Richard Nixon took office just eight years later—following Lyndon Johnson's Great Society initiative—the number of programs had grown to 400! By 1981, that number had risen to about 540, but it then fell to 400 by 1986 under Ronald Reagan. Then the number of grant programs rose again, to 478 in 1989 under George H. W. Bush and to 660 in 2000 under Bill Clinton.[19] In 2006, under George W. Bush, there were about 814 grants-in-aid programs.[20] In 2010, the federal government's grants portal "Grants.gov" showed the availability of over 1,000 grants distributed by 26 different agencies worth over $500 billion.[21]

In terms of dollars, federal grants-in-aid accounted for about $7 billion in 1960; the amount approached $24 billion by 1970, grew to $91 billion by 1980, and reached $135 billion in 1990.[22] In 2000, the federal grant program had risen to $300 billion,[23] and in fiscal year 2009 the dollar amount peaked at an estimated $568 billion.[24] As a percentage of federal government outlays, grants grew from 7.6 percent in 1960 to 15.9 percent in 2000[25] but fell to an estimated 14.2 percent in FY 2009.[26]

Not all federal money comes packaged in the same way or with the same restrictions. Federal aid can be classified either by how the money is distributed or by how the recipient spends the money. Federal funds are distributed in two ways:

1. *Formula grants* provide funds to local governments automatically on the basis of an administratively or legislatively prescribed formula. All block grants and about 30 percent of categorical grants are distributed according to some predetermined formula. This approach to distributing federal dollars has grown in popularity: in fiscal year 1975, about two-thirds of federal grants-in-aid were distributed by using a formula, but by fiscal year 2000, the percentage had grown to 90 percent.[27]

2. *Project grants* are awarded competitively—that is, at the discretion of the granting agency—and must be applied for by the recipient government. Project grants are the most numerous, accounting for about 72 percent of all categorical grants.[28]

When considered from the viewpoint of how local governments can spend the money, federal grants take two forms:

1. *Categorical grants* may be spent only for narrowly defined purposes, and often recipient governments must match a portion of the federal funds. About 82 percent of the money that state and local governments receive from the federal government is in the form of categorical grants.[29]

2. *Block grants* combine several related categorical grants in the same functional area or grants-in-aid in related functional areas into a single grant program. Although the federal government can provide some direction in spending, historically, the recipients of block grants have had considerable leeway in shifting money around within a broadly defined area. Approximately 18 percent of all federal grants-in-aid dollars are allocated through block grants.[30]

Most of the criticism of federal financial assistance is directed at categorical grants (which represents about 98 percent of all federal grant programs),[31] especially categorical project grants. From an urban management perspective, as the number of grants multiplied exponentially in the 1960s, the list of complaints grew about such problems as overlap, duplication, excessive categorization, insufficient information, varying matching and administrative requirements, arbitrary federal middle-management decisions, and grantsmanship—the art of writing successful proposals. In addition, grants must be applied for (constantly it seems), implemented, and evaluated; many grants require citizen participation and other conditions-of-aid that must be met and managed. But the money is welcome, even with strings attached; cities scramble for the newly available federal dollars.

Beyond the immediate financial relief they provide for hard-pressed cities, categorical grants can be defended from an economic point of view. Many governmental activities provide benefits, called *spillover effects*, for those who do not live within the boundaries of the government providing the service. Education, pollution prevention, parks, and recreation services are just a few examples. Local voters, to the extent that they recognize the situation, may be reluctant to fund activities that offer advantages to people who do not pay for the service. Categorical grants allow the federal government to support local programs that produce large external benefits.[32]

Despite the continued existence of a host of categorical federal programs, considerable change has taken place in federal urban aid in recent years. First, more and more, federal grants provide funds to individuals rather than to state and local government programs. About 64 percent of federal aid now goes for individual needs such as medical payments (Medicaid) or income support (unemployment compensation or welfare), whereas in 1980, only 36 percent went to people instead of programs.[33] Second, the use of block grants have provided cities with more flexibility and latitude to spend the federal funds they do receive. Block grants—especially the Community Development Block Grant (CDBG)—are popular among local officials. In the words of William Althaus, mayor of York, Pennsylvania, CDBG is "our last little baby."[34]

The Housing and Community Development Act of 1974

The passage of the Housing and Community Development Act in 1974 (Public Law 93–383) is often viewed as a significant development in federal support for cities. Originally a three-year program with an $11.3 billion budget, the act consolidated a number of categorical urban development programs—Model Cities, urban renewal, neighborhood facilities, open-space land, public-facility loans, water and sewer facilities, and code enforcement—into a block grant. Eligible activities for funding must (1) benefit low- and moderate-income persons, (2) aid the prevention or elimination of slums and blight, or (3) meet other urgent development needs that the jurisdiction is not able to fund on its own. Regardless of the principal focus, at least 70 percent of the grant funds received in a one-, two-, or three-year period must benefit low- to moderate-income persons.[35]

All cities with populations of 50,000 or more and urban counties with at least 200,000 residents—or about 1,209 jurisdictions—are automatically eligible for funds. Originally, the formula for grant distribution considered a community's population, the number of persons living in poverty, the extent of overcrowded housing, and the amount of housing built before 1940. Today, however, these entitlements are calculated by means of two formulas, and the metropolitan city or urban county receives the greater of the amounts calculated. The three factors and their weights for the first formula are: population (.25), extent of poverty (.50), and overcrowded housing (.25). The second formula also includes three factors, including growth lag (the lag in population growth from 1960 to the present), poverty, and age of housing, weighted at .20, .30, and .50, respectively. For fiscal year 2010, funding for this part of the program was estimated to be about $2.8 billion.

In addition to the entitlement program, beginning in 1981 Congress amended the original CDBG act to allow state governments, instead of officials in the Department of Housing and Urban Development (HUD), the opportunity to administer the nonentitlement or discretionary funding portion of the CDBG program. Cities with populations under 50,000 and counties with 200,000 or fewer residents could receive grants based on funding priorities and award criteria established by *state governments*. The funding under this part of the CDBG program is not an entitlement, for the state governments have discretion in choosing grant recipients. Small cities and counties are not required to match grant funds with local funds in order to be eligible for these CDBG funds. As in the entitlement program, however, states must ensure that "maximum feasibility priority" goes to funding programs that benefit low- to moderate-income persons and that prevent or eliminate slums or blight. Funds are allocated to each state government using the same method as described earlier for entitlement cities and counties: whichever of the two formulas provides the greater amount of funding is used. Currently, forty-nine states and Puerto Rico participate in the state-administered, nonentitlement CDBG program, for which the FY 2010 appropriation totaled about $1.2 billion. One state, Hawaii, chooses not to administer the small cities program, so HUD continues to assume programmatic jurisdiction there, awarding approximately $7 million to three counties (Kauai, Maui, and Hawaii) in fiscal year 2010.

Community development grants have spawned an enormous range of improvements, from spruced-up storefronts, freshly painted homes, and new sidewalks in New Haven, Connecticut, to lights for baseball fields in affluent Scottsdale, Arizona.[36] The mayor of Cleveland called CDBG a "catalyst" to garner support from banks, businesses, and foundations—without it, he remarked, Cleveland would be a disaster area.

Nonetheless, an early evaluation of the CDBG by the General Accountability Office raised questions about the program's targeting capacity. It found that cities often spread funds too widely, thus diluting their effect on revitalization.[37] Other critics, noting the considerable increase in support for economic development projects in recent years, complain that downtowns get too much of the action, without offering proof that lower-income people will benefit. They maintain that cities should be required to show how downtown projects will provide jobs, business opportunities, or training programs for the less advantaged.[38] In spite of these targeting problems, most observers consider the CDBG program a solid success.

Urban Enterprise Zones

Should small distressed areas be carved out of large cities and given special tax breaks to stimulate economic redevelopment? This is the essence of the various proposals urging the creation of "urban enterprise zones." In March 1982 President Reagan unveiled what he termed the linchpin of his urban policy: a proposal to establish enterprise zones in twenty-five American cities. The cities were to be chosen on the basis of a package of tax and deregulation incentives; local areas might offer reductions in local taxes and less stringent zoning, building codes, and licensing requirements. The target areas had to have sustained high levels of poverty, unemployment, and general distress.

Although federal legislation establishing enterprise zones did not make it through Congress, a number of states adopted variations of this idea. In general, these programs often did not create the islands of unfettered enterprise envisioned by the early Reagan proposal. Instead they relied heavily on traditional tax incentives granted to businesses, coupled with extensive public support in the delineated areas—infrastructure investment, training of disadvantaged workers, business loans, and technical assistance, for example.[39]

The original enterprise zone concept, although attractive to many, had its detractors, including those who argued that tax incentives may be nice, but venture capital is the key need of small businesses.[40] One assessment of enterprise programs operating in several states found a reduction in taxes to be about the only principal provision retained by many of the states; thus these programs do not represent a real alternative to the more traditional approach to urban revitalization.[41] Roy Green and Michael Brintnall, however, take exception to the negative press associated with state enterprise zones. They assert that "the states are at it again—experimenting, adapting, sometimes disagreeing, but in particular innovating with a timely policy issue."[42]

The EZ/EC Program

The Omnibus Budget Reconciliation Act of 1993, passed during the Clinton administration, created the Empowerment Zone and Enterprise Community (EZ/EC) Program. Coming in the wake of the 1992 Los Angeles riots, this ten-year, $3.5 billion program provided federal grants to distressed urban and rural communities for social services and community redevelopment. In addition, EZ/EC funds provided tax and regulatory relief for attracting and/or retaining businesses.

Funding for the program came primarily through the Social Services Block Grant Program administered by the Department of Health and Human Services. Responsibility for designating Empowerment Zones (EZs) and Enterprise Communities (ECs) devolved to officials in the Department of Housing and Urban Development (HUD) and the

U.S. Department of Agriculture (USDA). In December 1994 the secretaries of the two departments designated nine EZs and ninety-five ECs. Specifics of the EZ/EC program included the following effects:

- Six big-city empowerment zones—Atlanta, Baltimore, Chicago, Detroit, New York City, and Philadelphia/Camden, New Jersey—were created. Each EZ could receive grants totaling $100 million and tax breaks worth between $150 million and $250 million.
- Three rural empowerment zones—Kentucky Highlands, Mid-Delta in Mississippi, and Rio Grande Valley in Texas—were created. Each of the rural EZs could receive $40 million in grants and $150–$250 million in tax breaks.
- Los Angeles and Cleveland were designated Supplemental Empowerment Zones. Los Angeles received $450 million in grants and tax incentives, and Cleveland received $174 million.
- Sixty-five of the ninety-five ECs were located in big cities and the remaining thirty in rural areas. Each received grants and tax incentives worth about $6 million.
- Four "enhanced enterprise communities" were also created—Boston, Houston, Kansas City, and Oakland, California. The aid package for each was about $47 million.[43]

The two "supplemental" EZs and four "enhanced" ECs were added to address "disappointments" among areas that had been left out of original funding decisions. This is not to suggest that politics dominated the selection process. Recent research by Marc Wallace finds support for HUD Secretary Henry Cisneros' claim that "a city's degree of need and its revitalization approach was paramount to its selection."[44] In 1998 a second round of competitions was held, in which twenty new Empowerment Zones—fifteen urban and five rural—and twenty new rural Enterprise Communities were chosen.[45]

RC/EZ/EC: The Next Round

Building upon previous programs in this policy area, in December 2000 Congress passed the Community Renewal Tax Relief Act to create forty Renewal Communities (RCs)—twenty-eight in urban areas and twelve in rural areas—and to fund eight new Empowerment Zones (EZs)—six in urban areas under HUD and two in rural areas under USDA.[46] Accompanying the legislation was about $17 billion in tax incentives to be used for wage credits, tax deductions, capital gains exclusions, and bond financing. HUD Secretary Mel Martinez claimed, "These tax incentives couldn't come at a better time. This critical partnership between the public and private sectors will give local businesses in distressed neighborhoods an economic boost to help drive revitalization, provide jobs and ultimately build a foundation for stronger communities."[47]

The eight new EZs are located in Pulaski County, (Ark.); Fresno, (Calif.); Jacksonville, (Fla.); Syracuse, (N.Y.); Yonkers, (N.Y.); Oklahoma City, (Okla.); San Antonio, (Texas); and Tucson, (Ariz). The forty new Renewal Communities (RCs) are located in twenty different states. In addition to big cities such as Los Angeles, San Francisco, Detroit, and Chicago, a number of counties and parishes (primarily in the states of Alabama, Kentucky, Louisiana, and Mississippi) and the Turtle Mountain Band of Chippewa in North Dakota participate as RCs. New RCs and third-round EZs carried their designations until December 2009.

How have the various federal economic stimulus/revitalization programs fared? Marilyn Gittell and her associates examined the first-year experiences of the six urban EZ areas to determine the extent to which the program had enhanced civic opportunity.[48] They found variation in citizen participation levels among the six EZs—local political elites' control of the program had stifled the expansion of civic opportunity in some communities. These researchers urged caution, however, about a hasty evaluation of the EZ program with respect to expanding opportunities for community and citizen participation, pointing out that greater community capacity takes time to develop.

Community activists in EZ cities have also offered a mixed report card for the EZ program.[49] In Camden, New Jersey, Yvonne Haskins, an attorney who helped to write the EZ plan for the city, voiced concerns about fighting among participants over who got what and about the lack of concrete accomplishments. Gerald Roper, president of the Chicagoland Chamber of Commerce and a member of the city's thirty-nine-member EZ board, offered a similar story for Chicago. More positive assessments of the program came from Detroit and Baltimore. In the final analysis, perhaps Richard Nathan, director of the Rockefeller Institute of Government, provides an appropriate assessment of the program: "I'd give it a B-plus overall because this is a very ambitious agenda. . . . These things don't happen overnight."

In March 2004 the General Accountability Office (GAO) published an extensive review of federal revitalization programs in the area of community development.[50] As part of the report, the GAO laments the lack of tax benefit data that could be used by HUD and the USDA to "administer and evaluate the [EZ/EC/RC] programs."[51] The GAO report offers summaries of eleven studies focusing on EZs, ECs, and RCs, many of them highlighting the issues of citizen participation, citizen involvement, and community capacity in the revitalization programs. The number of participants, depth of participation, and sustainability of citizen involvement vary across the studies and across the sites studied. Some studies report minimal citizen involvement, some that citizen participation waned as the projects moved from planning to implementation, and some that citizen participation reached "moderate to substantial" levels. Another study reports that employment grew faster in four of the six EZ zones than in demographically similar neighborhoods, that large businesses are more likely to take advantage of tax incentives offered under the program, and that the number of business establishments owned by zone residents increased.

These community development programs, which are likely to remain part of the urban fabric for the foreseeable future, merit investigation to determine their effectiveness. After all, extensive local resources—time, effort, and money—are required to manage the programs. On the other hand, as academics, perhaps we focus too much on issues and problems and not enough on success. For those of you who think so, the U.S. Department of

Housing and Urban Development website offers over 100 "Community Renewal Good Stories" from EZs and RCs in over 30 states. These are real stories by real people about real successes (see www.hud.gov/offices/cpd/economicdevelopment/programs/rc/tour/gsindex.cfm).

The Local Response to Federal Assistance

We noted earlier that federal aid is a mixed blessing; the outside money is welcome, and often desperately needed, but the red tape, delays, and changing federal requirements frequently frustrate city officials. Complaints about federal programs abound. Local officials, for example, express concern about the administrative complexity associated with grant implementation. They note the need for improved communication between federal and local personnel, more timely information on new programs, and knowledge about similar programs administered by different federal agencies.[52] Robert Agranoff suggests that the cooperative federalism of the 1930s to 1960s has given way to even more federal control and bureaucratic management: "The actions of Congress, the Supreme Court, and presidential administrations appear to have introduced more supervisory than collegial behavior, funneled through an increasingly directive bureaucratic administration."[53]

Here we should note that localities are not as helpless in the face of federal grant requirements or mandates as they might seem. A great deal of bargaining and negotiation commonly occurs among levels of government; federal enforcement efforts are often weak; and cities can frequently shape grant programs to suit local needs, regardless of federal intent. As public administration scholars Jane Massey and Jeffrey Straussman point out, some grant requirements provide a range of compliance choices or allow different levels of compliance. Local governments, then, do not simply comply or fail to comply with grant mandates; instead they choose the method and/or degree of compliance.[54] We have more to say about federal and state mandates on local governments later, but first we examine the relationship between state governments and their legal offspring.

THE STATES AND THE CITIES

Like parents and their children, states and cities have nearly always had a love-hate relationship. States provide financial support for urban areas, but they are also the source of limitations and constraints. As legal creatures of the state, cities are subject to a number of potential controls and regulations. In the late 1860s, Judge John F. Dillon promulgated the most famous rule of law upholding total state sovereignty. Dillon's rule says in effect that cities owe their origins to and derive their powers solely from the state, which has the right to abridge and control those powers. Under this rule, cities have only those powers expressly granted to them by the state constitution or legislature, or any other powers that can be fairly implied from those specific grants of authority. Although this narrow perspective on municipal powers still prevails in some states, other state courts have taken a more liberal view of the powers of a municipal corporation, especially where the state constitution provides for a home-rule charter. (We examine the impact of home rule and the legal limitations that still surround city government in chapter 3.) Nonetheless, cities remain very much subject to state control in a variety of ways.

Although federal grant programs receive more attention, states actually provide more money to cities than does the national government. By 2007, state assistance as a proportion of *municipal general revenue* had increased to about 20 percent[55]—up from 16 percent in 1960. For all local governments (counties, municipalities, townships, special districts, and school districts), state transfer payments equaled almost 33 percent of local government general revenue in 2007. More than one-half (55 percent) of these dollars went to school districts.[56]

Because of the growing emphasis on decentralization and the accompanying loss of federal funds, states have been asked to do even more to help their cities. How have states responded? Do they have the capacity to meet the challenge? Capacity means more than money, of course; it means management skills and political will as well.[57]

During the early years of the Reagan budget cutting, some states stepped in to help fill the gap, but most made only modest efforts to replace the lost federal funds.[58] By the middle of the 1980s, as states began to grapple with their own budget shortfalls, state aid to localities slowed down.[59] The states' fiscal problems continued through the early 1990s, until, as the national economy registered steady improvement over the latter half of the decade, state finances also rebounded. Most of the new money went for traditional state services—education, prisons, and Medicaid captured the lion's share of spending growth. Then, the twenty-first century welcomed American cities with yet another wave of budget woes. Michael A. Pagano, writing in a research report entitled *City Fiscal Conditions in 2004* for the National League of Cities, notes:

> While economists announced the end of the recession two years ago, a fiscal recession continues in America's cities. Ongoing economic struggles, combined with soaring health care and pension costs, marked declines in state aid to local government, and other factors continue to cause serious fiscal problems for municipalities across the country. . . . Cities are responding to the deteriorating fiscal conditions in a variety of ways. The most common response has been to raise or institute new fees and charges for services. Cities have also increased productivity levels and reduced city employment, service levels and operating spending.[60]

The "marked declines in state aid" Pagano refers to represented a loss to cities of about $2.3 billion, or 9.2 percent, in FY 2004. This loss came on top of a 2.1 percent decline in state aid to cities in FY 2003, and a marginal growth rate of 0.3 percent in FY 2002. As Christopher Hoene noted in *American City and County* in 2003, "When it comes to financial matters, the bad news just keeps on coming for local governments."[61] And, indeed it did. As noted in chapter 1, in 2009 and 2010, collectively state governments experienced massive shortfalls. The National Council of State Governments in 2009 noted for the combined fiscal years 2009 and 2010 there were revenue shortfalls of $291 billion, with an estimated decline of $55 billion in 2011 and $69 billion in 2012.[62] On July 1, 2010, the first day of the new fiscal year, *Governing Daily* reported that the State of California began the new year without a plan to address a $19.1 billion budget deficit. The next day, Governor Arnold Schwarzenegger sent a letter to State Controller John Chiang requesting that the pay for most state hourly workers (about 200,000 state employees) be set at the minimum federal wage of $7.25 until the budget is restored.[63] Clearly, at least for the foreseeable future, cities will exemplify the fend-for-yourself intergovernmental environment that has slowly emerged since the late 1970s.

Before examining how cities manage relationships among themselves (interlocal relations) in metropolitan areas, a brief discussion of federal and state mandates is warranted.

FEDERAL-CITY AND STATE-CITY RELATIONS: THE ISSUE OF MANDATES

A *mandate* is "a constitutional provision, a statute, an administrative regulation, or a judicial ruling that places an expenditure requirement on a government. That requirement comes from outside the government forced to take the action."[64] In intergovernmental relations, mandates flow downward, from the federal to the state and local levels or from the state to the local level. Also, courts have become increasingly active in the mandate process, requiring various actions on the part of state and local governments (such as addressing prison/jail overcrowding). Mandates are especially troublesome for local governments, which are on the receiving end of most of them, because invariably they seem to require the expenditure of money. Thus the burden of dealing with many social ills falls disproportionately on those governments least able to absorb the shock because their revenue sources are the most restricted.

Although Congress drastically reduced aid to states and localities during the 1980s, federal lawmakers were reluctant to relinquish control over certain national programs. Therefore, as money dried up, mandates exploded—much to the displeasure of local officials. "Basically, it's a matter of buck-passing," complained Mayor Victor Ashe of Knoxville, Tennessee, chairman of an advisory board for the U.S. Conference of Mayors. "Congress has decided it can impose anything that it wants just by writing its goals into a law and then passing the costs on down to state and local governments. . . . Carried to its logical extreme, it's going to drive us all into bankruptcy."[65]

Mandates typically cover valuable and even popular programs. Most of these direct orders concern civil rights and environmental protection. Various pollution mandates require states or localities to comply with federal standards for clean air, pure drinking water, and effective sewage treatment. Another major mandate protects the rights of the disabled. The 1990 Americans with Disabilities Act (ADA), requiring businesses as well as state and local governments to provide equal access for the disabled, became one of twenty mandates enacted in that year.[66] Many times, the real question associated with mandates is not so much the desirability of the policies as who should pay for implementation.

When Republicans gained control of Congress in 1994, the pleas of state and local officials received a sympathetic hearing. The result was the Unfunded Mandates Reform Act (UMRA) of 1995. The law was not retroactive, and it exempted unfunded mandates covering civil rights.[67] Still, it represented a major shift in the relationship between the national government and state, local, and tribal governments. Basically, the act declared that Congress cannot pass any unfunded mandate without first submitting it for cost estimates to the Congressional Budget Office (CBO). If the CBO finds that the cost of the mandate exceeds an estimated $50 million (or $100 million for the private sector), Congress must specify the source of the additional money to support the legislation. The 1995 act did not end mandating, but, at least in principle, it should have substantially slowed the congressional tendency to impose these fiscal burdens on subnational governments. Did it succeed?

In May 2001 the Congressional Budget Office offered a five-year (1996–2000) report on its activities under the UMRA. The report notes, "Numerous pieces of legislation that originally contained significant unfunded mandates were amended to either eliminate the mandates or lower their costs. In many of those cases, information about mandate cost provided by the Congressional Budget Office (CBO) clearly played a role in the Congressional decisions. In those respects, title I of UMRA has proved to be effective."[68] The report further notes that during the five-year span only two intergovernmental mandates with costs exceeding the $50 million threshold became law—an increase in the minimum wage in 1996 and a reduction in federal aid to support the food stamp program in 1997.

Another study completed by the General Accountability Office in May 2004 was less sanguine about the effectiveness of the UMRA. The GAO suggested that the "identification and analysis of federal mandates on state, local, and tribal governments or the private sector is a complex process under UMRA."[69] There are multiple steps and multiple tests to pass before a law or regulation is tested against UMRA standards: "For example, UMRA does not require CBO to review potential mandates in appropriation bills, and UMRA does not apply to final rules that agencies issue without having published a notice of proposed rulemaking or to any rules issued by independent regulatory agencies."[70] The GAO report noted that the No Child Left Behind Act of 2001 did not meet the definition of a mandate because compliance with requirements in the act were a condition of receiving federal aid. In short, the UMRA has not been the panacea that state and local officials had hoped for because few actions trigger UMRA review. During the first three years of the act, only three federal actions were judged to impact subnational governments enough for UMRA review.[71] In the legislative years 2001 and 2002, only 5 of 377 statutes enacted and only 9 of 122 economically significant rules issued by federal agencies were deemed to have mandates applicable for UMRA review.[72]

What about state governments and their propensity to place mandates on their legal offspring? One might think that since the states are on the receiving end of federal mandates, they might "go easy" when imposing them on local governments. Unfortunately, this is not the case. Nicholas Henry, for example, notes, "On average, a fifth of the hundreds of measures introduced each year in state legislatures directly affect the authority, procedures, and finances of local governments," and "one careful review of this issue has labeled efforts to measure the cost of state mandates a 'fool's errand.'"[73]

INTERLOCAL RELATIONS

About 80 percent of the U.S. population lives in metropolitan (metro) areas.[74] These metro areas, however, comprise less than 20 percent of the nation's total land area. Metropolitan areas abound with local governments—counties, cities, school districts, and special districts—as is reflected in table 2-1.

Notice, for example, that the Chicago metropolitan area has over 1,400 units of local government—9 counties, 455 cities and towns, 662 special districts, and 330 school districts—but Pittsburgh has more governments per 10,000 residents. These statistics reinforce a basic truism about American politics: Political power in the United States is highly fragmented. The relationships that exist among all of the thousands of local jurisdictions tend to be informal and voluntaristic; no single political structure encompasses the entire metropolitan area in most parts of the country. For years various groups have decried this proliferation of autonomous political units, urging in its place a more unified, centralized political structure.

Just how serious is the multiplicity of local governments in the metropolis? According to some authorities, the political balkanization of the metropolitan area contributes to the following problems:

- Municipal services are provided less efficiently because of overlapping jurisdictions, duplication of services, and lack of economies of scale.
- Political accountability is reduced because citizens are confused as to which government is responsible for which activities.
- Area-wide planning is impossible—the lack of an area-wide government precludes a coordinated attack on problems (transportation, pollution, housing) that transcend local boundaries.
- Fiscal disparities are created between central city and suburb.
- Great variations in service levels occur among parts of the metropolis.
- The inability of the metropolitan area to handle its own problems compels state and federal intervention and reduces local initiatives and options.

In short, reformers blame many of the problems associated with big cities on the faulty metropolitan political structure. In an earlier period, local reform groups often urged the creation of some form of government that would encompass an entire metropolitan area, perhaps through city-county consolidation. But in this country, far-reaching structural changes almost always require voter approval, and over the years voters have not been kind to proposals that would drastically reshape government in metropolitan areas. Few city-county

Table 2-1 Local Governments by Number and Type in Selected Metropolitan Areas, 1997

Metropolitan Area	Land Area (sq. mi.)	1996 Population (thousands)	Total	Counties	Cities and Towns	Special Districts	School Districts	Governments per 10,000 Residents
Northeast								
Baltimore[a]	2,619	2,502	81	6	20	55	0	0.32
Boston[a]	1,836	3,209	260	3	106	129	22	0.81
New York[a]	1,145	8,643	201	3	80	65	53	0.23
Philadelphia[a]	3,870	4,953	845	8	354	296	187	1.71
Pittsburgh	4,637	2,379	858	6	412	334	106	3.61
Midwest								
Chicago[a]	5,103	7,734	1,456	9	455	662	330	1.88
Cleveland[a]	2,718	2,233	345	6	200	55	84	1.54
Minneapolis	6,061	2,765	519	13	331	97	78	1.88
St. Louis	6,396	2,565	788	11	300	357	120	3.07
South								
Atlanta	6,150	3,541	263	20	107	109	27	0.74
Houston[a]	5,961	3,792	802	6	79	669	48	2.12
Memphis	3,013	1,078	92	5	40	41	6	0.85
Miami[a]	1,955	2,076	36	1	27	6	2	0.17
West								
Denver[a]	3,755	1,867	430	4	31	378	17	2.30
Los Angeles[a]	4,070	9,128	378	1	88	196	93	0.41
Phoenix	14,470	2,747	215	2	32	105	76	0.78
Portland[a]	5,019	1,759	282	6	56	163	57	1.60
Total								
All metro areas > 1 million	254,490	132,355	15,844	295	5,540	6,902	3,000	1.20
All metro areas	707,211	211,231	35,024	780	12,915	15,310	6,019	1.66
Total United States	3,538,624	263,256	87,453	3,043	36,001	34,683	13,726	3.32

SOURCE: Calculated from U.S. Bureau of the Census, *1997 Census of Governments*, vol. 1, *Government Organization* (Washington, D.C.: Government Printing Office, 1999). Reprinted with permission from Michael J. Rich, "The Intergovernmental Environment," in John P. Pelissero, ed., *Cities, Politics, and Policy: A Comparative Analysis* (Washington, D.C.: CQ Press, 2003), p. 39.

[a] Primary metropolitan statistical area. All other areas are metropolitan statistical areas.

consolidation efforts have been successful. Only seventeen of the eighty-three referenda proposed on city-county consolidation passed between the years 1921 and 1979; seven out of twenty-seven passed in the 1980s, two in the 1990s, and one in 2003. Since the early 1900s, only four consolidations of a large city (250,000 or more people) and a county have been approved: Nashville–Davidson County, Tennessee, in 1962; Jacksonville–Duval County, Florida, in 1967; Indianapolis–Marion County, Indiana (imposed by the state legislature), in 1969; and Louisville–Jefferson County, Kentucky, in 2003. Historically, fewer than one-quarter of the consolidation issues placed on the ballot have been approved by the voters.[75]

Reorganization Successes and Failures

Why have far-reaching changes occurred in some places and not in others? There is no simple answer. Perhaps voter approval can be won only under unique, crisis-related circumstances. Or, as some contend, a crisis may be a necessary but not a sufficient reason for change. A variety of other forces—in particular strong local leadership from influential segments of the community—must converge if reorganization is to succeed.[76]

Which groups customarily oppose one another over the issue of metro reform? The central-city business elite, civic organizations, big-city newspapers, and reform groups often support reorganization, while suburban newspapers, mayors and employees of small towns, fringe-area business people, and central-city blacks often lead the opposition. Despite the endorsement of what seem to be powerful local groups, the status quo usually carries the day. In addition, the confusion and distrust created by reform opponents frequently induce voters to take the traditional way out. The adage, "Better the evil that is known," and the rule of thumb, "When in doubt, do nothing," are probably decisive for many voters.[77]

Centralization versus Decentralization

Not everyone favors increased governmental centralization in metropolitan areas. In recent years, certain groups, minorities in particular, have urged just the opposite—greater decentralization and increased citizen participation. This movement grew out of the maximum-feasible-participation requirements associated with the Johnson administration's War on Poverty. In general, traditional metro-centralization proposals omit any consideration of what many feel is an equally important need: providing a mechanism for individuals to exercise a greater degree of control over certain services and facilities serving their own neighborhood.

Support for metropolitan decentralization also comes from scholars who, committed to the public-choice tradition, favor competition in public service. They suggest that the fragmented metropolis is analogous to a market system in which cities compete with one another for customers by offering appropriate packages of urban services. Presumably, residents can select the particular community in the metropolitan area that most nearly provides the public services they need. Municipalities then are forced to compete by offering attractive services and low tax rates.

Decentralization offers the following advantages as well, according to critics of metropolitan reform:

- Services provided by smaller units frequently receive more favorable citizen evaluations than those offered by larger jurisdictions.[78]
- Economies of scale are not universally achieved with greater size; in fact, some services may be less costly when offered by smaller units.[79]
- The existence of a large number of local governments may provide greater citizen access to political authority and thus reduce feelings of apathy, isolation, and anomie.[80]

Even though city-county consolidation has not swept the country, mechanisms are available for ensuring some measure of coordination among local governments in metropolitan areas. Before examining councils of governments and metropolitan planning organizations as coordination mechanisms, we should consider local governments that further decentralize administrative and political power: special districts.

SPECIAL DISTRICTS: A "SPECIAL" TYPE OF DECENTRALIZATION

Over the past several decades, special districts have been the most rapidly growing type of government in the United States, increasing in number from 18,323 in 1962 to 37,381 in 2007. Although they represent 42 percent of all local governments, they do not include towns, municipalities, or school districts. Only one of ten provides services beyond a single county (they serve a limited area) and 90 percent of them deliver only one service (they serve a limited function). They are highly dependent on federal aid: 11 percent of their revenues come directly from Washington, "the largest proportion for any type of local government."[81] These governmental units are often highly criticized, for a variety of reasons:

> Excessive reliance on single function special districts has led to lack of coordination in local service provision, use of public funds to further private development interests, decrease in public accountability, and decreased capability of general-purpose governments to enact effective area-wide policies.[82]

Special districts offer a wide array of activities and services, including cemeteries, housing and urban renewal, soil conservation, sewers, water supply, electric power, transit, drainage, and irrigation. Operating largely outside the control of general-purpose government and public scrutiny, these "shadow" governmental units allow cities to do things they could not do otherwise because of state constraints on debt limits. Most special districts have taxing authority, and some even have the ability to issue revenue bonds.

So, then, are special districts "good" or "bad"? The answer depends, of course, on the politics of the creation of a particular special district. If politics allocate values, and if we value open, participatory government, then the development of a citizen-controlled, single-purpose water district in a rural area to lay pipes that enable citizens to enjoy safe, clean water is good. If, on the other hand, a special district is created to foster the politics of exclusion, to bypass public dialogue about an issue or problem, then the special district distorts the democratic process. Perhaps Nancy Burns summarizes the crux of the argument best in her important book on the topic of special districts, *The Formation of American Local Governments: Private Values in Public Institutions:*

> The benefits of special districts are that they can fund and provide services and infrastructure; they are able to get things done in a fragmented American polity. The difficulties are two: They do this while no one watches except interested developers, and they are gradually becoming the realm where much of the substance of local politics happens. Thus local politics becomes quiet, not necessarily through . . . consensus, but rather through the invisibility of special district politics.[83]

MECHANISMS FOR COORDINATION: COGS AND MPOS

Aside from the few successful instances of genuine metropolitan reorganization, about the only means of bringing about greater governmental centralization in metropolitan areas has been some form of voluntary cooperation. A host of interlocal agreements (special districts, contractual arrangements, and so on) characterize every large urban area, but the major development in effecting greater governmental coordination has been the creation of councils of government (COGs) and metropolitan planning organizations (MPOs). Few such arrangements existed prior to the mid-1960s. The real impetus for the formation of COGs came with the Demonstration Cities and Metropolitan Development Act of 1966, which required that a number of federal urban development grants be subject to review and comment by some area-wide organization. The most prominent mandate for area-wide review to help coordinate federal grants in metro areas is called the "A-95 review power" (after a budget agency document with that number).[84] Although the actual A-95 clearinghouse expired in 1982 under the Reagan administration, similar review processes have been established in all the nation's metropolitan areas (central cities and their surrounding areas), in the form of either COGs or MPOs—both of which are sometimes called *regional councils*.

Metropolitan planning organizations, like COGs, are primarily the product of federal legislation, but they are more recent in terms of development. In the early 1990s, a number of laws making amendments to the Clean Air Act and the Transportation Equity Act for the 21st Century required that metropolitan areas develop metro-wide transportation plans.[85] This led to the creation of MPOs. Often this metro-wide transportation planning function is housed in the local COG, however, and for this reason, the remainder of the discussion here focuses primarily on COGs.

Though stimulated and nourished by federal requirements, regional councils are voluntary in nature. They are not true governments because they lack taxing and legislative power. Organizationally, COGs consist of elected officials from member governments, primarily cities and counties in the region. In the early 1970s, about 50 percent of regional councils had a one-government, one-vote arrangement, although provisions for population-weighted voting have become common.

COG Activities and Funding

Regional councils essentially perform three functions: they prepare plans, oversee grant applications, and provide technical assistance to member governments, especially in grant preparation. The area-wide review-and-comment role gave COGs their greatest potential leverage for bringing about some measure of metropolitan area coordination. After President Reagan revoked the provisions of the A-95 review power, state governments were asked to develop their own procedures for reviewing federally funded activities. Under this order, federal agencies are still required to make every effort to accommodate state and local recommendations concerning federal programs affecting their jurisdictions. Almost every state has now implemented its own version of the review-and-comment function, in many cases essentially continuing the system in place under federal guidelines.

Today there are about five hundred regional councils; after the hard years in the 1980s, when many COGs closed their doors and cut staff, the number has stabilized.[86] Most of the planning done by COGs is for physical development; water-and-sewerage, land-use, open-space, transportation, and solid-waste planning are the most prevalent issues. Some economic development planning also occurs. But COGs are notorious for avoiding politically sensitive problems that might involve social change, such as metropolitan approaches to low-income housing and school desegregation.

In the past, most regional councils received the bulk of their planning and operating funds from federal sources, but that, too, has changed in recent years. Instead, the state and local governments in affected areas have had to come up with an ever-larger portion of their COGs budget.

Evaluating the COGs

How successful have COGs been in bringing about some measure of metropolitan centralization? The assessment of COGs varies considerably. The federal-COG partnership peaked in 1977; since then, COGs have been engaged in a continuing quest to redefine their role and their relationship to local governments. Even though these organizations now provide more direct delivery of services and offer more management support services than before, former COG official Charles Shannon believes they have declined in importance. Writing in 1986, he noted that COGs have served as vehicles for incremental change, but "they have not met the more fundamental tests of equitably redistributing public resources, including attendant metropolitan financing methods, nor have they fulfilled comprehensive regional planning needs. . . . Two and a half decades of search for relevance, legitimacy, and authority have yielded only crumbs and tokens."[87] Twenty-five years later, his assessment still holds true, in our opinion.

Retrenchment and redefinition of mission are the major challenges facing regional organizations today. Most supporters have abandoned hope that COGs can evolve into genuine metropolitan governments.

SUMMARY

The social, economic, and political context in which urban managers must function is a complex one. Especially in larger urban areas, the world of municipal governance has grown even more complicated and demanding in recent years. As population shifts accentuate the special needs of disadvantaged groups even as they decrease the resource base, city governments are finding it increasingly difficult to manage the seemingly endless service demands of the urban populace. Having sustained cuts in many federal aid programs, some cities have had an especially tough time adjusting to the new fiscal realities. But some observers contend that by relying more on their own resources—in many instances increasing taxes or fees to maintain service levels—cities have become stronger than they were ten or twenty years ago. They have had to grow stronger in an era of "fend for yourself" federalism.

The urban manager's intergovernmental environment is not by any means confined to higher levels of government. A bevy of local jurisdictions, often in competition with one another, is found in virtually every metropolitan area of any size. Questions of metropolitan government reform arise periodically, but Americans seem to like fragmented government and local control—and this is not a feature of politics American-style that is likely to change. Perhaps the best we can hope for is to address area-wide concerns in metropolitan areas through COGs and MPOs.

As we discuss in greater detail in chapter 4, systems management requires the urban administrator to recognize *and* manage the "big picture." Many factors act as inputs into the local political system. Some of these factors the urban executive can control, but many cannot be controlled. Among the inputs that are really beyond local control are actions taken by other governments vertically (federal and state policies) and actions taken by other governments in a metropolitan area (horizontal intergovernmental relations); political power is fragmented. Still, the message of this text is that local officials do not simply "deal with" these factors—they *manage* them.

SUGGESTED FOR FURTHER READING

Burns, Nancy. *The Formation of American Local Governments: Private Values in Public Institutions.* New York: Oxford University Press, 1994.

Conlan, Timothy, and Paul L. Posner, eds. *Intergovernmental Management for the 21st Century.* Washington, D.C.: Brookings Institution, 2008.

Government Accountability Office (GAO): various reports that are accessible online at: www.gpoaccess. gov/gaoreports.

Government statistical documents online, where they are readily accessible 24/7:

—*Census of Governments* at www.census.gov/govs.

— *County and City Databook* at www.census.gov/statab/www/ccdb.html.

—*State and Local Government Finance* at www.census.gov/govs/estimate.
—*State and Metropolitan Databook* at www.census.gov/compendia/smadb.
—*The 2010 Statistical Abstract: National Data Book* at www.census.gov/compendia/statab.
O'Toole, Laurence J., Jr. ed. *American Intergovernmental Relations: Foundations, Perspectives, and Issues.* 4th ed. Washington, D.C.: CQ Press, 2007.
Publius: The Journal of Federalism: an academic journal devoted to the study of federalism and intergovernmental relations.
Walker, David B. *The Rebirth of Federalism: Slouching toward Washington.* 2nd ed. New York: Chatham House, 2000.

NOTES

1. For an excellent discussion of the debate concerning the nature of federalism at the Constitutional Convention, see chapter 2 of David B. Walker, *The Rebirth of Federalism: Slouching toward Washington,* 2nd ed. (New York: Chatham House, 2000).

2. David Osborne, *Laboratories of Democracy* (Boston: Harvard Business School Press, 1990).

3. U.S. Census Bureau, *Statistical Abstract of the United States: 2010* (Washington, D.C., 2009), table 416, p. 261.

4. The classic article upon which all others are based is Morton Grodzins, "The American System," in *Classics of Public Administration*, 5th ed., ed. Jay M. Shafritz, Albert C. Hyde, and Sandra J. Parkes (Belmont, Calif.: Wadsworth/Thomson Learning, 2004), 233–237. Also see Deil S. Wright, *Understanding Intergovernmental Relations*, 2nd ed. (Monterey, Calif.: Brooks/Cole, 1982); and Walker, *Rebirth of Federalism*.

5. Discussion of the various eras of federalism comes from Nicholas Henry, *Public Administration and Public Affairs*, 9th ed. (Upper Saddle River, N.J.: Pearson Education, 2004), 382–383.

6. Ibid., 382.

7. William Anderson, *Intergovernmental Relations in Review* (Minneapolis: University of Minnesota Press, 1960), 3, as quoted in Michael E. Milakovich and George J. Gordon, *Public Administration in America*, 7th ed. (Boston: Bedford/St. Martin's, 2001), 109.

8. Milakovich and Gordon, *Public Administration in America*, 129.

9. Henry, *Public Administration and Public Affairs*, 383.

10. *Statistical Abstract: 2010*, table 419, p. 262.

11. Ibid.

12. The over 1,000-page law can be found and its implementation followed daily, aggregately, and by state, at www.recovery.gov/Pages/home.aspx.

13. An excellent summary of the provisions of the law can be found at House Speaker Nancy Pelosi's website www.speaker.gov/newsroom/legislation?id=0273. Also see "Aid to State and Local Governments," pages 247–314, in *Analytical Perspectives: Budget of the U.S. Government, Fiscal Year 2011,* found at the Office of Management and Budget portal, www.whitehouse.gov/omb/budget/fy2011/assets/spec.pdf.

14. Lori Montgomery, "Obama Pleads for $50 billion in State, Local Aid," *Washington Post,* June 13, 2010.

15. Ibid., quoting Steny Hoyer.

16. Deil S. Wright, "Federalism, Intergovernmental Relations, and Intergovernmental Management: Historical Reflections and Conceptual Comparisons," in Shafritz, Hyde, and Parkes, *Classics of Public Administration*, 520.

17. Quoted in Jeffrey Pressman, *Federal Programs and City Politics* (Berkeley: University of California Press, 1975), 124.

18. This discussion and Mayor Garner's quote come from Donald F. Kettl, "Unconnected Dots," *Governing*, April 2004, 14.

19. Number of grant programs comes from Milakovich and Gordon, *Public Administration in America*, 116; and Henry, *Public Administration and Public Affairs*, 385.

20. Chris Edwards, "Fiscal Federalism," *Downsizing the Federal Government*, CATO Institute, February 2009, at www.downsizinggovernment.org/fiscal-federalism.

21. See www.grants.gov.

22. Milakovich and Gordon, *Public Administration in America*, 116.

23. Michael J. Rich, "The Intergovernmental Environment," in *Cities, Politics, and Policy: A Comparative Analysis*, ed. John P. Pelissero (Washington, D.C.: CQ Press, 2003), 45.

24. *Statistical Abstract: 2010*, table 419, p. 262.

25. Rich, "Intergovernmental Environment," 45.

26. *Statistical Abstract: 2010*, table 419, p. 262.

27. Rich, "Intergovernmental Environment," 46.

28. Henry, *Public Administration and Public Affairs*, 385.

29. Ibid.

30. Ibid., 386.

31. Nicholas Henry, *Public Administration and Public Affairs*, 10th ed. (Upper Saddle River, N.J.: Pearson Education, 2007), 355.

32. George F. Break, *Intergovernmental Fiscal Relations in the United States* (Washington, D.C.: Brookings Institution, 1967), chap. 3.

33. Rich, "Intergovernmental Environment," 46.

34. Gary Enos, "CDBG Program 'Ain't Broke,'" *City & State*, June 17, 1991, 3.

35. Information about the CDBG program comes from U.S. Department of Housing and Urban Development, Community Development Block Grant (CDBG) Programs, at www.hud.gov/offices/cpd/communitydevelopment/programs.

36. These examples come from Neal Peirce, "CDBG Celebrates 10th Anniversary," *Public Administration Times*, January 15, 1985.

37. U.S. General Accounting Office, *The Community Development Block Grant Program Can Be More Effective in Revitalizing the Nation's Cities* (Washington, D.C.: GAO, April 30, 1981), i; see also Enos, "CDBG Program Ain't Broke."

38. Peirce, "CDBG Celebrates 10th Anniversary."

39. Marc Bendick Jr. and David Rasmussen, "Enterprise Zones and Inner-City Economic Revitalization," in *Reagan and the Cities*, ed. George Peterson and Carol Lewis (Washington, D.C.: Urban Institute, 1986), 114.

40. Neal R. Peirce, "Enterprise Zones Open Urban Opportunities," *Public Administration Times*, February 1, 1981, 2.

41. Bendick and Rasmussen, "Enterprise Zones and Inner-City Economic Revitalization," 119.

42. Roy E. Green and Michael Brintnall, "Reconnoitering State-Administered Enterprise Zones: What's in a Name?" *Journal of Urban Affairs* 9, no. 2 (1987): 159.

43. "Effects of Urban Federal Grant Efforts Argued," *Tulsa World*, December 26, 1997, A23.

44. Marc A. Wallace, "An Analysis of Presidential Preferences in the Distribution of Empowerment Zones and Enterprise Communities," *Public Administration Review* 63 (September–October 2003): 569.

45. U.S. Department of Housing and Urban Development, "Introduction to the RC/EZ Initiative," at www.hud.gov/offices/cpd/economicdevelopment/programs/rc/about/ezecinit.cfm.

46. Ibid.; also see U.S. Housing and Urban Development, "Welcome to the Community Renewal Initiative: HUD's Initiative for Empowerment Zones and Renewal Communities EZ/RC)," at www.hud.gov/offices/cpd/economicdevelopment/programs/rc/index.cfm.

47. Brian Sullivan, "Bush Administration Announces Community Revitalization Efforts—HUD Announces Eight New Empowerment Zones," U.S. Housing and Urban Development, News Release, January 15, 2002, at www.hud.gov/news/release.cfm?contentpr02–008.cfm, 1.

48. Marilyn Gittell, Kathe Newman, Janice Bockmeyer, and Robert Lindsay, "Expanding Civic Opportunity: Urban Empowerment Zones," *Urban Affairs Review* 33 (March 1998): 530–558.

49. Information in this paragraph comes from "Effects of Urban Federal Grant Efforts Argued," A23.

50. General Accounting Office, *Community Development: Federal Revitalization Programs Are Being Implemented, but Data on the Use of Tax Benefits Are Limited* (Washington, D.C.: General Accounting Office, March 2004).

51. Ibid., Highlights page.

52. David Walker provides an excellent and comprehensive discussion of issues and problems associated with intergovernmental relations in his historical overview of nearly four centuries of American federalism; see *Rebirth of Federalism*.

53. Robert Agranoff, "Managing within the Matrix: Do Collaborative Intergovernmental Relations Exist?" *Publius* 31 (spring 2001): 32.

54. Jane Massey and Jeffrey Straussman, "Another Look at the Mandate Issue: Are Conditions-of-Aid Really So Burdensome?" *Public Administration Review* 45 (March–April 1985): 292–300.

55. Calculated from data provided by U.S. Census Bureau, "Table 2. Local Government Finances by Type of Government and State: 2006–2007," at www2.census.gov/govs/estimate/07slsstab2a.xls.

56. Ibid.

57. Taken from John M. DeGrove, "State and Local Relations: The Challenge of New Federalism," *National Civic Review* 71 (February 1982): 75–83.

58. Richard Nathan, Fred C. Doolittle, and associates, *The Consequences of the Cuts* (Princeton, N.J.: Princeton Urban and Regional Research Center, 1983), 64.

59. Steven D. Gold and Brenda M. Erickson, "State Aid to Local Governments in the 1980s," *State and Local Government Review* 21 (winter 1989): 15. There is also a literature explaining state aid to cities; see, for example, David Morgan and Robert England, "State Aid to Cities: A Casual Inquiry," *Publius* 14 (spring 1984): 67–82.

60. Michael A. Pagano, *City Fiscal Conditions in 2004* (Washington, D.C.: National League of Cities, 2004), iii.

61. Data in this paragraph, and the quote, come from Christopher Hoene, *American City and County*, October 1, 2003, 1–2, at http://americancityandcounty.com/mag/government_states_decrease_aid/.

62. "Aid to State and Local Governments," 248.

63. *Governing Daily*, "California Budget Deadline Passes without a Budget," July 1, 2010, at http://now.eloqua.com/es.asp?s=1222&e=104768&elq=70491fb43e9940729f7f19f35c7176a7, and "California Governor Puts 200,000 Workers on Minimum Wage," July 2, 2010, at http://now.eloqua.com/es.asp?s=1222&e=105386&elq=f83ef8d5ea8546bb8d9bd21c1a6acfa7.

64. John L. Mikesell, *Fiscal Administration: Analysis and Applications for the Public Sector*, 6th ed. (Belmont, Calif.: Wadsworth, 2003), 531.

65. Quotations from William Tucker, "Cities Aim to Stop Federal Buck-Passing," *Insight*, September 6, 1993.

66. John DiIulio Jr. and Donald Kettl, *Fine Print* (Washington, D.C.: Brookings Institution, March 1, 1995), 41–42.

67. John Kincaid, "Intergovernmental Deregulation," *Public Administration Review* 55 (September–October 1995): 495–496.

68. Congressional Budget Office, *CBO's Activities under the Unfunded Mandates Reform Act, 1996–2000* (Washington, D.C.: Congressional Budget Office, May 2001), vii.

69. General Accounting Office, *Unfunded Mandates: Analysis of Reform Act Coverage* (Washington, D.C.: General Accounting Office, May 2004), 3.

70. Ibid., 4.

71. David H. Rosenbloom and Robert S. Kravchuk, *Public Administration: Understanding Management, Politics, and Law in the Public Sector*, 6th ed. (Boston: McGraw-Hill, 2005), 125–126.

72. General Accounting Office, *Unfunded Mandates*, Highlights page.

73. Henry, *Public Administration and Public Affairs*, 403.

74. John J. Harrigan and Ronald K. Vogel, *Political Change in the Metropolis*, 7th ed. (New York: Addison-Wesley, 2003), 25.

75. Ibid., 259–260.

76. Melvin B. Mogulof, *Five Metropolitan Governments* (Washington, D.C.: Urban Institute, 1972).

77. Scott Greer, *Metropolitics: A Study of Political Culture* (New York: Wiley, 1963), 196.

78. Elinor Ostrom, Roger Parks, and Gordon Whitaker, "Do We Really Want to Consolidate Urban Police Forces? A Reappraisal of Some Old Assertions," *Public Administration Review* 33 (September–October 1973): 423–432.

79. Elinor Ostrom, "Metropolitan Reform: Propositions Derived from Two Traditions," *Social Science Quarterly* 53 (December 1972): 474–493.

80. Thomas R. Dye, "Metropolitan Integration by Bargaining among Sub-Areas," *American Behavioral Scientist* 5 (May 1962): 11–13.

81. Henry, *Public Administration and Public Affairs*, 402.

82. Scott A. Bollens, "Examining the Link between State Policy and the Creation of Local Special Districts," *State and Local Government Review* 18 (fall 1986): 117.

83. Nancy Burns, *The Formation of American Local Governments: Private Values in Public Institutions* (New York: Oxford University Press, 1994), 117.

84. Harrigan and Vogel, *Political Change in the Metropolis*, 293.

85. Ibid., 299.

86. Henry, *Public Administration and Public Affairs*, 405.

87. Charles Shannon, "The Rise and Emerging Fall of Metropolitan Area Regional Associations," in *Intergovernmental Relations and Public Policy*, ed. J. Edwin Benton and David Morgan (New York: Greenwood Press, 1986), 77.

CHAPTER 3   URBAN POLITICAL STRUCTURE

A s we begin the second decade of the twenty-first century, the structure for local governance continues to be a topic of discussion in local government circles. In Africa, Asia, and Eastern Europe, newly formed democratic governments continue to look to the political structures in place in American cities to find models of best practices that may contribute to governmental effectiveness and efficiency. The choice of political structure has certainly been the key decision for municipalities throughout the past century. Local interest groups that want governmental change often argue for the need for new organizational arrangements, and, although the relationship between form and function undoubtedly has been overestimated, local political structure does indeed matter. The form and powers of municipal government and the institutional arrangements for citizen input into policymaking represent part of the local "rules of the governmental game." As in any game, rules make a difference.[1] They favor some groups and put others at a disadvantage, although it is sometimes difficult to know the extent to which structures advantage one group over another.

Twentieth-century reform groups in particular had exceptional faith in the efficacy of particular forms of governmental institutions. These groups recognized that merely "throwing the rascals out" might not be enough. If local government was to be improved permanently, basic institutions had to be changed. And so, in the name of good government, reformers fought the battle for basic changes in urban structure, and their impact is still felt in this new century.

THE REFORM MOVEMENT

What has been labeled the urban reform movement was largely a product of the Progressive Era in the United States—a period that ran from the late 1880s through the 1920s, when the muckrakers and other reformers aroused public opinion with their exposés on dishonesty, greed, and corruption in public life. Unsavory politics was not confined to urban areas, of course, but the physical development of the city during the latter half of the nineteenth century provided abundant opportunities for the buying and selling of contracts for paving streets, installing lighting, and building water and sewage systems.[2] Reacting to this graft and corruption, reformers searched for ways to eliminate the excesses and to oust unscrupulous profiteers from city halls and state capitals around the country.[3]

By the late nineteenth century, the problem of corruption had been compounded by the growth of the political machine. By means of political organization, those holding office in many large cities had found it possible to remain in power indefinitely. Now the reformers had to contend not just with corruption but also with the potential for long-term control by self-perpetuating, machine organizations dominated by political bosses.

Why were political machines so successful in a number of large cities? Many scholars contend that the machine succeeded because it distributed material incentives to its political and business supporters and to those citizens who voted for them.[4] The machine clearly did not make its appeal on issues or ideology; favors and protection—with a special human touch—were the order of the day. One of the most colorful and enlightening accounts of a machine's operation comes from the famous Tammany sage George Washington Plunkitt, who became a millionaire during his forty-year service with the Tammany organization in New York. He had this to say about how the machine was able to gain such widespread support:

> There's only one way to hold a district; you must study human nature and act accordin'. You can't study human nature in books. . . . To learn real human nature you have to go among the people, see them and be seen. . . .
>
> For instance, here's how I gather in the young men. I hear of a young feller that's proud of his voice, thinks he can sing fine.
>
> I ask him to come around to Washington Hall and join our Glee Club. He comes and sings, and he's a follower of Plunkitt for life. Another young feller gains a reputation as a baseball player in a vacant lot. I bring him into our baseball club. That fixes him. You'll find him workin' for my ticket at the polls next election day. Then there's the feller that likes rowin' on the river, the young feller that makes a name as a waltzer on his block, the young feller that's handy with his dukes—I rope them all in by givin' them opportunities to show themselves off. I don't trouble them with political arguments. I just study human nature and act accordin'.[5]

Now, of course, the machines have largely withered away, although not necessarily because of the reformers. Not that the reform movement had no impact on twentieth-century urban politics—to the contrary, the reform heritage is impressive. The decline and near-demise of the political machine, however, generally is thought to have resulted from other, more fundamental influences. Edward C. Banfield and James Q. Wilson, for example, indicate that voters gradually became less interested in what the machines had to offer: "The petty favors and 'friendship' of the precinct captains declined in value as immigrants were assimilated, public welfare programs were vastly extended, and per capita incomes rose steadily."[6] Banfield and Wilson emphasize the importance of the assimilation of lower-class people into the middle class, and the growing acceptance of the middle-class political ethos: "The central idea of which is that politics should be based on public rather than on private motives and, accordingly, should stress the virtues of honesty, impartiality, and efficiency."[7]

Perhaps the reformers were not instrumental in bringing down the bosses and their organizations. In fact, Steven Erie argues that machine bosses had a very limited supply of rewards to meet the demands of their supporters. He contends that the demise of machines was as much a response to the changing relationship between party resources and claimants as it was to the actions of reformers.[8] Still, many of the changes sought by reform groups were implemented in city after city across the land.[9]

THE GOALS AND ASSUMPTIONS OF MUNICIPAL GOVERNMENT REFORMERS

City governments perform two basic functions: they provide services and they manage local political conflict. To many, this second task is far less legitimate than the first. Perhaps it would be unfair to say that the municipal government reformers of the Progressive Era wanted to eliminate politics from city government altogether; but clearly they felt there was no room for party politics in municipal government. Obviously a city must provide fire and police protection, water and sewage facilities, and other essential services, but party influence was not appropriate to the exercise of any of these functions. "There is no Democratic or Republican way to pave a street," the old saying goes. Moreover, according to these reformers, partisan politics had led to abuses by the bosses and their machines, which contributed to corrupting the cities. It seemed impossible, then, to eliminate graft and corruption—to rid the cities of the machines—without freeing city government from partisan politics. These reformers' basic objective was to eradicate corruption; the means to that end was the exclusion of political parties from local public affairs. But eliminating corruption was just one goal of the early urban reform movement.

Making government more efficient was another goal of reformers. If the primary purpose of city government was to provide services, the Progressive Era reformers held, this function ought to be performed as economically and efficiently as possible. According to Lawrence J. R. Herson, "In the period just prior to the First [World] War, a new concern moved toward the top of the [reformers'] agenda: rationalized management of urban government. . . . The new reforms were a mixture of the business ethic and Taylorism, the new science of managerial efficiency."[10] The reformers found in the business corporation the ideal model for streamlining and rationalizing the municipal administrative process. The city-manager plan seemed to offer what was needed: an elected local council would choose an outside administrator on the basis of managerial experience and skill. The city government, then, not only needed rescuing from the baneful effects of partisan politics; it also needed restructuring to operate as efficiently as possible. These urban reformers were not apolitical; in fact, a political economy explanation of the urban reform movement is now widely accepted.

In a classic article, Samuel P. Hays dispels the myth that the municipal government reform movement was a product of the working and/or middle class, arguing that, instead, the driving force came from business and professional groups.[11] In fact, according to political scientists Dennis Judd and Todd Swanstrom, the recommended changes in structure and electoral rules were an attempt to undercut the political strength of lower-class groups.[12] Certainly one purpose was to curtail corruption and compel city governments to operate more efficiently, but Judd and Swanstrom contend that upper-income and business groups sought a local political climate that would be favorable to growth and economic development. These were not true social reformers, who would have wanted lower utility rates, safer and more affordable housing, or additional public services to improve the lives of the poor. Instead, the structural reformers were interested primarily in more efficient government and lower taxes as a way of advancing the political agenda of the business community.

Another reform goal was greater popular control of local government. Banfield and Wilson suggest that the reform movement was concerned that local government be more democratic.[13] The reformers felt that greater popular participation was a primary means of weakening the political machine. If only the political process at the grassroots could be opened up—removed from the smoke-filled back rooms—perhaps the people could regain control of city hall. To this end, Progressive Era reformers pushed for the initiative, referendum, recall, and the direct primary.

Behind these three goals—elimination of corruption, greater efficiency, and more democracy—lay a basic presupposition regarding the nature of city government. The reformers assumed that a single public interest existed for the city as a whole and that this interest should prevail over competing, partial, and usually private interests.[14] This larger community interest presumably could be discovered and agreed on if rational, well-intended people could free themselves from narrow partisan or geographic ties. The "best" people should be elected to municipal office regardless of where they lived. Therefore, at-large elections became an essential part of the reformers' search for rational, efficient local government. In addition, they believed that destroying the ward system would free council members from petty ward politics. Elected officials would no longer be required to serve as political brokers, exchanging services and favors for votes. Mutual accommodation, or logrolling, among council members would cease.

THE CHARACTERISTICS OF REFORM GOVERNMENT

Over time, a number of proposals were advanced by reformers to reorganize the structure of city government formally. Although modern reform groups have focused on somewhat different governmental features, one constant characteristic in the municipal reform model had emerged by the 1920s and 1930s: a dual emphasis on rational decision making and on increased efficiency in providing services.

How does the reform model compare to the more political model? Robert Boynton contrasts the reform model of city government with a political model.[15] The *reform model* embraces council-manager government; nonpartisan ballots; at-large elections; the separation of municipal elections from state and national elections; merit systems; and the initiative, referendum, and recall petition processes. We examine several of these features, particularly the ballot type and method for selecting council members, in the sections that follow. Here we should note that separating city elections from state and national elections presumably is an additional means (beyond removing party labels) of isolating local elections, thus lessening the influence of political parties and their organizations. Merit systems, of course, are the obvious answer to the spoils and patronage arrangements so crucial to the success of the political machine. Putting legislation or propositions on the ballot through a referendum petition is an attempt to make local government more responsive to the people. The same is true of the recall process, whereby a petition containing a sufficient number of names can force a new election for city council positions.

What other features of today's city governments reflect reform ideals? For one, a short ballot avoids fragmented executive authority. Also, reformers generally favor small councils to avoid potential divisiveness and cumbersome decision processes. Finally, no premium is placed on concurrent council terms: "On the contrary, overlapping terms are thought of as providing stability and continuity in decision making and are encouraged in the reform model."[16]

Boynton's *political model*—the opposite of the reform ideal—is committed to providing maximum representation for various community interests, especially those with some geographic base. The model's structural arrangements also enhance the conflict-managing capacity of city government. Its characteristics include a strong mayor–council form of government, partisan elections, ward representation, coterminous council elections, and a relatively large council. In the political model, a directly elected strong mayor is responsible for taking the lead in policymaking and controlling the administrative apparatus of the city. The council is relatively large (and elected from geographic constituencies), so that all legitimate community groups are represented. And the political party is a legitimate, if not essential, mechanism for aggregating and articulating competing local interests.

As with all ideal types, Boynton's two models seldom appear in their pure forms. Still, certain reform mechanisms commonly are found together. Overall, 66 percent of cities use the at-large election system, 17 percent elect by district, and another 17 percent have a mixed system in which some seats are elected by district and others in an at-large fashion.[17] For example, among council-manager cities, 72 percent utilize at-large elections, compared to just 51 percent of mayor-council cities.[18] Reform structures, moreover, are apt to be found in certain kinds of cities. Historically, very large cities resisted reform structures. As recently as 2001, only 25 percent of cities over 500,000 used the council-manager plan.[19] However, by 2006, 55 percent had adopted the plan. As table 3-1 reveals, the next largest category of cities—those with 250,000–500,000 residents—are the least attracted to the council-manager plan (35 percent in that category). Council-manager cities are much more common in the population range of 25,000–250,000—small to medium-sized cities. In smaller cities (less than 25,000), the odds are about even that the city adopted the council-manager form of city government or another governmental form, such as the mayor-council arrangement.[20] But most cities—regardless of size—now employ nonpartisan ballots.[21] This does not mean that all city elections are free of party influence; such influence is simply more subtle.

Table 3-1   **Municipal Reform Characteristics by City Population, 2006**

Population of Cities (number studied)	Council-Manager Form (percentage)
Over 500,000 (11)	55
250,000–499,999 (17)	35
100,000–249,999 (100)	70
50,000–99,999 (227)	67
25,000–49,999 (424)	63
2,500–24,999 (2,590)	52
Under 2,500 (495)	50
Total (3,864)	55

SOURCE: Evelina R. Moulder, "Municipal Form of Government: Trends in Structure, Responsibility, and Composition," *2008 Municipal Year Book* (Washington, D.C.: ICMA, 2008), 28. Adapted and reprinted with the permission of the International City/County Management Association, 777 North Capitol Street, N.E., Suite 500, Washington, D.C., 20002. All rights reserved.

Region and type of city (central city, suburb, or independent) are also linked to reformism.[22] Sunbelt and Pacific Coast cities are more likely to employ the council-manager form of government. Nonpartisan elections are likely to be used in all regions, except the Mid-Atlantic. Whereas central cities are somewhat more likely to adopt the council-manager plan (63 percent) than are suburban cities (53 percent),[23] central cities are much less likely to use at-large elections.

Urban research has long validated the connection between certain social and economic characteristics and a city's form of government.[24] Cities with more homogeneous populations find the reform model's emphasis on efficiency and businesslike practices more to their liking. Indeed, growth-oriented middle-class cities and cities with mobile populations tend to embrace the council-manager plan. Ethnically and religiously diverse, non-mobile populations, and industrial cities lean more toward the mayor-council form.

THE IMPACT OF REFORM

Except in bigger, more socially diverse cities, Progressive Era reform efforts begun at the onset of the twentieth century had largely succeeded in depoliticizing municipal government by the century's end, an achievement that has had several effects. What have been the effects of these reforms? For one, certain reform arrangements—nonpartisan ballots, the council-manager form, short ballots, and nonconcurrent elections—tend to depress voter turnout in city elections. Since lower levels of voter participation often work to the advantage of the well-to-do and the middle class, reform city governments may not be as responsive to the interests of the less advantaged. Ward-based elections, in contrast to at-large systems, produce more representative city councils. African Americans, for example, are much more likely to be elected to city councils in cities using ward-based as opposed to at-large elections.[25] This is generally also true for Latinos, who have made gains in representation with changes to district (or mixed) systems.[26] Election of Asians to city councils, however, appears to be unrelated to method of representation.[27] And the representation of females on city councils does not appear to be affected by electoral structures.[28]

Reformed structures also may affect municipal policy outcomes. Perhaps the major study on this issue was done by political scientists Robert Lineberry and Edmund Fowler, who examined two hundred cities of 50,000 or more inhabitants. They hypothesized that the policymaking of reformed city governments would differ from that of unreformed city governments. Indeed, they found lower levels of taxation and expenditures among reform cities, even when the social and economic characteristics of the cities were taken into account. In addition, the policies of unreformed cities were more responsive to socioeconomic cleavages in their environments. The authors conclude: "If one of the components of the middle-class reformer's ideal was to 'seek the good of the community as a whole' and to minimize the impact of social cleavages on political decision making, then their institutional reforms have served, by and large, to advance that goal."[29] Others, however, question the relationship between political structures and taxing and spending patterns in cities. Using a time-series analysis, for example, David Morgan and John Pelissero matched eleven cities that had changed political structure with eleven that had not. They found that taxing and spending differences were largely unaffected by changes in city government structure.[30] This research has largely been confirmed by later studies on the same question.

Perhaps the linkage between political structure and public policy is through representation. Unreformed political structures apparently enhance minority representation, and research shows that representation does have an impact on public policy outputs. Case studies have found, for example, that the election of black mayors can lead to substantive changes in public policies in a city.[31] For instance, a study by Albert Karnig and Susan Welch found that the election of a black mayor may result in higher levels of municipal spending on social welfare programs.[32] Other research shows that minority elected officials increase employment of minorities in municipal government.[33]

Some observers of city politics believe that city governments are not equally responsive to low-income and minority groups as to other groups in the city, and often blame the reform legacy for contributing to the problem. Their criticism often is directed at municipal bureaucrats whose power is enhanced under reform institutions. With the passing of political machines, the governance of cities increasingly has been influenced by bureaucratic independence and expertise. So some critics fault the merit system and the professionalized civil service for depersonalizing city government and isolating it from the individual citizen. Middle-class city dwellers do not suffer unduly from this situation because they have fewer needs for public services and are reasonably well positioned to make the system respond. Low-income residents, however, often have complicated social and economic problems that may require extensive governmental help. For these groups, the red tape, the delays, the innumerable offices and programs make it much more difficult for the disadvantaged to obtain needed assistance.

The extent to which the blame for bureaucratic inertia, insensitivity, and red tape should be assigned to the reformers is debatable; but the municipal reform movement did place its faith in a bureaucratic rather than a political process for identifying the public interest. And although city governments now may be more efficiently run, some authorities contend that large cities, in particular, are poorly governed. Chief executives today lack the power to control the autonomous agencies—the islands of functional power—because reform institutions, according to critics, destroyed the informal centralizing influence of the political party. Although municipal reform may contribute to more businesslike management of a city, it does so at a price—less responsiveness to disadvantaged groups within the community and more control by autonomous bureaucrats.[34]

FORMS OF CITY GOVERNMENT

What are the key differences between the mayor-council government and the council-manager plan? In this section, we contrast these basic forms of municipal government, and offer some new alternatives that have emerged in practice.[35]

MAYOR-COUNCIL GOVERNMENT

We can identify the two variations most commonly found in mayor-council government: the weak-mayor and strong-mayor forms. Essentially, the two types differ in degree only, and few cities reflect an extreme version of either type. The mayor-council form of government, which is used by nearly 34 percent[36] of cities, preserves the basic separation of powers between the legislative and executive branches. Historically, owing to widespread suspicion of concentrated executive power, councils were the dominant force in city government, but gradually, as cities grew and government became increasingly complex, more concentrated authority was put in the hands of the chief executive. Now, most authorities favor the strong-mayor variation as a way of providing the political leadership thought to be crucial, especially for larger cities. For smaller communities, the weak-mayor form still remains popular.

The Weak Mayor–Council Form

The weak mayor–council plan is a product of Jacksonian democracy, which held that if politicians have few powers and many checks upon them, they can do relatively little damage—if one politician becomes corrupt, he or she will not necessarily corrupt the whole city government. The following features distinguish this severely decentralized form:

- The council, which possesses both legislative and executive authority, may appoint several important administrative officials and invariably must approve the mayor's appointees.
- The mayor, whose appointive powers are restricted, may share power with the city council, and sometimes with other boards or commissions made up of elected or unelected city officials.

- The council exercises primary control over the municipal budget, often through the operation of a city council budget or finance committee.

Figure 3-1 illustrates the essence of the weak-mayor form. Notice that the voters elect both the mayor and the city council; in some cities, voters may also elect several other administrative officials, such as a clerk or treasurer. Moreover, the council has considerable appointive power itself and, if the mayor does choose department heads or appointees to various boards and commissions, city council approval is usually required. Clearly, this arrangement establishes no single administrative head of city government; power is fragmented, and the mayor is severely hemmed in. The mayor is "weak" because he or she lacks administrative power over the daily affairs of city government.

The weak-mayor plan was designed for an earlier era, when cities were smaller and government simpler. Today it seems especially ill-suited for large cities, where centralized political and administrative leadership is vital. Many of the nineteenth-century machines evolved under the weak-mayor structure because its lack of administrative centralization was an open invitation for external direction and control. Fragmented authority at the top also encourages greater bureaucratic independence. As Lana Stein has observed, "Despite the variations in institutional structure, a mayor has to be able to negotiate and compromise with key players in his or her environment in order to implement an agenda. In the American system of divided government, few elective executives can move forward by fiat."[37] The effect of autonomy is to make city government into a series of many little governments rather than a single coordinated one. For a number of reasons, then, larger cities have searched for ways to bring about more central control of administrative activities.

Figure 3-1   **Weak Mayor–Council Form of Government**

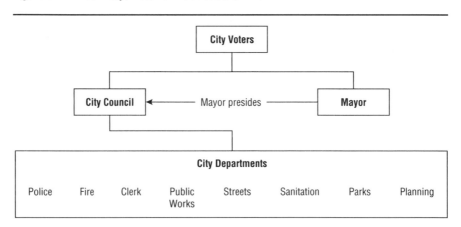

SOURCE: Reprinted with permission from John P. Pelissero, "The Political Environment of Cities in the Twenty-first Century," in John P. Pelissero, ed., *Cities, Politics, and Policy: A Comparative Analysis* (Washington, D.C.: CQ Press, 2003), p. 15.

The Strong Mayor–Council Form

The strong mayor–council government represents a significant contrast to the fragmented executive office of the weak-mayor plan. It includes the following features:

- The mayor has almost total administrative authority, including the power to appoint and dismiss virtually all department heads without council approval.
- The mayor prepares and administers the budget.
- A short ballot restricts the number of elected administrative officials.
- Policymaking is a joint enterprise between mayor and council.

Strong mayors are likely to have a veto power that usually can be overridden only by a two-thirds or three-fourths majority of the council. Because of this commanding legal position, the mayor becomes the dominant force in city government, as figure 3-2 illustrates.

The strong-mayor form is subject to criticism. First, it requires that the mayor be both a good political leader and a competent administrator—two traits that are not always found in a single mayoral candidate. In addition, much as in national government, conflict can erupt periodically between a strong, politically ambitious mayor and a recalcitrant council. Therefore, a legislative-executive deadlock remains a continual threat. In some large strong-mayor cities, the first potential shortcoming of the plan—the need to combine a good administrator and a good politician in the same office—is being rectified by a new development: a chief administrative officer (CAO) is appointed by the mayor to serve at his or her pleasure. The CAO may supervise department heads, prepare the budget (under the mayor's direction), coordinate various departments in the performance of day-to-day activities, and give technical advice to the mayor. By assigning these more mundane responsibilities to the CAO, the mayor frees time for two other

Figure 3-2   Strong Mayor–Council Form of Government

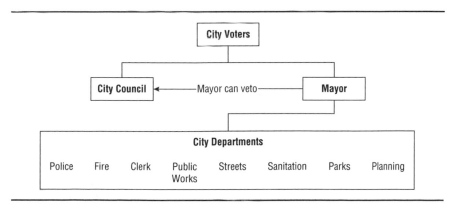

SOURCE: Pelissero, "The Political Environment of Cities," p. 15.

major jobs: serving as ceremonial head of the city and providing broad policy leadership. The CAO remains the mayor's deputy because she or he is responsible only to the mayor, not to the council. It is this mayoral control that distinguishes the job of the CAO from that of the city manager.

More recent research suggests that we need to expand our understanding of the variations in mayor-council governments.[38] In addition to traditional strong or weak mayor–council governments, there are now strong-mayor governments with managers or CAOs in 3 percent of cities and weak-mayor governments with CAOs in 17 percent of cities.[39] Political scientists Kimberly Nelson and James Svara recently published new findings on nearly 3,000 cities and found that 48 percent of mayor-council governments in their survey had a CAO appointed by either the mayor or the council.[40] With or without the CAO, the strong-mayor form is especially suitable to large cities with diverse populations, where strong political leadership is required to arrange compromises and arbitrate struggles for power among contending interests.

COUNCIL-MANAGER GOVERNMENT

In 1913 Dayton, Ohio, became the first city of any size to successfully adopt the council-manager form of government. Since then, with the approval and ardent support of reform groups, the plan has spread rapidly; today, 55 percent of cities with populations over 2,500 use this form.[41] The council-manager plan includes the following basic characteristics:

- A small city council, usually five to seven people, is elected, usually at-large, on a nonpartisan ballot.
- The council has responsibility for making policy, passing ordinances, voting appropriations, and overall supervision of the administration of city government.
- A full-time, professionally trained city administrator is hired to serve at the pleasure of the council, with full responsibility for managing day-to-day city operations (including hiring and firing department heads without council approval).
- An executive budget is prepared and administered by the city manager.
- A mayor performs largely ceremonial duties and has little or no involvement in the city's administrative affairs.

This description represents the plan as ideally conceived (and as shown schematically in figure 3-3); usually only slight deviations are found in actual practice. The council-manager plan departs most drastically from American government tradition in its abandonment of the doctrines of separation of powers and checks and balances. All executive and legislative authority resides in the council alone. The manager is essentially the council's hired hand and has no direct responsibility to the citizenry. Originally, reformers feared that the mayor might be tempted to interfere in the administrative affairs of city government unless mayoral powers were circumscribed strictly. The solution was to make the mayor

Figure 3-3   Council-Manager Form of Government

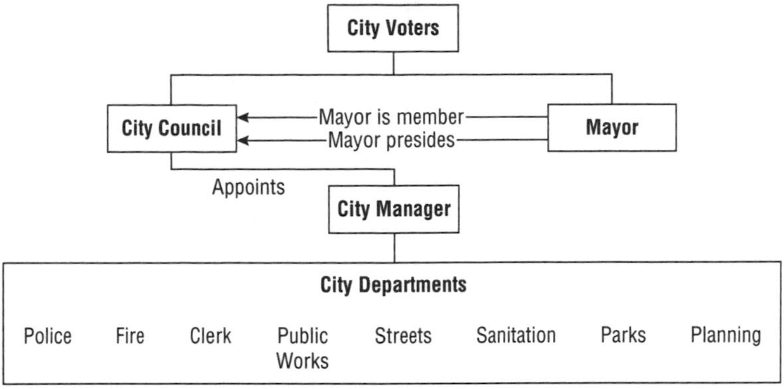

SOURCE: Pelissero, "The Political Environment of Cities," p. 16.

responsible to the council rather than to the people. Over time, this view has undergone modification, so that today about 65 percent of council-manager cities provide for direct popular election of the mayor.[47]

Strengths of the Form

The council-manager plan's main attribute is its businesslike approach to city government, which presumably maximizes efficiency and technical expertise. In fact, in many places, this form has been supported by business groups, which tout— perhaps excessively—the potential for saving taxpayers' money. These groups argue that professional administration reduces waste and inefficiency and thereby realize great savings. The plan's reputation for efficiency makes it appealing in the upper- and middle-class suburbs that so many business executives call home. And, unmistakably, the council-manager system of government has achieved considerable success in areas with little community diversity, where a high degree of consensus exists over the proper scope and function of city government.

Adopting the council-manager plan appears to lead to greater use of modern electronic government tools. As shown in the case study presented in box 3.1, council-manager governments have embraced the development of "e-government" more enthusiastically than have mayor-council cities.

Limitations of the Form

A reading of the reform literature and regular research reports from the International City/County Management Association (ICMA) would suggest that the council-manager system is the best form of government. But despite its obvious popularity, there are

ALL E-GOVERNMENT IS NOT CREATED EQUAL

The race to extend government to the Internet has proved to be a marathon, not a sprint, and many cities around the country are struggling to get past the starting line. While some municipalities have developed expansive online webs of information and transactions between governments, citizens, and businesses, many others struggle to even keep their contact information up-to-date.

Christopher G. Reddick set out to explain this variance by testing an empirical framework of e-government development in cities across the country. He began by integrating models of e-government developed separately in research by Karen Layne and Jungwoo Lee; Janine S. Hiller and France Belanger; and Richard T. Watson and Bryan Mundy. Reddick sought to determine what stage of e-government growth each local government had so far attained, and what factors facilitate the growth of e-government at the local level. He discovered that many governments have a long way to go in e-government development, but he found a surprising level of success in e-government development by council-manager governments.

Reddick uses Layne and Lee's work to show that the first stage of e-government development is the cataloging of information on a website. This cataloging stage involves presenting basic information about a government's activities, it is uni-directional and non-traditional in nature. The second stage of e-government growth, then, is the development of the capability for allowing citizens to transact with government electronically. This transaction stage enables citizens to pay taxes, fines, or fees online, for example. Layne and Lee also identified two additional stages: vertical integration with other levels of government and horizontal integration within the same government.

Reddick examined the results of the International City/County Management Association's 2002 e-government survey. Focusing on cities across the country with populations over 2,500, the survey asked local officials about the status of e-government capabilities in their municipality. The responses were characterized by the stage of the e-government relationships identified by Hiller and Belanger: government-to-citizen, government-to-business, and government-to-government.

Reddick found that most local governments are just past the minimum qualifications of the first stage in government-to-citizen activities—having little more than an initial web presence of catalog information. Still, a strong contingent of local governments had succeeded in reaching the second, transaction stage of e-government development.

Per the survey, local governments that have gotten to the transaction stage most likely have the following attributes: they use a council-manager form of government, are situated in the western United States, have populations greater than 250,000, and maintain separate IT departments. It seems only logical that such large cities (and thus cities able to afford separate IT departments), would be more successful in e-government development—it is simply a question of resources. What is striking, however, is the relationship between the council-manager form of government and e-government success.

Noting the dominance in this study of the council-manager or council-administrator form in e-government development, Reddick concludes that success in this endeavor depends on having a champion of the technology in a prominent position. After investigating two cities with strong levels of development—Roanoke, Virginia, and Colorado Springs, Colorado—he finds that the city manager or administrator can act as that champion in the pursuit of good government practices. Such leadership increases the level of prestige of the e-government initiative, concludes Reddick, and ultimately leads to its success. However, the efforts

(continued)

BOX 3.1   Policy and Practice (continued)

of such a champion can go only so far, as the barriers of cost, privacy, and security can still derail many e-government efforts.

SOURCE: Christopher Reddick, "Empirical Models of E-Government Growth in Local Governments," *e-Service Journal* 3, no. 2 (2004): 61–86.

potential shortcomings in the council-manager form. For instance, its sharp distinction between policymaking and administration is unrealistic. We look at the policymaking relationship between manager and council in chapter 4; here we should stress that the full-time professional manager inevitably will provide considerable policy advice to the part-time amateur council. Yet council members may not be certain just what the policy relationship between themselves and the manager should be. Citizens also may wonder who is really in charge of city affairs. Should administrative problems be brought to the mayor or to the city manager? And if a council merely rubber-stamps a manager's recommendations, then the manager—who is not directly accountable to the people — may seem to have too much power. Obviously, this confusion cannot improve a government's responsiveness.

However, the major potential limitation of the council-manager plan is its lack of formal provision for strong policy leadership: theoretically, at least, the council is a group of equals, the mayor is limited to a ceremonial role, and the manager presumably serves only in an advisory role. But what happens in practice often deviates from theory. The mayor or one of the council members may emerge as a policy leader, but "more likely, the council will flounder about or turn to the manager."[43] Sometimes, mayors can help managers to be more successful—with the council and with the public. The mayor can be a "stabilizer" who allows the municipal system to operate better[44] or can form a policymaking team with the city manager.[45] New research shows the trend toward more powerful roles for mayors in the council-manager system. A 2010 research article found that over 1,000 cities with the council-manager plan (about 63 percent) had a directly elected mayor.[46] The case study of Oakland, California, provided in box 3.2 exemplifies this trend.

An argument can be made, of course, that the experienced professional manager is in a better position than the council to interpret the needs of the community and thus should take the lead in policy formulation. But what does this do to the idealized role of the council? The issue is easy to resolve, and we return to it in the next chapter.

BALLOT TYPE

One goal of the Progressive reformers was to remove the partisan influence on local elections. In 1910 almost no cities held nonpartisan elections, but by about twenty years later, more than half of all cities with populations over 30,000 used nonpartisan ballots.[47]

BOX 3.2   Policy and Practice

RE-FORMING THE REFORM IN OAKLAND

Like many American cities, Oakland, California, found the spark of reform in the early twentieth century. In 1931, faced with growing instances of corruption in the executive, the city abandoned its mayor-commission form of government for the reform movement's popular council-manager plan. The new city council arrangement would keep a check on mayoral power, while an appointed city manager directed the day-to-day operations of the city.

By 1998, however, Oakland leaders had become disenchanted with their reformed system. The same business community that had called for the change to a council-manager form of government was finding a fractious, argumentative, and leaderless council inefficient at pursuing the economic development policies it had hoped for. City Manager Robert Bobb was working hard at going after slumlords and making the city more "customer friendly," but progress was slow, and he found great political resistance from council members.

In the midst of the mayoral election that year, former California governor Jerry Brown took up the "reform of the reform" cause and integrated it into his campaign for mayor. Brown had big plans, which he said would require strong leadership to move forward. Oakland residents wanted results and accountability, Brown argued, and those features were lacking in the current system. Brown began to champion a proposal known as Measure X, to amend the city charter to create a six-year experiment with a strong-mayor form of government—a system that he said would give him the power he needed to run the city. The voters agreed and passed Measure X, and they put Brown at the helm.

What was wrong with Oakland? Had the voters not learned from its troubles with a strong-mayor system in an earlier era? Would not Mayor Brown turn city government into an extension of his campaign? Would not efficiency drop as the mayor intervened in day-to-day workings? Would the mayor's highly politicized office block the manager's good-government reforms?

Surprisingly, no. What did happen, in fact, was a fusing of executive power that created a strong force for change. City Manager Bobb, kept on by Brown, found new power and comfort in tackling what the two saw as an entrenched status quo. One of the first acts by Bobb was to send a blunt letter to every city department head. "This is to notify you," it read, "that the city is contemplating possibly separating you from service in the near future." In the end, three department heads, including the popular police chief, were asked to resign, and a fourth was reassigned. Had Bobb targeted these departments on his own authority under the old council-manager system, the city council, outraged by his actions, would have had his head. But now Bobb only had to report to Mayor Brown, who wasn't afraid of a fight. In the four years they worked together, Brown and Bobb improved Oakland's fiscal situation and business environment and reduced the crime rate. There was great hope for the city and for this new style of strong mayor/strong manager relationship.

But while the first few years went smoothly for the new system, the story does not have a happy ending for the pair. By fiscal year 2003, the city began to face the prospect of large deficits, as new spending was not met with new revenue. Eventually, even the strong mayor/strong manager coalition would break up, as the two leaders disagreed on a major policy proposal, and the friction of their row finally generated enough heat to drive Bobb out of Oakland. Many observers have attributed the breakup to the proposed development of a downtown baseball park for the Oakland A's, at which point, despite Bobb's strong objections, Brown approved a housing project on the most likely site for the ballpark. In July 2003, Brown axed Bobb, citing a need for change.

(continued)

BOX 3.2   Policy and Practice (continued)

The honeymoon with the system appeared to be over. Politics began to creep back into the mayor's office and to stymie the new manager's efforts. The mayor's ability to consolidate power created an imbalance in city government and left little room for resistance, as he all but ignored the city council. City deficits were ballooning and major problems in the schools persisted.

Still, the voters of Oakland saw the venture as worthwhile. Many craved leadership and saw the strong and visible mayoral position as a necessary means for accountability in city government. In March 2004, Oakland residents voted to make the new strong-mayor system permanent.

SOURCES: Rob Gurwitt, "Mayor Brown & Mr. Bobb," *Governing* 13 (January 2000): 16–20; Anya Sostek, "The Big Breakup," *Governing* 17 (January 2004): 60; and "Oakland, California; Tax Secured, General Obligation," *Standard and Poor's, Ratings Direct,* July 15, 2003, at www.oaklandnet.com.

Today, nearly one hundred years after the highpoint of reformers' efforts, over 80 percent of American cities of all sizes use nonpartisan ballots.[48] As often happens with any reform, however, unanticipated side effects have developed. Reform groups wanted to get the political party out of municipal government as a way of destroying bosses and machine politics. Moreover, they considered parties irrelevant, if not harmful, to providing services; experts and professionals should determine the service needs of the populace. But evidence now reveals that nonpartisanship has other effects as well, some of which are of dubious value. Before examining the consequences of removing party labels in municipal elections, we should mention that much of the research done on nonpartisan elections focuses on cities that also have adopted other reform features, namely the council-manager plan and citywide elections. Therefore, in some instances it is difficult to separate the effects of nonpartisan ballots from other influences.

Some early research suggested that nonpartisan ballots gave a slight edge to Republicans.[49] Recent evidence, however, indicates that this relationship is not clear-cut. Relying on surveys from about 1,000 city council members from around the nation, political scientists Susan Welch and Timothy Bledsoe report that a significant Republican bias appears only in smaller communities and in cities that have both nonpartisan elections and at-large balloting.[50] Nonpartisanship also tends to produce elected officials who are more representative of the upper socioeconomic strata than of the general populace, especially when combined with at-large elections: "When nonpartisan and at-large structures are combined, both lower income and lower educational level groups and Democrats are disadvantaged."[51]

Ballot type does not seem to make a difference with respect to reelection of council members—the incumbents overwhelmingly win reelection regardless of ballot type. An ICMA survey showed that ballot type is not related to the election of women or minorities to city councils, although Hispanics fared a little better in nonpartisan elections.[52] Welch and Bledsoe report no differences in the level of conflict between partisan and nonpartisan elected council members. The nature of conflict on partisan versus nonpartisan councils was distinct, however: a "Democratic versus Republican rivalry was the most commonly cited principal source of factionalism among partisan council members, but the least commonly cited among those that are nonpartisan."[53]

ELECTORAL SYSTEMS

Citywide or district elections—which should a city have? Again, there is no simple answer. We know that at-large elections are used in 66 percent of cities, compared to just 17 percent that divide the balloting by districts or wards.[54] Proponents of at-large elections argue that they offer the following benefits:

- Council members in an at-large system can rise above the limited perspective of the ward and concern themselves with the problems of the whole community.
- Vote trading and logrolling are minimized.
- The chance of domination by a machine is lessened.
- Better-qualified individuals are elected to the council.

In contrast, those advocating ward-based elections insist on the following points:

- District elections give all legitimate groups, especially those with a geographic base, a better chance of being represented on the city council.
- Ward council members are more sensitive to the small but frequently important little problems that people have (neglected potholes, needed stop signs).
- Ward-based elections reduce voter alienation by bringing city government close to the people.

Because of the apparent strengths and shortcomings of both electoral systems, various combinations of the two have developed in about 17 percent of cities.[55] In one combination, council members are nominated by district and then elected citywide. This arrangement ensures geographic representation but also forces selected officials to think about the needs of the whole city; it also guarantees that the larger community will have the dominant voice in choosing representatives from each district. Blacks have objected to the arrangement, however, claiming that it can be confusing and potentially divisive for the minority community.[56]

A second combination requires that a certain number of the council members be elected from wards, while others run at-large. For example, a city might be divided into four wards, and one council member elected from each ward; then, three or four additional council members would be voted on by the entire city. This combination, too, is open to criticism: members elected at-large may consider themselves more important than the others and in some cases may see themselves as rivaling the mayor.[57] In cities that use this mixed system, on average, two-thirds of the council members are elected from districts and one-third at-large.[58]

The method of choosing council members—either by ward or at-large—does affect who is elected. As noted earlier, citywide elections tend to disadvantage blacks and other geographically concentrated minority groups. On the other hand, research shows that women do slightly better in at-large electoral systems, particularly if the city has a large council.[59] Additional evidence indicates that ward-based elections provide a greater opportunity for people of lower income and education levels to be elected, regardless of race.[60] Welch and Bledsoe note that council members elected at-large are better educated and are "less likely to focus on representing a neighborhood, ethnic, or party group and more likely to focus on the city as a whole."[61] They also report less conflict on councils where members are elected at-large instead of from wards.[62]

JUDICIAL AND LEGISLATIVE INTERVENTION

The importance of electoral structure is demonstrated by a series of recent legal battles over equal representation, many of which involve either ward-based or at-large elections.[63] In most cases, the plaintiffs are ethnic and racial minorities, seeking greater representation in city councils. After decades of controversy, a court decision forced Springfield, Illinois, to change from an arrangement in which four officials were elected at-large to a mayor-council form in which ten aldermen would be chosen by wards.[64] To avoid litigation, Tulsa, Oklahoma, decided to move from a commission form of government with at-large elections to a strong-mayor form with ward-based elections. Perhaps the city that has received the most public attention in recent years is Dallas, Texas. Through a series of contentious court battles with sharp racial overtones, that city's wholly at-large electoral system was changed in 1975 to a mixed system, with both at-large and single-member districts, and then in 1990 to an all-district system (except the mayor). In 2010 the council was composed of seven white, four black, and three Hispanic council members; a woman, Laura Miller, was elected mayor in 2002.[65]

Recent changes in government structures, and especially electoral systems, have been aided by legislation and a changing U.S. Supreme Court position on the issue. Originally, the Court found the issue of fair representation for minorities to be a slippery one. By a 6–3 vote in *Mobile v. Bolden* (1980), the Court overturned a lower court opinion that had forced the city of Mobile to abandon its historic three-member commission form mandating at-large elections, which had never produced a black commissioner. In effect, the higher court's decision forced protesting groups to prove that at-large elections were *designed* to discriminate against minorities—that is, the plaintiffs had to demonstrate that there had been *intent* to discriminate. This would be a heavy burden of proof against electoral systems, many of which were put in place at the turn of the century, during the heyday of the reform movement.

In response to the *Mobile* decision and over the vigorous objections of the Reagan administration, in 1982 Congress amended the Voting Rights Act to require that courts

look not only at intent to discriminate but also at the results or effects of political structures. In 1986, in *Thornburg v. Gingles*, the U.S. Supreme Court therefore moved beyond the
judicial restraint position that had obtained in the *Mobile* decision. In striking down some
multimember state legislative districts in North Carolina, the Court analyzed a number of
factors:

> ... the degree of historical discrimination; the degree of racially polarized block voting; racial
> appeals in political campaign rhetoric; the proportion of minorities elected to public office
> (although the Court made it clear that minorities do not have a right to have a fixed percent-
> age of elected positions); and the extent to which there is responsiveness to minorities on the
> part of public officials in a community.[66]

Post-*Gingles* court decisions suggest that the federal judiciary is willing to enforce the
Supreme Court's more activist position. And even where a court case is not at issue, racial
and ethnic minorities continue to try to force cities away from at-large elections.

At-large or district elections, which is preferable? The court cases and the debate continue. In *Protest Is Not Enough*, Rufus Browning, Dale Rogers Marshall, and David Tabb
demonstrate, however, that black and Latino council members can successfully join with
liberal whites to create winning electoral coalitions.[67] Minority political incorporation
results in more responsive city management.[68] Although about two-thirds of all cities
were using strictly at-large elections in the early 1980s, a trend toward ward-based and,
especially, mixed systems is clear. For example, by 2001 only 65 percent of all cities used
strictly at-large elections, whereas 15 percent used ward-based elections and 20 percent,
used mixed elections.[69]

THE INITIATIVE, THE REFERENDUM, AND THE RECALL

When political machines controlled cities, reformers searched for various ways to
circumvent boss-dominated local councils and return control of government to the people.
One way to do this was to allow citizens to petition for a communitywide vote on various
local propositions.

The *initiative* enables a legally determined number of electors, by means of a petition, to
force the placement of a charter amendment or city ordinance on the ballot for a vote by the
people. The city council is not involved in the process and cannot prevent the vote except
by challenging the validity of the petition in court. The *referendum* allows a prescribed number or percentage of qualified voters, by means of a petition, to force a vote on a legislative
measure after it has passed the council. If no emergency clause is attached (attesting to
the urgent need to protect the public health, safety, or welfare), city ordinances often do
not take effect immediately. This delay gives a disenchanted group the opportunity to
collect signatures and bring the ordinance to a popular vote. *Recall* provides a mechanism
for voters to remove an unsatisfactory council member before the official's term expires.
Again, a petition is required.

Proponents of direct democracy contend that these devices are essential to keep legislative bodies in check and to provide the opportunity for citizens to act directly on local policy issues. Skeptics feel that most voters are not sufficiently well informed to vote intelligently on the kinds of matters often placed on these ballots. Indeed, some referendum items are complex and esoteric, and many voters simply are not interested in them. The result frequently is to turn the initiative and referendum into tools for special interests that have the time and money to take advantage of the process. According to some critics, then, the process has deleterious effects on the normal legislative process.[70] Defenders counter that these voting procedures should not be condemned because of occasional misuse—that, in fact, they represent an effective means to enhance citizen control of local government.[71]

Regardless of the pros and cons, a recent ICMA survey shows staunch popular support for direct democracy. Over 62 percent of cities report some provision for referendum procedures, and recall elections are allowed in 61 percent. More than half (58 percent) of over 4,200 responding cities allow initiative petitions.[72]

HOME RULE AND THE LEGAL STATUS OF THE CITY

Despite the restricted view of municipal power reflected in Dillon's rule—that cities derive their powers solely from the state, which has the right to abridge and control those powers (see chapter 2)—courts permit cities with home-rule charters to exercise a greater degree of control over strictly local affairs. Municipal home rule provided by state law or constitution ensures that cities have "the right to make decisions on local matters without specific grants of authority and . . . limits the power of the state to intervene in local matters."[73] Such autonomy may be granted to all cities or to just a few, generally on the basis of population. In Oklahoma, for example, any incorporated place with a population of 2,000 or more can adopt a home-rule charter by following certain procedures spelled out in the state constitution. In contrast, Illinois' constitution awards home rule to cities with populations of 25,000 or more and permits smaller cities to achieve home rule through local referendum. Among other powers, a home-rule charter allows a city to determine its own form of government, type of ballot (partisan or nonpartisan), and method of electing council members (ward or at-large). In effect, the charter becomes the basic law, or constitution, of the city. Home rule for cities is available in forty-eight states.

Does home rule really give cities greater independence? Apparently so, at least in some areas of governance. Clearly, home-rule cities are free to choose the form of government they want. Morton Grove, Illinois, for example, used home-rule authority in the 1980s to enact local gun control.[74] Smoking bans in public places have been adopted under home rule in cities from New York to California. In other areas, such as finance, however, charter cities may have not much more authority than other cities. For example, in Pennsylvania, home-rule cities can set property-tax rates, but the state's general assembly retains the power over taxation and rates of taxation on nonresidents.[75] Also, states can always preempt local powers or determine that state and local governments may exercise some powers concurrently. In effect, then, home-rule powers are largely subject to restraints imposed by state legislatures.[76] But administrative flexibility is only one aspect of home rule; its greatest importance may be psychological. Home rule encourages state legislators to stay out of local affairs for fear of interfering with the rights of local self-government—of violating "the principle of home rule."[77]

Traditionally, home-rule supporters have feared state encroachment. In the past twenty years, however, even more concern has been expressed over federal preemption of local law. In a landmark decision affecting state and local governments, *Garcia v. San Antonio Mass Transit Authority* (1985), a divided (5–4) Supreme Court ruled that federal wage and hour standards apply to states and their local governments. The Court reasoned that the political process followed by Congress in passing laws provides sufficient protection to ensure that states and localities will not be unduly burdened. Although legislation lessened the impact of the *Garcia* ruling, critics point to other instances of federal intrusion on local affairs.

Today, above all, local officials complain of unfunded federal mandates, which force cities to comply with certain costly provisions of federal law. Many of these mandates relate to environmental protection—for example, requirements imposed by the Safe Drinking Water Act. Even efforts to abide by provisions of the 1990 Americans with Disabilities Act or the 2002 No Child Left Behind law regulating public schools may impose significant costs on local governments. In general, most municipal officials have little quarrel with the intent of these federal laws, but they do object to being forced to comply without being provided the funds to pay for the required improvements. Although local officials are now pursuing their complaints through the political process, relief may be long in coming. As one researcher has noted, "There's an iron law: When the easy money disappears, our federal system starts pushing things down, down, down."[78] Genuine home rule will probably continue to shrink as the federal government pursues deficit reduction and as some state governments contend with budgetary shortfalls.

SUMMARY

Today's city leaders owe much to the diligent efforts of past municipal reformers to professionalize city governments. The structural characteristics now found in most city governments—including the council-manager plan, nonpartisan ballots, at-large constituencies, and non-concurrent elections—were part of the reform agenda of the Progressive Era. Although all cities have embraced some degree of change, such reformist features are more likely to be found in certain kinds of cities—particularly white, suburban, middle-class cities, where greater consensus exists regarding the overall community interest. But this is not to say that larger U.S. cities have not embraced a heavy dose of reform, as well: these cities, for example, are largely staffed by employees selected through merit systems. And even in cities with the less reformed structures, today we find nearly half of mayor-council governments have chosen to appoint a chief administrator for the day-to-day management of its municipal affairs.

A consideration of the forms of city government and their accompanying electoral systems follows naturally from the discussion of the reform movement. The council-manager plan is now the most popular for cities with populations of 25,000–250,000, while mayor-council government remains more common in the smallest and largest municipalities. Debates persist over the alleged advantages and disadvantages of various electoral arrangements. Nonpartisanship is pervasive regardless of city size, but the at-large electoral form has not been as overwhelmingly adopted. The interest in city government structure is more than academic: although structure alone does not determine who gets what, certain arrangements may benefit some groups while working to the disadvantage of others.

Whereas cities remain creatures of the state, contemporary experience suggests that home-rule provisions have given municipalities greater freedom to frame their charters and choose their own forms of government. But with good reason, local government officials and scholars worry about growing federal preemption or intervention in local affairs, as well as about the impact of so-called unfunded mandates on the independence and fiscal health of America's cities.

SUGGESTED FOR FURTHER READING

Browning, Rufus P., Dale Rogers Marshall, and David H. Tabb, eds. *Racial Politics in American Cities*. 3rd ed. New York: Longman, 2003.

Burns, Nancy. *The Formation of American Local Governments: Private Values in Public Institutions*. New York: Oxford University Press, 1994.

Pelissero, John P., ed. *Cities, Politics, and Policy: A Comparative Analysis*. Washington, D.C.: CQ Press, 2003.

Svara, James H. *Official Leadership in the City: Patterns of Conflict and Cooperation*. New York: Oxford University Press, 1990.

Trounstine, Jessica. *Political Monopolies in American Cities: The Rise and Fall of Bosses and Reformers*. Chicago: University of Chicago Press, 2008.

Welch, Susan, and Timothy Bledsoe. *Urban Reform and Its Consequences: A Study in Representation*. Chicago: University of Chicago Press, 1988.

NOTES

1. For provocative analyses of community politics from a games perspective, see Norton Long, "The Local Community as an Ecology of Games," *American Journal of Sociology* 44 (November 1958): 251–261; and Paul A. Smith, "The Games of Community Politics," *Midwest Journal of Political Science* 9 (February 1965): 37–60.

2. This discussion draws on Lawrence J. R. Herson, "Pilgrim's Progress: Reflections on the Road to Urban Reform," in *Political Science and State and Local Government* (Washington, D.C.: American Political Science Association, 1973), 7–9.

3. For a popular account of the reform movement, see Richard Hofstadter, *The Age of Reform* (New York: Knopf, 1955).

4. For example, see Martin Meyerson and Edward Banfield, *Politics, Planning and the Public Interest* (New York: Free Press, 1955), 69–70.

5. William L. Riordan, *Plunkitt of Tammany Hall* (1905; repr., New York: Knopf, 1948), 33–34.

6. Edward C. Banfield and James Q. Wilson, *City Politics* (New York: Vintage, 1963), 121.

7. Ibid., 123.

8. Steven P. Erie, *Rainbow's End: Irish-Americans and the Dilemmas of Urban Machine Politics, 1840–1985* (Berkeley: University of California Press, 1988), 227.

9. See Jessica Trounstine, *Political Monopolies in American Cities: The Rise and Fall of Bosses and Reformers* (Chicago: University of Chicago Press, 2008).

10. Herson, "Pilgrim's Progress," 10.

11. Samuel P. Hays, "The Politics of Reform in Municipal Government in the Progressive Era," *Pacific Northwest Quarterly* 55 (October 1964): 157–189.

12. Dennis R. Judd and Todd Swanstrom, *City Politics: Private Power and Public Policy*, 3rd ed. (New York: Longman, 2002), 99–101.

13. Banfield and Wilson, *City Politics*, 138.

14. Ibid., 139.

15. Robert P. Boynton, "City Councils: Their Role in the Legislative System," *1976 Municipal Year Book* (Washington, D.C.: ICMA, 1976), 67–77.

16. Ibid., 69.

17. Evelina R. Moulder, "Municipal Form of Government: Trends in Structure, Responsibility, and Composition," *2008 Municipal Year Book* (Washington, D.C.: ICMA, 2008), 32–33.

18. Kimberly L. Nelson, *Elected Municipal Councils*, Special Data Issue no. 3 (Washington, D.C.: ICMA, 2002), 4.

19. Susan A. MacManus and Charles S. Bullock III, "The Form, Structure, and Composition of America's Municipalities in the New Millennium," *2003 Municipal Year Book* (Washington, D.C.: ICMA, 2003), 6.

20. Moulder, "Municipal Form of Government," 28.

21. International City/County Management Association, "Municipal Form of Government: Trends in Structure, Responsibility, and Composition" (Survey), 2006; and MacManus and Bullock, "Form, Structure, and Composition," 6.

22. Moulder, "Municipal Form of Government," 32.

23. Ibid.

24. Robert Alford and Harry Scoble, "Political and Socioeconomic Characteristics of American Cities," *1965 Municipal Year Book* (Washington, D.C.: ICMA, 1965), 82–97. Also see Thomas Dye and Susan MacManus, "Predicting City Government Structure," *American Journal of Political Science* 20 (May 1976): 257–271.

25. Richard L. Engstrom and Michael D. McDonald, "The Election of Blacks to City Councils," *American Political Science Review* 75 (June 1981): 344–354. See also Susan Welch and Timothy Bledsoe, *Urban Reform and Its Consequences: A Study in Representation* (Chicago: University of Chicago Press, 1988).

26. For examples, see Christopher L. Warren and Dario V. Moreno, "Power without a Program: Hispanic Incorporation in Miami," in *Racial Politics in American Cities*, 3rd ed., ed. Rufus Browning, Dale Rogers Marshall, and David H. Tabb (New York: Longman, 2003), 281–308; Rodney E. Hero and Susan E. Clarke, "Latinos, Blacks, and Multiethnic Politics in Denver: Realigning Power and Influence in the Struggle for Equality," in ibid., 309–330; and Katherine Underwood, "Ethnicity Is Not Enough: Latino-Led Multiracial Coalitions in Los Angeles," *Urban Affairs Review* 33 (September 1997): 3–27.

27. Nicholas O. Alozie, "The Election of Asians to City Councils," *Social Science Quarterly* 73 (March 1992): 90–100.

28. See Charles Bullock and Susan MacManus, "Municipal Electoral Structure and the Election of Councilwomen," *Journal of Politics* 53 (February 1991): 75–89; and Nicholas O. Alozie and Lynne L. Manganaro, "Women's Council Representation: Measurement Implications for Public Policy," *Political Research Quarterly* 46 (June 1993): 383–398.

29. Robert Lineberry and Edmund Fowler, "Reformism and Public Policies in American Cities," *American Political Science Review* 61 (September 1967): 716.

30. David Morgan and John Pelissero, "Urban Policy: Does Political Structure Matter?" *American Political Science Review* 74 (December 1980): 999–1006.

31. See William Nelson and Phillip Meranto, *Electing Black Mayors* (Columbus: Ohio State University Press, 1976).

32. Albert K. Karnig and Susan Welch, *Black Representation and Urban Policy* (Chicago: University of Chicago Press, 1980).

33. Peter K. Eisinger, "Black Employment in Municipal Jobs: The Impact of Black Political Power," *American Political Science Review* 76 (June 1982): 380–392; Kenneth R. Mladenka, "Blacks and Hispanics in Urban Politics," *American Political Science Review* 83 (March 1989): 165–191. For the latest studies on racial and ethnic politics in cities, see Browning, Marshall, and Tabb, eds., *Racial Politics in American Cities*.

34. Theodore Lowi, "Machine Politics—Old and New," *Public Interest* 9 (fall 1967): 83–92.

35. In addition to the mayor-council and council-manager forms of government, a small percentage of cities use the commission form (about 1 percent) and town meeting form (about 6 percent). See ICMA, "Municipal Form of Government," 2006, 1.

36. ICMA, "Municipal Form of Government," 2006, 1.

37. Lana Stein, "Mayoral Politics," in *Cities, Politics, and Policy: A Comparative Analysis*, ed. John P. Pelissero (Washington, D.C.: CQ Press, 2003), 150–151.

38. Kimberly L. Nelson and James H. Svara, "Adaptations of Models versus Variations in Form: Classifying Structures of City Government," *Urban Affairs Review* 45 (March 2010) 544–562. See also Bill Hansell, "Reforming the Reform, Part 2," *Public Management* 81 (January 1999): 28; Victor DeSantis and Tari Renner, "City Government Structures: An Attempt at Clarification," *State and Local Government Review* 34 (spring 2002): 1–10.

39. MacManus and Bullock, "Form, Structure, and Composition," 3–5.

40. Nelson and Svara, "Adaptation of Models versus Variations in Form," 555.

41. ICMA, "Municipal Form of Government," 2006, 1.

42. MacManus and Bullock, "Form, Structure, and Composition," 9.

43. Heywood T. Sanders, "The Government of American Cities: Continuity and Change in Structure," *1982 Municipal Year Book* (Washington, D.C.: ICMA, 1982), 181.

44. James H. Svara, "Mayoral Leadership in Council-Manager Cities: Preconditions versus Preconceptions," *Journal of Politics* 49 (February 1987): 207–227.

45. Nelson Wikstrom, "The Mayor as a Policy Leader in the Council-Manager Form of Government," *Public Administration Review* 39 (May–June 1979): 270–276.

46. Nelson and Svara, "Adaptation of Models versus Variations in Form," 555.

47. Welch and Bledsoe, *Urban Reform and Its Consequences*, 8.

48. ICMA, "Municipal Form of Government," 2006.

49. Willis D. Hawley, *Nonpartisan Elections and the Case for Party Politics* (New York: Wiley-Interscience, 1973), 33.

50. Welch and Bledsoe, *Urban Reform and Its Consequences*, 9–50.

51. Ibid., 53.

52. Susan A. MacManus and Charles S. Bullock, "Women and Racial/Ethnic Minorities in Mayoral and Council Positions," *1993 Municipal Year Book* (Washington, D.C.: ICMA, 1993), 78–79.

53. Welch and Bledsoe, *Urban Reform and Its Consequences*, 78.

54. Moulder, "Municipal Form of Government," 32–33.

55. Ibid.

56. William J. D. Boyd, "Local Electoral Systems: Is There a Best Way?" *National Civic Review* 65 (March 1976): 136–140, 157.

57. Ibid., 139.

58. ICMA, "Municipal Form of Government," 2001.

59. MacManus and Bullock, "Women and Racial/Ethnic Minorities," 78; Alozie and Manganaro, "Women's Council Representation," 395.

60. Timothy Bledsoe and Susan Welch, "The Effect of Political Structures on the Socioeconomic Characteristics of Urban City Council Members," *American Politics Quarterly* 13 (October 1985): 467–483.

61. Welch and Bledsoe, *Urban Reform and Its Consequences*, 42, 77.

62. Ibid., 102.

63. See Tari Renner, "Municipal Election Processes: The Impact on Minority Representation," *1988 Municipal Year Book* (Washington, D.C.: ICMA, 1988), 13–14.

64. This discussion is drawn from "At-Large Voting under Attack," *Governing* (November 1987), 8. See also "Election System Shot Down," *City & State* 5 (November 1990): 10.

65. City of Dallas, official website, www.dallascityhall.com.

66. Renner, "Municipal Election Processes," 14.

67. Rufus P. Browning, Dale R. Marshall, and David H. Tabb, *Protest Is Not Enough* (Berkeley: University of California Press, 1984), 166.

68. Browning, Marshall, and Tabb, *Racial Politics in American Cities*.

69. Nelson, *Elected Municipal Councils*.

70. Stanley Scott and Harriet Nathan, "Public Referenda: A Critical Appraisal," *Urban Affairs Quarterly* 5 (March 1970): 313–328.

71. George S. Blair, *Government at the Grass-Roots*, 2nd ed. (Pacific Palisades, Calif.: Palisades, 1977), 85–86.

72. International City/County Management Association, "Inside the Year Book," *The Municipal Year Book 2002* (Washington, D.C.: ICMA, 2002), ix.

73. David R. Berman, "State-Local Relations: Authority, Finances, and Cooperation," *2003 Municipal Year Book*, 52.

74. Bernard H. Ross, Myron A. Levine, and Murray S. Stedman, *Urban Politics: Power in Metropolitan America*, 4th ed. (Itasca, Ill.: F. E. Peacock, 1991), 82.

75. See Charles Hoffman, "Pennsylvania Legislation Implements Home Rule," *National Civic Review* 61 (September 1972): 390–393.

76. See, for example, the discussion in Samuel Gove and Stephanie Cole, "Illinois Home Rule: Panacea, Status Quo, or Hindrance?" in *Partnership within the States: Local Self-Government in the Federal System*, ed. Stephanie Cole (Urbana: Institute of Government and Public Affairs, University of Illinois; Philadelphia: Center for the Study of Federalism, Temple University, 1976), 158–161. The authors conclude that home rule has made some difference, but after five years the changes have not been dramatic (167).

77. Charles Adrian and Charles Press, *Governing Urban America*, 5th ed. (New York: McGraw-Hill, 1977), 142.

78. Quoted in Steven D. Gold, "Passing the Buck," *State Legislatures* 19 (January 1993): 37.

CHAPTER 4   **URBAN POLICYMAKING**

W E expect local elected and appointed officials to make, implement, and evaluate urban policy. In this chapter, we first provide a general overview of the public policy process, beginning with the observation that policymaking in the public sector tends to be democratic in nature and thus is typified by bargaining and compromise. This tendency has the effect of *lessening* the "rationality" (defined in the corporate sector as efficiency) of the process, but it enhances participation and input into the policy process (bringing accountability and responsiveness). Next, we examine three ways to look at public policy: as a generally stable, orderly process comprised of sequential steps or stages; as a disorderly, largely reactive process; and as a trifurcated process consisting of three basic types of policies—allocational, developmental, and redistributive.

In sections two, three, and four we identify and briefly differentiate the functions of local policymakers. We begin with chief executive officers—city managers and mayors—and, after examining the extant research on both, we discuss their interactions, manager/mayor relations. Next comes an introduction to the American city council, whose citizen-members give so much in the name of the public interest. Finally, we examine local bureaucrats' involvement in the policy process. Collectively, cities and towns across America employ over 11 million government workers to put out fires, pick up refuse, run water treatment plants, and provide a host of other services.

Section five of the chapter highlights the special role that citizens acting alone or through groups and neighborhoods play in local policymaking. This activity helps to define the very essence of democracy. The sixth section provides a brief summary of the chapter.

THE NATURE OF URBAN POLICY

At the outset, we should define the concept of *public policy*. James Anderson describes it as a "relatively stable, purposive course of action or inaction followed by an actor or set of actors in dealing with a problem or matter of concern."[1] He goes on to add that public policies are those developed by governmental bodies and officials. When the question arises as to whether deliberate inaction by government constitutes policy, most would answer yes. Anderson, for example, includes "inaction" as part of definition of public policy and emphatically notes, "Recall that public policy is determined not only by what government does do but also by what it deliberately does not do."[2] A conscious choice to take no action thus can be considered as endorsing or perpetuating existing policy. Political scientists

Peter Bachrach and Morton S. Baratz offer the classic statement of government's process of deciding not to take an action (which they call "nondecision-making") in their book *Power and Poverty*—it is "a means by which demands for change in the existing allocation of benefits and privileges in the community can be suffocated before they are even voiced; or kept covert; or killed before they gain access to the relevant decision-making arena; or failing all these things, maimed or destroyed in the decision-implementing stage of the policy process."[3]

How does *policymaking* differ from *decision making*? As the quote from Bachrach and Baratz suggests, the two terms often are used synonymously, but a difference of scope or degree does exist. In a narrow sense, decision making is choosing among competing alternatives; policymaking goes beyond this to include, in David Easton's words, "a web of decisions and actions that allocate values."[4] A *policy*, then, is a series of decisions that creates a comprehensive set of standards or guidelines for dealing with a subject. The line between basic policy and less comprehensive tactical or programmatic decisions may be difficult to draw in practice. But we can recognize the following distinction: "For those (actions) which have the widest ramifications and the longest time perspective, and which generally require the most information and contemplation, we tend to reserve the term policy."[5] In short, as noted in chapter 1, we think of policy as the response of a political system to the various supports and demands produced by its environment.[6]

Considerable agreement exists on one basic point about government policymaking: that it is not always a highly rational, scientifically based enterprise, but is, instead, essentially political in nature. This is not to suggest that systematic analysis has no place in the policymaking effort. We know, both from experience and from reading the literature, that governments at all levels expend considerable resources to improve their capacity for making informed choices—they hire analysts, retain consultants, and fund all kinds of sophisticated research in the quest for more effective policies. Sometimes the results influence major policy decisions significantly, as, for example, when a benefit-cost analysis results in the decision to go forward with a large public works project. Similarly, much of the focus of modern public management focuses on how to make government policies that are more efficient and effective.

Many times, however, the attempt to ensure more rational choices through analysis goes for naught, as a host of obstacles and/or unintended consequences interfere with the successful resolution of the problem. For example, in 1970, in the midst of the urban sprawl and suburbanization process in America, economist Anthony Downs noted that as soon as a major expressway was built, it quickly filled up with cars, leaving the community no better off than it had been before. This poor policy outcome occurred not because of bad planning, argued Downs, but because of a very rational response made by rush-hour drivers. This unintended consequence had been so automatic over the years that Downs formulated what he called the Law of Peak-Hour Traffic Congestion: "On urban commuter expressways, peak-hour traffic congestion rises to meet maximum capacity."[7] Three and one-half decades later, little has changed—just ask the daily commuter in Los Angeles, Chicago, Oklahoma City, or Phoenix.

Policy experts Charles Lindblom and Edward J. Woodhouse say we are of a mixed mind about rational policy and the influence of politics: "A deep conflict runs through common attitudes toward policymaking. People want policy to be informed and well analyzed, perhaps even correct or scientific; yet they also want policymaking to be democratic and hence necessarily an exercise of power."[8] This conflict is evident, for example, in policymaking for economic development. Some contend that an effective development policy can be produced only through extensive fact gathering, planning, and analysis, after which the final decisions rest in the hands of a small elite group with close ties to the business community. Others worry about the lack of popular participation in such an approach. Later in this chapter, we hear more from Paul Peterson, a contributor to this debate, who believes that economic development policymaking is so vital to a community's well-being that the local leadership will restrict the process to a few dominant interests, thus minimizing conflict among competing groups. First, though, we need to consider the steps in the policymaking process.

POLICYMAKING AS A RELATIVELY STABLE, ORDERLY SERIES OF EVENTS

Anderson's definition, cited earlier in this chapter, characterized public policymaking as a "relatively stable" course of action. And even though that course of action, as Lindblom suggests, is not always highly rational because in the public sector we must, at times, satisfy potentially competing values (such as efficiency and responsiveness), we still can identify several steps or stages in the process.[9] Briefly, these policy stages and the important issues or questions involved with each stage may be outlined as follows:

1. *Issue creation*. What gives rise to the problem? How does the issue get defined as a public matter?
2. *Agenda building*. How does the issue reach public decision makers? Who participates in the agenda-building process and how? What keeps problems off the public agenda?
3. *Issue resolution*. How do public officials respond to demands for problem resolution? How is the final policy choice made?
4. *Policy implementation*. What happens to the policy after it has been passed and given to the bureaucracy to be actually carried out? Are rules, regulations, or adjudicatory mechanisms needed to enforce the legislation? How are discretion and "decision rules" used by government officials in the implementation process? What outputs are associated with a policy?
5. *Policy outcomes, evaluation, and feedback*. What impact does the policy have on individuals or groups? Is the policy effective; did the policy reach its goals? Is the policy in need of change or should it be terminated?

Issue Creation

Political issues are created in various ways. Roger Cobb and Charles Elder emphasize the interaction of an initiator and a triggering device as the first step.[10] In the most common case, a person, organization, or group perceives an unfavorable distribution of resources and seeks government help to redress the imbalance. Such initiators may then search for allies or turn to the media in the hope of publicizing their cause. They may benefit from the help of a friendly officeholder who, for various self-serving reasons, wishes to adopt and push the cause of the aggrieved party. The critical step in issue creation may well be publicizing the issue—bringing the proposed solution of the problem to the attention both of those who are already aware of the problem and of those who will be concerned once they learn about it.

Triggering devices are largely unanticipated occurrences that create a problem requiring government response. External events—technological change, a natural disaster, or an unexpected human event (a riot or a sudden upsurge in violent crime or even a major court decision)—may give rise to a situation that stimulates a response by an affected group. The point is that a triggering mechanism and an initiator, such as an affected group, must converge to create a public issue.

Agenda Building

How does a problem or issue reach the public agenda, where some official response is expected? Not only must certain groups or powerful interests perceive the issue as a legitimate concern, but it also must be seen as an appropriate target for government action. This requirement may seem simple enough, but in fact one of the most effective strategies by those wanting to avoid official action is to argue that the issue lies outside the scope of government authority.[11] For example, those opposed to mandatory seatbelt or motorcycle helmet laws usually insist that these matters of "personal safety" should not be dictated by government policy.

Two factors seem especially important in determining who gets access to the public agenda. First, local officeholders have enormous discretion over which issues will be considered officially; they are not merely passive arbiters of problems brought to them by others. Elected officials, especially at the local level, frequently arrive at their own conclusions regarding the nature of local problems. As we discuss further later, city council members tend to see themselves not as politicians expected to respond to the pressures of group demands, but rather as nonpolitical "trustees" or "volunteers" who have been elected to pursue their own views of the public interest.

A second key factor in whether issues are placed on the public agenda is the nature of the proposing group. Some organizations have far easier access to public officials than do others. As might be expected, the more politically powerful or prestigious the group, the more likely its concerns are to find their way onto the action agenda. Elected officials also are much more likely to grant access to groups with whom they share values and interests. Not uncommonly, the politically powerful groups and the groups with views similar to those of council members are one and the same. Business interests, in particular, are likely to fall into this category, for their commitment to growth and investment is often viewed as being in the interest of the larger community as well.

Issue Resolution

The resolution stage is where some final outcome occurs. Does the issue become resolved with the adoption of a new policy or modification of an existing one? Or is the matter disposed of in some other way—formally rejected, passed to some other level of government, or postponed for some time? How are these decisions made? Because decision making is considered in some detail in the next chapter, at this point we only sketch briefly the process by which such choices might be made.

Charles Lindblom argues that policy is determined largely on the basis of interaction among contending interests.[12] How does one group or interest gain the upper hand—in other words, exert sufficient control or influence to achieve its objectives? Lindblom specifies the following methods of resolution:

- *Persuasion*. In many instances, one participant may be able to show another why the desires of the former will benefit the latter. We should not underestimate the power of persuasion.[13]
- *Threats*. Although not commonly used, threats may be resorted to by some groups. A threat may be as simple as telling officials that if they take a particular course of action, the group will feel compelled to oppose either their reelection or some action that the officials support.
- *Exchange*. The adoption of a mutually beneficial arrangement is a widely used political tactic. Officials frequently engage in "logrolling" (supporting another's project or proposal in direct exchange for that person's support of one's own project). Money is perhaps the most common medium of exchange, even in politics—not for bribes as such, but to buy influence, access, or services; as an organizational resource, money can work miracles.
- *Authority*. Public officials occupy positions of considerable authority, which can be an important resource. Their positions can enhance persuasive power and provide access to jobs and money, which may influence the actions of others.
- *Analysis*. The use of systematic analysis also can be listed among the influences shaping the final decision. It may provide just the ammunition needed by one side or the other to push its case. Certainly a well-conceived, accurate, and timely study may tip the scales on a closely contested issue. As Lindblom says, analysis is an indispensable element in politics: "It becomes a method of exerting control."[14]

Policy Implementation

The implementation stage is where administrators and the bureaucracy enter. Policy is inevitably modified, molded, and influenced by administrative implementation. We address bureaucratic behavior more completely later in this chapter, but we should note at this point that in large public organizations, policymaking, as Lindblom puts it, "rests overwhelmingly in the hands of the bureaucracy."[15] Administrative officials exercise an enormous amount of discretion in determining how policy is carried out. Bureaucrats also significantly impact policy by developing decision rules—devices to simplify and expedite decision making and reduce uncertainty. Finally, administrators are frequently the source of much of the analysis and advice that informs the policy choices made by legislators and the chief executive.

Two other features of policy implementation merit consideration. First, the implementation process may also be affected substantially by the need for coordination among fragmented agencies or with other governments, or even by the need to bargain with employee groups to secure the cooperation needed to ensure policy success. Second, within the context of systems theory, policy implementation represents an *output* of the political system. For example, after the council passes an ordinance, funds are expended to deliver a good or service (an output), or a rule or regulation (an output) is formulated by the administrative agency to ensure compliance with the new ordinance.

Policy Outcomes, Evaluation, and Feedback

The policy process does not end with implementation. Classic case study implementation analyses by Frank Levy, Arnold Meltsner, and Aaron Wildavsky in Oakland, California, and Robert Lineberry in San Antonio, Texas; integrative "third generation" implementation theory offered by Malcolm L. Goggin and his associates; and more recent scholarly research on bureaucratic rulemaking by Barry Bozeman and Cornelius Kerwin all suggest that policy implementation is associated with policy outcomes.[16]

Many public policies make a difference in the lives of ordinary citizens on a daily basis; policies have impacts. These impacts or outcomes *must* be evaluated to gain useful feedback about the nature of the policy itself. Is the bureaucracy, for example, delivering the policy in an efficient fashion? If not, perhaps a change in administrative practices or procedures is required. Is the policy reaching its intended legislative goals—that is, is it effective? If not, perhaps the policy can be modified to better meet such goals. Or, as James Lester and Joseph Stewart Jr. note, perhaps policy termination is necessary.[17] Questions such as these can be answered through properly designed and executed program evaluations. Finally, in a democracy we expect public officials to be accountable and responsive to the people. Systems theory *requires* a feedback loop by which the people can evaluate the adequacy of all stages of the policy process.

Even though a series of policymaking stages can thus be identified, the policy process is often not quite as stable, orderly, and rational as urban leaders would like it to be. This is particularly true when one examines policymaking in large cities, where sometimes the process appears chaotic—characterized primarily by a pattern of government reaction to a series of ever-changing external forces.

REACTIVE POLICYMAKING

In the late 1970s, political scientist Douglas Yates offered a rather complete, even entertaining, description of urban policymaking that emphasized its nonsequential and disorderly nature.[18] His basic point was that, given the level and range of demands placed on big-city officials and the instability in the local political environment, the prospects for orderly agenda building, planning, and implementation are very slim. Why? Yates insisted that a number of structural characteristics of urban government create a distinctive situation that makes comprehensive, systematic policymaking impossible. Without listing all of these characteristics, we might note that Yates emphasized service delivery as the basic function of urban government. Services are tangible, visible, and even personal in their impact; in many instances, they can be divided so that people in need receive more than others do. But citizens and an array of community organizations constantly press their service demands on the mayor and the urban bureaucracy, neither of which has the formal power or the resources to respond effectively to all these demands. This lack of administrative authority can result from the presence of independent boards, uncooperative and independent jurisdictions in the metropolitan area, and/or bureaucratic resistance and autonomy.

Yates went on to stress how fragmented authority creates chaos in urban policymaking, calling this unstable political free-for-all "street-fighting pluralism," which he defined as "a pattern of unstructured, multilateral conflict in which many different combatants fight continuously with one another in a very great number of permutations and combinations."[19] Because the demands from this unrestrained battle are not filtered, channeled, assigned priority, or otherwise mediated by formal political representatives, they create a constant stream of new and often bewildering issues for urban decision makers. In effect, urban policymaking becomes a reactive procedure by which the official leadership sets its agenda in response to the most dramatic problems and the loudest complaints. Yates compared the situation to a penny arcade's shooting gallery, where more targets than can be hit continually keep popping up on all sides.

This reactive model purports to describe politics in such major cities as Boston, Detroit, Cleveland, Chicago, and New York. In small or medium-sized cities—where fewer groups are involved, events are less pressing, and the degree of uncertainty and instability is lower—the model may not fit as well. But even in a slower-paced community, policymaking may at times be perceived as essentially reactive.

TRIFURCATED POLICYMAKING: ALLOCATIONAL, DEVELOPMENTAL, AND REDISTRIBUTIVE POLICIES

In his book *City Limits*, Paul Peterson challenges both the more traditional, open systems approach to understanding urban policymaking discussed earlier and Yates's model of urban policymaking, with its emphasis on fragmentation and street-fighting pluralism.[20] Peterson agrees with the assumption of both models that bargaining and compromise among contending interests may determine many of the most visible actions taken by city governments. But these *allocational policies* are not the most vital actions taken by the city. Above all, he says, the city is committed to protecting and promoting its economic well-being. To that end, it must pursue what Peterson calls *developmental policies*—decisions designed to further growth and expansion of business interests in the city. These issues are not subject to the ordinary pull-and-tug of pressure politics. Instead, they tend to be settled through highly centralized decision-making processes dominated by business and professional elites. Conflict is minimized, and the process is closed to outsiders. The result is a quiet drama "where political leaders can give reasoned attention to the longer range interests of the city, taken as a whole."[21]

The quest to improve the city's economic base may lead to measures that have adverse consequences for certain groups. For example, Peterson asserts that *redistributive policies* designed to benefit the poor do not promote the long-term economic welfare of the community, and, therefore, local officials should avoid them. Redistribution, he believes, should be dealt with at the national level, not by city governments. But surely local groups, such as minorities or the poor, will raise such a ruckus that city officials will be forced to deal with them? Not necessarily, according to Peterson. He insists that political party and group activity is so limited at the local level that community elites are largely free to concentrate on the city's economic growth. In effect, Peterson's model postulates that when a community's most vital interests are at stake, local policymakers act to further the long-term good of the city.

As urban politics scholars Bernard H. Ross and Myron A. Levine note, "Peterson's view of the limits of city politics has proven quite controversial."[22] The economic determinism of the model is simply too much for some. Empirical observation of the actions of local officials show that they do care about and pursue policies that benefit poor individuals and neighborhoods—that is, local leaders do engage in redistributive policies. They also note that the business community in a city is not a monolithic entity; businesses are not always united behind developmental projects. There may be competition among businesses representing different sectors of the economy—wholesale, retail, manufacturing, tourism—or among businesses that serve different parts of the city or metropolitan area—central business district, strip malls, megamalls, neighborhood boutiques, and so on. In the final analysis, Charles C. Euchner and Stephen J. McGovern suggest that Peterson "has over-stated . . . [his] case."[23] Still, "Peterson's theory remains valid as it points to an extremely strong and important tendency in municipal affairs: Cities tend to cater to the needs of the business community and of tax-paying, upper- and upper-middle-income residents."[24]

Perhaps we can better understand the process of policymaking if we examine the roles of those who officially are charged with formulating urban policy—chief executives, city council members, and local bureaucrats.

CHIEF EXECUTIVES

Urban chief executives, whether they are mayors or city managers, invariably play a prominent role in the policy process. Based on data gathered in 1985, public administration scholars David Ammons and Charldean Newell found that these officials worked hard: mayors in mayor-council and commission cities put in an average of sixty-six hours a week and city managers report an average workweek of about fifty-six hours.[25] More recently, a 2009 ICMA survey of city managers reports that 53 percent of the city managers who responded worked between 50–59 hours a week, with another 28 percent reporting a work week of 60–69 hours. The mean hours among the 369 managers who provided a finite number of working hours was 55.1 hours per week.[26] Much of the growth of executive power has come about unintentionally and despite traditional fears of executive authority. But cutbacks in federal funds and the demands of modern public management have made strong executive leadership indispensable.

Before we discuss the different types of chief executives, it may be helpful to consider the role of the strong mayor in the twenty-first-century city. Current or former mayors such as New York's Rudy Giuliani, Los Angeles' Richard Riordan, Philadelphia's Ed Rendell, Indianapolis' Stephen Goldsmith, Milwaukee's John Norquist, and Jersey City's Bret Schundler all made their reputations by appropriately blending—within the context of their city's political environment—"old ways" and modern management reforms, such as privatizing municipal services and adopting private-sector performance practices.[27] The case study presented in box 4.1 is the story of one of these former strong mayors—Rudolph Giuliani.

MAYORS

Perhaps David R. Morgan and Sheilah S. Watson best summarize the nature of the American mayor when they note:

> Every U.S. city has a mayor. There the similarities end. Incumbent officeholders differ markedly in their personality, style, energy, and effectiveness. More than this, the offices themselves reflect considerable variation. Some mayors are elected directly by the people; some are not. Some possess the veto power while others do not; appointment power fluctuates significantly—all of which may advance or impede the capacity of the mayor to offer productive policy leadership.[28]

As discussed in chapter 3, a mayor's powers are most restricted, of course, in the council-manager system, wherein the mayor's office is often, but not always (as we will see), largely

BOX 4.1   Policy and Practice

MAYOR GIULIANI MANAGES NEW YORK CITY: BLENDING THE OLD WITH THE NEW

In a well-developed case study, Lynne Weikart analyzes the extent to which former New York City mayor Rudolph Giuliani, an aggressive proponent of the reforms advocated by the New Public Management (NPM) agenda, was successful in his attempts to "implement abstract reform principles in a politicized environment."

Before examining the mayor's performance, Professor Weikart reviews five NPM reforms:

- *Downsizing.* The purpose of downsizing is to reduce the overall size and scope of government activity.
- *Managerialism.* The focus of managerialism is on accountability, both at the macro (organizational) and micro (individual) levels. Strategic management allows the organization to define its mission and to develop measures for periodically monitoring performance. At the individual level, employees' productivity should be measured to ensure accountability. Often managerialism requires "managed competition"—public employees compete with the private sector and/or nonprofit sector for the right to deliver goods and services.
- *Decentralization.* Service delivery agents in government agencies should be empowered to act as decision makers on their own; street-level bureaucrats should have the power to act based on their best judgment and professionalism. In addition, at the municipal level, decentralization means empowering community residents with more service delivery authority—which may involve creating more partnerships with neighborhood associations and thus moving power away from the central bureaucracy.
- *Debureaucratization.* This concept requires that government agencies focus on results instead of processes. Debureaucratization entails structural and procedural changes: hierarchies must be flattened and rulebooks thrown away. Once agency goals and objectives are determined, city workers should be set free to accomplish these goals free of unnecessary rules, policies, and procedures that impose significant constraints on organizational and individual productivity.
- *Privatization.* In government, the "P" word is often controversial, but NPM reforms place a heavy emphasis on "load-shedding," or contracting out government services to the private or nonprofit sectors. Load-shedding, for example, requires that city-owned housing stock be sold to private owners. Governmental contracting might replace the provision of snow removal services by city workers; the service would be financed by tax dollars or user fees, but a private-sector, for-profit firm or firms would provide the service with their own workers.

How well was Mayor Giuliani able to "walk the walk" in implementing these reforms? Weikart offers a mixed review. Giuliani did *downsize* New York City government through his tax cuts and by reducing the total city workforce. But he was not a major user of the business protocols associated with *managerialism.* Weikart argues that Giuliani resisted the use of performance measurement and failed to "capitalize on the opportunity to increase productivity during the negotiation with the sanitation union and several other union contracts" (371). Perhaps his least successful reform outcomes were in the areas of *decentralization* and *debureaucratization.* Giuliani's centralist governing style, Weikart argues, pulled him in the opposite direction to these two reform principles. "The mayor did not support decentralization. Several agencies were

(continued)

BOX 4.1 Policy and Practice (continued)

centralized" (376). Similarly, he "did not succeed in changing the structure of government [debureaucratization], emphasizing results rather than process. His emphasis was centralization and downsizing, with little interest in encouraging worker participation in agency transformation" (376). Giuliani was quite successful in his efforts to privatize some local services—especially in the policy areas of housing, parks, and homeless services. Judicial intervention prevented him, however, from "selling off the New York City water system" and from privatizing "the municipal hospital system" (374–375).

In the final analysis, "to resolve issues in running the city, the mayor sometimes turned not to the tools of NPM but to traditional strategies of New York City mayors who began their administrations as reformers but ultimately retained power by brokering agreements among major stakeholders, including unions" (365). Professor Weikart concludes her analysis by noting, "Mayor Giuliani embraced NPM principles when it suited his own political agenda and failed to embrace them when it was politically inconvenient. Mayor Giuliani compromised, but he did win reelection" (377).

As noted in chapter 1, managing the modern city requires all of the skills—old and new—that city officials can bring to the table.

SOURCE: Lynne A. Weikart, "The Giuliani Administration and the New Public Management in New York City," *Urban Affairs Review* 36 (January 2001): 359–381.

ceremonial. Under most mayor-council plans, chief executives are not officially members of the legislative body and cannot vote except to break a tie. A large-scale 2001 ICMA survey involving about 4,200 cities, for example, reports that in mayor-council plans, mayors are members of the council in only 41 percent of the cities.[29] In 55 percent of the cities, they can vote only to break a tie, and they cannot vote on any issue in another 17 percent of the cities. Mayors in council-manager cities, in contrast, ordinarily are members of the council (in 86 percent of the cities) and cast votes on all issues (in 73 percent of the cities). Mayors in both forms of government generally preside over council meetings. But veto power is rare among council-manager mayors (in 12 percent of cities), whereas a majority (58 percent) of mayors in mayor-council communities have that power.

In cities adopting the mayor council form of government, only 28 percent employ a full-time mayor, and this is most likely to happen in cities with at least 250,000 or more residents. The mayor is usually elected directly by the people (in 96 percent of the cities), does not face term limits (in 94 percent), and serves a four-year term (in 68 percent). A little more than half (58 percent) of the mayors have veto power; in 90 percent of these cities, a supermajority vote by the council is required to override the veto. Increasingly, and most noticeably in medium- to large-sized cities, mayors are receiving help in managing the city from one or more chief administrative officers (CAOs). These appointed officials, for example, often have overall responsibility for developing the municipal budget (in 28 percent of the cities), whereas this power is given directly to the mayor in 25 percent of the survey cities following the mayor-council plan of government. Most mayors are male

(87 percent) and white (96 percent). Regardless of gender, race, or ethnicity, mayors are more educated than the populations they represent.[30] In 2009 the average nationwide salary for a mayor was about $51,918. In mayor-council cities the mean salary was $63,241; in council-manager cities the comparable figure was a little more than $33,500 a year. In cities with 500,000 to one million residents, the average salary is $65,595; in cities with populations greater than one million people the mean salary is $156,481.[31]

The Prerequisites of Mayoral Leadership and Political Entrepreneurship

In a seminal article published in 1972 on the critical importance of the role played by American mayors in responding to the "urban crisis," Jeffrey Pressman argued that formal authority is only the foundation of the resources essential to mayoral leadership and political entrepreneurship.[32] Pressman listed a number of other institutional characteristics that are also necessary:

- Adequate financial and staff resources within the city government
- City jurisdiction over key policy areas—education, housing, redevelopment, and job training
- Mayoral jurisdiction within the city government in these key policy fields
- A full-time salary for the mayor along with sufficient staff for policy planning, speech writing, and so on
- Vehicles for publicity, such as friendly newspapers or television stations
- Political support groups, including a party, that can be mobilized to support the mayor's goals

As this list suggests, institutional barriers can substantially affect a mayor's capacity for leadership. But the personal qualities of the mayor are often of equal or greater importance. The pluralistic, dispersed nature of local government demands political leaders who can accumulate personal influence to supplement their limited formal authority.[33]

Recent Research on Mayors

As Melvin G. Holli suggests, historically we have learned about the American mayoralty from "monographs, urban biographies, . . . and studies of single cities and their mayors."[34] While this literature is rich in detail, informative, and at times even entertaining, it is also journalistic, anecdotal, and impressionistic—its findings can't be generalized beyond the single city and mayor studied. In recent years, a growing number of scholars of urban politics and management have conducted studies that examine the American mayoralty from a more empirical, systematic, and comparative perspective. As such, their findings are more able to be generalized, and the studies are less impressionistic and more scientific. A brief review of a few of these studies will provide a flavor of this important and developing research on the American mayor.

Research by P. Edward French and David H. Folz is particularly interesting because it attempts to discover whether differences exist in executive behavior and decision making between mayors and city managers in small U.S. cities (those with populations between 2,500 and 24,500).[35] Historically, urban studies have focused on big cities such as New York, Boston, or Chicago, or on a group of central cities that define what are called "metropolitan areas." These six hundred or so central cities must contain at least 50,000 residents and are where the vast majority of Americans live. But there are also over 5,000 cities in the United States with populations of less than 25,000 that have rarely been studied systematically. French and Folz selected a random sample of 1,000 of these cities and, by conducting two mailed surveys, secured a database that included about five hundred city managers and mayors.

Their findings suggest that city managers in small communities, like those in big cities, spend more of their time on management and on policy than do mayors.[36] This finding does not hold true, however, in those small cities in which the mayor is aided by a chief administrative officer (CAO). In these cities, the mayor spends about the same amount of time as the city manager does on policy activities. And in small cities in which the mayor does not have a CAO, the mayor spends about the same amount of time on management activities as does a big-city mayor. In terms of the four dimensions of the governmental process—mission, policy, administration, and management—both mayors and city managers believe that they are more extensively involved in mission and policy activities than in management and administrative activities. But city managers reported involvement in all four dimensions of the governmental process at levels that were higher to a statistically significant degree than those reported by mayors—and this difference held true regardless of whether the mayor was aided by a CAO or not. Research findings also suggest that "city managers are more likely than mayors to consult with key stakeholders before they reach a decision that affects a local service or project," and that "there were no statistically significant differences in how mayors and city managers rated the perceived level of influence that members of interest groups have on shaping their decisions" across six policy areas.[37]

Research by Zoltan L. Hajnal focuses on the election of black mayors: "The first and most obvious [lesson that can be drawn from this study] is that black representation does matter."[38] Hajnal uses a pooled sample of the American Election Study from 1984 to 1992 to assess changes in white attitudes and policy preferences of whites under black mayors. His findings suggest that "although white Republicans seem largely immune to the effects of black incumbency, for Democrats and independents an experience with a black mayoralty tends to decrease racial tension, increase racial sympathy, and increase support of black leadership."[39] On the other hand, John P. Pelissero, David B. Holian, and Laura A. Tomaka use an interrupted time-series design to determine whether the election of a city's first minority mayor (black or Latino) has any short- or long-term impacts on city fiscal policies. They did not find significant changes in city revenues or spending per capita during a twenty-one-year period as a result of electing a minority mayor.[40]

CITY MANAGERS

In council-manager cities, the mayor has extremely limited formal power and is forced to exercise political leadership by facilitating and coordinating the work of others. The original theory of this plan implied that the city council collectively would provide the initiative and leadership in policy formulation, and that a full-time professional administrator, the city manager, would then be employed to conduct the daily administrative activities of city government under the overall guidance of the council. In this way, the administration of city government would be divorced from politics and policymaking—a task that would be left primarily, if not solely, to the elected mayor and council. Indications are, however, that the plan has never, even in its early stages, worked in this idealized fashion. In recent years, overwhelming evidence has shown the prominent role city managers play in all four dimensions of the governmental process: helping to determine the *mission* (purpose and scope) of government, initiating and formulating *policy* recommendations, *administration* through policy and program implementation, and *management* through the day-to-day control of human, fiscal, and information/technology resources.

Public administration scholar John Nalbandian argues that today's complex urban environment compels city managers to become involved in community politics.[41] As appointed officials, though, managers had best avoid direct involvement in local elections. Their political role takes another form, and it extends beyond merely advising the council. Modern city managers have become full-fledged brokers, building coalitions and negotiating compromises among competing groups.

Who Are They?

Survey data show that local managers are an elite group that is unusually homogeneous with respect to gender, race, age, education, and experience. In 2000, for example, the ICMA surveyed all local government managers—city managers in council-manager cities, chief administrative officers in mayor-council cities, county executives/managers, town administrators, and so on—in cities and counties with a population of 2,500 (a total of about 6,395 jurisdictions). After a follow-up mailing, 51 percent of the managers responded. Thus, although the data that follows is not exclusively for city managers operating in council-manager cities, the survey results do represent the general pool of managers who serve as city and county managers and CAOs.[42]

The 2000 ICMA survey reported that 88 percent of local managers were male—a change from 95 percent in 1989 and 99 percent in 1974, indicating that gender diversification is taking place in the city/county management profession, albeit slowly. In a series of articles, Richard L. Fox and Robert A. Schuhmann study women as local managers. Based on data gathered in a 1996–1997 survey conducted under the auspices of the ICMA, they provide a demographic profile of women serving as local managers. Of the total 410 women serving in the United States at the time as local chief administrative officers, 257 responded to the ICMA survey.[43] About 87 percent of the women serve as local managers in cities with populations of 25,000 or less. The mean age of the women responding to the survey is 47.9 years. The representative female local manager is highly educated when compared to her gender group generally. For example, she is nine times more likely to have a master's degree than is a woman in the general population (35 percent versus 4 percent). Most of the women local managers are white (92 percent). The average time spent in their present position is about six years, but over half (51 percent) of the local managers indicate they have been in their present position four years or less. In terms of political ideology, 37 percent of the women self-identify as liberals, 35 percent as conservatives, and 28 percent as moderates. The greatest motivator for women administrators is their commitment to public service—seven in ten women identified this commitment as the primary reason they chose to be a local manager.

In another article, Fox and Schuhmann note that, compared with men, women city managers are (1) more likely to incorporate citizen input in their decisions, (2) are more likely to emphasize the importance of communication with citizens and with elected and appointed government officials in carrying out their duties, and (3) are less likely to see themselves as policy entrepreneurs and more likely to see their role as that of manager and facilitator. They note, "Women in this study were more likely to value citizen input and would prefer to be in the middle of a 'web' of interactions rather than to be on top of the hierarchy."[44]

Finally, Fox and Schuhmann contend that the slow inclusion of women into the field of city management may, in part, be explained by the mentoring experiences of women city managers, who are significantly more likely than men to rely on female mentors.[45] Also, significantly fewer women than men indicated that they had had male professors who mentored them. This gender divide presents an obstacle, since women have fewer choices and opportunities to meet women in high-level positions and in educational institutions. In the late 1990s, for example, the authors report that about 50 percent of all graduate students in public administration and public affairs programs were women, but only 24 percent of the faculty members were women.

Returning to our profile of local managers based on the 2000 ICMA survey, we find that 92 percent of local managers were between the ages of thirty and sixty—and 50 percent were between forty-six and fifty-five. Compared to the 99 percent of chief administrative officers in 1989 who were white, by 2000, 95 percent of the managers were white, 2 percent were Hispanic, and 2 percent African American, while the remaining 1 percent was made up of Asian Americans, Native Americans, and other ethnicities.

The typical manager had served in his or her present position for 6.9 years (up from 5.4 years in 1989) and had spent a total of 17.4 years as a local government executive (up from 10.1 years reported in 1989). This 28 percent increase in average tenure in a position and the 72 percent increase in average tenure in the profession both bode well for a profession that has been characterized as "serve and move." Job stability is now greater and should serve as an even stronger incentive for young people to enter the city management profession. However, as the average 6.9 years' tenure in position suggests, few city managers were spending too long in one city. Research on "long-serving" city managers (defined as at least 20 years of service in the same city) by Douglas J. Watson and Wendy L. Hassett finds that most of these managers serve in smaller cities (populations under 30,000) that are relatively homogeneous, politically stable, and committed to the principles of the reform movement.[46] These managers are well-educated and committed to public service and to "their communities, their staffs, and the elected officials for whom they work."[47]

In the 2000 survey, about 13 percent of the managers reported that they had changed positions in the past year; of these, 10 percent had done so voluntarily and 3 percent involuntarily. Of those moving of their own accord, 61 percent had done so for career advancement. Of the group who had been asked to leave, 10 percent were fired, 20 percent were forced to resign, and the remaining 70 percent reported being under pressure to resign. But, it is important to put these later percentages into perspective: 3 percent of the sample equals only about one hundred local managers who were forced to leave their positions.

The survey also found that local managers were a well-educated group: 89 percent held a bachelor's degree (up from 69 percent in 1971), 60 percent had a master's degree (up from 27 percent in 1971), and 3 percent had an earned doctoral degree (JD or PhD). Over the past several decades, academic areas of study for local managers have shifted substantially from preparation in engineering to preparation in public administration and business management. Finally, two-thirds of the city managers reported that they were highly satisfied (22 percent) or moderately satisfied (44 percent) with their jobs. These felt-satisfaction ratings may seem high, given the intense pressure and scrutiny under which local managers work, but local managers are paid relatively well. In 2009 the average city manager/CAO earned about $106,000. In cities with populations of over 50,000, the city manager/CAO, on average, was more likely to be paid about $154,000; in cities with populations between 100,000 and 500,000 the average salary was about $184,000; in America's big cities with 500,000 or more residents the mean salary for city managers is over $210,000.[48]

What Do They Do?

According to the official position of the ICMA, the following four essential responsibilities rest with city managers:

- Formulating policy on overall problems
- Preparing the budget, presenting it to the council, and administering it when approved by the council
- Appointing and removing most of the principal department heads in city government
- Forming extensive external relationships to deal with overall problems of city operations[49]

In addition, most city charters charge managers with the responsibility for executing policy made by the city council.

In a classic study, political scientist Deil Wright contends that city managers' duties can be grouped into three basic categories: managerial, policy related, and political.[50] Executing policy, budgeting, and controlling bureaucracy through appointment and removal are the key elements of the *managerial role*. The *policy-related role* involves managers' relationships with the council and mayor. In the *political role*, the manager is called on to negotiate not only with officials at other levels of government, particularly the state and federal level, but also with a bevy of nongovernmental groups and individuals throughout the community.

In Wright's survey of city managers in forty-five large cities, respondents were asked to indicate how they in fact allotted their time among the three basic roles and how they would like to allot their time. Survey results show that city managers said that they spent 60 percent of their time in the management role, 21 percent in the policy role, 16 percent in the political role, and 3 percent doing "other" tasks. They preferred, however, to spend less time in the administrative role (46 percent) and more time in the policy role (19 percent), the political role (19 percent), and their "other" role (9 percent). Most managers apparently wanted to spend more time interacting with the council and the larger public.

Twenty years after the Wright study, research by Charldean Newell and David Ammons found that the gap between what city managers do and what they want to do had narrowed.[51] Their 1985 sample of 142 city managers in cities with populations of 50,000 or more found that city managers devoted about half their time (51 percent) to administrative activities, 32 percent to the policy role, and 17 percent to the political role. Moreover, these actual role allocations matched almost perfectly their preferred role allocations. Based on a 2009 survey that included almost 400 city managers and CAOs, Jerri Killian and Enamul Choudhury report findings similar to Newell and Ammons in terms of actual time managers spent in their management, policy, and political roles. The 2009 study does depart, however, from the earlier Newell and Ammons study in terms of how managers prefer to allocate their time. The urban leaders desired to spend slightly less time in their management role and strongly wished to increase the amount of time they spend in their political role.[52] A recent study by David Ammons examines role similarities and differences between city managers and chief administrative officers (CAOs, also frequently called "city administrators") using 2004 survey data secured from persons who have served as both.[53] First Ammons discusses the debate surrounding whether city managers serving in council-manager municipalities and city administrators who provide broad administrative leadership in mayor-council cities are functional equivalents. Although he notes many similarities and differences, he defers offering a definitive response to this question to the conclusion of his article. Next, he reports the mean percentage of time devoted to the management, policy, and political roles for 275 executives when they were in their positions as city managers and when they served as CAOs. The time allocations are remarkably similar. When they served as city managers, the city executives declared they spent 53.2 percent in the management role, 29.0 percent in the policy role, and 17.9 percent in the political role. In their city administrator positions, the time allocations were 53.8 percent in the management role, 26.9 percent in policy role, and 19.0 percent in the political role. After a thorough analysis of perceived differences and similarities among those who served as both city managers and city administrators across a number of administrative, policy, political, job complexity, and career progression questions, Ammons concludes:

"[O]n several key dimensions—particularly on matters of budget and human resource management—they [survey respondents] reject the assertion of role equivalence. On these important dimensions, the city manager's influence and authority are perceived to be greater."[54] Furthermore, Ammons asserts, "Professionalism tends to be advanced by the appointment of a city administrator and advanced even further by the appointment of a city manager."[55] Research also shows that attitudes of city managers regarding role importance attitudes vary according to municipal, structural, and city demographic characteristics.[56]

Finally, in terms of what city managers do, James Svara argues that the three-role typology offered by Wright and later used by Newell and Ammons should be "reconceptualized" into four roles: mission, policy, administration, and management.[57] We agree; these "dimensions of the governmental process" are discussed further later in this chapter.

Even in an urban world less chaotic than the one depicted by Yates's model of street-fighting pluralism, city managers must play a complex policy role perhaps undreamed of by their early predecessors. In fact, many see the city manager engaging in behavior that was traditionally reserved for elected politicians. The manager, in the words of James Banovetz, must operate as a "catalyst in the formulation of urban policy, 'brokering' or compromising and satisfying the multitudinous and conflicting demands made by special interest groups."[58] Perhaps Camille Cates Barnett, who holds MPA and PhD degrees and is a former city manager of Houston, Austin, and Dallas, Texas, is prototypic of the new breed of city managers. Admitting that as a city manager she was a "facilitator" and "negotiator," she notes, "I think it's abdicating for a manager not to tell people what she thinks. But you don't ever want to upstage your council people."[59]

MAYOR-MANAGER RELATIONS

The relationship between mayor and manager has been the subject of considerable attention among urban scholars and practitioners.[60] The original council-manager plan envisioned a modest role, at best, for the mayor, but this expectation probably was unrealistic. Even in many smaller communities mayors have been known to exercise considerable influence on a host of municipal affairs. In fact, a classic study of several small communities in Florida published in the early 1960s revealed that an activist mayor—especially one who has been popularly elected—can pose a threat to a manager's tenure.[61] More recent research by Gordon Whitaker and Ruth Hoogland DeHoog confirms this finding.[62] In addition, these researchers aver that contrary to some findings, conflict is a frequent cause for turnover among city managers. They argue that city managers should attempt to better understand the role of conflict in community politics and should be better trained in conflict resolution techniques.

Still, with cooperation, the relationship between mayors and managers can and should be mutually beneficial. James Svara, for example, contends that the mayor in the council-manager plan plays a unique, albeit ambiguous, role in city affairs.[63] Svara creates a seven-category mayoral leadership typology based on combinations of twelve roles (activities) performed by mayors in North Carolina. He concludes that the mayor is the "stabilizer" in the council-manager plan: "He will be more or less central, more or less public, more or less assertive as conditions warrant. . . . Effective [mayoral] leadership is built upon strengthening the other participants in the governing process rather than controlling or supplanting them."[64]

David Morgan and Sheilah Watson draw on a national survey to analyze the way in which mayors and city managers often work together.[65] They find that in large cities, especially, the two officials often form teams or create partnerships, although the mayor took the lead in most cases. Among smaller communities, mayor-manager collaboration also appeared, but with somewhat less frequency. Here, the city manager was a bit more likely to emerge as the dominant leader of the mayor-manager team. Finally, the authors comment on the prevalence of what they call "caretaker" governments. In about a third of all cities, neither the mayor nor the manager possesses abundant power regardless of the frequency with which they interact. Consequently, neither official has sufficient authority to affect municipal policy decisively. Large council-manager cities, however, had far fewer caretaker regimes than did smaller communities.

THE CITY COUNCIL

Although the need for executive leadership remains crucial, representative government mandates an active policymaking role for the legislative branch. Who are these people at the municipal level? And what are they doing?

A large-scale 2001 ICMA survey of cities allows for a better understanding of city council members.[66] The average council size in the United States is six members. Of the more than 25,000 city council members who responded to the survey, 22 percent were female, up from 10 percent in 1976. Sixty-seven percent of all survey cities reported that at least one female serves on the council. Political scientists Susan MacManus and Charles Bullock, the authors of the ICMA study, suggest that the "biggest obstacle to women's election is their reticence to run. Female candidacy rates still lag behind those of their male counterparts."[67] Most council members (87.5 percent) were white; in 1986 the comparable percentage was 93.6 percent. African Americans represented about 5.6 percent of the council members, Hispanics approximately 2.6 percent. Native American council members showed a large increase in representation, from 0.3 percent in 1986 to 4 percent in 2001. In terms of age, serving on a city council tends to be the province of older citizens: 87 percent of the council members were forty years of age or older; of all council members, 27 percent were sixty or older, and 22 percent were retirees.

Sixty-four percent (up from 59 percent in 1991) of cities in the 2001 survey elected council members by means of at-large elections, compared to 14 percent (up from 11.7 percent in 1991) using ward- or district-based elections and 21 percent (down from 29.3 percent in 1991) using mixed elections.[68] As noted in chapter 3, previous studies suggest that minorities fare better in district-based and mixed-election cities, whereas women do slightly better under the at-large formats.

Few jurisdictions (9 percent, up from 4.2 percent in 1991) set term limits for council members. And those that did so tended to be cities with populations above 50,000 (so-called central cities) and cities located in the ICMA-defined Mountain region, consisting of the states of Arizona, Colorado, Idaho, Montana, Nevada, New Mexico, Utah, and Wyoming. Of the cities using at-large elections, about 60 percent employed four-year terms of office, and another 22 percent used a two-year term. Of the cities electing council members from districts or wards, 61 percent used four-year terms and 31 percent used two-year terms. Most cities (83 percent) staggered elections to ensure continuity, stability, and organizational memory on the council. Most councils met either once (20 percent) or twice (69 percent) a month. Similar to the U.S. Congress and state legislatures, more than half the cities (58 percent, up from 53 percent in 1996) had standing committees; the percentage in cities with populations above 250,000 was 75 percent. Finally, the urban reformers had apparently been successful in their efforts to promote the use of nonpartisan ballots to—theoretically anyway—remove politics from local government. In 2001, about 77 percent of cities selecting their council members by ballot were using nonpartisan ballots.

In a study commissioned by the National League of Cities in 2001, James Svara reports survey results from 664 council members serving in cities with populations of 25,000 or more.[69] Svara's findings provide useful information not included in the larger ICMA study. He notes, for example, that, compared to their fellow citizens, council members are generally well-educated. In 2001, 75 percent of the responding city council members had a college degree, and 40 percent had professional or graduate degrees. The average age of those serving on city councils was fifty-four. About 40 percent of the city council members reported their occupation as "manager or professional," while 21 percent were business owners, 21 percent were retired, 3 percent were "house spouses," 2 percent were blue-collar workers, 1 percent were clerical workers, and the remaining respondents were classified as "others."

Although council members in American cities are more likely than not to run on nonpartisan ballots, partisanship and political ideology are still part of what defines a council person. Svara reports that across all cities, 38.3 percent reported that they were Democrats, 30.9 percent were independents, and 30.8 percent were Republicans. Significant differences in partisanship existed by race, age, size of city, and ballot type.

According to survey data, most council races are not close contests. Almost half (45 percent) of council members reported winning by large margins, and 19 percent had run unopposed. Only 11 percent of the respondents said that their election was close. Fifty-six percent of the council members planned to run for another term, and about one in three (28 percent) expressed interest in running for a higher office.

Council members were fairly evenly divided in terms of years of service across categories used in the study. Twenty-four percent had served 0–2 years; 22 percent, 3–5 years; 28 percent, 6–10 years; and about one in three (29 percent) reported 10 or more years of service. A typical council member receives only modest compensation for services rendered, and salaries vary considerably by size of city and form of city government.

For example, in large cities (of 200,000 or more residents) 73 percent of the council members received $20,000 or more per year and 35 percent earned more than $40,000 per year; in contrast, in small cities (having 25,000–69,999 residents), less than 2 percent of council members received $20,000 per year. Council members in cities using the mayor-council versus the council-manager form of government are more likely to receive higher levels of pay. On the other hand, the time devoted to serving on a city council is significant regardless of the size of the city: the average city council member works on council-related matters twenty hours per week in small cities, twenty-five hours per week in medium-size cities (having 70,000–199,999 residents), and forty-two hours per week—a full-time job—in big cities.

Why do council members run for office? When provided a list that contained a variety of reasons for seeking office and asked to mark those that applied to them, about 80 percent of the respondents said they had run "to serve the city as a whole." The second most often cited reason for running was to "serve my neighborhood" (51 percent). Only 3 percent saw serving on the council as a stepping-stone to higher office.

Svara's research on city councils suggests that there is significant variation based on form of city government—mayor-council versus council-manager. Research by Timothy Krebs and John P. Pelissero captures many of these major differences, as shown in table 4-1.[70] Most of the characteristics shown in the table are fairly straightforward, but two of them require some elucidation. First, "representational style" refers to the classic discussion in political science about the role of a representative—should she act based on her own best judgment

Table 4-1   Common Characteristics of City Councils under Two Forms of Government

Characteristics	Mayor-Council Governments	Council Manager Governments
Size of council	Larger	Smaller
Nature of work	Full time	Part time
Compensation	Higher pay	Lower or no pay
Meeting	More frequent	Less frequent
Party roles	Partisan and nonpartisan	Nonpartisan
Representational method	District	At-large
Committees	More	Fewer
Staff	More	Smaller
Diversity	More	Less
Representational style	Delegates	Trustees
Constituency serivce	More casework	Less casework
Policymaking roles	Advocates-adopters	Respondents-adopters
Conflict	Higher	Lower

SOURCE: Reprinted with permission from Timothy B. Krebs and John P. Pelissero, "City Councils," in John P. Pelissero, ed., *Cities, Politics, and Policy: A Comparative Analysis* (Washington, D.C.: CQ Press, 2003), pp. 169–195. Reprinted with permission.

(a trustee role) or vote according to her constituents' desires (a delegate role). The second characteristic that may require a bit of explanation is "policymaking role." In cities operating under the council-manager form, council members are more likely to be part-time and either non-paid or low-paid, and they often defer or respond to the expertise of the city manager and the professional bureaucracy—thus, they are given the policymaking label of "respondents-adopters." The mayor-council form of government is more often found in larger cities, which are more likely to have legislative committees and full-time, paid council members. These big-city councils are likely to be large bodies—thus increasing the chances of differences in attitudes about what constitutes "good" policy. Their members are likely to be elected from districts or wards and to feel obligated to "take care of their own"—a politics that often results in a policymaking role called "advocates-adopters." Still, caution is required: as Krebs and Pelissero note, "If we have been able to learn one thing [from this study], it is that city councils in the United States are not all alike."[71] Generalizations are possible, but for every generalization, there is an exception to the rule.

COUNCIL-MANAGER RELATIONS

Almost from the beginning, the correct relationship between manager and council has been the subject of study and debate. For example, a symposium in the journal *State and Local Government Review* focused on "Conflict Management and Resolution in Cities," with the goal of "examining how interactions between council members and city managers can be managed to foster elective working relationships."[72]

Although the council-manager government appears, in theory, to support the almost total separation of policy and administration—the so-called politics-administration dichotomy—even the plan's early proponents saw the need for managerial involvement in policymaking. Or, as John Nalbandian so aptly reminds us: "It has been acknowledged for a long time that city and county managers play a prominent role in policymaking. It can be no other way."[73] Today, the debate essentially centers on the proper spheres of responsibility of the council and the manager. In the mid-1980s, James Svara offered what many consider a classic study to sort out this relationship.[74] His model remains, in our opinion, as instructive today as when first published.

Drawing on field observations in five large North Carolina cities in addition to other studies, Svara developed a dichotomy-duality model of policy and administration in council-manager cities. He divided the basic governing responsibilities into four categories: mission, policy, administration, and management. Then he used a curved line to graphically depict the typical division of responsibility between council and manager in each area. The basic model is shown in figure 4-1.

As briefly touched on previously in this chapter, *mission* refers to the organization's broadest goals and most basic purposes. It encompasses such matters as the scope of services provided, levels of taxation, and fundamental policy orientations. As the figure reveals, mission remains the overwhelming responsibility of elected officials. The manager is not powerless even here, of course—she or he will make recommendations,

Figure 4-1 **Basic Division of Responsibility between City Council and City Manager**

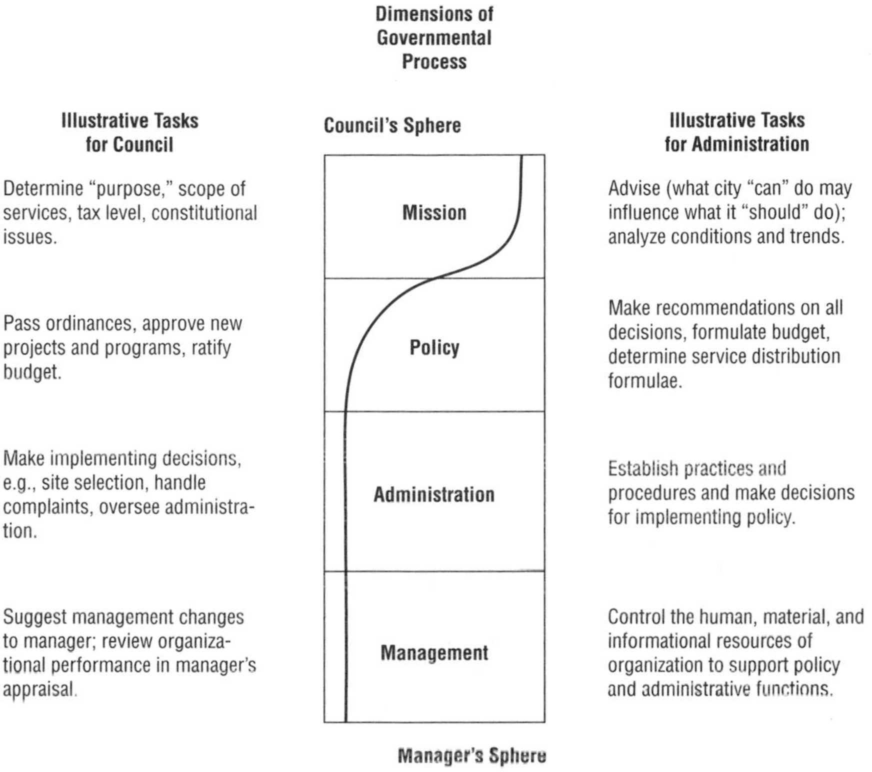
Dimensions of Governmental Process
Illustrative Tasks for Council
Council's Sphere
Illustrative Tasks for Administration
Determine "purpose," scope of services, tax level, constitutional issues.
Mission
Advise (what city "can" do may influence what it "should" do); analyze conditions and trends.
Pass ordinances, approve new projects and programs, ratify budget.
Policy
Make recommendations on all decisions, formulate budget, determine service distribution formulae.
Make implementing decisions, e.g., site selection, handle complaints, oversee administration.
Administration
Establish practices and procedures and make decisions for implementing policy.
Suggest management changes to manager; review organizational performance in manager's appraisal.
Management
Control the human, material, and informational resources of organization to support policy and administrative functions.
Manager's Sphere

SOURCE: "Dichotomy and Duality: Reconceptualizing the Relationship between Policy and Administration in Council-Manager Cities," by James H. Svara, *Public Administration Review*, 1985, 45, 228. Reprinted with permission from *Public Administration Review* © by the American Society for Public Administration (ASPA), 1120 G Street NW, Suite 700, Washington, D.C. 20005. All rights reserved.

undertake studies, and engage in planning—but mission lies predominantly in the council's sphere.

The term *policy* is narrowly applied here to middle-range issues and problems, the "redistribution" questions in Paul Peterson's formulation. The annual budget certainly reflects these mid-range decisions—which programs or services to expand or cut, whether to contract out to the private sector or to undertake a new service responsibility. Notice in figure 4-1 that the curved line almost bisects this sphere, although slightly more space is given to the manager. Indeed, the city manager is expected to play a prominent role here, proposing and recommending a variety of policy measures. The council, of course, must ratify the budget, pass ordinances, and approve new service initiatives. But in many cities, the initiative for such activities lies with the city manager.

As we move downward to the areas of administration and management, the manager's sphere naturally expands. According to Svara, *administration* refers to the specific decisions and practices employed to achieve policy objectives. The governing body still has some influence here. It may choose to specify the specific administrative techniques to be used, or it may intervene in service delivery, perhaps in response to constituent demands or to ensure that some special need of a council member's ward is met. Finally, at the bottom of the figure we come to *management*, where we expect to find little council involvement. These are the very immediate actions taken by the city manager to control and allocate the organization's human and material resources. The council may play an oversight role here, offering suggestions or passing along citizen complaints, but the boundary between elected officials and administrators in the management arena is usually fairly clearly defined and widely acknowledged.

As figure 4-1 shows, a dichotomy of sorts does exist, but only at the mission and management levels. In between, in policy and administration, considerable sharing of responsibilities is called for. Svara readily admits that this schematic does not apply to all council-manager cities. He identifies several variants to the model—the strong-manager model, where the line is shifted to the left, and the "council incursion" model, where the council frequently moves more prominently into the administrative sphere. In general, however, the model shown in figure 4-1 represents a reasonably typical, if not ideal, arrangement by which councils and city managers both divide and share responsibility for the basic tasks of urban governance and management.

More recently, Svara has argued that the "myth" of the politics-administration dichotomy should be replaced by a model that he labels "complementarity of politics and administration."[75] This interdependent (versus dichotomous) model suggests that policymaking should be—and in reality is—shared between elected officials (mayors and city council members) and administrators (city managers and local bureaucrats). Research by Sally Coleman Selden, Gene A. Brewer, and Jeffrey L. Brudney supports Svara's complementarity model. Based on a survey of about 1,000 city managers, these researchers found that while city council members possess considerable means to control city managers' actions through evaluations, oversight, and even termination, most council members "opt for less complex solutions involving trust and role sharing."[76]

But it is important to remember that city managers do often find themselves thrust into the policy arena. Among the possible reasons are these:

- The failure of mayors and councils to play their idealized leadership roles
- The full-time nature of the manager's job compared with the part-time involvement of council members
- The manager's experience and/or specialized training in problem solving
- The staff specialists, technicians, and department heads available to assist the manager

- The manager's role in preparing the city budget
- The manager's position at the apex of an information network, which allows the manager to channel, control, and veto options offered by others

There are limits on the city manager's domination of municipal policy. First, most managers are cognizant of the need to keep their councils satisfied, and they recognize that councils usually frown on too much policy activism. Second, even in the management profession, the dominant feeling is that managers should not publicly espouse a view contrary to a stated council position. Finally, in large council-manager cities, city managers frequently must share their policy role with the mayor. As noted earlier, Morgan and Watson report that mayor-manager "governing coalitions" are frequently found in larger cities. To the extent that such a situation prevails, these council-manager cities are not so different from mayor-council cities that employ a full-time professional administrator (CAO). One final note is in order. Regardless of how hard a local executive tries to develop an appropriate working relationship with his or her city councils, sometimes city manager turnover is the result of systemic changes in the local political and economic environment of the municipality. For example, in a recent pooled cross-sectional time series analysis of 143 U.S. cities with populations of 75,000 or more residents, Barbara Coyle McCabe, Richard C. Feiock, James Clingermayer, and Christopher Stream examine the impact of local "push" (e.g., turnover among elected council members and short term economic change) and "pull" (e.g., a positive economic growth trend over time, large and fast-growing communities) factors that may explain city manager tenure.[77] Findings suggest that substantial turnover on a city council increase the likelihood of more city manager turnover. "By holding other factors affecting manager tenure constant, our empirical results demonstrate the powerful, direct, and independent effect of political change on city management tenure."[78] In addition, data show that communities that experience short-term economic declines or long-term economic growth have slightly higher manager turnover.[79]

Thus far we have examined mayors and city managers as chief executives, mayor-manager relations, and council-manager relations. The case study provided in box 4.2 shows the interaction of all three groups of policymakers in council-manager cities—mayors, managers, *and* council members—as they attempt to implement current administrative reforms.

BUREAUCRATS AND POLICY

Bureaucrats—the city staff and operating departments—participate prominently in policymaking, both in its formulation and in its implementation. In terms of the policy-making role of the bureaucracy, Charles E. Lindblom and Edward J. Woodhouse offer the following assessment:

Indeed, if it were possible to count all the policy-making acts in any political system— choices made, attempts at persuasion, agreements reached, threats and promises made,

---

BOX 4.2   Policy and Practice

THE IMPACT OF MAYORS AND CITY COUNCILS ON CITY MANAGERS' "MANAGING FOR RESULTS" REFORM INITIATIVES

In 2001, a year after their research project introduced in the case study entitled "Incidence, Predictors, and Consequences of Reinventing Government" (box 1.1), professors Richard Kearney and Carmine Scavo offered findings of another systematic, comparative analysis of reinventing government (REGO) actions at the local level. This study attempted to answer two questions in council-manager (reformed) cities: "First, what are the correlates and extent of REGO actions by managers, mayors, and councils? Second, what is the nature of REGO interactions among managers, mayors, and councils?" The answer to the first question was that REGO actions are a function of city managers' support of the reinvention ideology and of the municipal government characteristics of wealth of the city, number of full-time employees, and location in the Sunbelt.

When mayoral and council characteristics were added to the analysis (regression equation), several new variables reached statistical significance as predictors of council members' agreement with managers' budget recommendations for managing for results initiatives: "A large, racially homogeneous city council facilitates the implementation of REGO policies, but a strong and active mayor [measured by his or her ability to appoint department heads] with increasing ties to citizens' groups and the public as a whole makes REGO less likely" (62). The authors speculate that racially diverse city councils may evoke more conflict than more homogeneous councils and impede reform policy adoption. Or, perhaps, minority council members may regard the management initiatives as more citywide in scope and therefore a threat to local constituencies.

In explaining their findings related to mayors, Kearney and Scavo suggest that "managers may have less influence over department heads appointed by the mayor than they have over those whom they hire themselves" (63). Also, mayors who are more active with various citizen groups and with the public as a whole may pursue agenda items that simply are not as management related; involvement in determining the "mission" of the government may be more forthcoming from this type of mayor.

In short, while city managers may be very supportive of reinventing government in theory and even in action, they must interact with councils and mayors, both of which can have a significant impact on implementing management reform initiatives. In the words of Kearney and Scavo, city managers "can only accomplish what their community, governmental, and political environments permit" (63).

SOURCE: Richard C. Kearney and Carmine Scavo, "Reinventing Government in Reformed Municipalities," *Urban Affairs Review 37* (September 2001): 43–66.

---

authoritative commands given or received—one would find that, so defined, policy making rests overwhelmingly in the hands of the bureaucracy.[80]

Kenneth J. Meier agrees. He argues that bureaucracies, like legislative bodies, authoritatively allocate values and in doing so engage "in politics of the first order."[81]

Bureaucrats have become key policy figures for several reasons. First, they are the source of much of the technical and highly specialized information that is so essential for making decisions. Second, legislative bodies increasingly find it necessary to write laws in terms broad enough to permit flexibility in their application; this practice obviously increases the authority of those who implement the laws—the bureaucrats. Finally, many bureaucrats, especially at the urban level, are in constant contact with the public in a variety of situations in which judgment and discretion are necessary to resolve problems, disputes, and complaints.

Although, bureaucrats "are central to policy formulation,"[82] most observers would probably agree that bureaucrats have their major effect on policy during the implementation phase.[83] We can identify two principal means by which they exert their influence: through the development of decision rules that guide administrative behavior, and through the exercise of discretion in dealing with people at the street level.

BUREAUCRATIC DECISION RULES

First, to understand how and why bureaucrats develop decision rules, we must understand something about the psychological needs of bureaucrats themselves. In a classic study of bureaucratic decision making in the city of Oakland, California, Frank Levy, Arnold Meltsner, and Aaron Wildavsky observe that, like most of us, bureaucrats want to work within a relatively secure, stable organizational environment. To keep their relationships as predictable and orderly as possible, bureaucrats rely on what the Oakland study calls the "Adam Smith rule." This decision rule, in keeping with its laissez-faire orientation, says: when a "customer makes a 'request,' take care of him in a professional manner; otherwise, leave him alone."[84] Bureaucrats employ the Adam Smith rule, coupled with a heavy reliance on professional standards, as a way of routinizing and stabilizing the decision-making process.

Levy and his colleagues demonstrate how bureaucratic decision rules affect the operation of several city departments, beginning with libraries. There, the Adam Smith rule would dictate that new acquisition funds be allocated to those branches with the highest circulation: the more books the patrons take out, the more money their branch receives. In the street department, the rule would require that money be spent to repair streets primarily on the basis of complaints received. On the surface, these decision rules sound reasonable and defensible, but, as the Oakland study points out, they often harbor a hidden allocational bias. In the case of libraries, certain low-circulation branches, particularly those serving low-income and minority populations, thereby failed to obtain the resources to provide new materials to serve the changing needs of their customers. In the street department, evidence suggested that concentrating resources on heavily traveled roads tended to benefit well-to-do commuters (including those living outside Oakland), while poorer citizens were left with few street improvements.

BUREAUCRATIC DISCRETION

Some public employees also affect policy implementation through the exercise of discretion in their daily dealings with the public. Michael Lipsky calls these people "street-level bureaucrats"—a phrase that would apply to the officer on the beat, the classroom teacher, and the welfare caseworker.[85] Lipsky argues that these bureaucrats operate under considerable stress owing to inadequate resources, threats (physical and psychological) or challenges to their authority, and ambiguous job expectations. Accordingly, they develop mechanisms or defenses for reducing job-related stresses.

Unfortunately for many of those with whom these officials interact (especially low-income and minority groups), their stress-reducing efforts often take the form of routinized responses to client or public demands. For example, stereotyping and other forms of racial, gender, or class bias may come to play a significant part in bureaucratic behavior. Such bias or discrimination may not be overt or even intentional; it may simply be institutional.[86] One way to address this problem is by ensuring a representative bureaucracy—that is, the demographic make-up of those who constitute public bureaucracies should mirror that of the general local population in terms of race, ethnicity, gender, age, disability, and so on. Since different social groups have different socialization patterns, values, mores, attitudes, and behaviors, a representative bureaucracy can help to overcome race-, gender-, or class-based biases. A significant literature has developed that supports the positive impact of a representative bureaucracy.[87] Other defensive bureaucratic devices involve attributing responsibility for all actions to the clients—blaming the victim—or, conversely, assuming that the clients are so victimized by social forces that they cannot be helped by the service being offered.

At the street level, no group exercises more discretion than the police officer on the beat. As a presidential crime commission acknowledged in the 1960s: "Law enforcement policy is made by the policeman."[88] The reason is simple: officers are confronted with so many offenses that they cannot arrest everyone involved; instead they use their discretion, particularly in matters of maintaining order.

In short, bureaucratic discretion is a powerful policy implementation tool in the hands of street-level bureaucrats. Problems arise from the use of defensive psychological mechanisms. A distortion of reality can make bureaucrats less effective in performing their jobs as a result of institutional discrimination, blaming the victim, or producing a work environment defined by hopelessness. On the other hand, bureaucratic discretion allows the local worker on the street latitude to "bend the rules," "to go above and beyond the call of duty," and to challenge operating procedures and organizational cultures that are in need of changing. What we have here is a case of the proverbial two-edged sword; which side of the blade is used is dependent on the "discretion" of the street-level bureaucrat.

CITIZENS' INFLUENCES ON CITY GOVERNMENT

Citizens can make their voices heard at city hall in several basic ways. The most obvious and widely employed means is voting, but several other options are available as well: organizing or joining some group or political party, and contacting city officials with complaints or requests for services.

ELECTIONS AND VOTING

The first and perhaps most significant thing we can say about municipal elections is that most Americans do not vote in them. Moreover, to our knowledge, there is no source that provides a definitive "average turnout" for city elections. Average for what—big cities, small cities, all cities? Since over 35,000 cities and towns in the United States hold their elections at different intervals and at different times of the year, calculating an "average" is not something the academic community has ventured to do. Elaine Sharp does note that one recent national survey reports, "Only 35 percent of respondents indicated that they always vote in local elections."[89] The comparable figure for respondents who said they always vote in national elections was 58 percent. Similarly, Sharp points to research that shows a 47 percent turnout in Chicago in 1991 and a 53 percent turnout in the 1989 Cleveland mayoral race. But turnout rates for school board elections "can run as low as 10 to 15 percent—and sometimes even lower!"[90] Therefore, the basic generalization about turnout in local elections is that it is distressingly low.

Obviously, local elections are not as exciting or dramatic as national contests, and the stakes seem seldom as high. Perhaps Charles Adrian and Charles Press said it best many years ago:

> The principal reason for apathy in municipal elections, in fact, is likely to be a pervasive consensus, that is, there may be widespread agreement in the community as to the kinds of persons who are wanted in public office, as to expenditure levels, and as to public policies. Under such circumstances, little incentive exists for any but the most conscientious voter or the chronic dissenter to go to the polls.[91]

What difference does voter turnout make? In a democracy, elections provide a vital mechanism for controlling the political system, shaping policy alternatives, and expressing community values. But in whose interests? Not those of the entire community it seems. Research repeatedly shows that those who do not vote have less education and income than do members of the active electorate. Thus, the lower the turnout, the more likely the election will reflect the preferences of the well-to-do. Some might argue that the politically active should have more to say about community affairs—certainly, local officials are especially sensitive to the preferences of the attentive public. Still, we should remember that the election process reveals only a partial picture of the values and preferences of the whole city.

Voter participation is affected significantly by the characteristics of the municipal government itself. As noted in the previous chapter, "reformed" governmental practices, such as at-large and nonpartisan elections, scheduling of municipal elections at times different than national and state elections, and the council-manager form of government "have come at a price. Turnout in local elections is typically lower in cities with such reform-style institutions than it is in cities with unreformed governing institutions."[92] Similarly, after acknowledging the many positive gains in urban management associated with the reform movement, Ross and Levine also lament that one of the movement's legacies is that it "diluted the power of lower-class and minority voting groups."[93]

Elections are only one means by which citizens affect local policy. Participation in party or group activity may represent an even more direct means of exercising influence.

POLITICAL PARTIES AND INTEREST GROUPS

As noted, a supermajority of city elections today are nonpartisan. There was a time when political parties played a powerful role in local politics—sometimes as handmaiden to the local political machine—but the changing social and economic character of many cities, coupled with the successful efforts of urban reformers, has dealt a deathblow to most big-city machines. The major vehicles for accomplishing that objective were the introduction of nonpartisan ballots, the direct primary, and adoption of the merit system in personnel management.

Most ordinary citizens probably see the diminution of party influence at the local level as a plus; not all scholars would agree. In political scientist Bryan Jones's words, "Political parties are the mainsprings of mass democracy."[94] Unlike most other organizations interested in public affairs, parties are committed to getting out the vote. Moreover, each party makes some attempt at addressing issues and developing some agreement on those issues among candidates running on its label. Granted, parties in this country have never been very successful in inducing elected officeholders to adhere to their platforms or programs. But many political scientists believe that the alternative is worse—elected officials pursuing the dictates of their own consciences without regard to consequences or unconstrained group influence.

Organizing like-minded citizens or joining an active interest group represents a popular means by which citizens make their wishes known to city officials. Which groups at the local level are particularly visible and important? One way to determine this level of efficacy is to ask local representatives what they think. In the 2001 National League of Cities survey of city council members discussed above, council members were asked to identify the groups they believed it was important to represent. The groups identified— "listed in rank order based on the proportion of all council members who considered representation of that group to be very important"—were these: neighborhoods (68 percent); the elderly (37 percent); racial minorities (26 percent); women (24 percent); ethnic groups (21 percent); business (21 percent); municipal employees, "other," and environmentalists (each at 17 percent); labor unions (8 percent); realtors/developers (7 percent); and political parties (4 percent).[95] When council members were asked which local groups they believed had a great deal of influence on council decisions, once again the top-rated group was "neighborhoods" (54 percent), followed by business interests (28 percent), the elderly (24 percent), realtors/developers (16 percent), municipal employees and racial minorities (each at 14 percent), women and "other" (each at 13 percent), environmentalists (10 percent), ethnic groups (9 percent), labor unions (8 percent), and political parties (7 percent).

Several observations can be made about group influence. First, although business is usually acknowledged as the most powerful interest, its role differs among cities and among issues within a single city.[96] Labor, conversely, rarely commands much influence in municipal politics; its interests normally lie at the state and national levels. The city council perspectives reported above indicate that neighborhoods are not only what they believe it is important to represent, but are also believed to be the most influential group impacting city council decisions. Historically, the demands made by neighborhood groups and homeowners have been narrowly focused on discouraging city policies and actions that would adversely affect their particular slice of the community—"Not in my backyard" (NIMBY) has been a frequent rallying cry.

But this parochialism may be changing. Nowadays, neighborhoods are making fewer claims on city governments; instead, they are looking to city halls for partnerships. As Jeffrey Katz reports, as of 1989, "community-based development organizations had built nearly 125,000 units of housing in the United States—mostly for low-income residents. They had developed 16.4 million square feet of retail space, offices, and other industrial development."[97] Neighborhoods are asking that city governments empower them; instead of confrontation, neighborhood representatives seek collaboration. Government in Dayton, Ohio, for example, "runs on citizen power": seven area councils called "priority boards" working with city officials help to determine how not only Community Development Block Grants but also city-generated CD funds are to be spent.[98] According to Rob Gurwitt, by the early 1990s, similar neighborhood empowerment activities were under way in cities such as San Antonio, Denver, Phoenix, Indianapolis, Richmond (Va.), Santa Clarita (Calif.), Minneapolis, and Portland (Ore.).[99] The case study in box 4.3 based in the Netherlands demonstrates that emerging dynamic partnerships between local officials and neighborhoods is global in scope.

CITIZEN PARTICIPATION (REDUX) AND CITIZEN CONTACTS WITH LOCAL GOVERNMENT

Citizen Participation

As noted in chapter 1, and as Nancy Roberts tells us, "Citizenship participation is the cornerstone of democracy. . . . Direct democracy keeps community life vital and public institutions accountable."[100] Using the words of Enlightenment and social contract theorist Jean-Jacques Rousseau, Professor Roberts also warns of the consequences of not taking seriously the right to participate in our government: "As soon as public service ceases to be the main business of the citizens, and they prefer to serve with their pocketbooks rather than with their persons, the State is already close to its ruin."[101]

Fortunately, with advances in technology it has never been easier for people to connect with government. Instead of "We the People," James Scott at the Truman School of Public Affairs at the University of Missouri calls electronic participation "'E' the People."[102]

BOX 4.3   Policy and Practice

CITIZEN-GOVERNMENT COLLABORATION IN TWO DISADVANTAGED NEIGHBORHOODS IN THE NETHERLANDS: THE ADVANTAGES OF PARTICIPATORY DEMOCRACY

The importance of citizens working with public officials at the neighborhood level in two Dutch communities illustrates the transformative power of citizen participation in the governance of modern cities. In his excellent case study, Dutch Professor Hendrik Wagenaar of Leiden University tells about The Night Prevention Project in the Schilderswijk neighborhood in The Hague and the six Neighborhood Councils in the mid-sized town of Deventer located in the middle of the Netherlands. Before examining the consequences of these neighborhood interventions, a brief background of both cases is in order.

The case of the Schilderswijk neighborhood is a familiar tale. A low-income, blue-collar neighborhood begins a downward spiral of "decay, crime, and loss of social cohesion. Drug dealing, burglaries, street robberies, violence, and public nuisance were more and more common." Many old-time residents fled. Those residents who were left behind complained to the neighborhood police officer. He did his best to keep order, but was simply overwhelmed. City hall denied the problem, which left neighborhood residents feeling abandoned by authorities and angry that the neighborhood they had grown up with had been taken from them. Janny, one of the original residents, and her neighbors started keeping a "black book" that documented the physical and social decline of the neighborhood.

At a community meeting Janny complained about the "invisibility" of the neighborhood cop, who, in turn, suggested that residents join him on patrol one night to get a better view of his onerous job. They accepted his challenge. Out of this "spontaneous initiative" grew The Night Prevention Project in which residents, "mostly housewives," began to patrol the streets at night. They became "the eyes and ears" of the police. Janny and her friends also became skilled at creating links with city hall administration and with the local alderman. About a decade later, in 2001, the Night Prevention Project received the national prize for the most innovative crime prevention initiative in the nation. Crime was reduced and social cohesion was increased.

The City of Deventer is defined by six institutionalized neighborhood councils, which were initiated by local officials. In these neighborhood councils, administrators, professionals, and residents follow a rather formal process to flag problems and find solutions to them. "Most problems concern public safety, traffic nuisance, street crime, garbage in the streets, and quality of life." The councils are charged with the responsibility of maintaining and improving the quality of life in their community, transmitting problems to city hall, and enhancing social integration and "connectedness" in the neighborhoods. Each neighborhood has a neighborhood team comprised of and selected by local residents. In dialogue with neighborhood residents, the team formulates an annual plan to address local issues and receives roughly 30,000 Euros to put the plan into action. The central administration assigns a "neighborhood administrator" to each council to serve as a liaison between city hall and the neighborhood residents. For many, council meetings have become a social meeting place and have enhanced interest in neighborhood issues.

According to Professor Wagenaar these two case studies are examples of citizens and public officials collaborating to create "participatory, discursive democracy." They have created a "participatory society . . . which fosters a sense of political efficacy, nurtures a concern for collective problems and contributes to the formation of a knowledgeable citizenry capable of taking a sustained interest in the governing process." The case studies also demonstrate the global power of "neighborhoods" as the basic building blocks of cities.

SOURCE: Hendrik Wagenaar, "Governance, Complexity, and Democratic Participation: How Citizens and Public Officials Harness the Complexities of Neighborhood Decline," *The American Review of Public Administration* 37 (March 2007): 17–50.

Professor Scott studied the extent to which the websites of the principal cities in the 100 largest metropolitan statistical areas, as defined by the 2000 U.S. Census, facilitated public involvement in government. He found that the city portals (with over 3,000 web pages on 100 websites) "offer surprisingly rich and diverse information for interested users."[103] The sites, for example, included real-time traffic and transportation updates, Internet-based interactive mapping programs, city services available for various population subgroups (e.g, youth, families, and seniors), city organizational structures, the historical and cultural background of the locality, and key issues facing the city. Most of the sites allowed citizens to interact directly with appointed and elected city officials via e-mail or comment forms. About 60 percent of the cities posted their council agendas on the web and more than 50 percent provided the minutes of these meetings online. Over 80 percent of the big cities also included on their web page links to different charities, religious organizations, arts and culture groups, and voluntary associations. This "horizontal communication," according to Scott, leads to greater local social capital and civic engagement. [104] The research also found that most cities' web page supports direct democracy activities. The municipalities "run rather extensive programs designed to recruit, prepare, motivate, and manage public-service volunteers. These programs include neighborhood watch and beautification, mentoring, foster grandparents, and arts and culture specialists."[105] Many of these volunteers serve on city boards, commissions, and task forces that make significant policy decisions. Another broad-based survey of public participation in U.S. cities also found the extensive use of the Internet to communicate with citizens.[106] Of the 249 high–level city leaders responding to the survey, 39.8 percent "strongly agreed" and another 41.8 percent "agreed" (for a total of 81.6 percent) that they used the Internet as a citizen participation mechanism. Only two other citizen participation mechanisms scored a higher use, public hearings (96.9 percent) and community or neighborhood meetings (87.4 percent).[107] Surely, it seems, professor Scott is correct in his assessment that "web technology will likely redefine the relationship between citizens and government and help foster more engaged citizens."[108]

CITIZEN CONTACTS WITH LOCAL GOVERNMENT

In the daily course of events, a number of people call, write, or visit city hall—to complain about such problems as uncollected trash, or loose dogs, or an unusually large pothole in a nearby street. Or they may be seeking some sort of information—where to go to receive a health service or how to inquire about employment. In the past few years, considerable attention has been devoted to the nature of these contacts with local government.

Who are these people? Two characteristics heavily influence individual citizens' contact with local government: social class and need. As with voting, better-educated and more affluent citizens are the most likely to understand the system and to feel comfortable contacting local officials for a variety of purposes. But need for service may be even more critical, according to several studies.[109] Some local agencies distribute their services in response to observed demand, which apparently relates more to citizens' perceptions of the need for service (in the form of complaints) than to their income or education.[110]

What do these people want? Urban scholar Elaine Sharp's study of citizen-government contacts in Kansas City revealed that citizens have quite high expectations about the problems local government should solve, particularly in the areas of community services and public safety.[111] Responses to the question, "What do you think is the most important problem that you have in your neighborhood?" most frequently concerned what Sharp calls community services (flooding, trash piles, barking dogs); next were safety problems (crime, fear of walking the streets at night); social problems (undesirable neighbors, unsupervised juveniles) were least often mentioned. More important, people tended to think local government should do something about these matters—especially service and safety problems. A public ethic has evolved in this country, according to Sharp, that not only encourages the translation of personal problems into demands for public service but also fosters the expectation that city government is indeed responsible for resolving most of these problems. Sharp's concern is that these heightened citizen expectations may lead to disappointment and disillusionment whenever city hall fails to deliver as expected.

SUMMARY

Public policymaking at any level will always remain something of a mystery. So many potential groups can be involved and external conditions can vary so greatly that the process can be extraordinarily difficult to comprehend. And yet, as with any other enigmatic but important process, we continue to try. In this chapter we have considered the basic stages of community policymaking, emphasizing the political nature of the process. No matter how much we crave rational and efficient policy, the nature of democratic policymaking—with its heavy reliance on bargaining, negotiation, and compromise—virtually guarantees a messy process whose outcomes seldom satisfy everyone. Some scholars even offer formal descriptions of policymaking that stress the reactive role played by public officials and agencies, a process that one expert calls street-fighting pluralism. Others contend that where policy affects the city's most fundamental interests, business elites dominate the process to promote the economic well-being of the community.

No matter what form it takes or what impact it has, policy is made by people. At the urban level, the official policymakers include the chief executives, city councils, and bureaucracies, as well as the citizens acting at the ballot box, organizing in interest groups, or living in their neighborhoods. Policy initiation and leadership must come from somewhere; increasingly, the chief executive, whatever the form of government, is playing a more visible and vigorous policy role. Executive leadership often emerges because legislative bodies, especially those composed of amateurs working part-time, find it difficult either to acquire the expertise or to devote the time necessary to cope with ever more complex issues. The career civil service also plays a prominent role in policymaking and policy implementation.

Understanding the various ways in which bureaucratic influence operates has become increasingly important.

Finally, we cannot forget the people. Citizens influence local government in a number of ways. They vote, but generally not in the same numbers as turn out for state and national elections. Citizens also participate through interest groups, neighborhood associations, via city web pages, and by contacting local government officials.

SUGGESTED FOR FURTHER READING

Dalton, Russell J. *Citizen Politics*. 4th ed. Washington, D.C.: CQ Press, 2006.

Frederickson, H. George, and John Nalbandian, eds. *The Future of Local Government Administration: The Hansell Symposium*. Washington, D.C.: ICMA, 2002.

Garson, G. David. *Public Information Technology and E-Governance: Managing the Virtual State*. Sudbury, Mass.: Jones and Bartlett, 2006.

Meier, Kenneth J., and Laurence J. O'Toole Jr. *Bureaucracy in a Democratic State: A Governance Perspective*. Baltimore: The Johns Hopkins University Press, 2006.

Peters, B. Guy. *American Public Policy: Promise and Performance*. 6th ed. Washington, D.C.: CQ Press, 2004.

Peterson, Paul E. *City Limits*. Chicago: University of Chicago Press, 1981.

Ross, Bernard H., and Myron A. Levine. *Urban Politics: Power in Metropolitan America*. 7th ed. Belmont, Calif.: Thomson Wadsworth, 2006.

Yates, Douglas. *The Ungovernable City*. Cambridge, Mass.: MIT Press, 1977.

NOTES

1. James E. Anderson, *Public Policymaking: An Introduction*, 5th ed. (Boston: Houghton Mifflin, 2003), 2.

2. Ibid., 100.

3. Peter Bachrach and Morton S. Baratz, *Power and Poverty* (New York: Oxford University Press, 1970): 44.

4. David Easton, *The Political System*, 2nd ed. (New York: Knopf, 1971), 130.

5. Raymond E. Bauer, "The Study of Policy Formation: An Introduction," in *The Study of Policy Formation*, ed. Raymond Bauer and Kenneth Gergen (New York: Free Press, 1968), 2.

6. See David Easton, *A Framework for Political Analysis* (Englewood Cliffs, N.J.: Prentice Hall, 1965), and *A Systems Analysis of Political Life* (New York: Wiley, 1965).

7. Anthony Downs, *Urban Problems and Prospects* (Chicago: Markham, 1970), 176.

8. Charles E. Lindblom and Edward J. Woodhouse, *The Policy-Making Process*, 3rd ed. (Upper Saddle River, N.J.: Prentice Hall, 1980), 7.

9. This discussion of stages or steps in the policy process draws on a number of sources, including Thomas R. Dye, *Understanding Public Policy*, 11th ed. (Upper Saddle River, N.J.: Pearson Prentice Hall, 2005), primarily chapter 3; Anderson, *Public Policymaking*, especially chapters 3, 4, 6, and 7; James P. Lester and Joseph Stewart Jr., *Public Policy: An Evolutionary Approach*, 2nd ed. (Belmont, Calif.: Wadsworth Thomson, 2000); and B. Guy Peters, *American Public Policy: Promise and Performance*, 6th ed. (Washington, D.C.: CQ Press, 2004).

10. Roger Cobb and Charles Elder, *Participation in American Politics: The Dynamics of Agenda-Building* (Boston: Allyn and Bacon, 1972), 84–85.

11. Ibid., 86.

12. Charles Lindblom, *The Policy-Making Process*, 2nd ed. (Englewood Cliffs, N.J.: Prentice Hall, 1980), 48–49.

13. See Richard E. Neustadt, *Presidential Power* (New York: Wiley, 1964), for a classic argument concerning the power of persuasion.

14. Lindblom, *Policy-Making Process*, 28.

15. Ibid., 68.

16. See Frank Levy, Arnold Meltsner, and Aaron Wildavsky, *Urban Outcomes* (Berkeley: University of California Press, 1974), 229; Robert L. Lineberry, *Equality and Urban Policy: The Distribution of Municipal Public Services* (Beverly Hills, Calif.: Sage, 1977); Malcolm L. Goggin, Ann O'M. Bowman, James P. Lester, and Laurence J. O'Toole Jr., *Implementation: Theory and Practice* (Glenville, Ill.: Scott, Foresman/Little, Brown, 1990); Barry Bozeman, *Bureaucracy and Red Tape* (Upper Saddle River, N.J.: Prentice Hall, 2000); and Cornelius M. Kerwin, *Rulemaking: How Government Agencies Write Law and Make Policy*, 3rd ed. (Washington, D.C.: CQ Press, 2003).

17. Lester and Stewart, *Public Policy*, 155.

18. Douglas Yates, *The Ungovernable City* (Cambridge, Mass.: MIT Press, 1977).

19. Ibid., 34.

20. Paul E. Peterson, *City Limits* (Chicago: University of Chicago Press, 1981).

21. Ibid., 109.

22. Bernard H. Ross and Myron A. Levine, *Urban Politics: Power in Metropolitan America*, 7th ed. (Belmont, Calif.: Thomson Wadsworth, 2006). See also the critique of developmental politics offered in a three-article series in *Urban Affairs Quarterly* 22 (June 1987): Heywood Sanders and Clarence N. Stone, "Developmental Politics Reconsidered," 521–539; Paul Peterson, "Analyzing Developmental Politics: A Response to Sanders and Stone," 540–546; and Sanders and Stone, "Competing Paradigms: A Rejoinder to Peterson," 548–551.

23. Charles C. Euchner and Stephen J. McGovern, *Urban Policy Reconsidered: Dialogues on the Problems and Prospects of American Cities* (New York: Routledge, 2003), 26.

24. Ross and Levine, *Urban Politics*, 72.

25. David N. Ammons and Charldean Newell, *City Executives* (Albany: SUNY Press, 1989), 61.

26. Jerri Killian and Enamul Choudhury, "Continuity and Change in the Role of City Managers," *2010 Municipal Year Book* (Washington, D.C.: ICMA, 2010), 15.

27. Ross and Levine, *Urban Politics*, 226.

28. David R. Morgan and Sheilah S. Watson, "Mayors of American Cities: An Analysis of Powers and Responsibilities," *American Review of Public Administration* 26 (March 1996): 121.

29. Statistics in this section, unless otherwise noted, are for the year 2001 and come from Susan A. MacManus and Charles S. Bullock III, "The Form, Structure, and Composition of America's Municipalities in the New Millennium," *2003 Municipal Year Book* (Washington, D.C.: ICMA, 2003), 3–13. We should note that Evelina R. Moulder provides 2006 data for *some*, but not all, of these statistics in "Municipal Form of Government: Trends in Structure, Responsibility, and Composition," *2008 Municipal Year Book* (Washington, D.C.: ICMA, 2008), 27–33. In general, the percentages do not vary much between the 2001 and 2006 surveys. Given the more complete reporting of data in the former than the latter article, we decided to report the 2001 statistics.

30. Susan A. MacManus and Charles S. Bullock III, "Women and Racial/Ethnic Minorities in Mayoral and Council Positions," *1993 Municipal Year Book* (Washington, D.C.: ICMA, 1993), 70–84.

31. Rollie O. Waters and Joyce C. Powell, "Salaries of Municipal Officials, 2009," *2010 Municipal Year Book*, 76, 79.

32. Jeffrey L. Pressman, "Preconditions of Mayoral Leadership," *American Political Science Review* 66 (June 1972): 511–524.

33. Terrell Blodgett, "Beware the Lure of the 'Strong Mayor,' " *Public Management*, January 1994, 11.

34. Melvin G. Holli, "American Mayors: The Best and the Worst since 1960," *Social Science Quarterly* 78 (March 1997): 149–150.

35. P. Edward French and David H. Folz, "Executive Behavior and Decision Making in Small U.S. Cities," *American Review of Public Administration* 34 (March 2004): 52–66.

36. Ibid., 57.

37. Ibid., 59, 60–61.

38. Zoltan L. Hajnal, "White Residents, Black Incumbents, and a Declining Racial Divide," *American Political Science Review* 95 (September 2001): 613.

39. Ibid., 603.

40. John P. Pelissero, David B. Holian, and Laura A. Tomaka, "Does Political Incorporation Matter? The Impact of Minority Mayors over Time," *Urban Affairs Review* 36 (September 2000): 84–92.

41. John Nalbandian, "Tenets of Contemporary Professionalism in Local Government," *Public Administration Review* 50 (November–December 1990): 654–662.

42. Unless otherwise cited, all data in this section come from Tari Renner, "Local Government Management Profession at Century's End," *2001 Municipal Year Book* (Washington, D.C.: ICMA, 2001), 35–46. In the *2010 Municipal Year Book,* Jerri Killian and Enamul Choudhury in "Continuity and Change in the Role of City Managers," pp. 10–18, report the findings of a much smaller survey of city managers and chief administrative officers (CAOs) conducted in 2009. The data is for about 400 city managers and CAOs, Given the larger scope (a sample size of about 3,000 managers) and greater detail in findings of the 2000 versus the 2009 survey, we report the 2000 findings here.

43. Robert A. Schuhmann and Richard L. Fox, "Women Chief Administrative Officers: Perceptions of Their Role in Government," *1998 Municipal Year Book* (Washington, D.C.: ICMA, 1988), 16–22.

44. Richard L. Fox and Robert A. Schuhmann, "Gender and Local Government: A Comparison of Women and Men City Managers," *Public Administration Review* 59 (May–June 1999): 231–242.

45. Richard L. Fox and Robert A. Schuhmann, "Mentoring Experiences of Women City Managers: Are Women Disadvantaged?" *American Review of Public Administration* 31 (December 2001): 381–392.

46. Douglas J. Watson and Wendy L. Hassett, "Long-Serving City Managers: Why Do They Stay?" *Public Administration Review* 63 (January–February 2003): 71–78.

47. Ibid., 77.

48. Salary statistics come from Waters and Powell, "Salaries of Municipal Officials, 2009," 76.

49. Laurie Frankel and Carol Pigeon, "Municipal Managers and Chief Administrative Officers: A Statistical Profile," *Urban Data Service Reports* (Washington, D.C.: ICMA, 1975), 3.

50. Deil S. Wright, "The City Manager as a Development Administrator," in *Comparative Urban Research: The Administration and Politics of Cities,* ed. Robert T. Daland (Beverly Hills, Calif.: Sage, 1969), 218.

51. Charldean Newell and David N. Ammons, "Role Emphases of City Managers and Other Municipal Executives," *Public Administration Review* 47 (May–June 1987): 250.

52. Killian and Choudhury, "Continuity and Change," 16–17.

53. David N. Ammons, "City Managers and City Administrator Role Similarities and Differences: Perceptions Among Persons Who Have Served as Both," *The American Review of Public Administration* 38 (March 2008): 24–40.

54. Ibid., 39.

55. Ibid.

56. Charldean Newell, James J. Glass, and David N. Ammons, "City Manager Roles in a Changing Political Environment," in *Ideal & Practice in Council-Manager Government,* 2nd ed., ed. H. George Frederickson (Washington, D.C.: ICMA, 1995), 53–67.

57. James H. Svara, "Dichotomy and Duality: Reconceptualizing the Relationship between Policy and Administration in Council-Manager Cities," *Public Administration Review* 45 (January–February 1985): 221–232.

58. James M. Banovetz, "The City: Forces of Change," in *Managing the Modern City,* ed. James M. Banovetz (Washington, D.C.: ICMA, 1971), 42.

59. As quoted in Alan Ehrenhalt, "The New City Manager Is: (1) Invisible (2) Anonymous (3) Non-political (4) None of the Above," *Governing,* September 1990, 43–45.

60. Information in this section and the next on "Council-Manager Relations" draws heavily from Robert E. England, "City Managers and the Urban Bureaucracy," in *Cities, Politics, and Policy: A Comparative Analysis,* ed. John P. Pelissero (Washington, D.C.: CQ Press, 2003), 200–207.

61. Gladys Kammerer, Charles Farris, John DeGrove, and Alfred Clubok, *The Urban Political Community* (Boston: Houghton Mifflin, 1963), 197–198.

62. Gordon Whitaker and Ruth Hoogland DeHoog, "City Managers under Fire: How Conflict Leads to Turnover," *Public Administration Review* 51 (March–April 1991): 162.

63. James H. Svara, "Mayoral Leadership in Council-Manager Cities: Preconditions versus Preconceptions," *Journal of Politics* 49 (February 1987): 224.

64. Ibid., 225.

65. David R. Morgan and Sheilah S. Watson, "Policy Leadership in Council-Manager Cities: Comparing Mayor and Manager," *Public Administration Review* 52 (September–October 1992): 438–445.

66. MacManus and Bullock, "Form, Structure, and Composition," 13–17.

67. Ibid., 16.

68. An ICMA study reporting electoral systems used in 2006 in about 4,000 cities show only modest changes in the use of electoral systems took place between 2001 and 2006. Sixty-six percent of the governments report the use of at-large elections, 17 percent employ ward/district elections, and 17 percent prefer a combination of at-large and district elections. See Moulder, "Municipal Form of Government," 32.

69. James H. Svara, *Two Decades of Continuity and Change in American City Councils* (Washington, D.C.: National League of Cities, September 2003), at www.nlc.org/content/Files/RMPcitycouncilrpt.pdf.

70. Timothy B. Krebs and John P. Pelissero, "City Councils," in Pelissero, *Cities, Politics, and Policy,* 169–195.

71. Ibid., 189.

72. "Conflict Management and Resolution in Cities," *State and Local Government Review* 31 (fall 1999): 158–213.

73. John Nalbandian, "The Manager as a Political Leader: A Challenge to Professionalism?" *Public Management,* March 2000, 7–12.

74. James H. Svara, "Dichotomy and Duality: Reconceptualizing the Relationship between Policy and Administration in Council-Manager Cities," *Public Administration Review* 45 (January–February 1985): 221–232; see also William Browne, "Municipal Managers and Policy: A Partial Test of the Svara Dichotomy-Duality Model," *Public Administration Review* 45 (September–October 1985): 620–622.

75. See James H. Svara, "The Politics-Administration Dichotomy as Aberration," *Public Administration Review* 58 (January–February 1998): 51–58; James H. Svara, "The Myth of the Dichotomy: Complementarity of Politics and Administration in the Past and Future of Public Administration," *Public Administration Review* 61 (March–April 2001): 176–183.

76. Sally Coleman Selden, Gene A. Brewer, and Jeffrey L. Brudney, "The Role of City Managers: Are They Principals, Agents, or Both?" *American Review of Public Administration* 29 (June 1999): 124.

77. Barbara Coyle McCabe, Richard Feiock, James C. Clingermayer, and Christopher Stream, "Turnover among City Managers: The Role of Political and Economic Change," *Public Administration Review* 68 (March/April 2008): 380–386.

78. Ibid., 384.

79. Ibid.

80. Charles E. Lindblom and Edward J. Woodhouse, *The Policy-Making Process,* 3rd ed. (Upper Saddle River, N.J.: Prentice Hall, 1993), 59.

81. Kenneth J. Meier, *Politics and the Bureaucracy: Policymaking in the Fourth Branch of Government,* 4th ed. (Fort Worth, Tex.: Harcourt, 2000), 7.

82. Peters, *American Public Policy,* 63.

83. Dye, *Understanding Public Policy,* 52.

84. Levy, Meltsner, and Wildavsky, *Urban Outcomes,* 229.

85. Michael Lipsky, "Street-Level Bureaucracy and the Analysis of Urban Reform," *Urban Affairs Quarterly* 6 (January 1971): 391–409.

86. For a discussion of institutional discrimination at the local level in school systems, see Kenneth J. Meier, Joseph Stewart Jr., and Robert E. England, *Race, Class, and Education: The Politics of Second-Generation Discrimination* (Madison: University of Wisconsin Press, 1989), 29–30.

87. See, for example, Julie Dolan and David H. Rosenbloom, eds., *Representative Bureaucracy: Classic Readings and Continuing Controversies* (Armonk, N.Y.: M.E. Sharpe, 2003).

88. President's Commission on Law Enforcement and Administration of Justice, *The Challenge of Crime in a Free Society* (Washington, D.C.: Government Printing Office, 1967), 10.

89. Elaine B. Sharp, "Political Participation in Cities," in Pelissero, *Cities, Politics, and Policy,* 70–71.

90. Ross and Levine, *Urban Politics,* 207.

91. Charles Adrian and Charles Press, *Governing Urban America,* 5th ed. (New York: McGraw-Hill, 1977), 104.

92. Sharp, "Political Participation in Cities," 71.

93. Ross and Levine, *Urban Politics,* 225.

94. Bryan D. Jones, *Governing Urban America: A Policy Focus* (Boston: Little, Brown, 1983), 135.

95. Svara, *Two Decades of Continuity and Change*, 15–19.

96. Jones, *Governing Urban America*, 159.

97. Jeffrey L. Katz, "Neighborhood Politics: A Changing World," *Governing*, December 1990, 48–49.

98. Rob Gurwitt, "A Government That Runs on Citizen Power," *Governing*, December 1992, 48.

99. Ibid., 48–54.

100. Nancy Roberts, "Public Deliberation in an Age of Direct Citizen Participation," *American Review of Public Administration* 34 (December 2004): 315.

101. Jean-Jacques Rousseau as quoted in Roberts, "Public Deliberation."

102. James K. Scott, "'E' the People: Do U.S. Municipal Government Websites Support Public Involvement? *Public Administration Review* 66 (May/June 2006): 341–353.

103. Ibid., 346.

104. Ibid., 348.

105. Ibid.

106. Xiaohu Wang, "Assessing Public Participation in U.S. Cities," *Public Performance & Management Review* 24 (June 2001): 322–336. The sample included 46 percent of all U.S. cities in the late 1990s with populations of 50,000 or more residents.

107. The use of citizen advisory boards was tied with the Internet (81.6 percent) as a means of fostering citizen participation in these central cities.

108. Scott, "'E' the People," 349.

109. See John C. Thomas, "Citizen-Initiated Contacts with Governmental Agencies: A Test of Three Theories," *American Journal of Political Science* 26 (August 1982): 504–522; Elaine B. Sharp, "Citizen Demand Making in the Urban Context," *American Journal of Political Science* 28 (November 1984): 654–670; and Michael W. Hirlinger, "Citizen-Initiated Contacting of Local Government Officials: A Multivariate Explanation," *Journal of Politics* 54 (May 1992): 553–564.

110. Bryan D. Jones, *Service Delivery in the City* (New York: Longman, 1980), 89.

111. Sharp, "Citizen Demand Making," 664–669.

CHAPTER 5 **URBAN PLANNING**

AND DEVELOPMENT

Mᴏʀᴇ than a century has passed since town planners, social scientists, and city engineers recognized the need for cities to follow a plan. Prior to the mid- to late-1800s, the infrastructure of most American cities, big and small, was not well developed. Once focused almost exclusively on the physical development of cities, today's urban planners develop a comprehensive approach to planning that incorporates physical, social, economic, sustainability, and services management in cities and metropolitan areas. Recognizing the importance of urban planning, however, does not mean that urban areas and their government officials do it well. Urban encroachment, highway congestion, sprawling subdivision and exurban development, inadequate transit design, and environmental degradation are just a few of the persistent problems and nagging concerns that remain to be addressed by urban planning and development.

We begin this chapter with an overview of the nature and evolution of the urban planning function, and then we move on to consider the specific activities and strategies it involves. What issues are involved in organizing for planning at the municipal level? Why has economic development come to dominate the planning activities in so many cities? And finally, what relation do planning and development bear to politics? What are the political barriers to effective planning and development? These are some of the questions to be explored in this chapter.

THE NATURE OF CITY PLANNING

City planning is a particular kind of urban management that focuses on the physical use of land. Many planners would be quick to point out that their responsibility today embraces much more than land use. Although there is truth in this claim, most city planning in one way or another affects the use of land, and how far the planner's function should move beyond this traditional concern for physical space is still debated.

Urban planning has been defined as a "process of preparing in advance, and in a reasonably systematic fashion, recommendations for programs and courses of action to attain the common objectives of the community."[1] Obviously, plans must be prepared in advance of some expected future development. But just how systematic or scientific can city planning be? Everyone does agree that planning is advisory—regrettably, perhaps, planners are never in a position to implement their own programs and courses of action, because final planning decisions at the municipal level always rest in the hands of elected public officials. But before any of the planning process can begin, the common objectives of the relevant community must be defined by politicians and planners.

Several city-planning perspectives have evolved in this country. An early one began with the City Beautiful Movement that developed around the turn of the twentieth century. Emphasis here was on the physical design of the community: "Physical order equalled social order."[2] Environmental determinism held sway during this period—by changing the physical features of urban life, early planners hoped to cure many of the social and economic ills of the city. As the planning discipline developed, it absorbed many of the assumptions underlying the municipal reform movement. First, politics had no place in planning. Second, the notion of a unitary public interest was widely accepted, so planning was to be based on a rational pursuit of the best interests of the whole community. Although other conceptions of the planning function have evolved, this traditional view has had enormous impact, and many of its tenets are still widely accepted.

Looking back over more than a century of urban planning, many authorities agree that this nonpolitical, comprehensive approach does not work as intended. The classical model has been undermined considerably by the growing realization that politics does have a significant effect on the implementation of plans. As their fully formed plans lay fallow, planners began to realize that the political environment could not be ignored, but this awareness has so far failed to alter to a significant degree the day-to-day reality of city planning. The comprehensive plan, with its commitment to long-range rational goals, remains the primary model for many, if not most, contemporary planning agencies.

NEWER APPROACHES TO PLANNING

Planning experts have been disenchanted with the traditional comprehensive plan for some time, but finding a satisfactory alternative has not been easy. Susan Fainstein, an expert on urban issues, has written of the "reinvigoration" of urban planning theories in recent years, describing three new approaches that have emerged.[3]

The Communicative Model

Pragmatic approaches to planning in which the planner regularly interacts with others are indicative of the communicative model. Fainstein describes the planner's role here as "negotiator and intermediary among stakeholders,"[4] bringing professional expertise both to guide planning and to act as a broker among competing interests. Judith Innes has referred to this model as the emerging paradigm in planning theory.[5]

The New Urbanism Model

Noting that the new urbanism approach has roots in the design focus of early planning leaders such as Frederick Law Olmsted, Fainstein describes this model as a spatial building approach for neighborhoods. "The new urbanists call for an urban design that includes a variety of building types, mixed uses, intermingling of housing for different income groups, and a strong privileging of the 'public realm.'" Although popular among architects and journalists, this approach lacks a solid theoretical foundation—emphasizing the plan more than the methods of implementation. Nonetheless, Fainstein notes that it has become the founding basis for some new neighborhoods and towns such as Seaside, Florida.[6]

New emphasis on environmental sustainability also fits within the new urbanism model. Creating more green spaces within cities; adding rooftop gardens to commercial buildings in urban centers; requiring construction of LEED-certified[7] buildings; and promoting a culture of reuse, recycling, and ecological consciousness are among the contemporary hallmarks of urban planning.[8] One of the challenges with incorporating sustainability into city planning is the lack of agreement on what sustainability means. A recent study in the San Francisco area, for instance, showed that sustainability to city officials could apply to urban design, economic development, or civic engagement.[9] Knowing what the goals for sustainability are intended to achieve can result in a better planning model for cities.[10]

The Just City Model

The "just city" approach has been championed in different ways by a variety of groups: political economists (like Fainstein), neomarxists, radical democrats, and those who would prefer to be labeled simply "advocacy planners." Increasing public involvement in planning is one part of the approach, which includes calls for participation by those who have been relatively powerless in cities and a focus on achieving greater equity in planning outcomes.[11] Some American critics might describe the goal as utopian, but there have been some concrete examples of the approach in practice, such as Amsterdam, a city not so far away from the United States in the global village of today. But in a less radical style, Michael Vasu argues that advocacy planners work toward the ideal that dispossessed urban groups—the poor and minorities—should have the chance to challenge the unitary plans developed by planning professionals.[12] This objective requires funding a separate neighborhood planning function so that, with the help of a planning expert, these isolated groups can present their own plans and proposals for consideration. This approach is based on a pluralistic view of society, and it places the planner in an overtly political role. As Paul Davidoff aptly remarked decades ago: "Pluralism in support of political contention describes the process; advocacy describes the role played by the professional in the process."[13] As Vasu puts it, "In effect, the advocacy movement in planning replaced a faith in comprehensiveness with a faith in pluralism."[14] And the approach clearly legitimizes an active political role for urban planners.

POLICY PLANNING

Some planners have argued that planning should not be a method of describing an ideal state of affairs but a process of decision making that culminates in a statement of policy.

The basic purpose of this approach to city planning is to facilitate the achievement of certain community goals and objectives. Increasingly, the traditional view that the city plan could capture some larger community-wide interest has given way to a more open, democratic process of developing statements of purpose and strategic policies for reaching those goals. In effect, policy planning stresses the formulation of various policy statements for guiding urban development rather than a single comprehensive land-use plan for controlling growth and development. Policy statements, then, should be the basis for choosing among alternative courses of action; they are not simply statements of conditions about which everyone agrees. For example, "The city should preserve its older neighborhoods" is not a policy statement because it offers little guidance for decision making. Seattle is one large city that has used the policy planning approach in its downtown development.[15]

Some policy planners have argued for a comprehensive, regional approach to planning in major metropolitan areas. In this model, land use, transportation, education, housing, economic development, and sustainability, and so on are examined in a large regional context and an effort is made to achieve a level of buy-in from multiple government jurisdictions for coordinated planning. An excellent example is the Chicago Metropolis 2020 project, whose planning effort involves more than two hundred members, including representatives from business, labor, civic, and religious organizations as well as local and state governments.[16]

OBSTACLES TO PLANNING

Those who call themselves planners have had a difficult time deciding what they should be doing. How far should their interests extend? What methods should they employ? Who are their clients? The job is further complicated by the political environment in which it takes place. As Thad Beyle and George Lathrop see it, in our political system "planning may well be impossible."[17] Some of the problems commonly encountered are these:

- The fragmented nature and the functional autonomy of our governmental system make it impossible to devise long-range, centralized solutions to social problems.
- Local governments seldom have sufficient funds to make major commitments to the large-scale investments proposed by planning agencies.
- Continuity in political leadership is so uncertain that continuing support for particular planning activities is always threatened.
- Planners frequently find themselves in an untenable middle position between their commitment to a long-range, comprehensive approach and the necessity to respond to decision makers' concerns for shorter-range policy issues and problems.

The basic problem: "Planners propose and politicians dispose." Despite these troubling issues, planning has continued and the demand for planners has increased.

PLANNING IN A POLITICAL ENVIRONMENT

Early proponents of city planning wanted that activity removed from politics as much as possible, which seemed to demand the creation of a separate and presumably nonpolitical board—the planning commission. This group of respected community members would make its recommendations directly to the elected governing board. Reliance on such a semi-independent commission dominated the planning scene for years, and the mechanism is still used in a number of cities. Planning commission members are appointed for long, overlapping terms and are difficult to remove except for cause. This secure tenure gives them a measure of political independence from any given city administration. In theory, commission members themselves, perhaps with the aid of a planning staff that reports directly to them, develop plans and proposals; final decisions, of course, are to be made by a legislative body. In fact, however, few planning commissions actually prepare plans themselves; instead, the bulk of their time is spent in reacting to development proposals offered by others, mostly private developers and individual citizens. Figure 5-1 represents a simplified organization chart for a semi-independent planning commission.

How useful is the planning commission form? In some cities it is very political, whereas in others the commission can be viewed as politically weak. But the most frequently cited objection to its use assumes that planning should be part of the municipal executive staff, not a semiautonomous function. Proponents argue that planning involves policy formulation as broad as the scope of municipal government and therefore should be thoroughly integrated with that government. Furthermore, implementation of plans and policies requires a close working relationship between planners and municipal decision makers.[18]

Figure 5-2 shows how the planning function can be organized under a municipal chief executive—the form that most large cities are using today. The planning department reports directly to the mayor or city manager. Where a planning commission is retained,

Figure 5-1   **A Semi-Independent Planning Commission**

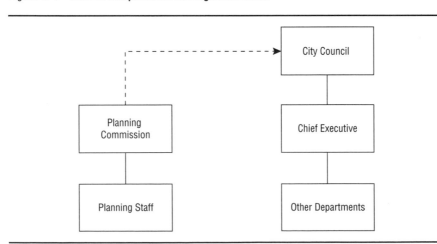

Figure 5-2   **A Planning Department under a Chief Executive**

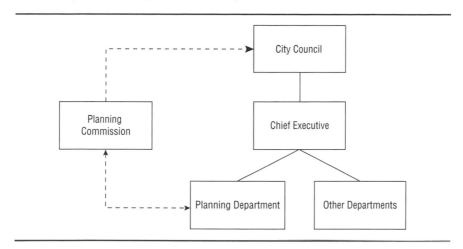

it is essentially a citizens' advisory board that looks to the planning department for technical expertise and assistance before it makes its recommendations to the city council. This
configuration gives the chief executive responsibility for coordinating overall community
planning.

Even where the planning department reports to the chief executive, the mayor or manager may not, in practice, play a prominent part in making the planning decisions. Instead,
the routine work of planning (zoning and subdivision regulation) is handled by the planning commission, which receives recommendations from the staff of the planning department and then offers its own proposals to the city council. The legislative body then has two
sets of recommendations before it—those of the planning department staff and those of
the planning commission. Very often, the recommendations are the same; planning commissions generally endorse staff proposals, especially where an issue is not controversial.
Thus, in routine matters, the chief executive may have virtually no input.

Whatever the organizational form of the planning function in a particular city, departmental planners and planning commissions operate solely in an advisory capacity, either
to the chief executive or to the city council.

PLANNING AND POLITICS

Planning is not a value-free technical enterprise. Every basic planning decision requires
a choice among competing values. In this sense, there is no escape from politics and political influence in urban planning. As Robert Linowes and Don Allensworth observe:

> Planning is a distinctly political activity. . . . Different groups in the planning process
> view the ends and means of planning differently. Unanimity does not exist and cannot be
> expected. A certain degree of conflict is healthy, and in a democracy it will be found whether
> it is healthy or not. It is this conflict that makes for politics.[19]

Still, some planners and planning commission members clearly believe that politics gets in the way of rational planning.

Most planning decisions do not engulf the whole community in political conflict. Some groups are much more likely to be concerned with urban planning than are others; some projects or planning actions may evoke considerably more controversy than do others. Zoning requests that threaten single-family interests seem to raise the most controversy. In the central city, urban redevelopment can stir up this same type of controversy.

But planning has become more important to citizens as the environmental awareness has increased. More and more, citizens expect to have opportunities to engage with city officials in the planning and development processes of their communities. More and more, city officials want an engaged citizenry to develop, comment, and inform the planning process. At a minimum, city planners may believe that civic participation is essential to achieve what political scientist Kent Portney calls a "durable and operational definition of sustainability."[20] In his examination of 41 U.S. cities, he found that 28 cities (nearly 70 percent) promote civic participation in the sustainability planning process, including Seattle's development of its comprehensive plan in 2000.[21]

Planning's heritage is fundamentally antipolitical. Its early association with the reform movement reinforced the notion that planning was above opportunism, compromises, bargains, and political deals. It was to be a profession—one in which technical ideals would guide a rational search for solutions to benefit the entire community. But years of frustration created by watching comprehensive plans collect dust on the shelves have compelled planners to become more interested in policy and the political process.

Planners and Political Roles

Where there is community consensus and the governing ideology favors planning, the technician role can work well. In other places, planners who want to see their plans consummated may have to assume a more active role. Political scientist Francine Rabinovitz identified two active roles for planners: the broker and the mobilizer.[22]

The *broker* appears in a political environment in which several major competitive interests exist. In politically competitive communities, the prospects for effective urban planning may not be good, especially if large interests oppose some proposal.

In a politically fragmented community where decision making is highly decentralized, the planner becomes a *mobilizer*, displaying bold initiative to overcome the natural inertia of the developmental situation. A mobilizer must also be willing to face conflict, because getting things done in these circumstances will require generating support from a variety of sources while pushing specific proposals, some of which will undoubtedly draw opposition. At this point, the broker's skills may again become essential to effectively mediate conflict. Mobilizers must not only maintain alliances but also activate sufficient resources to support change—they must be skilled in the art of the possible. This balancing act is obviously risky: a series of attacks from opponents could jeopardize their legitimacy as unbiased experts. If they lose too often, the planning program may be seriously undermined, and the planners themselves could be looking for other jobs.

By heritage, training, and sometimes temperament, planners often lack the requisite skills to become effective political participants. What skills do they need? Research shows that, above all, planners need social-process skills. Implementation of plans demands the capacity to create cooperative networks of interested groups. Successful planning means building coalitions of experts and nonexperts, of interest groups and activists who have the leadership capabilities and resources to organize and sustain a fragile and difficult process.[23] Coalition building itself demands other skills—a talent for persuasion and manipulation, experience with client analysis, and information and communication proficiency.[24]

To what sorts of groups in particular must planners relate? A number of different community interests emerge periodically, depending on the specific issues under consideration. But in many communities, only a relatively narrow range of interests evidence a continuing concern for planning and developmental decision making.

Groups in the Planning Process

Especially in suburbs and growing communities, two interest groups are prominent: developers and neighborhood associations.[25] The first group—land developers, realtors, landowners, and home builders—favor policies that promote growth and development. These interests do not oppose planning and land-use controls so long as they work for pro-development ends. They also favor federal grants that promote development, such as subsidies for water and sewer construction.

Realtors are not as politically influential as the other members of this coalition, because they serve two masters: those who build homes and those who buy and live in them. The former favor more development; the latter usually oppose it. Realtors also may be concerned that growth will alter a community's social, economic, and racial patterns, which might work against the interests of their existing clients. In the end, realtors usually support development policies, but cautiously.

In many places, citizens' groups have become more vocal in recent years, partly as an outgrowth of the activism of the sixties. When these citizens' or homeowners' associations are found in higher-income areas, they are especially likely to be concerned with land-use decisions, particularly rezoning questions and the location of highways. Any change considered a threat to the residential character of a neighborhood or to property values will be resisted vigorously.

Although few admit it, most citizens' groups are antidevelopment. They may support new construction that is comparable to their own—especially if it is large-lot residential—or favor open-space and recreational development, but they nearly always oppose commercial and industrial uses, low-income housing, mobile home parks, new roads, even public facilities, at least in their own neighborhoods. The basic fear is economic: they want nothing to happen that might in any way jeopardize their property values. This fear has been described as the NIMBY effect—citizens' propensity to support certain land uses only if they are "not in my back yard."

On occasion, the two major groups—developers and citizens' associations—come into direct conflict. Both groups are distinct minorities, concerned essentially about protecting and advancing their own economic interests. Planners must recognize that most community conflicts over land-use decisions reflect such group interests. Understanding the nature of these groups and their objectives can help public officials to devise appropriate strategies for coping with the political environment in which planning must function.

PLANNING ACTIVITIES

The ICMA produces a popular series of management texts called the "Green Books." The newest green book on planning[26] introduces new chapters on contemporary issues, such as sustainability, smart growth, and healthy cities. However, despite the increasing number of subjects now covered in that text and others, most city planning is devoted to a fairly limited range of activities. City planners spend most of their time and effort on city-wide and project planning, which includes both comprehensive and area-wide planning. Zoning and subdivision regulation are the next most important operations, based on staff time consumed. Most planners do not spend the bulk of their time formulating plans and policies for future development; much of their day-to-day activity is devoted to evaluating planning proposals advanced by others. Zoning and subdivision regulations, for example, would fall into the category of planning evaluation.

In general, however, the planning process involves the following steps:

1. *Research*: conducting an inventory and analysis of existing conditions, collecting baseline data, and so on
2. *Goal establishment*: determining the needs and preferences of the citizenry, perhaps through opinion surveys
3. *Plan and policy formulation*: preparing a host of plans, programs, and projects for land use, transportation, community facilities, and other uses
4. *Plan implementation*: devising tools and techniques—zoning ordinances, subdivision regulations, housing codes, and the like—to carry out the plans

The first three planning steps would be performed, at least initially, during the process of preparing a community's comprehensive plan. It is important to note, finally, that although the planning department may devise plan implementation tools and techniques (step 4), most planning agencies do not have enforcement responsibilities or powers. Even though some have criticized the concept of comprehensive planning as an impossible ideal, most cities still engage in the activity. In fact, in many places, something called the *comprehensive plan*, master plan, or general plan still forms the core of all planning activity.

COMPREHENSIVE PLANNING

Until the early 1960s, comprehensive planning—or "master planning," as it was called then—was virtually synonymous with physical planning. Alan Black described the basic rationale as follows: "The local government needs an instrument which establishes long-range, general policies for the physical development of the community in a coordinated, unified manner, and which can be continually referred to in deciding upon the development issues which come up every week."[27] Many planners now feel that economic and social planning should also be part of the process, but even in the twenty-first century, most comprehensive plans revolve around the physical development of the community. In older communities, the principal thrust may be conservation and renewal; in declining cities, it is likely to be redevelopment of land uses; in the established suburbs, it may emphasize protection; and in the urban fringe areas, growth management.

The plan ordinarily consists of three basic components: land use, transportation, and community facilities. In addition to its focus on physical development, the comprehensive plan is long-range—often a period of twenty or twenty-five years is projected—and general in nature. At least the following elements are likely to be included:

- *Population*: a study of population characteristics, distribution, and trends
- *Economic base*: an analysis of the community's economic characteristics, with particular attention to the tax base
- *Land use*: a survey of existing and projected uses, and a color-coded map to reveal variations in land use
- *Transportation and circulation*: an investigation of existing facilities and projections of future needs
- *Community facilities*: a range of public services—schools, fire and police protection, libraries, water and sewerage—along with future requirements
- *Capital improvement plan*: a strategy for including projected capital needs into the municipal budgetary system
- *Regulatory measures*: certain legal tools to carry out planning—at the least, a zoning ordinance (with map) and subdivision regulations[28]

The land-use segment of the comprehensive plan can be developed before or in conjunction with the transportation plan, while the community facilities portion of the document would come later. The land-use plan normally requires a careful analysis and delineation of existing uses of land within the city. Special attention is accorded to the intensity of use, density, drainage, and traffic patterns. At a minimum, land use is assessed in terms of the following categories: residential, commercial, industrial, public buildings, vacant, and perhaps agricultural; within each category are levels of density. All of this information is color-coded on a large map of the community.

In addition to existing land patterns, the plan should project future uses—approximate or recommended locations for major streets and highways, large shopping centers, schools, public facilities, and parks, for example. Clearly, no planner, no matter how skilled or dedicated, can anticipate how certain developments will occur in a dynamic community. The preferences of land developers, for instance, may not coincide with what the land-use plan dictates. Also, private landowners are given the major voice in determining how their land will be used, and this factor remains a serious constraint on land-use planning by local government.

Just how far can a government go in restricting the use of private land? It can condemn, tax, and regulate within reasonable bounds, and it retains the sovereign power to supervise land use in the name of public health, safety, and welfare. Some of the more interesting battles involving public versus private control of land have arisen where municipalities have attempted to limit population growth by such means as refusing to issue building permits or prohibiting the construction of apartment complexes.

The government is allowed to take land for public purposes as long as just compensation is provided to the private owner—this is the *law of eminent domain*. This power has long been invoked to permit cities to acquire needed land for transportation rights-of-way; it was used extensively for urban renewal in the 1950s and 1960s; and in recent years it has been a tool for development of facilities ranging from airports to sports stadiums to shopping malls. Although eminent domain is widely accepted as an efficient and often fair way to acquire property needed for public purposes, many city managers report that they approach its use with caution. As Matthew Cypher and Fred Forgey demonstrate in a national survey of city managers, many officials express concern about the matter of equity to property owners and developers that is often involved in eminent domain actions.[29]

Despite the best of intentions and inclusive planning processes, comprehensive plans do not always achieve their desired results. Part of the problem is the political environment in which urban planning takes place—a subject we consider in more detail later in this chapter. But there are a number of other problems and limitations associated with comprehensive planning, including the following:

- A comprehensive plan, which by its nature embraces a single perspective ("the public interest"), cannot really accommodate the varying, conflicting interests of a pluralistic community. As one analyst commented, "Differing perspectives lead to clashes of social interests that are usually capable of being resolved only through processes of negotiation, bargaining, and political pressure."
- Long-range plans are too dependent on external forces and conditions that cannot be controlled or foreseen.
- Planners have little more than fragmentary knowledge of complex situations. Their intuition and views can be and often are challenged successfully by groups with an effective veto over specific decisions.
- Comprehensive planners assume a capacity for central control and coordination that rarely exists in fact.
- The logic of rational, long-range goal setting is inconsistent with the normal imperatives for action. To act demands a focus on limited, short-range, opportunistic objectives that may be contrary to more distant goals.[30]

These shortcomings have led to an interest in other approaches to planning, such as the policy planning discussed earlier in this chapter. Some writers have called for *continuous planning*, an approach that is as comprehensive as long-range planning, but in a different way.[31] This approach envisions a city plan, adopted annually, that would go beyond the traditional concern for urban physical development to incorporate the budgets, operating plans, and longer-range goals and objectives of all municipal departments. Such continuous city planning would involve current data, analyses, and information about a wide range of conditions and events as the basis for creating intermediate-term plans.

ZONING

Most citizens do not distinguish between planning and zoning. Technically, of course, zoning is a major tool for implementing plans, regulating the use of private land and development by requiring that similar uses be grouped together. The legal basis for zoning—ordinarily provided in state law—rests with the police power that allows a city to protect the health, safety, and welfare of its inhabitants. Zoning ordinances remain the most common form of land regulation; in fact, zoning can be found in every city of any size in the United States except one: Houston. Indeed, planning commissions, if not planning departments, spend up to half their time on zoning matters. What, then, is zoning meant to accomplish?

Purposes of Zoning

A basic purpose of zoning is to maximize the value of private property. It has been suggested that zoning first caught on as an effective technique to further an eminently conservative objective: the protection of single-family neighborhoods. From this perspective, zoning simply requires that certain noxious uses of land (heavy industry, for example) be separated, if not isolated, from other uses so as not to create a nuisance or lower property values. In effect, this rationale makes zoning an adjunct to market forces because it operates to protect the market from imperfections in the natural operation of supply and demand.[32]

A second, opposing view holds that zoning attempts to adjust and modify market outcomes. Presumably, zoning can be used to allocate land in accordance with certain community values and objectives that the unregulated market might ignore.[33] In combination with other regulatory instruments—such as subdivision controls and building codes—zoning could be used to protect the environment, enhance community character, and preserve key land parcels (prime industrial land, airport sites, scenic places, and historical locations).

The Zoning Ordinance

Cities use elaborate color-coded maps and a text (or legend) to visually illustrate a local zoning ordinance. A simplified zoning map using three shades of gray for the Village of

Skokie, Illinois, is shown in figure 5-3. The map shows the three general land uses in the village—residential (light gray), business commercial (medium gray), and industrial/office (dark gray)—to which each parcel of land has been assigned. The zoning map is similar to the land-use map, but exact land uses may not be reflected on it. Some so-called nonconforming uses may exist within certain zoning categories; these are likely to be activities that existed before the land was assigned to a particular zone.

Depending on the size and complexity of the community, the zoning ordinance may include a number of classifications—residential, commercial, industrial, and so on—much as the land-use map does. In most cases, however, the zoning ordinance offers even more categories, to allow subtle distinctions among potential land uses. For instance, if a color map had been used in figure 5-3 for the Village of Skokie, land-use classifications could have been broken down further to include:

- single-family and limited other residential units
- two-family units
- general residential (multiple family residences with three or more units)
- elderly and disabled subsidized housing
- service commercial
- business
- regional shopping
- downtown
- medical hospital
- office research
- office assembly industry
- light industry
- industry[34]

The ordinance text may include a multitude of regulations covering such matters as front-yard setback lines, side-yard setbacks, rear-yard requirements, lot widths, intensity of use (ratio of floor area to lot area), off-street parking requirements for commercial and industrial property, height regulations, uses permitted or prohibited, and so on. The ordinance also includes a section on administration that lists methods for appeal.

Problems with Zoning

To the extent that zoning attempts to compel decisions that run contrary to private interests, it bucks a potent force. If it significantly affects the market price of land, zoning forces buyers and owners to accept a less advantageous outcome than they might otherwise receive. But research developed over several decades suggests that zoning actually has little impact on the real estate market; it does not seem to alter the total supply of land available for private uses. Of course, in any number of specific instances, zoning has served to change land-use decisions, and, as any planning commission or city council can readily testify, proposed zoning changes can provoke intense reaction from neighbors who fear

Figure 5-3   **Zoning Map for Skokie, Illinois**

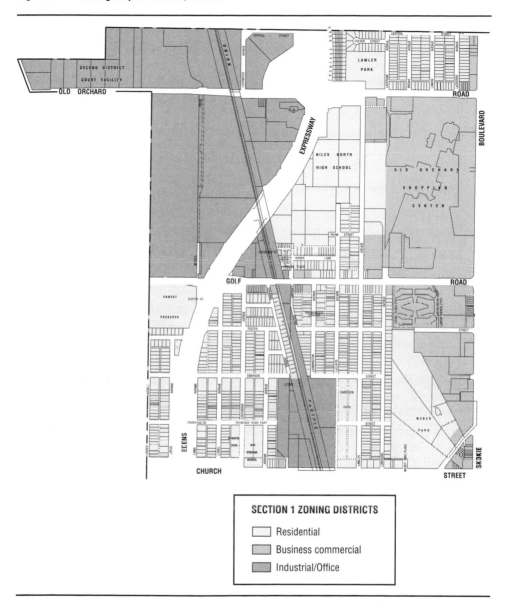

SECTION 1 ZONING DISTRICTS

☐ Residential
▨ Business commercial
■ Industrial/Office

SOURCE: Village of Skokie, Illinois.

possible adverse consequences. But from a larger point of view, zoning seems to have a fairly minor effect on total land use.

What about "snob zoning"—the effort by high-status suburbs to zone out undesirable uses? Here, evidence, including court cases if nothing else, suggests that cities have used zoning for exclusionary purposes on occasion; a typical action would mandate large lot sizes and perhaps a large floor area for dwellings. Such exclusionary zoning remains controversial. Not only does it tend to bar the poor and minorities—although racial motivations are hard to prove—but it can contribute to urban sprawl, inefficient land use, and more costly transportation systems. Some critics even charge that large-lot zoning reinforces class and racial segregation, thereby fundamentally contradicting our democratic values of fair play and equal opportunity. In fact, it has been argued that all zoning is essentially class-biased and parochial, designed to protect the status quo and to discourage diversity.[35]

Other authorities recognize possible drawbacks in current zoning practices—problems created by administration or ordinance failure to reflect up-to-date zoning concepts and techniques—but defend zoning otherwise. They argue that zoning is better than its alternatives, such as private covenants.

Use of Codes

Most cities also have a series of codes covering standards for building construction and electrical, plumbing, heating, and air-conditioning installations. Housing codes, designed to provide minimum standards for the safety, health, and welfare of housing occupants, are also common. These rules can affect the facilities in the structure supplied by the owner (toilets, baths, sinks); the level of maintenance, both structural and sanitary; and occupancy levels (the number of people who may live in dwelling units and rooms). Where these standards exist, however, they apparently are not widely enforced; like all plans and regulations, they mean very little unless they can be implemented. Although this is the area in which planners have been most criticized, it seems illogical to blame them for lax enforcement of housing codes. Planners are advisers; politicians and administrators are the actors who should be held accountable for enforcement.

In most cities, one of the key aspects of planning is community development, especially economic development. In the balance of this chapter, we take a closer look at the significant role that strategies for economic development have played in the planning for cities over the past quarter century.

URBAN ECONOMIC DEVELOPMENT

Development of the local economy continues to be a contentious battle across communities, states, and regions. The question of who wins, who loses, and why when it comes to local economic development continues to be one of the most compelling urban issues in the twenty-first century. The lingering national recession that characterized the end of the first decade—affecting housing, banking, personal and property equity, and jobs—also hit hard the budgets of most U.S. cities. As such, communities have become extremely interested in economic development; indeed, Paul Peterson, in a classic and provocative book, argued that it was *the* primary interest of all cities.[36] And, because virtually every community wants its share of the economic pie, we find local public officials and business leaders alike pursuing various plans and projects designed to make their areas more attractive for development. The objectives: to create more and better jobs, revitalize downtowns, redevelop older neighborhoods, and establish stronger tax bases. And every community sought help with development from the federal government through the stimulus funds and projects supported through the American Recovery and Reinvestment Act of 2009.[37]

ECONOMIC DEVELOPMENT AS A PROCESS

What is economic development and why do cities need it? Basically, *local economic development* is a process for achieving and maintaining the economic health of a community by means of the retention, expansion, and attraction of commerce and industry. The more specific purposes of economic development (ED) may vary by community. Development specialist Robert Weaver articulated a useful distinction between two basic types of communities—"haves" and "have nots."[38] The "haves" see ED as a tool for *managing* growth; the "have nots" initiate programs to *encourage* growth. The "haves" tend to be communities where considerable economic or residential expansion is under way, such as the larger suburbs of a major metropolitan area or a city such as Austin, Texas, which has benefited greatly from high-tech industry. The main objective here may be to establish policies that will channel growth into the kinds of development and areas of the community where it will cause the least harm to the quality of life and will produce the greatest net gain in local revenue.

The typical "have-not" community, in contrast, may be suffering from a declining or stagnant population and tax base. With little new growth and development to manage, it is much more interested in policies designed to reduce unemployment and to expand and diversify the local economy. Frequently, such a locality is burdened with special problems: it may be overly dependent on a single industry or economic sector; it may lack transportation facilities or a skilled labor pool; or it may be experiencing business disruptions resulting from changing national or international trade practices. In many instances, these economic difficulties are rooted in conditions over which the community has little control—the movement of industry overseas, a decline in manufacturing jobs, a drop in world oil prices, or a negative export/import ratio.

Economic development and entrepreneurship have moved to the top of the municipal agenda for at least two other reasons. The first is recent changes in federal policy. Even as cities were becoming more self-sufficient in the final decades of the twentieth century, the federal government pushed them further in that direction, instructing them to wean themselves from dependence on federal aid and to prepare themselves for free-market competition.[39] Under this philosophy, cities were urged to gain control over their own destinies, make themselves attractive to business, compete with one another, and adapt to changing national and international economic trends. City officials were asked to become more than experts at grantsmanship; they were asked to become entrepreneurs.[40] This "fend-for-yourself" trend toward self-sufficiency continues today. The second reason for the enormous interest in ED is that development is one means of raising local government revenue without increasing taxes. As public officials are forced to retrench while holding the line on services, anything that promises a little fiscal relief is most welcome.[41]

Paul Peterson has made the case that development is the product of three interrelated variables: land, capital, and labor.[42] Cities directly control the land and its uses; capital and labor can be leveraged, but these elements are controlled by private forces. ED involves planning for the most effective and efficient ways to maximize the economic potential of land, capital, and labor in the city, metropolitan area, or region.

THE ECONOMIC DEVELOPMENT PLAN

Planning is essential to successful economic development. By 2009, 56 percent of local governments had a specific written plan for economic development—a proportion that is still smaller than expected.[43] Each community must make a conscious decision to create a stronger local economy and to build community support for it. A series of steps such as the following will likely be necessary to establish a development plan.[44]

Step 1: Analyzing Local Attributes

Three activities can be undertaken to develop the knowledge necessary to decide which ED strategies fit a given community best: an economic base analysis, a business survey, and a community survey. A big city may elect to hire a consulting firm to perform its economic base analysis, given the complexity of such a task in a large community. The essential purpose, however, is straightforward: to determine which businesses and industries make up the economic base of the community and whether they are *export* or *nonexport* firms. Export industries sell goods and services to customers outside the community, whereas nonexport firms concentrate on sales inside the community. Export industries are the most valuable because they bring dollars into the community, which in turn helps to generate new jobs and economic growth. Export activity thus has a multiplier effect.

Economic base analysis requires tracking the performance of local industries over time, using census data in addition to local sources of information. The undertaking may include comparing the percentage of workers employed locally in a particular industry to the percentage employed nationally in that industry. Such factors as growth rates and the mix or diversity of industrial types may be addressed. An ICMA study declares, "The economic base study serves as the starting point for formulating an effective local economic development strategy."[45]

Conducting a business survey is an effective way of gathering information about the plans and priorities of existing businesses. Such information may be collected through door-to-door, telephone, or mail surveys of all businesses over a certain size. Topics covered in a survey might include type of business, number of employees, growth and location plans, needs for land and buildings, and satisfaction with city services.

The purpose of a community analysis is to collect information on the community. What attributes does the community possess that might be considered attractions for business and industry? What are its negative features? Considerable research emphasizes the critical importance of the labor force, transportation facilities, and access to materials and markets. Additionally, the quality of life, educational facilities, possible financial incentives, and even the physical appearance of the community may affect industrial location or expansion decisions.

Step 2: Setting Goals

Goals and priorities may be established by an "action team" made up of key leaders from local government, business and finance, and community organizations, as well as local university personnel. The ICMA stresses the importance of involving representatives of the banking community because they have the most detailed knowledge of business activity in the community; they continually monitor the local economy by reviewing loan requests and deposit trends, they regularly talk with other business leaders, and they can provide "the skills in packaging loans, examining business plans, and assessing the management capabilities of entrepreneurs."[46]

The action team examines and analyzes the information collected in the light of current local and national economic trends. Broad economic goals may be formulated at this point, to be followed by a set of strategies and objectives that should move the community in the proper direction. Although the goal-setting process may seem relatively straightforward, disagreements over priorities and specific interests will undoubtedly arise, requiring negotiation and compromise.

Step 3: Formulating Development Strategies

Essentially, three principal strategies are available to enhance the economic vitality of the community: retain and expand existing industries, attract outside businesses, and provide development programs for new businesses. Although, in the past, many cities concentrated on attracting enterprises from outside the community, considerable research has shown that most new jobs are created by the expansion of existing industry and the start-up of new businesses. Retaining and boosting existing businesses may require reducing barriers to expansion—such as an inadequate labor force, lack of sites for expansion, and, most often, a shortage of capital—and stimulating demand for their products.

Encouraging the start-up of new businesses may take several forms. Leveraging funds from federal grants—such as the Community Development Block Grant (CDBG) discussed in chapter 2—can play a vital role, since access to capital funds is probably more critical to emerging entrepreneurs than to existing businesses. The use of community development corporations, which are usually private, nonprofit entities, may also prove beneficial in getting new enterprises off the ground. The next section of this chapter examines specific tools and strategies at greater length.

Although most authorities agree that attracting new industry should not be the cornerstone of an economic development plan, most communities include such an effort as part of their overall scheme, if only because every other place does so and they want to be competitive. It may also be a good way to diversify the community's economic base. The ICMA emphasizes the importance of building on the community's existing assets in efforts to attract outside firms.[47]

Step 4: Identifying and Overcoming Obstacles

The last step in the overall effort at economic development requires monitoring, feedback, and modification of the program. Implementation does not take place automatically or without hitches. Some activities may pay off quickly, whereas others may lag or encounter unexpected obstacles. A process of continually assessing and reassessing how the overall effort is working ultimately may be the best assurance of success. Community resistance is one of the biggest and most difficult obstacles to overcome. The ICMA urges a "can do" attitude on the part of the development team, partly as a means of promoting a positive attitude toward development within the community.[48]

STRATEGIES AND TOOLS FOR ECONOMIC DEVELOPMENT

By the end of the twentieth century, the leaders and managers of cities had developed an almost boundless array of strategies, tools, and activities for ED. But a review of economic development strategies in cities and how they changed from 1994 to 2004 shows that at the beginning of the twenty-first century, cities have "diversified their economic development strategies."[49] Today they range from the creation of community development corporations to tax incentives, job-training programs, and the leveraging of state and federal funds. And greater emphasis is being placed on business retention, quality of life, and regional cooperation (as opposed to competition).[50] Despite the greater diversity of economic development strategies, we still find three basic categories of strategies that communities can and do pursue: financial incentives, public improvements, and public-private partnerships.

Financing Economic Development

If a community is to pursue economic development seriously, it must create mechanisms to finance various projects and activities early in the game. We are speaking here mainly of tax incentives or other government-provided financial subsidies that may be necessary to get a project off the ground or otherwise make the community attractive for private investment. Financial incentives—especially tax abatements—are often controversial, and considerable research indicates that financial inducements are quite low on the list of state and community characteristics considered important in business location or expansion decisions.[51] Nonetheless, local governments continue to offer financial inducements regularly. Eighty-six percent of cities responding to a 2009 nationwide ICMA survey stated that they use municipal revenue to support their economic development programs, a percentage that has steadily increased over three decades.[52]

Businesses do not consider tax advantages or financial incentives decisive in their decision process because other locational characteristics invariably outweigh them. Influences generally thought to be more critical than taxes or monetary incentives include availability of labor, transportation, and land; energy costs; and the quality of life of an area. Probably the biggest reason that cities nonetheless continue to offer financial incentives is fear of the competition—the stakes are high.

Because everyone else does it, communities must compete so as not to put themselves at a comparative disadvantage. Moreover, evidence does show that if a business is considering various locations within a specific geographic region, the importance of taxes and fiscal incentives increases. The two most common kinds of financial inducement are fiscal incentives and the use of public funds to leverage sizable private investments.

Fiscal Incentives

Of the several possibilities for offering financial incentives, a common technique has been the issuance of local industrial revenue bonds (IRBs), also known as industrial development bonds. These bonds are often issued by a local government or some other local public authority created by the city or county government, without a vote by the people. The ICMA survey found that about 8 percent of responding cities used revenue bonds and nearly another 11 percent used special assessment district revenue to finance economic development projects.[53] The purpose of these instruments is to provide a pool of money to buy land, construct buildings, and purchase capital equipment. IRBs are tax exempt, and the lower costs are passed on to the borrower.[54] The principal advantages of IRBs are access to long-term financing, low interest, and the absence of federal income tax on the interest earned by the bondholder.

Because the U.S. Treasury is affected by the issuance of IRBs, the federal government has imposed a number of restrictions on the way these bonds may be used. The Tax Reform Act of 1986, for example, eliminates a number of uses of IRBs and establishes a state-by-state limit on the amount of private-purpose bonds that may be issued; no longer may tax-exempt bonds be used to finance sports stadiums, convention centers, parking facilities, or industrial parks.

A second device employed as a fiscal inducement for ED is tax increment financing (TIF). The idea of TIF originated in California in the 1950s, although most TIF districts were created in the 1980s.[55] The 2009 ICMA survey found that 35 percent of responding cities used TIFs in their development efforts, a proportion that has increased in just five years.[56] This device requires the creation of a special district or area to which the increased taxes received by the local government as a result of economic expansion are returned to finance public improvements in that specific area. The additional tax receipts (the increment) may be used to fund improvements on a pay-as-you-go basis or may be pledged to repay revenue bonds issued for long-term improvements.[57]

Currently forty-eight states allow their cities to use tax increment financing. Whereas TIFs are often good for the city government, TIF districts may result in the loss of revenue for counties and school districts, which do not get a share of the new revenue until the TIF bonds are paid off. But as economic development expert and political scientist Richard Bingham noted, "TIFs are now the most popular form of economic development financing in major metropolitan areas."[58]

Cities may also offer tax abatements (or exemptions) to private firms in accordance with state law. In many instances, such tax breaks are granted as part of an urban empowerment zone program. It is worth noting that the incentives offered by local governments to spur development are often driven by underlying socioeconomic conditions in the community as much as by its economic health. For example, Paul Lewis's study of California city managers revealed that their cities' propensity to offer incentives for development are highly linked to "past growth patterns," such as residential affordability, time spent commuting, and the ratio of jobs to workers. Moreover, the congestion that can be produced by growth can be a strong predictor of a tendency toward slow or no-growth policies.[59]

It is worth noting that the financial tools to stimulate economic development need not ignore issues of sustainability. In a 2010 book, law professor Joan Fitzgerald demonstrates that financial and policy incentives for development can be implemented in ways that achieve goals for both economic progress and urban sustainability.[60] Success will vary, but local leadership is a key factor in achieving green goals along with economic development.

Public Improvements

Cities often finance a host of public improvements, from streets to sewers to parking garages or recreation facilities, as a major strategy for supporting economic development. Some of these actions—perhaps most—are directly tied to the investment of private capital, and the primary purpose often is reduction of overall private development costs. Public spending for development-related infrastructure must compete, of course, with other potential uses for those dollars. The expectation of new tax revenues and expanded tax bases is the primary factor in a city government's decision to spend public funds for projects designed primarily to facilitate or aid private development. New tax revenue may be generated in several ways, not only from the construction of new buildings but also from the creation of new jobs and the inducement of surrounding businesses to upgrade and improve their structures. Job creation in itself certainly represents another common argument in favor of public support for ED.

Making public improvements may take forms other than providing infrastructure or assembling land parcels. Research by the American Planning Association shows that the way a community handles enabling powers such as zoning, eminent domain, code enforcement, and enforcement of development regulations can greatly encourage or discourage private development. And smart growth can be facilitated by reform of land-use ordinances and codes.[61] Some cities now have one-stop permit centers, and many places have begun to reexamine the whole set of regulations in the hope of removing impediments and streamlining the city's role in the development process. Milwaukee and Dayton are just two examples of large cities that have recently completed major revisions of their codes and zoning regulations.[62]

Public-Private Partnerships

One could make the case that, almost by definition, urban economic development requires a partnership between the public and private sectors. Certainly, the preceding discussion suggests the extent of the public-private collaboration that is frequently essential for successful development. Here we examine public-private partnerships that take a somewhat different and, in some instances, more enduring form.

Economic Development Corporations

Quasi-public economic development corporations have sprouted up all over the country, primarily to provide a permanent planning and financing structure to facilitate ED. Arranging the financial package necessary for development is a prime responsibility of such organizations, which are especially useful because laws in some states prohibit cities from providing direct funding for business development. Many observers praise these quasi-public economic development corporations for their capacity to raise money and expedite the development process, while others criticize them because—although they normally include both business leaders and public officials on their boards of directors— they are not under direct public control. Political scientist Robert Stoker calls them "shadow governments," partly because they are designed to operate out of the public eye and limit popular participation.[63] (More attention is devoted to this issue in this chapter's final section, on the politics of development.)

Employment and Job Training

Another arena in which collaboration between the public and private sectors can be effective is employment assistance and job training. Cities pursue a range of strategies in the effort to link the public and private sectors for employment and training purposes. Attempting to meet the needs of hard-to-employ groups, dealing with layoffs from corporate mergers and plant closings, developing retraining programs, and working with new and small businesses to create or retain jobs are among the many activities being undertaken in various communities.

Public-Private Cooperation in Infrastructure Development

We usually think of infrastructure improvements as solely the responsibility of the public sector, but this is not necessarily so. A growing number of cities now recognize that the quality of life they offer can help or hinder their economic development efforts, particularly if they are trying to woo high-tech industries that can pick and choose among various desirable locations.[64] Therefore, cities are beginning to consider improving the "amenity infrastructure" as part of the ED strategy—an ambitious undertaking that requires substantial public-private cooperation. The amenity infrastructure can include a wide range of facilities: civic and convention centers, sports arenas, venues for the performing and visual arts, culture, and museums. As Mark Rosentraub found, many cities use these developments as tools to restore confidence in the city and its downtown vitality.[65]

Public-private partnerships have also included the creation of so-called Economic Development Banks, by which public funds are made available to nonprofit organizations in order to spur development. Whereas these banks can encourage the private sector to help in carrying out public objectives with public funds, there is no guarantee of success. A study of the innovative Los Angeles Community Development Bank, which was created to help disadvantaged neighborhoods recover from the riots of 1992, revealed that the bank suffered significant losses in its often failed efforts to effectively stimulate development by disbursing $435 million in federal money.[66] Its failures raise important questions about the wisdom of such public-private partnerships. But new approaches to public-private partnerships that emphasize economic and environmental development may offer models for new collaborations. The case of Portland, Oregon's public-private partnership is one example and it is discussed in the case study in box 5.1.

ORGANIZING FOR AND MANAGING ECONOMIC DEVELOPMENT

Cities appear to follow one of two primary approaches to organizing for economic development. As outlined earlier, one involves the creation of a quasi-official economic development corporation to handle the operation, perhaps working closely with certain agencies of city government. The second approach places the responsibility for development directly upon city government, although the model chosen by a given community will depend on a variety of local conditions and past history. Chicago combined its planning and development departments into one super department; and in recent years its website promoted its economic development mission first, mentioning planning almost as an afterthought. Alan Gregerman, research director of the National Council of Urban Economic Development, suggests that the public approach may work well in cities where the local government has given a high priority to ED and the private sector is already actively involved.[67] In contrast, he says, a quasi-public corporation may be more effective where development is not a top municipal priority or where the private sector is uneasy about working directly with local government. Increasingly, Gregerman notes, communities are pursuing the quasi-public route—not without opposition from some quarters, however. In Chicago, for example, the late Robert Mier, who was appointed the first economic development commissioner by Mayor Harold Washington, expressed concern over the idea of putting too much power in the hands of a private body. "The major question," opined Mier, "is the degree to which economic development gets privatized. The city must retain responsibility for policymaking, and it must remain accountable for its use of public resources."[68] Cities do devote considerable fiscal and human resources to economic

DEVELOPMENT PLANNING IN PORTLAND, AN ICON OF SUSTAINABILITY

Cities across the United States are actively promoting sustainable development in their local planning. From Maine to California, economic development planning has embraced tools to integrate environmental sustainability in redevelopment and new development projects.

One city that has been called the "greenest city" for its wide-ranging and aggressive approaches to sustainability is Portland, Oregon. Mayor Sam Adams and city planners in this West Coast city believe that their city can emerge from the recession with green economic policies. "We aspire to this driving Portland as an icon of sustainability," said Lisa Abuaf, a senior project manager with the Portland Development Commission, the city's urban renewal agency.

Portland planners are partnering with major corporations, such as General Electric Company (GE) to achieve new sustainability goals and provide economic benefits, including new jobs to offset Portland's high unemployment rate. One project with GE involves construction of a "triple-net-zero" building. What is being called the Oregon Sustainability Center will provide commercial office space in a complex that produces its own electricity, draws its water from rain, and processes all of its wastewater. The plan for this project focuses on three inter-related aspects of sustainability—economic, environmental, and social.

The Portland Bureau of Planning and Sustainability is a key piece of the public-private partnership with GE. The Bureau represents the public interest in planning and any commitment of taxpayer funds, whereas the corporation provides the technology and corporate resources to achieve sustainability. Constructing this office complex will not only help to achieve many of the environmental and economic goals of the public partners, it plays to the corporation's long-term strategy, too. GE hopes that a successful sustainability development in Portland will become a model for the ways it could partner with other U.S. cities. Though it may take some selling to other cities for this model to catch on.

For one, the construction of a LEED certified (Leadership in Energy and Environmental Design) building will be more expensive. It may cost as much as 15 to 20 percent more than a similar size building that does not include sustainable components. This is driven by more windows, solar panels, special air handling systems, and even a cistern in the basement to store rain water for the building. These design features could save 60 percent of the energy that would normally be consumed in a conventional building.

But another challenge is the social aspect of sustainability. "Additional savings needed for the project to achieve net-zero energy consumption must come from behavioral changes—such as having cleaning crews come during daylight hours, persuading occupants to take the stairs and adjusting the temperature set points seasonally." These are no small challenges. But successful achievement of these objectives will help the partners sell this model to other cities' planners.

For Portland, this is just one project in the city's sustainability agenda. The city wants to implement a major overhaul in the way it uses energy and protects the environment. Portland hopes to do this through the design of five pilot EcoDistricts. Each will change the conventional approaches to power usage, waste disposal, and transportation. According to Michael Armstrong, a senior planning manager for Portland, "We want to do at a district scale what green building has done at a building scale."

Mayor Adams believes the overall strategy will attract and retain businesses and jobs for Portland. And he thinks the city can do this and reduce greenhouse gas emissions by 80 percent over the next 40 years. As the mayor explains, "Our goal is to be more economically successful and equitable in the pursuit of environmental sustainability." This could become the new model for sustainable economic development in U.S. cities.

SOURCE: Adapted from Michael Burnham, "Bold Public-Private Venture Aims to Make Ore. City an 'Icon of Sustainability,'" *New York Times*, July 7, 2010.

development efforts. An ICMA survey found that in 2009, on average, cities were spending $1,300,232 a year for economic development.[69]

LEADING AND MANAGING

Regardless of the organizational structure used, aggressive foresight, planning, and leadership may spell the difference between success and failure. If so, whose job is it to provide that leadership? Many, such as Mier, would argue that the city government must do it—especially the mayor, and perhaps the city manager. Apparently, however, that does not always happen. The ICMA survey asked cities to report who participates in developing their economic development strategies, and nearly all of them named the city government as the primary actor. But participation by other actors was quite varied, involving, for example, the chamber of commerce (65 percent), private businesses (40 percent), development corporations (44 percent), citizen advisory groups (36 percent), and colleges (30 percent).[70]

Coordination would likely be severely impaired if no single person or group were in charge, and it would seem difficult to achieve such a condition if the key responsibility for development were to lie within the business community generally. Yet private organizations and corporations—even the local chamber of commerce—are leading the development effort in many communities, and city hall may acquiesce willingly. In fact, a private organization can be the focal point of various public-private cooperative ventures. For example, in Denver, Mayor Federico Peña announced in July 1984 that the city and the Denver Partnership, the downtown development corporation, would collaborate on a downtown master plan to promote and direct development in and around the central business district. Denver's downtown planner explained that the Denver Partnership would take the lead in the downtown plan because "we just didn't have the core staff or the money to do it ourselves."[71]

Technology has also contributed to innovation in the new management approaches to development. In recent years, the development efforts of city governments have included creating websites, establishing online services for such functions as submission of permit applications, installing fiber optic networking, and employing hand-held computers in the permitting and inspection processes.[72] Sometimes, reinventing government through technological innovation is a fundamental feature of an economic development strategy.

In some instances, the city manager may be a key figure in facilitating economic development. Most of the literature suggests that such an essentially political position is best reserved for elected officials. But, given the high stakes involved in ED, communities with city managers may also find these individuals in the thick of the fight.

THE POLITICS OF URBAN DEVELOPMENT

Like the practices of urban planning, economic development is not beyond controversy, especially when questions of tax relief or control of the process arise. Indeed, political disputes may be unavoidable. And as Harold Wolman has pointed out, the politics of economic development is often studied from the systems model by looking at the forces behind development activity, the objectives sought by the activity, and the environment of the city that shapes the wide variation in development policy.[73]

At least three issues bear on the political dimension of ED. One is how to build the political consensus necessary for success. The other two are more fundamental questions of values and ideology—who participates in the process and who benefits.

CONSENSUS BUILDING

Development requires teamwork and cooperation if it is to be successful. Creating an action team may be a way of involving certain groups in the community who have a stake in the process. Identifying key team members from the city government may not be too difficult—most likely the city manager or mayor, accompanied by certain staff or technical specialists such as the planning director or the head of an ED department or division. But what about those outside the municipal government? Part of the answer here depends on where the idea originated. If the business community has taken the lead, its representatives in effect may invite or urge city officials to join the effort. In such instances, the city's participation may be secondary to the main enterprise being directed by business interests. The city's cooperation will be needed, of course—perhaps to issue bonds or to provide public works improvements and technical assistance—but municipal officials may be limited to a distinctly supporting role.

No matter who takes the lead, even when general agreement about the course of development has been reached, it is often difficult to achieve the necessary consensus on specific activities. One of the basic problems, according to Weaver, is that "various local interests can look at the economy of the city and arrive at very different conclusions about its economic development needs and goals."[74] Thus, consensus building may become a difficult process in which some person or group must be called in to broker the various interests. The city manager may play this role, as in the Cincinnati case, or the mayor may be a more appropriate broker in some communities. As we see later, whether the business community or the city government takes the lead, the larger public or affected neighborhood groups may not follow, at least not willingly.

WHO PARTICIPATES AND WHO BENEFITS

The push for economic development is based on a fairly simple model: business investment leads to more jobs and an expanded tax base, from which everyone in the community benefits. As political scientists Dennis Judd and Margaret Collins have observed, "It is easy to understand how downtown business interests equate their own investment decisions with the general public good and why they become infuriated when 'minority factions' get in the way of progress."[75] Yet, as John Schwarz and Thomas Volgy, authors of *The Forgotten Americans: Thirty Million Working Poor in the Land of Opportunity* (1993), argue in an article in *Governing* magazine, that there "is little evidence that the billions of dollars spent annually on economic development by states and localities have resulted either in higher wages or fewer working poor."[76] Similarly, in an empirical study of 212 U.S. cities, Richard Feiock found that "local economic development policies have a significant effect on capital investment but little effect on employment growth."[77]

What some see, in effect, is an unbalanced public-private partnership, which in a number of cities permits development decisions with far-reaching consequences to be made by a business-dominated elite, with very little input from the larger community. Based on an extensive case study of neighborhoods and public-private partnerships in Pittsburgh, for example, sociologist and urban affairs expert Louise Jezierski offers this assessment of the process: "Partnerships alter the governing structure of a community by limiting participation to enhance efficiency."[78] Jane Grant's analysis of the process involved in locating a General Motors truck plant in Fort Wayne, Indiana, reaches a similar conclusion: public input was limited.[79] Perhaps Max Stephenson best captured the essence of the controversy in his critical overview of public-private partnerships:

> Partnerships are unlikely to vanish from the nation's political scene soon. Their apparent promise is simply too great and city needs too vast for officials to ignore the very real economic and political benefits that such efforts may bring. But great uncertainty exists about the issue of whether such arrangements can address the long-term needs of the community and not simply fulfill the agendas of the best organized groups within them.[80]

Some would argue that there are good reasons why development decisions are not widely shared. Peterson, for example, identified two related reasons for limiting public participation in ED policymaking. First, by keeping mass involvement at a minimum, the city can avoid conflict over "economically productive policies." He argues that development is so fundamental to a city's well-being that it should not be derailed by disagreement and dissension. And second, Peterson thinks, the development process can be accomplished more effectively when conducted out of the public eye, relying on "highly centralized decision-making processes involving economic elites."[81] When consensus has been obtained, broader support may be sought.

Peterson's description of developmental politics contrasts sharply with the nature of allocational politics. These stark differences have prompted urban affairs expert Elaine Sharp to offer a "bifurcated model" of politics as a way of understanding who rules in urban America.[82] The particulars may vary from community to community, of course, but frequently the politics of development is relatively closed, nonconflictual, and elite-dominated; the players are prominent economic interests: bankers, land developers, corporate leaders, and downtown business representatives. In contrast, the politics of allocation is more open, conflictual, and pluralistic. Here various interests compete over the most routine issues and problems involved in service delivery.

In addition, ED projects may well produce unintended consequences. For example, an analysis of casino development in Atlantic City indicated that substantial social costs have accompanied the immediate gain in jobs and taxes.[83] Increased land values may bring higher taxes or rents, possibly threatening residents on fixed incomes. New job opportunities may not go to inner-city dwellers but to suburbanites. High-rise development may discourage the street trade that many small retailers rely on. As political scientist Clarence Stone asks, "Why should a city government embrace policies that help some people while neglecting or harming others?"[84] Or, at the least, are these not matters that should be considered openly in a forum accessible to all who might be affected?

It is also worth noting that the concept of a unitary interest among pro-development business interests is faulty. Research on 350 U.S. and Canadian cities by political scientists Laura Reese and Raymond Rosenfeld reveals that development is less driven by any cohesive private business objective than by the underlying civic culture that dominates the community.[85]

The position one takes on how much politics should affect the development process may depend ultimately on one's ideology. No one expects all decisions involving the obligation of public funds to be put to a vote—that is why we have a representative democracy. And almost everyone recognizes that a substantial private commitment is a must for development to work. The local government, however, clearly has a role to play. Should it initiate and direct the process, or should it be a mere handmaiden to decisions made behind closed corporate doors? Can a true balance be achieved? These questions are not easily answered, but the proper relationship between the public and private sectors is a legitimate concern for all who are committed to economic development.

SUMMARY

Local government officials and citizens alike would likely agree that urban or city planning represents a vital and essential activity. At the same time, they would admit that development and the planning associated with it are often beset by difficulties. As planning evolved in the past century, its practitioners struggled to agree on its role. Early on, urban planning was identified with the City Beautiful Movement, with its emphasis on environmental determinism. It also had close connections with urban reformers who stressed rationality, efficiency, and a unitary public interest. Both of these movements were essentially antipolitical, and their tenets held that planners were advisers, not doers.

As alternative approaches to traditional comprehensive planning were developed, new ways of thinking also affected the organization of the planning structure. The separate, nonpolitical planning commission increasingly became advisory in nature, and the planning function became the province of professional planning staffs responsible directly to municipal chief executives.

The function of planning agencies ranges from comprehensive planning (land-use, growth-control, and areawide planning) to zoning, to a host of other regulatory activities. Always, however, their role remains advisory; planning implementation rests with elected legislative bodies. This does not mean that planning agencies are never political, for if their plans are to be realized, political action may be essential.

Economic development—being entrepreneurial and competitive—has become almost synonymous with planning in many cities. Yet it is also a narrowing of what planning should try to accomplish in urban areas. What has caused this narrowing? Some communities have had a harder time than others in coping with the reduction of federal aid that began in the 1980s—they have lost population and jobs over the past few decades, their inner core has collapsed, their tax base has seriously eroded. They have been deeply impacted by the national recession that characterized 2008–2010. Economic development has become their preferred strategy to improve the economic base and make the community more attractive to new private investment. In short, in many communities, economic development now occupies a niche at or near the top of municipal priorities.

Despite special federal government assistance to stimulate the economy (such as the American Recovery and Reinvestment Act), federal aid has been declining for three decades. Yet, cities continue to use what federal and state funds they do receive as a way of leveraging private investment for development. A variety of other strategies and techniques are widely used as well, including embracing the technologies of the twenty-first century that may allow cities to be more innovative with development. Some strategies involve financial incentives from the local treasury or require the obligation of local funds for public works improvements. Much of this activity takes place under the umbrella of a "public-private partnership." Although most observers recognize that both sectors must participate for many projects to succeed, some have raised questions about the proper relationship between the public and private sectors. One group contends that privatizing development reduces delays and red tape, allowing the whole process to occur more efficiently. Others fear that business dominance, perhaps operating largely out of the public eye, keeps the process from being accountable to the larger community.

What is certain for the near future is that urban planning will continue to be directed toward activities that support the economic development of communities and metropolitan areas. And as we enter the second decade of the twenty-first century, urban planning and development will continue to evolve in strategic ways that will support development, but do so in ways that promote urban sustainability.

SUGGESTED FOR FURTHER READING

Blair, John P. *Local Economic Development: Analysis and Practice*. Thousand Oaks, Calif.: Sage, 1995.

Fitzgerald, Joan, *Emerald Cities: Urban Sustainability and Economic Development* New York: Oxford University Press, 2010.

Hack, Gary, Eugenie L. Birch, Paul H. Sedway, and Mitchell J. Silver, eds., *Local Planning: Contemporary Principles and Practice*. Washington, D.C.: ICMA Press, 2009.

Peterson, Paul. *City Limits*. Chicago: University of Chicago Press, 1981.

Portney, Kent E. *Taking Sustainable Cities Seriously: Economic Development, the Environment, and Quality of Life in American Cities*. Cambridge, Mass.: MIT Press, 2003.

Stone, Clarence N., and Heywood T. Sanders, eds. *The Politics of Urban Development*. Lawrence: University Press of Kansas, 1987.

NOTES

1. Coleman Woodbury, ed., *The Future of Cities and Urban Redevelopment* (Chicago: University of Chicago Press, 1953), quoted in Anthony J. Catanese, *Planners and Local Politics* (Beverly Hills, Calif.: Sage, 1974), 43.

2. John L. Hancock, "Planners in the Changing American City, 1900–1940," *Journal of the American Institute of Planners* 33 (September 1967): 293.

3. Susan S. Fainstein, "New Directions in Planning Theory," *Urban Affairs Review* 35 (March 2000): 451–478.

4. Ibid., 454.

5. Judith Innes, "Planning Theory's Emerging Paradigm: Communicative Action and Interactive Practice," *Journal of Planning Education and Research* 14 (1995): 183–189.

6. Fainstein, "New Directions in Planning Theory," 461–462.

7. LEED: Leadership in Energy and Environmental Design, sponsored by the U.S. Green Building Council, non-profit organization (see www.usgbc.org).

8. For examples, see Kent E. Portney, *Taking Sustainable Cities Seriously: Economic Development, the Environment, and Quality of Life in American Cities* (Cambridge, Mass.: MIT Press, 2003); and Eugenie L. Birch and Susan M. Wachter, eds., *Growing Green Cities: Addressing Urban Environmental Issues in the Twenty-first Century* (Philadelphia: University of Pennsylvania Press, 2008).

9. Eric S. Zeemering, "What Does Sustainability Mean to City Officials?" *Urban Affairs Review* 45 (November 2009): 247–273.

10. Other research on urban sustainability includes Mathew E. Kahn, *Green Cities: Urban Growth and the Environment* (Washington, D.C.: Brookings Institution Press, 2006); and Daniel A. Mazmanian and Michael E. Kraft, eds., *Toward Sustainable Communities: Transition and Transformations in Environmental Policy*, 2nd ed. (Cambridge, Mass.: MIT Press, 2009).

11. Fainstein, "New Directions in Planning Theory," 468.

12. Michael L. Vasu, "Planning Theory and Practice in the 1980s," *Urban Affairs Quarterly* 17 (September 1981): 109–114.

13. Paul Davidoff, "Advocacy and Pluralism in Planning," *Journal of the American Institute of Planners* 31 (November 1965): 333.

14. Vasu, "Planning Theory and Practice," 111.

15. Charles J. Hoch, "Making Plans," in *The Practice of Local Government Planning*, 3rd ed., ed. Charles J. Hoch, Linda C. Dalton, and Frank S. So (Washington, D.C.: ICMA, 2000), 25–27.

16. Elmer W. Johnson, *Chicago Metropolis 2020: Preparing Metropolitan Chicago for the 21st Century* (Chicago: Commercial Club, 1999).

17. Thad Beyle and George Lathrop, "Planning and Politics: On Grounds of Incompatibility," in *Planning and Politics: Uneasy Partnership*, ed. Beyle and Lathrop (New York: Odyssey, 1970), 1–12.

18. David C. Ranney, *Planning and Politics in the Metropolis* (Columbus, Ohio: Merrill, 1969), 57.

19. R. Robert Linowes and Don Allensworth, *The Politics of Land Use* (New York: Praeger, 1973), 23.

20. Kent Portney, "Civic Engagement and Sustainable Cities in the United States," *Public Administration Review* 65 (September/October 2005): 583.

21. Ibid., 587.

22. Francine Rabinovitz, *City Politics and Planning* (Chicago: Aldine, 1969), chap. 4.

23. Richard Bolan and Ronald Nuttall, *Urban Planning and Politics* (Lexington, Mass.: Heath, 1975), 147.

24. Dennis Rondinelli, "Urban Planning as Policy Analysis: Management of Urban Change," *Journal of the American Institute of Planners* 39 (January 1973): 13–22.

25. This discussion is based on the significant work of Don T. Allensworth, *The Political Realities of Urban Planning* (New York: Praeger, 1975), 166–183.

26. Gary Hack, Eugenie L. Birch, Paul H. Sedway, and Mitchell J. Silver, eds., *Local Planning: Contemporary Principles and Practice* (Washington, D.C.: ICMA Press, 2009).

27. Alan Black, "The Comprehensive Plan," in *Principles and Practice of Urban Planning*, ed. William Goodman and Eric Freund (Washington, D.C.: ICMA, 1968), 351.

28. These elements are modified from the classic work of Herbert H. Smith, *The Citizen's Guide to Planning* (West Trenton, N.J.: Chandler-Davis, 1961), 35–36.

29. Matthew L. Cypher and Fred A. Forgey, "Eminent Domain: An Evaluation Based on Criteria Relating to Equity, Effectiveness, and Efficiency," *Urban Affairs Review* 39 (November 2003): 254–268.

30. Adapted from John Friedmann, "The Future of Comprehensive Planning: A Critique," *Public Administration Review* 31 (May–June 1971): 317–318.

31. Melville C. Branch, *Continuous City Planning: Integrating Municipal Management and City Planning* (New York: Wiley, 1981), 82–83, 96–101.

32. Richard F. Babcock, *The Zoning Game* (Madison: University of Wisconsin Press, 1966), 117.

33. Steven Maser, William Riker, and Richard Rosett, "Municipal Zoning and Real Estate Markets," *State and Local Government Review* 9 (January 1977): 7–12.

34. Village of Skokie, www.skokie.org/villagecode.cfm.

35. Linowes and Allensworth, *Politics of Land Use*, chap. 3.

36. Paul Peterson, *City Limits* (Chicago: University of Chicago Press, 1981).

37. Up-to-date information on the act's effectiveness is available at www.recovery.gov.

38. Robert R. Weaver, *Local Economic Development in Texas* (Arlington: Institute of Urban Studies, University of Texas at Arlington, 1986), 4–6.

39. Dennis Judd and Randy Ready, "Entrepreneurial Cities and the New Politics of Economic Development," in *Reagan and the Cities*, ed. George Peterson and Carol Lewis (Washington, D.C.: Urban Institute, 1986), 210.

40. John P. Pelissero and Robert E. England, "State and Local Governments' Washington 'Reps': Lobbying Strategies and President Reagan's New Federalism," *State and Local Government Review* 19 (spring 1987): 68–72.

41. Roger L. Kemp, "Economic Development: Raising Revenue without Increasing Taxes," *Public Administration Survey* 34 (autumn 1986–winter 1987): 1–2.

42. Peterson, *City Limits*.

43. ICMA, "Economic Development 2009 Survey Summary," p. 2. Available at http://icma.org/Documents/Document/Document/107026.pdf.

44. This discussion of development planning is drawn from ICMA, "Strategies for Local Enterprise Development," *MIS Report* 18 (February 1986): 1–7; and *Making Sense Out of Dollars: Economic Analysis for Local Government* (Washington, D.C.: National League of Cities, 1978), 5–6.

45. ICMA, *Making Sense Out of Dollars*, 6.

46. ICMA, "Strategies for Local Enterprise Development," 2.

47. Ibid., 7.

48. Ibid.

49. Lingwen Zheng and Mildred E. Warner, "Local Economic Development, 1994–2004: Broadening Strategies, Increasing Accountability," *2010 Municipal Year Book* (Washington, D.C.: ICMA Press, 2010), 8.

50. Ibid., 9.

51. For example, see Michael Kieschnick, *Taxes and Growth: Business Incentives and Economic Development* (Washington, D.C.: Council of State Planning Agencies, 1981), 87.

52. ICMA, "Economic Development 2009 Survey Summary," p. 3.

53. Ibid.

54. The discussion of IRBs comes from Wardaleen Belvin, "Industrial Revenue Bonds," in *Local Economic Development*, ed. Sherman Wyman and Robert Weaver (Arlington: Institute of Urban Studies, University of Texas at Arlington, 1987), 52.

55. An excellent summary of TIFs can be found in Richard D. Bingham, "Economic Development Policies," in *Cities, Politics, and Policy: A Comparative Analysis*, ed. John P. Pelissero (Washington, D.C.: CQ Press, 2003), 237–253.

56. ICMA, "Economic Development 2009 Survey Summary," 3.

57. For a general discussion of TIF issues and methods, see Don Davis, "Tax Increment Financing," *Public Budgeting and Finance* 9 (spring 1989): 63–73.

58. Bingham, "Economic Development Policies," 248.

59. Paul G. Lewis, "Offering Incentives for New Development: The Role of City Social Status, Politics, and Local Growth Experiences," *Journal of Urban Affairs* 24 (April 2002): 143–157.

60. Joan Fitzgerald, *Emerald Cities: Urban Sustainability and Economic Development* (New York: Oxford University Press, 2010).

61. See American Planning Association, *Codifying New Urbanism: How to Reform Municipal Land Development Regulations* (Chicago: APA, 2004).

62. ICMA, "Smart Growth and Code Reform," issue summary paper, 2005.

63. Robert Stoker, "Baltimore: The Self-Evaluating City?" in *The Politics of Urban Development*, ed. Clarence Stone and Heywood Sanders (Lawrence: University Press of Kansas, 1987), 258.

64. This section draws on Rita J. Bamberger and David Parham, "Leveraging Amenity Infrastructure: Indianapolis's Economic Development Strategy," *Urban Land* 43 (November 1984): 12.

65. Mark S. Rosentraub, *Major League Winners: Using Sports and Cultural Centers as Tools for Economic Development* (New York: CRC Press, 2010), 245–250.

66. Julia Sass Rubin and Gregory M. Stankiewicz, "The Los Angeles Community Development Bank: The Possible Pitfalls of Public Private Partnerships," *Journal of Urban Affairs* 23 (April 2001): 133–153.

67. From Ruth Knack, James Bellus, and Patricia Adell, "Setting Up Shop for Economic Development," in *Shaping the Local Economy*, ed. Cheryl A. Farr (Washington, D.C.: ICMA, 1984), 43.

68. Quoted in ibid., 43.

69. ICMA, "Economic Development 2009 Survey Summary," 3.

70. Ibid.

71. Quoted in Judd and Ready, "Entrepreneurial Cities," 226.

72. Ibid.

73. Harold Wolman, with David Spitzley, "The Politics of Local Economic Development," *Economic Development Quarterly* 10 (May 1996): 115–150.

74. Weaver, *Local Economic Development in Texas*, 45.

75. From Dennis Judd and Margaret Collins, "The Case of Tourism: Political Coalitions and Redevelopment in the Central Cities," in *The Changing Structure of the City*, ed. Gary Tobin (Beverly Hills, Calif.: Sage, 1979), 183.

76. John E. Schwarz and Thomas J. Volgy, "Commentary: How Economic Development Succeeds and Fails at the Same Time," *Governing*, November 1992, 10–11.

77. Richard C. Feiock, "The Effects of Economic Development Policy on Local Economic Growth," *American Journal of Political Science* 35 (August 1991): 653.

78. Louise Jezierski, "Neighborhoods and Public-Private Partnerships in Pittsburgh," *Urban Affairs Quarterly* 26 (December 1990): 242.

79. Jane A. Grant, "Making Policy Choices: Local Government and Economic Development," *Urban Affairs Quarterly* 26 (December 1990): 48–69.

80. Max O. Stephenson, "Wither the Public-Private Partnership: A Critical Overview," *Urban Affairs Quarterly* 27 (September 1991): 123.

81. Peterson, *City Limits*, 129–132.

82. Elaine B. Sharp, *Urban Politics and Administration* (New York: Longman, 1990), 261.

83. Cited in Clarence N. Stone, "The Study of the Politics of Urban Development," in Stone and Sanders, *Politics of Urban Development*, 7.

84. Ibid., 8.

85. Laura A. Reese and Raymond A. Rosenfeld, "Reconsidering Private Sector Power: Business Input and Local Development Policy," *Urban Affairs Review* 37 (May 2002): 642–674.

CHAPTER 6

DECISION MAKING AND ANALYSIS

D ECISIONS, decisions. Public organizations face a never-ending round of decisions, and urban managers inevitably play a major part in the decision-making process. Students of management frequently list decision making as one of the basic managerial functions, along with planning, organizing, staffing, controlling, and budgeting.[1] In fact, decision making is the core process—it ties the other functions together. There is even widespread agreement that, above all, managers are judged by the decisions they make.

A good deal has been written about the decision process, and a number of techniques have been suggested over the years to improve it. Several scholarly disciplines—business administration, sociology, political science, psychology, and public administration—evidence a concern for how decisions are made within an organizational setting. Obviously, we cannot review all the theories and issues found in this disparate literature; instead, in the first section of this chapter we focus on four decision-making approaches most commonly found in the areas of political science and public administration. Next we examine some quantitative and nonquantitative decision-making tools. The third section offers a discussion of program analysis, providing a fairly comprehensive discussion of the analysis process and the issue of its political feasibility. Next we consider analysis applications, including an overview of the use of geographic and management information systems and computers at the local level. The chapter concludes with a few thoughts about the contributions and limitations of analysis.

APPROACHES TO DECISION MAKING

To some extent, each of the four basic approaches to decision making—rational-comprehensive, incremental, mixed scanning, and garbage can—purports to describe reality, to represent reasonably how decisions actually are made. At the same time, each approach has normative overtones, especially the rational-comprehensive approach.

THE RATIONAL-COMPREHENSIVE APPROACH

The rational-comprehensive—also known as economic, or classical—approach to decision making is widely known and accepted. It is the way management textbooks say decisions should be made. Observers and even participants in decision making frequently hold up the rational-comprehensive model as an ideal against which the actual decision process should be compared and evaluated.

As in our discussion of policymaking as a stable, orderly series of events in chapter 4, rational-comprehensive decision making is often described as a process requiring sequential action. For instance, a decision might be made using the following steps:

1. Recognize the problem.
2. Agree on facts and overall objectives.
3. Identify alternative solutions, analyze the alternatives, and assess the consequences (both short- and long-term) flowing from each.
4. Choose.
5. Implement.
6. Evaluate.

Although the decision-making process is often not this orderly, adherents to the rational-comprehensive approach generally believe that executive decision making can be improved through careful fact-gathering and precise analysis.

Rational-Comprehensive Decision Making in Action

Some years ago Brian Rapp and Frank Patitucci described a step-by-step decision-making process that a strong mayor might pursue to improve municipal performance.[2] The process has not changed. Assume the role of mayor as you work through the sequence of events.

Step 1: Identify opportunities. You ask your staff to prepare a list of opportunities for improving city government, based on information and ideas generated during your campaign for office. You instruct the staff to look at the causes underlying observed conditions and estimate the consequences if changes are not made. Three weeks later, staff members present to you the results of their preliminary study.

Step 2: Determine responsibility. The staff identifies possible improvements, but you are surprised to find that many of them may not be within the mayor's power to bring about. Various external groups, ranging from civic organizations to the state or federal government, may be extensively involved, either as a financing source or as a possible veto threat. You decide to concentrate on those improvement items that you believe you can change, and, accordingly, you ask the staff to indicate for each item whether the mayor's responsibility is direct or indirect. Other possible participants—city council, municipal unions, corporate business leaders—are to be identified as well. You realize, of course, that you cannot really command others' cooperation; persuasion, negotiation, and compromise will be required.

Step 3: Order opportunities according to their impact on performance. Next, the various opportunities or needed changes are placed in order of priority on the basis of their potential impact on municipal performance. This can be done by answering the simple but important question "So what?" You instruct the staff to group activities into three basic categories of impact: significant, moderate, and low.

Step 4: Reorder priorities on the basis of available resources. Reviewing the prioritized list, you recognize immediately that, given resource limitations, many of these identified opportunities just cannot be implemented. Therefore, you must distinguish between what is desirable and what is doable. Working with staff, you reorder the problems according to your perception of which ones have the best chance of being implemented.

Step 5: Develop an action plan. Now that the final list is complete, you ask your staff to convert those in the top category ("most significant" and "most doable") into specific action plans. Each plan should answer certain questions: "What objectives are to be achieved? When are they to be achieved? What results will be produced? What resources will be required to produce these results? Where will these resources be found? Who will be held accountable for converting resources into results?"[3]

As Rapp and Patitucci suggest, a decision to adopt a new budgetary system or to develop a downtown mall will have little effect unless you know the steps required to complete the project, how much it will cost, who will be responsible, and when it will be finished.

Strategic Planning and Strategic Management

The decision scheme outlined above clearly reflects an attempt to decide rationally what needs to be done and how to go about doing it. In practice, this process may occur rather informally, depending on the style of the decision maker and the complexity or magnitude of the problem. Some contend, however, that important decisions should be made in a more consciously systematic fashion, one that relies heavily on a formalized planning process.

In general, planning is figuring out what you want to do and how to do it. At the municipal level, as discussed in chapter 5, planning is often associated with decisions related to land use and zoning. Historically, city planning departments have prepared comprehensive or master plans, which form the basis for subsequent decisions relating to the community's economic base, transportation network, and capital needs, in addition to decisions affecting land use and zoning. Such all-encompassing plans have been criticized for their static nature, their relatively narrow focus on physical development, and the difficulties that arise in their implementation. As a result, in recent years, interest has grown in planning as a process rather than as the production of a comprehensive document. Some call this "policy planning," but the term most frequently used is *strategic planning*.

Developed in the private sector, and in particular by General Electric in the late 1950s and early 1960s, strategic planning is "a disciplined effort to produce fundamental decisions and actions that shape and guide what an organization (or other entity) is, what it does, and why it does it."[4] The management technique is based on systems theory, as outlined in chapter 1. Systems theory requires that the "organization's objectives and steps to achieve those objectives are seen in the context of the resources and constraints presented by the organization's environment."[5]

Strategic planning involves the following specific, sequential stages of action:

1. Identify the mission of the organization.
2. Establish a set of goals and priorities to be achieved.
3. Assess the organization's environment, including the individuals and groups whose support will be crucial.
4. Develop a set of measurable objectives for goal attainment.
5. Devise various strategies or action plans for achieving the objectives.
6. Agree on a timetable for implementation.
7. Create an information system to monitor and evaluate progress.[6]

These steps are quite similar to those enumerated earlier in outlining the rational-comprehensive approach to decision making, but several points should be made about strategic planning specifically. Disagreement exists about how the process should take place. Public administration specialist Robert Denhardt thinks most cities lack sufficient internal expertise to conduct strategic planning without help, and so he suggests bringing in an outside consultant.[7] Others agree, noting that local government officials should not make a large investment in the technique unless they have sophisticated managerial capabilities.[8] Denhardt also favors creating a planning group of some sort to carry out the process. Depending on the scope of the goals being considered, this group might be composed of high-level city staff or it might extend beyond city government to include representatives of business, finance, labor, and neighborhood associations. Todd Swanstrom echoes this inclusive approach.[9] Lamenting the elitist/technical nature of a process that often produces an economic growth bias, Swanstrom argues that strategic planning should not overlook the values of democratic participation and the need for checks and balances. Furthermore, in the public sector, one cannot forget politics. Indeed, political scientist John Gargan insists that planning proposals must be "technically feasible, fiscally feasible, and politically feasible."[10] Since strategic planning ultimately involves value judgments about the use of scarce resources, some disagreement, conflict, and political battles may be unavoidable, and the best-laid plans may never become reality. Research suggests that one of the best predictors of the presence of conflict (and cooperation) in decision making is the form of government used in a city (see box 6.1).

How many cities develop strategic plans? A 2009 ICMA survey that included 2,214 U.S. cities with 2,500 or more people (a 26 percent response rate), found, surprisingly, that only 62 percent of the localities reported having a strategic or long-range plan.[11] As one might assume, as the population size of the city decreases, the propensity to develop a strategic plan also decreases. Ninety-four percent of municipalities with 500,000 to one million residents had a strategic plan; the statistic for cities sized 250,000 to 499,999 people was 86 percent. Among the 80 Mid-Atlantic cities, only 38 percent of the jurisdictions had created a strategic plan. For the other eight ICMA-designated regions, in two regions more than one-half of the cities had strategic plans; and in six regions, over 60 percent of the

BOX 6.1   Policy and Practice

COOPERATION AND CONFLICT IN GOVERNMENTAL DECISION MAKING IN 165 MEDIUM-SIZED AMERICAN CITIES

Reflect for a moment about the *process* of decision making in your own life. This process is often defined by the levels of "cooperation" or "conflict" that accompany the decision. The presence of one characteristic, say cooperation, does not preclude the presence of the other—conflict, or vice versa. Nevertheless, you will probably attach a label to describe a decision-making experience as *more* cooperative or conflictual in nature. Cooperation means "positive interactions or active contributions that strive to take participants' preferences into account." Conflict "results from negative interactions, which include blocking behavior when some participants seek to impose their preferences on others." Now, apply this decision-making process to mid-sized U.S. cities, with populations greater than 50,000 but less than 250,000. There are 562 such cities in America. Participants involved in the decision-making calculus include mayors, city council members, and either a city manager in council-manager cities or a chief administrative officer in communities employing the mayor-council form of government.

Using survey data collected in 2006 and an intuitively appealing research design that measures the ability of 11 independent variables to predict conflict or cooperation (the two dependent variables) among the triangle of decision makers (mayors, city council members, and city managers/CAOs), Professor Karl Nollenberger finds that the "form of government is the only statistically significant factor to account for levels of conflict and cooperation in the decision-making process" in 165 medium-sized cities. More specifically, multiple regression analysis showed that the council-manager form of government is significantly associated with lower amounts of conflict in the decision-making process than the mayor-council form of government. When the analysis was expanded to include three forms of government—council-manager, mayor-council *with* a chief administrative officer, and mayor-council *without* a chief administrative officer— findings show that the "mayor-council form with a CAO position has less conflict and more cooperation than the mayor-council form without a CAO." The impact of this variable that measures three forms of city government (as opposed to just the dichotomous city-manager versus mayor-council designation) was statistically significant.

The other variables included in the analysis that did not show independent and significant impacts on the presence of conflict and cooperation in the decision-making process across the 165 cities were:

- Size of city, between 50,000 and 250,000 as measured by the 2000 census
- Location of city, whether it is a central city or suburb
- Fiscal condition of city, as measured by major bond rating organizations
- Socioeconomic conditions
  - Ethnicity, percentage of white population
  - Income level, average family income
  - City growth, population growth or decline during previous decade
  - Educational level in city, percentage of college graduates
- Method of council elections
  - Size of city council
  - Electoral system, district versus at-large elections
  - Ballot type, partisan or nonpartisan elections

(continued)

BOX 6.1   Policy and Practice (continued)

- Form of government
  - Mayor-council or council-manager.
  - And in the expanded analysis, mayor-council with a CAO, mayor-council without a CAO, and council-manager.

What should one make of these findings? Is the council-manager form of government superior because cooperation in decision making is enhanced and conflict is attenuated? As Nollenberger reminds us, this is not the case. Cities choose a form of government to maximize certain values. The city manager form of government was created at the turn of the twentieth century to minimize conflict and run cities like a business. And while times have changed and city managers are very much policy leaders in American cities today, they still remain facilitators "to help promote problem solving and develop consensus among interests." After all, city managers serve at the pleasure of the council; as such, it makes little sense to antagonize your "boss." In contrast "the mayor-council form of government, in which the mayor sees leadership as the acquisition and use of power, functions through the separation of powers and thus creates an environment for competition and disagreement similar to that found on the national level." Finally, with respect to the "calming" influence of the CAO in the mayor-council form of government, this professional may play a similar role to the one he or she plays in a council-manager system.

An insightful student may ask the question, "If we already know what values are maximized under various forms of government, why did Professor Nollenberger conduct the study? This is a good question. The study was undertaken to empirically test, using a systematic, comparative research design, a research question that had been previously examined using mostly case studies. The present study allows for the generalizability of research findings, one of the principle advantages of systematic hypothesis testing over the case study methodology.

SOURCE: Karl Nollenberger, "Cooperation and Conflict in Governmental Decision Making in Mid-Sized U.S. Cities," *2008 Municipal Year Book* (Washington, D.C.: ICMA, 2008), 9–15.

---

localities had a similar document. Sixty-seven percent of cities operated under the council-manager plan had developed a strategic plan, compared to 56 percent of mayor-council communities. Evelina Moulder also notes that a frequent criticism of strategic plans is that they "sit on a shelf."[12] Data from the ICMA survey suggest otherwise. Fifty percent of the cities with a strategic plan had revised their documents since the economic recession starting in early 2008. If strategic plans are intended to reflect current and future conditions, then, logically, they must be updated to reflect significant environmental changes.[13] Others would argue that the best way to make strategic plans more usable is to change how they are developed.

As part of the New Public Management reforms beginning in the 1980s, *strategic management* began to replace strategic planning as a process. Unlike strategic planning, which concentrates on making "optimal strategy decisions," strategic management focuses on strategic results—"more attention is paid to implementation because of the human factors present in the organization culture and affecting its management."[14] Owen Hughes, a major proponent of the NPM reforms, suggests that the strategic management model is more political in nature than strategic planning, since it is based on the assumption that one "must be cognizant of the exercise of political authority."[15] It also places a greater emphasis on awareness of those factors external to the organization (called "environmental scanning"), because it is guided by "an external perspective emphasizing not adapting to the environment but anticipating and shaping environmental change."[16]

The six steps of strategic management, as defined by Paul C. Nutt and Robert W. Backoff, include the following actions:

1. Depict the organization's historical context in terms of trends in its environment, its overall direction, and its normative ideas.
2. Assess the immediate situation in terms of current strengths and weaknesses and future opportunities and threats.
3. Develop an agenda of current strategic issues to be managed.
4. Design strategic options to manage priority issues.
5. Assess the strategic options in terms of stakeholders affected and resources required.
6. Implement priority strategies by mobilizing resources and managing stakeholders.[17]

Juxtapose, if you will, the steps involved in strategic management with the points in the more traditional strategic planning model outlined earlier. While the second, third, and fourth points associated with the strategic management model are similar to strategic planning, the first step and the last two steps are more much more political and contextual in nature, requiring that significant attention be paid to environmental scanning and stakeholders, both internal and external to the organization. Noting that "organizations have a history and a culture, both of which need to be considered in formulating strategy," Hughes claims that a real difference in the model "is in recognition of stakeholders and using them to implement strategy."[18]

Survey research reported in the *2002 Municipal Year Book* on the use of strategic planning at the local level suggests that a strategic management focus might improve the viability of plans.[19] The survey of appointed and elected senior officials in U.S. cities with 25,000 or more residents found that as part of the strategic planning process, a number of the municipalities had *not* evaluated internal strengths and weaknesses (41 percent), assessed external threats and opportunities (44 percent), or determined the feasibility of proposed strategies (63 percent). In short, as Gregory Streib and Theodore Poister observe, survey findings reveal that some municipalities use strategic planning "to help chart a clearer course and strengthen community ties without making direct linkages to ongoing management process."[20] As noted above, linking the planning process to the management process through environmental scanning and stakeholder analysis is one of the primary goals of strategic management.[21]

Strategic planning obviously involves an attempt to formalize a rational approach to decision making. But just how rational can the process be when problems are complex, information is scarce, time is limited, and various competing interests have a stake in the outcome? Even two of the most ardent supporters of strategic planning as a form of "anticipatory government" note its limitations. In their book *Reinventing Government*, David Osborne and Ted Gaebler note, "Strategic planning is the antithesis of politics. It assumes a thoroughly rational environment—something that never exists in government."[22]

Charles Lindblom agrees. He has argued for some years that the rational approach to decision making suffers from a number of limitations.[23] First, he believes that human intelligence—or problem-solving capacity—is too limited to encompass all of the options and potential outcomes of the alternatives generated by the rational approach. And, in any case, it is not possible to gather enough information to assess all options accurately. Furthermore, in Lindblom's view, comprehensive analysis requires too much time and is too expensive. Finally, he argues, facts and values cannot be neatly separated as required by the comprehensive approach. In fact, Lindblom insists, real decision makers recognize many of these shortcomings and invariably search for simpler, more realistic ways to solve problems.

INCREMENTALISM

Lindblom goes beyond a critique of the rational-comprehensive approach by offering an alternative decision-making theory that is variously called "incrementalism," "the science of muddling through," "successive-limited comparisons," and "decision making at the margins." Briefly, it includes these essential features:

- Goals are not isolated and determined before analysis begins. Goal determination and analysis are closely intertwined, even simultaneous. The means often affect the ends, and vice versa.
- Decision makers usually consider only a limited number of alternatives—ordinarily only those that differ marginally from existing policy.
- All consequences, even of the more restricted options, are not evaluated. All consequences cannot be known, and the time and effort required for comprehensive assessment normally are not available.
- Since means and ends are inseparable, problem redefinition is continuous; analysis is never-ending, and policy is never made once-and-for-all but is remade endlessly.[24]

Incremental problem solving enormously reduces the range of investigations undertaken by decision makers, and it greatly reduces the cognitive strain of comprehensive evaluation. Its basic assumption is that many public policy problems are too complex to be understood, much less mastered. Therefore, managers must search for strategies to cope with problems, not to solve them. If an issue is not resolved by the original solution, or if a new problem arises from the initial effort, it is dealt with at a later point.

Lindblom offers several arguments in behalf of the incremental approach. First, non-incremental decisions may be unpredictable in their consequences, especially if they represent a significant departure from existing policy. Second, errors are much easier to correct when decisions are successive and limited. Finally, incremental decisions are likely to be more acceptable politically than are the far-reaching changes that can result from comprehensive analysis.

Twenty years after publication of his original article, Lindblom proffered a reassessment of incrementalism entitled, "Still Muddling, Not Yet Through,"[25] in which he recommended some modifications and refinements but continued to support the basic approach. His follow-up treatise suggests a continuum of decision-making constructs, ranging from "grossly incomplete analysis" on one end to "comprehensive and scientific analysis" on the other (see figure 6-1). Although he continues to argue that comprehensive analysis is unattainable, in retrospect he contends that decision makers can aspire to something he calls "strategic analysis," which he defines as any calculated or thoughtfully chosen set of stratagems to simplify complex problems—that is, to shortcut comprehensive, "scientific" analysis. Lindblom insists that decision making can be improved by moving toward strategic analysis and away from ill-defined, makeshift problem solving. Yet even for complex problems, he thinks the use of formal analytic techniques—systems analysis, operations research, or computer modeling—should be focused on strategies rather than used as attempts at rational comprehension.

Decision makers in municipal government quickly learn that a variety of influences and interests affect a decisional outcome. Could (or should) a democracy be run any other way? Probably not. A recent case study of nonincremental policy change in Michigan's state-wide Medicaid managed-care program showed, for example, that while the "ambitious statewide effort to enroll all Medicaid clients in managed care succeeded in its goals," success came at a price—"namely, stakeholder dissatisfaction, mistakes, and lack of public involvement."[26]

Figure 6-1   **Lindblom's Continuum for Decision Making**

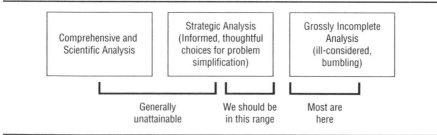

A few years after Lindblom's original attack on rationalistic decision making, sociologist Amitai Etzioni offered a widely cited critique of incrementalism.[27] Although he agrees with Lindblom that rational decision making has its limitations, Etzioni contends that incrementalism does as well. First, decisions made as the outcome of give-and-take among numerous groups necessarily reflect the interests of the most powerful; the demands of the underprivileged and the politically unorganized are usually underrepresented. Second, incrementalism does not provide any guidance or direction for organizational innovation or change—it is action without direction. Etzioni writes that even incrementalists recognize that the approach is not applicable to the process of making a large or fundamental decision, such as a declaration of war. And he insists that the number and role of far-reaching decisions are significantly greater than incrementalists admit.

MIXED SCANNING

To the rational and incremental approaches, Etzioni proposes an alternative—mixed scanning—that incorporates elements of both. He uses the analogy of a person with two cameras, one with a broad-angle lens to capture the big picture and a second with a telephoto lens that can zero in on the details overlooked by the first. Etzioni does not reject incrementalism's concern for minor changes at the margin, but he does insist that periodically, at least, an all-encompassing scan of the larger situation should be undertaken to avoid straying too far from some wanted objective.

Etzioni's defense of mixed scanning identifies quite a few instances in which the approach seems to operate. One example he mentions is the court system, where higher courts (like higher executives) reserve for themselves the fundamental decisions and expect the lower courts to practice incrementalism.[28]

Mixed scanning is an attempt to combine the best features of both rational and incremental decision making. Yet it remains essentially a compromise between the rational and incremental approaches, with few guidelines for how and when it should be employed.

THE GARBAGE-CAN MODEL

A model that moves beyond Lindblom's incrementalism reflects an even stronger sense of nonrationality. The "garbage-can model" contends that the rational approach and even incrementalism depict a decision-making world that is unrealistically coherent and orderly, that both methods err in assuming too much certainty and knowledge in decision making. In reality, most decision-making situations are plagued by ambiguities of all sorts: objectives are unclear; organizational preferences are not ordered; causality is obscure; attention and participation of key actors are uncertain; and outcomes are unknown.[29] In metaphorical terms, the garbage-can model views a choice opportunity as "a garbage can into which various problems are dumped by participants. The mix of garbage in a single can depends partly on the labels attached to the alternative cans; but it also depends on what garbage is being produced at the moment, on the mix of cans available, and on the speed which garbage is collected and removed from the scene."[30]

Michael Cohen, James March, and Johan Olsen, the organizational theorists who developed this model, call the situation "organized anarchy"[31] and say that decisions are made essentially in one of these three ways: by oversight, without any attention to existing problems and with a minimum of time and energy; by flight (or avoidance), postponement, or buck-passing; or by resolution, which occurs generally only when the flight option is severely restricted or when problems are relatively minor or uncomplicated.[32]

According to the garbage-can model, oversight and flight dominate organizational decision making. Jay Starling agrees, and his analysis of decision making in Oakland, California, offers considerable support for this approach.[33] Starling observes that decision makers discard the tactics of avoidance and delay only when forced to do so by great need or compelling circumstance. Then, they generally make only limited responses, based on routine, past experience, and training, and even these more active tactics often include selecting courses of action that appear ambiguous to outsiders, are readily reversible, or both.

One final word about the garbage-can model. The name does not imply that decisions made are "garbage" or necessarily bad; even successful organizations make decisions in this rather haphazard way. Instead, the garbage-can model may merely reflect the nature of large-scale organizational *culture*, which is, in turn, "intangible, rarely written down or discussed but still a potent force in shaping and controlling [organizational] behavior: it is an observable and palpable phenomenon, reflected in the shared philosophies, ideologies, myths, values, beliefs, assumptions, and norms of the organization."[34]

Now that we know various *approaches* to decision making, we should look inside the urban manager's decision-making "toolbox," to find helpful methods and practices that can be employed to make "better"—that is, more efficient, effective, responsive, and/or equitable—decisions.

DECISION-MAKING TOOLS

Urban managers are, above all, problem solvers: managing problematic situations means making tough choices among alternative solutions. Resources are limited, time is crucial, alternatives may be hazy, and objectives may be ill-defined, but decisions must be made. The process can be reactive, erratic, and unpredictable—leading to muddling through rather than a rational choice among clearly defined options. Both public and private managers have long searched for ways to improve the management process, and so have developed a variety of tools—both quantitative and nonquantitative aids—to help the urban executive to make more effective decisions.

QUANTITATIVE AIDS

According to Theodore Sorenson, decision making is not always a highly rational process: "Decision-making is not a science but an art. It requires, not calculation, but judgment."[35] Still, as Etzioni and others suggest, analysis may help. Indeed, a wide body of business management literature is devoted to the tools and techniques that assist managers in making better decisions. Many of these tools are complex, but we can briefly review several basic techniques that are applicable and useful to both public and private decision making. For example, both payoff matrices and decision trees are simple graphic displays that lay out alternative decisions and likely outcomes.

The Payoff Matrix

The *payoff matrix* is a way of displaying choices and results to make a simple decision. For example, assume that a city is planning to construct a new swimming pool; how big a pool should it build? Prospective swimmers will want it to be as large as possible, but too big a pool would cost more than the city should spend. Although this type of facility is rarely expected to pay its way, taxpayers should not be expected to provide too large a subsidy. But a small pool, though cheaper to build and operate, would not meet the likely demand. The payoff matrix shown in figure 6-2 depicts the two possible choices—building a large pool or building a small one—and the results of those choices, consisting of the four possible outcomes based on the two choices and the two levels of use. If a large pool is built and heavily used, everyone will be satisfied; if a large pool is built and usage is low, the city will incur excessive costs. If a small pool is built and usage is low, again everyone will be satisfied; but if a small pool is built and used heavily, the swimmers will not be happy and the city will not receive as much revenue as it would have if it had built the larger pool.

The Decision Tree

As a part of formal decision theory, decision trees are based on *utility theory*, which assigns numerical values to decision-makers' preferences, and *probability theory*, which assigns numbers in accordance with the likelihood that certain events will occur in the future.[36]

We can see how a *decision tree* works by adding some financial data to our swimming pool problem. First, we must consider the probabilities associated with the use of the pool. Assume that the city manager consults with the parks and recreation director. Together they arrive at estimates of usage based on the potential growth of the area to be served and

Figure 6-2   **A Payoff Matrix**

		Possible outcomes	
		Low Usage	High Usage
Choice	Large pool	Swimmers happy; income low, costs high	Swimmers happy; income high, costs high
	Small pool	Swimmers happy; income low, costs low	Swimmers unhappy; income low, costs low

the usage of other city pools. They may use such qualifiers as "probably" and "less than likely" in their estimates, or they may use more precise terms, such as "a 60 percent likelihood" or "a 60 percent chance."

By applying such numerical probabilities to the swimming pool decision, we can create a *decision tree* (see figure 6-3). Again, there are two basic choices: building a large pool for $300,000 or building a small one for $150,000. Customarily, boxes represent decision points in a tree diagram, while the circles, or nodes of the tree, depict possible choices, in this case based on level of usage. Probabilities for level of use in terms of each possible choice are shown along the lines of each branch of the tree. In this case, the manager and the recreation director estimate the probability of high usage with a large pool at .6, or a 60 percent chance. If a small pool is built, they figure that there is a 70 percent chance that low usage will result.

But what about costs and anticipated revenue under these various conditions? This information is shown to the right of the tree, where, for example, the annual income from high usage of a large pool is estimated at $40,000, whereas that from low usage is estimated at only $25,000. But the probabilities of usage must be taken into account to obtain the total estimated financial yield, as follows:

$$(\$40,000 \times .6) + (\$25,000 \times .4) = \$34,000$$

Applying the same procedure to the decision to build a small pool produces the following calculation:

$$(\$20,000 \times .3) + (\$15,000 \times 7) = \$16,500$$

Figure 6-3   **A Simple Decision Tree**

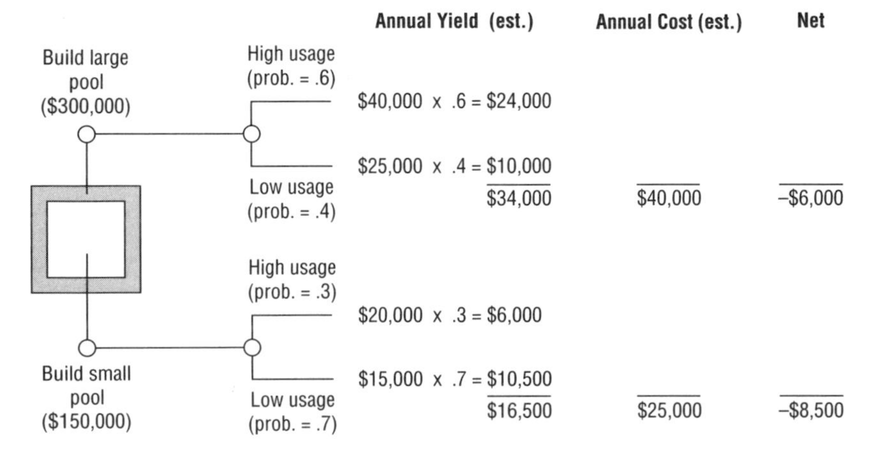

		Annual Yield (est.)	Annual Cost (est.)	Net
Build large pool ($300,000)	High usage (prob. = .6)	$40,000 x .6 = $24,000		
	Low usage (prob. = .4)	$25,000 x .4 = $10,000		
		$34,000	$40,000	−$6,000
	High usage (prob. = .3)	$20,000 x .3 = $6,000		
Build small pool ($150,000)	Low usage (prob. = .7)	$15,000 x .7 = $10,500		
		$16,500	$25,000	−$8,500

Notice that the probabilities, as well as the estimated revenue, are different for the small pool decision. When the estimated annual costs are figured in, we obtain the following results:

	Annual Revenue	Annual Cost	Net
Large pool	$34,000	$40,000	−$6,000
Small pool	$16,500	$25,000	−$8,500

In this case, the manager would recommend to the council that the large pool be built, because it would likely lose less each year than the small pool.

For purposes of illustration, we have kept this example quite simple. We could have added a middle option, in pool size and in usage. With each additional option, the branching would extend considerably.

Decision trees have obvious limitations: probabilities are only estimates based on human judgment, and quantifying individual preferences is always a tricky business. Still, the form can help decision makers to be more precise in their calculations and to think more carefully about a series of options and possible consequences. As James Vaupel argues, "The phrase 'an 80 percent chance,' even if it only means 'roughly an 80 percent chance,' conveys much more information than a sloppy, ambiguous term like 'probably,' which can mean anything from a 51 percent chance to more than a 90 percent chance."[37]

The payoff matrix and the decision tree are only two fairly unsophisticated examples of the many quantitative techniques designed to help decision makers; later, we discuss some more complex models, such as program analysis and benefit-cost analysis.

NONQUANTITATIVE AIDS

As Herbert Simon reminds us, we should keep the potential usefulness of quantitative aids in perspective: "Many, perhaps most, of the problems that have to be handled at middle and high levels in management have not been made amenable to mathematical treatment, and probably never will."[38] In such cases, various nonquantitative aids are also available to aid the urban executive in choosing among alternative courses of action.

The Delphi Technique

The *delphi technique*, which originated as a tool for forecasting future events, combines two methods used by executives to gather information: the use of experts and the committee system. It generally requires the use of a panel of experts who are asked to respond anonymously to a survey instrument that includes a series of questions and statements regarding a particular problem. When the questionnaires are returned, the responses are tabulated by a steering committee, which then tries to clarify responses by editing existing items and adding new items to the list.[39] Then a second and, usually, a third wave of questionnaires are sent to the experts to get a greater consensus on the options being considered. In some cases, one best recommendation is sought; in other instances, only a ranking of options is desired.

The basic idea in use of the delphi technique is that experts may consider possibilities they had not thought of previously at the same time that they benefit from the views of other authorities. Preserving the panel's anonymity presumably avoids some of the negative consequences of committee activity, such as the bandwagon effect or the dominance of the group by one or two strong-willed members.[40]

The Scenario

A *scenario* is essentially an attempt to picture some future state of events by means of a written narrative. It requires projections of existing trends and predictions of future occurrences in whatever areas decision makers want to explore. One or more scenarios may be prepared by a group of experts and offered in several different versions. Sometimes the device is used in connection with other analytic techniques, particularly those of a quantitative nature. The application of scenarios might work in this way:

> Scenarios could be used in developing and analyzing transportation policies or transportation systems. Starting with various philosophical assumptions and introducing technological, social, political, economic, and physical factors and events, alternative urban futures could be developed. . . . These environments might depict the preferred or optimal urban future, the worst possible future, or both, and numerous other futures in between. Various policies and systems could then be tested in terms of their effectiveness in achieving the optimal future.[41]

PROGRAM ANALYSIS AND OTHER SYSTEMATIC APPROACHES TO DECISION MAKING

Most of the decision-making aids considered here—both quantitative and non-quantitative—were developed either in defense-related enterprises or in the private sector. Some are more suitable for the public sector than are others. Regardless, today's economic environment requires measuring results and performance and making decisions that enhance efficiency; public managers are under ever more pressure to adopt private-sector models and methods. Analysis is the name of the game, and a host of systematic decision-making methods are available to the modern manager.

Program analysis is one such method for improving public decision making. By providing a means of systematically comparing alternatives in the light of their costs and consequences, this approach can help decision makers to choose among possible courses of action. As a methodology, program analysis is a form of *systems analysis*, which itself is more "a mosaic [of methods] than a specific analytical technique."[42] Often, "managers and analysts use the terms 'systems analysis,' 'policy analysis,' 'cost-benefit analysis,' and others, almost synonymously."[43] For our current purposes, we use the definition of systems analysis offered by Michael E. Milakovich and George Gordon: any "analytical technique designed to permit comprehensive investigation of the impacts within a given system of changing one or more elements of that system."[44] This definition seems to closely match our discussion of systems theory as outlined in the first chapter.

The purpose of most analysis is to provide a scientific basis for choosing among the alternative actions available to decision makers, thereby reducing much of the confusion and uncertainty associated with organizational decision making.[45] Although, as noted earlier, the two terms most commonly used to describe this process in the public sector are sometimes used interchangeably, *policy analysis* is more often applied to fairly broad or complex problems involving a variety of external interests and groups (such as revising a city's general planning document), while *program analysis* is more limited in scope, referring to a narrower problem with fewer external actors (such as deciding where in the city to build three government-subsidized rental houses). We should also note that program analysis is not the same as program evaluation: analysis attempts to project what may happen at some future time if certain choices are made; evaluation assesses how effectively a particular program, already implemented, has met its intended objectives.

THE ANALYSIS PROCESS

Any form of analysis involves a series of steps, or component actions. Although the components displayed in schematic form in figure 6-4 may not be observed unfailingly in every instance, the analysis procedure generally includes the following steps:

1. Clearly defining the *problem* or need
2. Stating the specific *objectives* being sought
3. Identifying *constraints* that could limit the proposed courses of action
4. Identifying and describing the key features of the various *alternatives* for attaining the objectives
5. Devising appropriate *selection criteria* for choosing among the alternatives
6. *Analyzing* the alternatives and *selecting* the best alternative according to the accepted criteria
7. *Implementing* the selected alternative
8. *Evaluating* the results and determining the extent to which the objectives have been attained; providing *feedback* to previous steps and revising if necessary[46]

Defining the Problem

Defining the problem may seem to be the easiest part of analysis, but this is seldom so. Just as in decision making, where often the most difficult task is to secure consensus concerning the goals or objectives of a program, the most difficult step in program analysis may be defining the need to be met. Three experimental studies involving the ICMA demonstrate that urban officials have a tendency to generalize problems, making it difficult to state needs in a sufficiently specific form for analysis purposes.[47] Where local

Figure 6-4   **Components of Analysis**

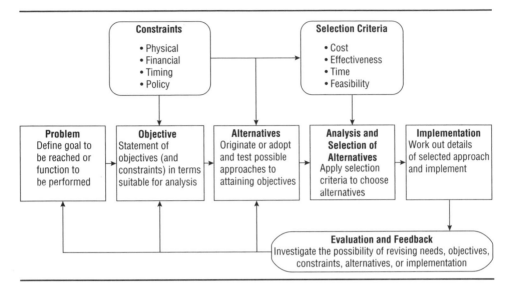

SOURCE: Adapted from "Introduction to Systems Analysis," by J. K. Parker, Appendix C to *Applying Systems Analysis in Urban Government: Three Case Studies* (Report prepared by the International City Management Association for HUD, March 1972), 5. Reprinted by permission.

government does not have staff expertise in program analysis, outside experts may have to be employed to assist in defining the problem.

Because the task of problem formulation is difficult and obviously crucial to what follows—a solution to the wrong problem cannot be of much help—an issue paper may be prepared. An issue paper is as complete of an assessment of all that is currently known about the problem or issue as the readily available data allow.[48] It may include the following kinds of questions:

- What are the sources of the problem? What forces are contributing to it?
- What is the magnitude of the problem? How many people or groups are affected? What will the problem's dimensions be in the future?
- Which specific groups (clientele) are affected by the problem? If other than the general public, what are the special characteristics (age, minority status, geographic location, income, education level) of the affected groups?
- Which other groups or agencies—particularly public ones—are working on the problem?
- Does the problem have political overtones?

An issue paper can go beyond problem definition to include objectives, evaluation criteria, alternatives, and recommendations for follow-up action. But its primary purpose is to present the dimensions of the problem carefully thought through and stated in terms amenable to analysis.

Whether or not an issue paper is prepared, a problem must be defined as specifically as possible. For example, the generalized problem that a community has too little housing for low- and moderate-income families might be stated in more specific terms as the goal or objective of constructing 1,500 standard-quality rental housing units each year.[49] Or, if the general problem is a rising crime rate, the stated objective might be to reduce serious juvenile crimes by 20 percent within a two-year period.

We should make two other points about problem definition. First, it is essential that the problem be one that is under the control of the city government. Although this may sound obvious, it is not always taken into account. For example, the general problem of unemployment in the city may not be something the city government by itself can realistically undertake to correct. Second, problem definition is a responsibility of top management and should not be left to technical specialists. This is not to say that analysts cannot help; experienced analysts can be of considerable value to decision makers in narrowing and identifying a problem. But the final definition must rest with top officials.

The following are examples of issues or problems that could be treated successfully with program analysis as a form of systems analysis:

- What is the most effective way of deploying limited police personnel? By geographic location? By time of day? By reported crime incidence?
- How many fire stations are needed? Where should they be located?
- What mix of health treatment programs is needed to serve a particular clientele?
- What specific equipment and routing should be used in the collection and disposal of solid waste?
- What type and size of recreation facilities should be provided, and where should they be located in the community?[50]

Stating the Objectives and Constraints

In the second step, the problem or need is converted into a set of measurable objectives that, when met, presumably will solve the problem. Statements of public policy objectives are likely to be vague and conflicting,[51] so they must be translated into goals that are specific enough to be measurable, ordinarily in quantitative terms. Some possible objectives are these:

- Reducing traffic fatalities by 10 percent
- Reducing the average response time of a fire company by 10 percent
- Increasing the reading comprehension level of students finishing elementary school by 20 percent
- Reducing the number of complaints of missed garbage collection by 30 percent

Clear, straightforward formulations of objectives, such as these, develop from analysts' experience or from extensive discussion with decision makers and others knowledgeable about the topic. It is very important that objectives do not predetermine which alternative will be used to deal with the problem. Whether means and ends can be effectively separated in complex problems is debatable; still, an objective should say nothing about the means to be used in achieving the end.

At this point in the analysis, more specific consideration of the needs of client groups is necessary. If program analysis is to be sensitive to the political environment, which may well determine just how effective its outcome will be, particular attention must be paid to those who will benefit and those who potentially stand to lose from the program effort. Jacob Ukeles, former director of the Mayor's Management Advisory Board in New York City, refers to this process as *client analysis*. He argues that groups should be differentiated by the degree to which they are likely to be affected by a decision: "Trade-offs are constructed on the basis of the net benefits and losses to the most highly impacted groups."[52] Among other possible benefits, this focus on the differential effects of programs may bring to the analysts' attention groups that are not particularly vocal in the political arena. Client analysis should be a continuous process, and it should begin in earnest at the point of specifying objectives. Citizen surveys, discussed in the next chapter, can serve as a useful aid in collecting information from clients.

Constraints also must be considered at this stage. Such factors as time limits, finances, and physical conditions, as well as the restrictions imposed by past policies, must be taken into account. How much time is available, both for the analysis and for the implementation? What kinds of personnel needs will be involved? What is the budget, both for the analysis and for the problem resolution? Will new or remodeled physical structures be necessary? Do past municipal policies or commitments limit this particular administration? All these considerations must be fed into the analysis at the time the objectives are established.

Generating Alternatives

Various potential courses of action must be developed within the existing constraints. How do analysts develop alternatives? There are a number of possible sources: guidance from top officials, brainstorming, consultation with other municipalities that have faced the same problem, discussion with governmental departments knowledgeable in the area, suggestions from interested community groups, professional literature, and suggestions from vendors and suppliers. For example, if the objective is to reduce juvenile car theft, analysts might develop alternatives by consultation with the police department; with officials in the courts, in the welfare department and other social service agencies, and in the school system; and with the juveniles themselves.[53]

Developing Selection Criteria and Analyzing Alternatives

After a sufficient number of alternatives have been generated, each must be evaluated using appropriate criteria. This is a fairly straightforward step, which involves assessing each alternative's probable performance against each criterion and comparing the alternatives with one another on the basis of performance against the criteria. At least four broad criteria are found in any analysis program: effectiveness, cost, time, and feasibility.

To gauge *effectiveness*, we must devise measures that reveal how well an alternative achieves a program's objective. For example, does it increase the health and safety of citizens? Does it improve the condition of the streets? Does it increase citizens' satisfaction with recreational opportunities? In developing measures of program effectiveness, an analyst may select workload measures of physical capacity or change: tons of garbage collected, number of clients served, number of hospital beds filled, acres of park land. These indicators can be useful as a first step in assessing governmental performance, but they provide little or no information about effectiveness—how well a program's objectives are being met or how satisfied citizens are with public facilities and activities. The following factors are some potential measures of urban service effectiveness:

- *Public safety measures*: average police response time; crime rates; crime clearance rates; number of traffic accidents, injuries, and fatalities; average response time for first-arriving fire company; and fire loss, including dollar value of property, injuries, and fatalities
- *Public health measures:* communicable disease rate; infant mortality rate; air-quality standard
- *Public works measures:* missed garbage collections per total collections; cleanliness of streets; smoothness of streets
- *Leisure and recreation measures*: circulation of library books and number of persons participating in recreational programs per 1,000 population[54]

Estimates of *costs* are essential in evaluating alternatives. This sounds simple: just add up the costs of personnel, materials, and overhead. Unfortunately, however, analysis incorporates several kinds of costs—opportunity costs, indirect costs, and capital versus operating costs, to name a few. Some guidelines for figuring the costs of an alternative are these:

- Separate capital from operating expenses. Where capital costs are necessary, they may have to be prorated over a period of several years.
- Identify both direct and indirect costs. Indirect costs are easy to overlook, but expenditures for staff support, fringe benefits, maintenance, and usage of space should be included in the total cost.
- Omit sunk costs—costs that have been previously incurred. In this regard, analysis differs from strict cost accounting.
- Consider funds required over a multiyear period to obtain a complete picture of an alternative's cost commitment.
- Indicate the source of funding. An alternative may be paid out of several identifiable sources, such as state or federal project grants. Some types of funds are easier to obtain than others.[55]

Opportunity costs and external costs are important. The use of resources in a particular way precludes their use for some other purpose. Thus, forgone opportunity costs must be estimated. Although not a perfect measure, one way of measuring opportunity costs, particularly for developmental policies where the city has funds to invest, is to compare the return to the city from a project with the return on the funds if they had been invested otherwise—say, in a pension fund. At a minimum, the true cost of a multiyear project must be calculated. It is not true, for example, that a $100,000 project that generates $10,000 per year will pay for itself in ten years.

Before an assessment of options is complete, some effort can be made to relate costs to benefits. If dollar figures can be assigned to all costs and all benefits, a benefit-cost ratio can be calculated. Often, genuine benefit-cost analysis is beyond the capability of city staffs because it requires a greater knowledge of applied economics than these staffs have. (We discuss this issue at greater length in a later section.)

The final two criteria for evaluating alternatives are *time* and *feasibility*. Time can be thought of as a cost, of course. Beyond that, some options may take considerably longer to meet the objective than will others. This factor is especially important if public officials are under pressure to produce quick results.

Considering feasibility means carefully assessing potential veto points along the way to implementation. For example, who has to agree to this proposal? Which groups will oppose the alternative? Will the city council buy this solution? Which political pitfalls await this option? The best solution imaginable is of no value if it cannot be implemented. (The political feasibility of a project is so important to its success that we consider it in a separate section at the end of this overall discussion of the analysis process.)

Implementing the Selected Approach

Whenever possible, a pilot implementation of a preferred alternative should be tried before the solution is adopted on a continuing or permanent basis.[56] Where this is not feasible, the alternative should be implemented on a careful, planned basis, with constant monitoring and evaluation. Implementation does not follow automatically once a policy has been formulated; it is often difficult and frustrating, full of pitfalls.

Analysis can help to uncover potential pitfalls by identifying the issues and problems that may affect the implementation of a selected alternative.[57] Among the questions to be asked in this context are these:

- How many agencies (internal and external to the city) must participate or cooperate to ensure successful implementation?
- Does the selected alternative visibly affect certain clientele groups in an adverse way? (Is there a cutback in services, for example?)
- Does the alternative threaten the power or privileges of important officials? Are employees' jobs threatened? If so, what reaction might be expected from employees' organizations?

- Are there complicated legal questions?
- To what extent has public debate galvanized opinion for or against the alternative?[58]

Because analysts often fail to appreciate the potential implementation difficulties that may arise when a new program is undertaken, some authorities suggest that municipalities prepare an *implementation feasibility analysis*. The problems of implementation are not overstated; the lack of concern for implementation feasibility is a primary cause of unsuccessful program analyses.

Evaluating and Providing Feedback

One of the final steps in the analysis process is the careful, continuous evaluation of the implemented alternative. Is the program alleviating the original problem? Analysis does not stop at implementation; it is a dynamic process that requires ongoing assessment of consequences. The feedback arrows in figure 6-4 graphically convey this notion. In fact, an iterative approach is a basic characteristic of analysis for policy decisions. "If none of the alternatives originally considered can achieve the goals, further alternatives must be sought and, if that fails, the goals must be reexamined and possibly lowered."[59]

ANALYSIS AND POLITICAL FEASIBILITY

Although feasibility was identified as one of the critical criteria for evaluating alternatives, the preceding discussion did not do justice to its enormous significance. At first glance, it may sound simple enough to consider who might or might not support a given policy option or what group might have enough power to block a particular course of action. But the history of program analysis clearly reveals otherwise; the primary reason many programs never see the light of day is not poor technical quality but lack of political feasibility. Arnold Meltsner, a specialist in the study of policy analysis, argues that one of the difficulties in considering political feasibility is the lack of a convenient methodology. He offers a three-step approach, as follows.[60]

The first step requires *determining the relevant environment*. The analyst begins by defining a policy space or policy issue area. An issue area goes beyond what the need or problem is to include the publics and actors that dominate this area. If the issue area is economic development, for example, community financial interests certainly have to be taken into account. Or, if the city is interested in private collection of solid waste, the group most clearly affected is the municipal employees who might lose their jobs.

The second step in determining political feasibility is *organizing political information*. Meltsner recommends the paper-and-pencil scenario as an organizing device. As we noted earlier, preparing a scenario of the future is more an art than a science; it requires speculation and conjecture based on the best knowledge available. The task can be made easier, however, by developing a set of basic categories about which information is needed: actors, motivations, beliefs, resources, sites, and exchanges.

- *Actors* are the individuals, groups, and coalitions most likely to be affected by and interested in the policy problem. At first, three groups are likely to appear: friends, enemies, and fence-sitters. Soon, the dynamics of the process push fence-sitters to take sides. Some actors, of course, have much more to gain or lose than others, but it may not be easy to determine just how strong the concerns of particular actors are.
- What are the *motivations* of the various policy actors? What do they really want? What will they settle for? What will it take to mobilize a fence-sitter? The problem here is that the more a clever political actor can mask his or her policy preferences, the better his or her bargaining position will be in many cases.
- Closely related to an actor's motivations are *beliefs, values, and attitudes*. People perceive the political world through a particular frame of reference or belief system, which may be encapsulated in a few dominant phrases, such as "local control" or "the advantages of competition."
- Almost every policy actor possesses something another actor may want. These incentives are considered *resources* and are used to satisfy another actor's motivations. Resources range from the material (such as a job with higher wages) to the symbolic (such as appointment to a prestigious committee). Information and even political skill might be among the resources available to some policy activists. The analyst must try to determine which specific resources the skillful actor may use to gather support and build coalitions.
- Meltsner mentions the *site* for the final decision as another important element in political analysis. He is referring not only to the arena (such as a city council committee) but also to the location in time.
- Finally, we come to *exchanges*. The analyst must predict or estimate likely outcomes based on all the information available. In particular, he or she must identify the possible areas of agreement or conflict so that alternative proposals that will achieve the requisite political support can be considered. From this perspective, developing alternatives implies anticipating the sorts of coalitions that are likely to form around a particular option. Such coalitions are built mostly through a series of exchanges— side payments, trade-offs, or policy modifications. The analyst tries to ascertain what exchanges might be needed to produce a certain outcome. Which group wants what? How much will this group accept? How much political support from certain actors is critical for success? Nothing is exact here; the analyst must rely on experience and judgment, while hoping that most of the relevant facts have been collected.

The third and final step in the assessment of political feasibility is to *incorporate the knowledge of the political process* into the analysis itself. How should this be done? Much depends on the local situation, of course, but two general possibilities exist. The analyst may make a decision based on quantitative or economic reasoning and then modify that answer in the light of political considerations. The more difficult but also probably more effective strategy is to introduce politics at each stage of the analysis. Thus, the analyst would consider political feasibility in problem definition, in identification of alternatives, and in the recommendation of preferred policy alternatives.

ANALYSIS APPLICATIONS

Analysis does not have to be highly sophisticated to be useful. All too often, students of urban management and practitioners steer clear of analysis because they have heard terms such as "beta coefficients," "the linear model," "factor analysis," "time-series analysis," and so on. But, although many statistical techniques can take a while to learn, there are many more that can be mastered fairly quickly with a bit of patience and practice. For example, former city official and current professor of public administration and government David N. Ammons presents over thirty analytical techniques that can be used to solve real-world, everyday urban issues and problems in his book, *Tools for Decision Making: A Practical Guide for Local Government*.[61] These analysis tools range from graphic techniques—such as demand analysis, Program Evaluation Review Technique (PERT), and Critical Path Model (CPM)—to work-flow and work measurement methods (such as work-distribution analysis, using performance standards) to making comparisons (cost-effectiveness analysis, lease/buy analysis, calculating "go-away" costs for privatization decisions, and so on). In addition, discussion of each technique is grounded in an example, and, for many of the decision-making tools, a "how-to-do-it electronically" feature using a popular spreadsheet (Microsoft Excel) is offered. Box 6.2 presents a case study, adapted from Ammons's book, which illustrates the kind of analysis that takes place every day across urban America.

A more advanced type of analysis is *benefit-cost analysis*. Although few municipalities except the very largest are likely to undertake a formal, full-blown benefit-cost study, it is not unusual for this type of analysis to appear in studies done by outside consultants. And the method has long been applied to certain large-scale public improvements, especially water resource projects. Therefore, local public managers need to know something of what is involved in producing a benefit-cost study. In essence, the analysis calls for the calculation of a ratio that reflects the relationship between all foreseeable benefits and all known and estimated costs. If the benefits exceed the costs, presumably the project is worth pursuing; if not, a strong argument can be made against the undertaking.

Although, in theory, benefit-cost analysis seems functional, in practice it generates a number of problems. At least two basic limitations of this method are generally acknowledged.[62] First, the process can become subjective, especially where a number of intangible benefits accrue to the proposal: omit these potential benefits and the ratio may be badly biased; include them and you risk being arbitrary. Analysts, then, must use common sense in deciding what to include, especially in regard to potential benefits. A second problem relates to the issue of who pays the costs and who receives the benefits. It is very difficult to incorporate allocational and distributional considerations in benefit-cost analysis. For

---

BOX 6.2   Policy and Practice

CALCULATING A STAFFING FACTOR

Many of the services provided by local governments are not limited to a 40-hour-per-week operation. The municipal pool may be open 56 hours per week. Police and fire services must be provided around-the-clock, 168 hours per week. In order to determine the number of employees needed to fill a position to provide extended-hour or uninterruptible service, taking into account vacations, sick leave, holidays, and so forth, a "staffing factor" must be calculated. The staffing factor is the number of employees needed to provide full coverage of a position.

You are a policy analyst in the parks and recreation department. The city manager wants to know how many lifeguards are going to be needed to staff the new indoor municipal pool. You are told that there must be two lifeguards on duty at all times and that the pool will be open 8 hours per day, 7 days a week, year-round. A full-time lifeguard will receive one week of paid vacation and 5 days of sick leave per year; part-time lifeguards will receive the same benefits, prorated on the basis of number of hours worked. To avoid overtime pay, the assumption is that no employee will work more than 40 hours per week. How many lifeguards do you need?

The first step in the calculation of the staffing factor is based on the formula

$E = P - A$

where E = the number of hours actually worked by the average employee (that is, effective hours), P = the number of paid hours per employee per year, and A = the average number of hours of paid absences per employee per year (vacation, sick leave, and so on). In the example above, P = 40 hours per week × 52 weeks per year = 2,080. A = 40 hours of vacation and 40 hours of sick leave = 80. E = P − A = 2,000.

The second step uses E above to calculate the staffing factor:

$$\text{Staffing Factor} = \frac{\textit{Hours per year of operation}}{E}$$

From information supplied to you, hours per year of operation = 8 hours per day × 7 days a week × 52 weeks a year = 2,912.

$$\text{Staffing Factor} = \frac{2,912}{2,000} = 1.45$$

In order to staff one of the lifeguard positions, one full-time and one approximately half-time employee, or an equivalent combination of part-time employees, will be needed to provide extended, uninterrupted service. But because two lifeguards must be on duty at all times, you need the equivalent of 2.90 employees, or

$$\text{Staffing Factor} = \frac{\textit{Hours per year of operation}}{E}$$

16 hours per day × 7 days a week × 52 weeks = 5,824 hours

$$\text{Staffing Factor} = \frac{5,824}{2,000} = 2.90$$

SOURCE: This case is adapted from information and formulas provided by David N. Ammons, *Tools for Decision Making: A Practical Guide for Local Government* (Washington, D.C.: CQ Press, 2002), chapter 20.

example, if a proposal involves a redistribution of income, a straightforward summation of costs and benefits does not reveal the true impact of the project.

A quick example involving deregulation illustrates some of these problems.[63] A few years back, the National Highway Traffic Safety Administration (NHTSA) announced that it intended to either eliminate the front-bumper crash standard for automobiles or lower it from 5 miles per hour to 2.5 miles per hour. As a justification, the agency cited benefit-cost studies showing that scrapping the bumper standard would save consumers about $65 over a ten-year period, the result of increased gas savings from lighter cars. But the NHTSA's calculations omitted, among other things, an almost certain rise in auto insurance premiums if such a change were made. According to one insurance company, the $65 supposedly saved with lighter bumpers would end up costing $110 in increased insurance premiums over a five-year period.

The moral of this story, and the appropriate caveat for local decision makers, is that benefit-cost studies must be scrutinized carefully to ensure that all possible benefits and costs are included in the analyses.

GEOGRAPHIC AND MANAGEMENT INFORMATION SYSTEMS: FRIENDS OF ANALYSIS

Accurate analysis demands accurate information. But not only is information costly; it also is not easily available. Obtaining reliable, continuous, and systematic information for problem solving requires a conscious effort to develop an information-gathering process or system. It is little wonder that "information has become the lifeblood of government in the digital age."[64]

The terms electronic data processing (EDP) and automated data processing (ADP) generally refer to the same practice: the use of computers to process certain kinds of information. At a higher level are information systems, of which there are two basic types: the urban information system (UIS) and the management information system (MIS). The UIS essentially represents a data bank of wide-ranging information covering the city (or metropolitan area) as a whole; its primary purpose is to assist in planning and community development. Such a system may include a variety of census data, including some at the block level, and a multitude of items collected by the city on a geographic basis.

Geographic Information Systems

A type of UIS that is growing in popularity is the geographic information system (GIS), a computerized mapping system that aids in spatial analysis. As Boyce Thompson points out, "When you consider that at least 80 percent of the information collected by local governments relates back to a particular location, the management promise of GIS comes into sharper focus."[65] In Brevard County, Florida, a GIS is used to display parcels of land, roads, water and sewer lines, zoning, and topography. In addition, county officials can use the GIS for other management purposes. A point on the map can be accessed; and the road maintenance schedule can be determined. Decision makers employ GIS technology to optimize school bus routes and fire substation siting, to redraw political boundaries at reapportionment time, and to map the outbreak of diseases.

In a 1995 assessment of the use of geographic information systems in local government, Stephen Ventura notes that GIS vendors' reports and recent studies suggest that GIS adoption is "proceeding at a rapid rate."[66] But, in many cases, the use of GIS technology is limited to map query and/or geographic display applications and is not integrated into a broader information *analysis* and *management* system. In the cities that have integrated their GIS with other information communication technology (ICT), Ventura argues:

> a 'new way of doing business' seems to be emerging. GIS and related technologies have created the need for new structures for using information and new relations within and between agencies. GISs have provided the basis for 'one stop shopping'—services and products from many departments or agencies through a single point of contact. Local government can become more accessible, more efficient, and more effective if GIS is used as a means to such ends, not as a goal itself.[67]

More recently, two nationwide surveys were conducted in 1999–2000 to assess the use of geographic information technology (GIT) at the local level.[68] GIT includes three "distinct but increasingly integrated forms of technology": *geographic information system* (GIS), *global positioning system* (GPS), and *remote sensing*. The first two forms of technology are fairly straightforward. Remote sensing involves "methods of obtaining data about an object or environment that rely on a sensor that is not in contact with that object or environment. Such methods include satellite imagery, aerial photography, and use of other airborne data collection instruments."[69] The response rate (12 percent) to the national "imagery survey" was low, and the findings offered should be viewed as preliminary. The other national survey was a "coordination survey" sent to a targeted cluster of GIS users involved in interorganizational relationships. Of the 529 surveys mailed, 245 were completed and returned, for a respectable 46 percent response rate.

Results of the imagery survey suggest that "few local governments have taken advantage of these emerging technology resources. Much of this technology and data have not been made accessible in forms useful to local government, nor have most local governments had the capacity to use them fully."[70] Survey results do validate, however, the suggestion of previous studies that *planning and development* is the leading application of GIT in local governments: 76 percent of respondents indicated that they use imagery or a GIS or both for planning. GIT applications were also used in general and financial management (such as property tax assessment), public works and utilities (such as road construction and maintenance, rights-of-way management and maintenance), environmental and natural resources (such as parks management, pollution abatement), public safety and management (such as vehicle and hazardous material routing, services and facilities siting), and, to a lesser degree, human, health, and social services (such as creating service delivery systems based on location of public assistance recipients, predicting disease incidence using socioeconomic and environmental data).

In terms of local government coordination of GIT applications, responses to the second survey show that local governments do share GIT data with each other. However, results also "disturbingly reveal . . . that a relatively low level of internal and interorganizational cooperation exists in local governments regarding GIT."[71] More complex forms of coordination are more likely to occur internally within a jurisdiction rather than among multiple organizations. Formal instruments such as memoranda of understanding, intergovernmental agreements, and contracts are frequently used to coordinate the sharing of GIT among organizations (70 percent). Internal cooperation arrangements use these techniques much less frequently (24 percent) and are more likely to use informal procedures such as mutual rules and procedures and department director policies. Finally, in a study of Dutch public organizations, Guido Vonk, Stan Geertman, and Paul Schot aver: "Some 25 years after the introduction of the first geo-information technologies in public organizations, strategies to manage their diffusion are still inadequate."[72] To ameliorate this condition, Vonk and his colleagues argue for a knowledge management approach in which geo-information specialists and planners collaborate in the development of diffusion policies.

Clearly, local government officials are at the dawn of a new day with respect to adopting, implementing, and coordinating GIT technologies within city departments and with surrounding jurisdictions. GIT technologies are costly not only in terms of initial purchase outlays but also in requiring expenditures for maintenance and training. Research also finds that, in addition to financial considerations, "human factors" play a significant role in the adoption of GIS systems. Specifically, perceived relative advantage—a tangible personal gain such as a salary raise or promotion or an intangible gain such as personal satisfaction—strong computer background and experience, exposure to GIS technology, and active networking are important predictors of employees' willingness to use GIS technology.[73] That human factors impinge on the decision to adopt *and* implement GIT applications is not surprising, for, as we discuss in chapter 9, people, not technologies, drive city government. Technology is simply a tool to be used by the human resources.

Management Information Systems

The second major type of information system, the management information system (MIS), is a tool for internal decision making and control. In the early 1980s, for example, the city of Dearborn, Michigan, installed a microcomputer system called Public Services Network, which incorporates twelve terminals located in agencies that handle requests for service. When an operator keys in particular information, the system routes the problem to the proper agency, eliminates duplicate requests, and permits the aggregation of data that reveal how much time was spent on each request. Thus, at budget time, Dearborn's deputy director of public works was able to say, "Mr. Mayor, of the 40,000 requests for service that we received, 27 percent went to Parks. And we can say unequivocally, last year we spent $100,000 for tree removal and $50,000 for utility maintenance."[74]

David Landsbergen and George Wolken note that over the past fifty years, computing technology has evolved from large vacuum-tube macrocomputers to personal, desktop computers that allow each person in a government agency to collect and store data.[75] But it is the *networking* of computers that excites Landsbergen and Wolken: "Theoretically, networking makes it possible for the information and processing power of all of these desktop, mainframe, and super computers to become available on each individual's desktop."[76] With networking, moreover, comes interoperability—the ability of systems to work together and share information. The benefits of interoperability are threefold: effectiveness, efficiency, and responsiveness. More *effective* government requires integrated policy approaches and leveraging of information, knowledge, and technology across agencies and/or governmental jurisdictions. Once data is collected and stored electronically, it can be duplicated and shared easily through networked computers, thus enhancing *efficiency*. Finally, better access to information allows government workers to act quickly to identify and respond to public issues and problems, thus enhancing *responsiveness*.

In fact, Landsbergen and Wolken argue that computer networking and interoperability facilitate current government reform efforts by "reducing rules and encouraging entrepreneurial managers who are now held accountable to goals and measures and given the freedom to devise ways to achieve those goals using their entrepreneurial talents, creativity, and *information* [emphasis added]."[77] They note, finally, that a number of issues involving political (privacy, statutory authority, openness to public scrutiny), organizational (trust, lack of experience, lack of awareness of opportunities to share information), economic (lack of resources, low-bid procurement requirements), and technical (hardware and/or software incompatibility, public or private property-rights issues, and data-sharing standards) factors affect interoperability.

Barry Bozeman and Stuart Bretschneider offer several guidelines to public users of MIS.[78] First, MIS planning should proceed incrementally, primarily because of the need to be sensitive to external control and political change. Second, public use of information technology should be designed to anticipate extra-organizational linkages; otherwise, MIS can become a small fiefdom of knowledge used by insiders to pressure top management. Third, the MIS chief should not report to the highest level in the organization. Top officials' focus on political cycles and quick results can undermine the long-term objectives of the system. Fourth, MIS should not generally be used to enhance managerial control, because such efforts will likely meet with resistance, which may diminish the value of MIS as a managerial tool. The fifth guideline argues that MIS should not be justified on the basis of labor savings; although sometimes marketed that way, such systems have not been shown to bring significant labor-reduction benefits. Finally, MIS planning must be sensitive to staffing problems, given that public agencies often do not fare well when competing with the private sector for highly trained specialists. Staffing will not take care of itself; personnel agencies must be aware of the special problems of recruitment and retention of MIS specialists.

We might also note that Yong-Mi Kim recently asked the following question: Do council-manager and mayor-council types of city governments manage information systems differently?[79] Based on data from 232 council-manager and mayor-council cities, he found no statistically significant differences between mayor-council and council-manager cities in funds budgeted to information systems (IS) expenditures and to the presence of an independent IS department by form of government. The logic was that if a city emphasizes IS work, the function would find an autonomous home and not be assigned to another department, such as finance or general administration. Kim did find statistically significant differences in information systems between mayor-council and council-manager municipalities in three areas. First, council-manager cities were more likely to employ advanced IS functions (such as, application development, maintenance, and systems planning and management) that could perform city work more efficiently. City-manager cities allocated a higher percentage of its budget to these higher-level IS applications than did mayor-council cities. Third, IS managers in city-manager cities have fewer "transaction costs" than their counterparts in mayor-council cities. Specifically, the IS manager in a council-manager municipality has fewer hierarchical levels to go through to secure approval for spending.

THE CONTRIBUTIONS AND LIMITATIONS OF ANALYSIS

Experience with a variety of local government analysis efforts over the years has taught the following lessons about conditions that affect the success of analysis:

- Commitment from top management is crucial.
- Financial support is needed; analysis is often expensive and usually requires the use of outside consultants.
- If consultants are used, the user organization must be prominently involved with the project.
- The selection and definition of the problem are extremely important; but even top-level officials frequently have trouble identifying quantifiable objectives and defining constraints.
- Projects that are narrowly defined and have few social or political implications are more likely to be successful.
- The availability of quality data, especially over time, is always problematic.
- A basic conflict inevitably develops between the analyst's concern for a complete study and the decision maker's need for immediate results.

Because of these many limitations and constraints, skeptics often charge that analysis is not as helpful as it could be. As former Cincinnati city manager William Donaldson put it, "The core problem in municipal government is not knowing what to do but being able to do it. . . . [T]he ability to implement is a much more difficult skill to acquire than having the ideas in the first place."[80]

Analysis cannot replace judgment, eliminate value conflicts, or preclude the bargaining and compromises associated with the political process. As one practitioner reminded us many years ago:

The ultimate solutions and decisions to most complex urban problems involve value judgments. They require decisions as to which problems are assigned what priority, as to the level of taxes that can and should be levied, and as to the allocation of available fiscal resources to such problems. There is no question that management science is helping governments concerned with their urban problems to identify and define them better. . . . . However, the final decisions about such problems involve judgments as to what is "best" for the people. Under our form of government, these are political decisions, and despite the development of management science they will remain so.[81]

Despite problems and limitations, analysis will play an increasing role in the urban future. Muddling through is not enough though.

In the final analysis, perhaps, the bane of analysis is resistance to change. As David Ammons notes, "Analysts who have devoted hundreds of hours to a project only to see their recommendations rejected are sure to feel disappointment."[82] As someone who has been there, Ammons suggests that disappointment is natural, but warns that failure should not lead to discouragement. Resistance to analysis will always come from those who benefit from current policies or from current operational inefficiencies; those who fear new technologies or new operational methods; those who are or feel incapable of applying or understanding the results of analytic techniques; and those who dominate the decision-making process through charisma or brokering abilities and prefer not to have that dominance threatened by the introduction of a new element in the process.[83]

No one said it was going to be easy. Change never is—and change lies at the heart of analysis. Fortunately, however, as this chapter suggests, an abundance of analytical tools are available to help decision makers manage urban America.

SUMMARY

Decision making is a complex activity, whether it takes place at the individual, organizational, or community level. Is it a rational process? This question has been addressed by a number of theorists from various disciplines. As a result, we have several models that purport to describe how decisions really are made. The rational-comprehensive approach, incrementalism, mixed scanning, and even the garbage-can model all have their defenders, and each has certain attractive features. Perhaps, as the incrementalists argue, most decisions do come about by virtue of habit, inertia, muddling through, or whatever. But even the father of incrementalism, Charles Lindblom, agrees that governmental decision making can and should be improved.

And help is available. A variety of tools, quantitative and nonquantitative, have been developed over the years to assist those who want to make decisions more rationally. The payoff matrix and the decision tree help decision makers to put alternatives into a more systematic perspective. Nonquantitative aids, such as the delphi technique and scenario writing offer ways of approaching decisions that can provide useful information to public officials.

Analysis is a response to the demand for more than an incremental approach to urban decision making; it is based on the rational-comprehensive decision-making model. Regardless of whether the particular method chosen is systems analysis, policy analysis, or program analysis, each operates with basically the same procedure: the problem must be defined, objectives must be stated clearly, constraints must be identified, alternatives must be proposed in the light of appropriate selection criteria, analysis and selection must take place, and the solution must be implemented. And the process does not end there, for the implemented program must be evaluated, so that feedback can lead to revision where necessary.

What should we conclude about the place of analysis in urban management? First, good analysis is hard to do, but worth the effort. Given the complex environment in which analysis must take place, there are many reasons to expect urban analysis to fail, but we must maintain the expectation that it will succeed. Second, analysis is likely to be more successful under some conditions than under others—basically, the easier the problem, the greater the chance of success. Third, political feasibility is particularly critical for public-sector analysis. The crucial factor in successful implementation may be the analyst's skill in deciphering the complex political environment in which problem solving takes place.

But analysis should not be abandoned. We know how fragmented and disjointed the urban policymaking process can be. Although some of this confusion may be unavoidable, any technique that can give decision makers a larger, more comprehensive picture is helpful. And the systems approach represents a step in this direction. On a more immediate note, the continuing pressure on public officials to get more results for the dollar surely demands that some problems be attacked on a rational, systematic basis. Analysis and geo-informational technologies are tools that help foster change.

SUGGESTED FOR FURTHER READING

Ammons, David N. *Tools for Decision Making: A Practical Guide for Local Government*. 2nd ed. Washington, D.C.: CQ Press, 2008.

Fleming, Cory, ed. *The GIS Guide for Local Government Officials*. Washington, D.C.: ICMA, 2005.

Meier, Kenneth J., Jeffrey L. Brudney, and John Bohte. *Applied Statistics for Public and Nonprofit Administration*. 7th ed. Belmont, Calif.: Thomson Wadsworth, 2008.

Weimer, David L., and Aidan R. Vining. *Policy Analysis*. 5th ed. Boston: Longman, 2011.

Wholey, Joseph S., Harry P. Hatry, and Kathryn E. Newcomer. *Handbook of Practical Program Evaluation*. 3rd ed. San Francisco: Jossey-Bass, 2010.

NOTES

1. See, for example, chapter titles in Donald F. Kettl and James W. Fesler, *The Politics of the Administrative Process*, 4th ed. (Washington, D.C.: CQ Press, 2009); and Grover Starling, *Managing the Public Sector*, 8th ed. (Boston, Mass.: Thomson , 2008).

2. Brian W. Rapp and Frank M. Patitucci, *Managing Local Government for Improved Performance* (Boulder, Colo.: Westview, 1977), chap. 16.

3. Ibid., 329.

4. John M. Bryson, *Strategic Planning for Public and Nonprofit Organizations* (San Francisco: Jossey-Bass, 1988), 5.

5. Robert B. Denhardt, "Strategic Planning in State and Local Government," *State and Local Government Review* 17 (winter 1985): 175.

6. These stages of the strategic planning process are modified from John J. Gargan, "An Overview of Strategic Planning for Officials in Small to Medium Size Communities," *Municipal Management* 7 (summer 1985): 162; also see Gregory Streib and Theodore H. Poister, "The Use of Strategic Planning in Municipal Governments," *2002 Municipal Year Book* (Washington, D.C.: ICMA, 2002): 18–19.

7. Denhardt, "Strategic Planning in State and Local Government," 176.

8. Gregory Strieb, "Applying Strategic Decision Making in Local Government," *Public Productivity and Management Review* 15 (spring 1992): 341.

9. Todd Swanstrom, "The Limits of Strategic Planning for Cities," *Journal of Urban Affairs* 9, no. 2 (1987): 139.

10. Gargan, "Overview of Strategic Planning," 166.

11. Evelina R. Moulder, "Citizen Engagement: An Evolving Process," *2010 Municipal Year Book* (Washington, D.C.: ICMA, 2010), 28.

12. Ibid., 29.

13. Ibid.

14. Owen E. Hughes, *Public Management and Administration*. 3rd ed. (New York: Palgrave Macmillan, 2003), 135–136.

15. Ibid., 142.

16. Ibid.

17. Paul C. Nutt and Robert W. Backoff, *Strategic Management of Public and Third Sector Organizations: A Handbook for Leaders* (San Francisco: Jossey-Bass, 1992), 152, as quoted in Hughes, *Public Management and Administration*, 143.

18. Hughes, *Public Management and Administration*, 143.

19. Streib and Poister, "Use of Strategic Planning in Municipal Governments," 18–25.

20. Ibid., 18.

21. Hughes, *Public Management and Administration*, 142.

22. David Osborne and Ted Gaebler, *Reinventing Government* (Reading, Mass.: Addison-Wesley, 1992), 235.

23. Charles E. Lindblom, *The Intelligence of Democracy* (New York: Free Press, 1965), 138–143.

24. These characteristics are adapted from ibid., 143–148; and Charles E. Lindblom, "The Science of 'Muddling Through,'" *Public Administration Review* 19 (spring 1959): 79–88.

25. Charles E. Lindblom, "Still Muddling, Not Yet Through," *Public Administration Review* 39 (November–December 1979): 517–526. Figure 6-1 is adapted from this article.

26. Carol S. Weissert and Malcolm L. Goggin, "Nonincremental Policy Change: Lessons from Michigan's Medicaid Managed Care Initiative," *Public Administration Review* 62 (March–April 2002): 210, 206.

27. Amitai Etzioni, "Mixed-Scanning: A 'Third' Approach to Decision-Making," *Public Administration Review* 27 (December 1967): 385–397.

28. Amitai Etzioni, "Mixed Scanning Revisited," *Public Administration Review* 46 (January–February 1986): 8–14.

29. Harold Gortner, Julianne Mahler, and Jeanne Nicholson, *Organization Theory: A Public Perspective*, 2nd ed. (Fort Worth, Tex.: Harcourt Brace, 1997), 239.

30. Michael Cohen, James March, and Johan Olsen, "Garbage-Can Model of Organizational Choice," *Administrative Science Quarterly* 17 (March 1972): 1–25, as quoted in Gortner, Mahler, and Nicholson, *Organization Theory*, 239.

31. Cohen, March, and Olsen, "Garbage-Can Model of Organizational Choice."

32. Michael Cohen and James March, *Leadership and Ambiguity* (New York: McGraw-Hill, 1974), 83–84.

33. Jay D. Starling, *Municipal Coping Strategies* (Beverly Hills, Calif.: Sage, 1986), 22–27.

34. Florence Heffron, *Organization Theory & Public Organizations* (Englewood Cliffs, N.J.: Prentice Hall, 1989), 212.

35. Theodore C. Sorensen, *Decision-Making in the White House* (New York: Columbia University Press, 1963), 10.

36. Jack W. Lapatra, *Applying the Systems Approach to Urban Development* (Stroudsburg, Pa.: Dowden, Hutchinson and Ross, 1973), 46.

37. James W. Vaupel, "Muddling Through Analytically," in *Improving the Quality of Urban Management*, ed. Willis Hawley and David Rogers (Beverly Hills, Calif.: Sage, 1974), 187–209.

38. Herbert A. Simon, *The New Science of Management Decision*, rev. ed. (Englewood Cliffs, N.J.: Prentice Hall, 1977), 63.

39. Kenneth L. Kraemer, *Policy Analysis in Local Government* (Washington, D.C.: ICMA, 1973), 127.

40. For an example of a delphi process in the strategic planning process of a city, see David R. Morgan, John P. Pelissero, and Robert E. England, "Urban Planning: Using a Delphi as a Decision-Making Aid," *Public Administration Review* 39 (July/August 1979): 380-384.

41. Kraemer, *Policy Analysis in Local Government*, 131.

42. Starling, *Managing the Public Sector*, 290. See also Harry P. Hatry, "Can Systems Analysis Be Institutionalized in Local Government?" in *Systems Analysis for Social Problems*, ed. Alfred Blumstein, Murray Kamrass, and Armand B. Weiss (Washington, D.C.: Washington Operations Research Council, 1970), 52–79.

43. David I. Cleland and William R. King, *Systems Analysis and Project Management*, 3rd ed. (New York: McGraw-Hill, 1983), 83.

44. Michael E. Milakovich and George J. Gordon, *Public Administration in America*, 8th ed. (Belmont, Calif.: Thomson Wadsworth, 2004), 175.

45. Richard Rosenbloom and John Russell, *New Tools for Urban Management* (Boston: Graduate School of Business Administration, Harvard University, 1971), 6–7.

46. These steps are modified slightly from John K. Parker, "Introduction to Systems Analysis," in *Applying Systems Analysis in Urban Government: Three Case Studies* (Report prepared by the International City Management Association for HUD, March 1972), Appendix C, 4–10; and E. S. Savas, "Systems Analysis—What Is It?" *Public Management* 51 (February 1969): 4.

47. Parker, "Introduction to Systems Analysis," 3.

48. E. S. Quade, *Analysis for Public Decisions* (New York: American Elsevier, 1975), 69.

49. Adapted from Carter Bales and Edward Massey, "Analyzing Urban Problems," in Rosenbloom and Russell, *New Tools for Urban Management*, 280.

50. Taken from Harry Hatry, Louis Blair, Donald Fisk, and Wayne Kimmel, *Program Analysis for State and Local Governments* (Washington, D.C.: Urban Institute, 1975), 16–17.

51. Quade, *Analysis for Public Decisions*, 103.

52. Jacob Ukeles, "Policy Analysis: Myth or Reality," *Public Administration Review* 37 (May–June 1977): 227.

53. Parker, "Introduction to Systems Analysis," 7–8.

54. For a lengthy list of local public-service measures, see Robert Lineberry and Robert Welch Jr., "Who Gets What: Measuring the Distribution of Urban Public Services," *Social Science Quarterly* 54 (March 1975): 700–712. Also see Harry Hatry, Louis Blair, Donald Fisk, John Greiner, John Hall Jr., and Philip Schaenman, *How Effective Are Your Community Services?* 2nd ed. (Washington, D.C.: Urban Institute and ICMA, 1992).

55. Bales and Massey, "Analyzing Urban Problems," 286–287.

56. Parker, "Introduction to Systems Analysis," 9.

57. Quade, *Analysis for Public Decisions*, 259.

58. Adapted from Hatry et al., *Program Analysis*, 100–101.

59. Quade, *Analysis for Public Decisions*, 20.

60. This section is adapted from Arnold J. Meltsner, "Political Feasibility and Policy Analysis," *Public Administration Review* 32 (November–December 1972): 859–867.

61. David N. Ammons, *Tools for Decision Making: A Practical Guide for Local Government.* 2nd ed. (Washington: D.C.: CQ Press, 2008).

62. Michael J. White, Ross Clayton, Robert Myrtle, Gilbert Siegel, and Aaron Rose, *Managing Public Systems: Analytic Techniques for Public Administration* (North Scituate, Mass.: Duxbury, 1980), 292.

63. This example comes from "Tales from the Cost-Benefit Wonderland," *Consumer Reports,* June 1981, 338.

64. Guido Vonk, Stan Geertman, and Paul Schot, "New Technologies Stuck in Old Hierarchies: The Diffusion of Geo-Information Technologies in Dutch Public Organizations," *Public Administration Review* 67 (July/August 2007): 745.

65. Boyce Thompson, "The Dazzling Benefits (and Hidden Costs) of Computerized Mapping," *Governing,* December 1989, 43.

66. Stephen J. Ventura, "The Use of Geographic Information Systems in Local Government," *Public Administration Review* 55 (September–October, 1995): 462; see also Jeffrey L. Brudney and Mary M. Bowen, "Do Geographic Information Systems Meet Public Managers' Expectations?" *State and Local Government Review* 24 (spring 1992): 84–90.

67. Ventura, "The Use of Geographic Information Systems in Local Government," 467.

68. Timothy Haithcoat, Lisa Warnecke, and Zorica Nedovic-Budic, "Geographic Information Technology in Local Government: Experience and Issues," *2001 Municipal Year Book* (Washington, D.C.: ICMA, 2001), 47. A 2002 large-scale ICMA survey focusing on local e-government initiatives reports that fully 63 percent of the responding 2,969 jurisdictions use GIS technology; see Evelina R. Moulder, "E-Government: Trends, Opportunities, and Challenges," *2003 Municipal Year Book* (Washington, D.C.: ICMA, 2003), 45.

69. Ibid.

70. Ibid., 56.

71. Ibid., 57.

72. Vonk, Geertman, and Schot, "New Technologies Stuck in Old Hierarchies," 745.

73. Zorica Nedovic-Budic and David R. Godschalk, "Human Factors in Adoption of Geographic Information Systems: A Local Government Case Study," *Public Administration Review* 56 (November–December 1996): 554–567.

74. Quoted in Steven Vignet, "Computers and Productivity," *Public Productivity Review* 8 (spring 1994): 76.

75. David Landsbergen Jr. and George Wolken Jr., "Realizing the Promise: Government Information Systems and the Fourth Generation of Information Technology," *Public Administration Review* (March–April 2001): 206–218.

76. Ibid., 207.

77. Ibid., 208.

78. Barry Bozeman and Stuart Bretschneider, "Public Management Information Systems: Theory and Prescription," *Public Administration Review* 46 (November 1986): 475–487.

79. Yong-Mi Kim, "Do Council-Manager and Mayor-Council Types of City Governments Manage Information Systems Differently? An Empirical Test," *International Journal of Public Administration* 26 (Issue 2), 2003.

80. William V. Donaldson, "Donaldson on Policy Analysis," *The Bureaucrat* 10 (fall 1981): 57.

81. Reprinted from Matthias E. Lukens, "Emerging Executive and Organizational Responses to Scientific and Technological Developments," in *Governing Urban Society: New Scientific Approaches,* ed. Stephen Sweeney and James Charlesworth (Philadelphia: American Academy of Political and Social Science, monograph no. 7, 1967), 121.

82. Ammons, *Tools for Decision Making,* 221.

83. Ibid., 4.

CHAPTER 7　URBAN SERVICE DELIVERY

Good urban management depends on well-trained personnel, sound decision-making practices and valid analytical techniques. And this is particularly true when it comes to the key role of local governments—the development of programs and the delivery of services. Providing services has always been a major function of local governments, but in recent years governments have directed an even greater concern on service delivery, as budgetary pressures have forced city officials to reshape or end programs and to find ways to operate more efficiently.

Some of the most vital services provided by any level of government are the responsibility of municipalities, and these activities consume a great deal of urban managers' time and attention. Urban service delivery is not particularly exciting—collecting and disposing of solid waste, repairing streets, and providing water are not among the most dramatic events in the life of a city. But cities are more concerned than ever with issues of service efficiency and accountability, as they find themselves caught between strong opposing pressures. Municipalities must respond to all the problems that arise from an advanced state of urbanization even as they face shrinking resources, severe fiscal limitations, and public resistance to higher taxes.

In this chapter, we look at several characteristics of service delivery, beginning with the basic issues that cities must confront in providing even routine services. As we see, more is involved than just economy and efficiency. Citizens want city services to be responsive to their demands, and they also expect that services will be distributed in an equitable fashion. How do cities assess their service performance? How do they implement and evaluate new programs? What alternative service arrangements are being employed?

GOALS FOR SERVICE DELIVERY

Municipal experts are in wide agreement on four essential goals for urban service delivery: efficiency, effectiveness, equity, and responsiveness.

Efficiency involves maximizing output from a given amount of input or resources. How much does it take to obtain the intended result? Efficiency is a process-oriented concept that assesses how inputs are converted into outputs; it says nothing about the degree to which goals are achieved or about citizen reaction to the service being provided.[1]

Effectiveness, in contrast, is concerned with objectives; it reflects the extent to which goals are being met. It is a results-oriented concept focusing on how closely the desired outcome is being fulfilled, without regard for the cost involved or resources used.[2]

Equity has many dimensions. Service goals may include equal opportunity for the same level of service, equality based on how much one pays in taxes for services, or similar results or outcomes. These issues are discussed in detail later in the chapter.

Responsiveness is the goal of meeting citizens' demands and expectations for services that are provided by the city government. This is always a tall order, but many city governments work hard to provide responsive service delivery. We also discuss this effort later in the chapter.

Cities often attempt to achieve more than one of these goals in their service-delivery plans. As a national survey of solid-waste disposal and recycling policies shows, innovations in service delivery can address efficiency, effectiveness, equity, and responsiveness through one approach. The case study presented in box 7.1 thus reflects the multiple goals of many urban service programs.

Surveying the research on urban service delivery, one can surmise that these broad goals can be examined in many ways. Public management scholar David Ammons, for example, groups urban service research into four categories:

1. Inventories of service-delivery systems, which examine the nature and quality of urban services (effectiveness) or the approaches used to manage or deliver services (efficiency), such as intergovernmental or private-sector contracting.
2. Studies of service-delivery patterns, which tend to focus on the politics and socioeconomics of service delivery (responsiveness and equity) by examining the impact of factors such as political structure, leadership, and community demographics on the distribution of city services.
3. Analysis of the mechanics of managing services, which includes studies of the tools that can be used to deliver services, such as reinventing, reengineering, Total Quality Management (TQM), and volunteerism (efficiency and effectiveness).
4. Evaluation of service delivery, which focuses principally on the cost and quality of service delivery strategies, such as police patrols or contract arrangements (efficiency and effectiveness).[3]

Clearly, a study may cover several service-delivery goals while analyzing the same research. We begin our discussion by examining efficiency and effectiveness as goals for urban services.

MEASURING EFFICIENCY AND EFFECTIVENESS OF URBAN SERVICES

How do cities measure the efficiency and effectiveness of public services delivered? The private sector uses a variety of standard measures of performance: profit, sales, return on investment, and so on. There are far fewer commonly accepted measures of municipal performance to tell managers, political leaders, and citizens how city services are faring. Two reasons have been suggested for the general absence of municipal performance measures: that much of what cities do to improve the quality of community life is intangible, and that

BOX 7.1   Policy and Practice

CASH FOR TRASH?

Facing growing budget deficits and concerns about the environmental impact of excessive waste, many cities across the country are beginning to make their citizens put up cash to dump their trash. Proponents of such Pay-as-You-Throw (PAYT) policies—which forgo tax-based financing of trash collection in favor of variable rates that citizens pay based on the quantity of waste disposed—claim that there are many benefits to the program. Consistent research on the subject has lauded such policies for their potential to reduce solid-waste collection and disposal costs for the community, reduce the volume of waste generated by households, and increase the levels of solid-waste recycling and composting.

PAYT is just one of a number of tools governments have pursued that seek to take advantage of market forces to achieve environmental objectives. Other recent examples include investment tax credits for recycling, deposit-refund programs for beverage containers and batteries, pollution shares, emissions trading, carpool lanes, and so on.

But the question remains, do the PAYT policies truly have the desired impact of creating more environmentally friendly communities? Results so far have been mixed: some community studies have shown no change in waste disposal or recycling behaviors, while others have found dramatic improvements. The reasons for this inconclusiveness, according to David H. Folz and Jacqueline N. Giles, are that studies of single jurisdictions or small numbers of communities are not sufficient for constructing an accurate analysis of PAYT policies across the country, and that the literature reflecting this scattershot approach fails to satisfactorily address the success or failure of PAYT independently. These authors attempted to fill that gap in the literature by constructing an empirical analysis of PAYT usage nationwide. Using data from a national survey of cities with solid-waste recycling programs, they measured the effects of PAYT policies on outcomes—household waste disposal behavior (tons of solid waste disposed per household per year in a community), recycling behavior (mean tons of recyclable materials collected per household annually), and recycling diversion (the percentage of the total municipal solid-waste stream diverted from disposal by local recycling).

Folz and Giles discovered that there are three main types of PAYT policies implemented by local governments: (1) customers may be required to purchase approved bags, tags, or stickers that are to be affixed to containers set out for curbside pickup; (2) customers may subscribe to a waste-collection service level that varies in price based on the number or size of the containers used in curbside pickup; or (3) collection crews may actually weigh the solid waste disposed at curbside and charge customers based on this information.

The authors find that these PAYT policies have a significant independent effect on the amount of waste disposed per household: adopting such policies results in a mean reduction of 1.16 tons of solid waste disposed per household per year, regardless of other recycling program features or demographic characteristics. In addition, they found that households recycle about three hundred pounds more per year, on average, in cities with PAYT policies—thus confirming that PAYT is an incentive for households to recycle greater quantities of materials.

The final dependent variable examined by Folz and Giles was the diversion rate—the percentage of the total municipal solid-waste stream diverted from disposal by local recycling. This data offers further support that PAYT policies help to boost recycling in a community, when controlling for the effects of the type of recycling participation, the level of citizen support for the program, and other demographic characteristics. Cities with PAYT have a mean level of recycling diversion that is about 2.49 points higher than in cities without

(continued)

BOX 7.1   Policy and Practice (continued)

such policies. That means, for example, that a city with a mean recycling level of 26.4 percent could expect to see an increase to about 29 percent, regardless of other factors, by adopting PAYT policies.

The authors conclude that in PAYT cities, households generally dispose of less solid waste and recycle more, regardless of other policies or demographics. These policies also lead to a greater level of waste diversion through recycling. As a result, trash pickup will most likely be more efficient, as a reduced load can lead to longer routes and fewer personnel needed for the job. Also, landfill life will be extended because of the lower rate of waste coming in. Recycling programs will also be more effective. All these environmental impacts of greater recycling and less waste disposal are positive goals for which communities should strive.

SOURCE: David H. Folz and Jacqueline N. Giles, "Municipal Experience with 'Pay-as-You-Throw' Policies: Findings from a National Survey," *State and Local Government Review* 34 (spring 2002): 105–115.

political leaders resist the establishment of measures that constituents might use to hold them accountable.

Cities do rely on some urban service indicators. *Input measures*, for instance, specify the level of resources committed to a particular activity. In the police service, these indicators might include the number of full-time officers assigned to an area or the number of patrol cars available during a designated period of time; in the field of public works, they could take the form of tons of asphalt used, cubic yards of concrete poured, or gallons of paint sprayed. Input measures are often criticized because they may bear little relation to output or level of performance, but they are useful to administrators who need to show that all neighborhoods are receiving approximately equal resources or treatment. Input measures can prove valuable, then, when issues of equity arise.

Closely related to input measures, are *workload indicators*, which are probably the most widely used yardsticks of service delivery. These measures are often reported in terms of the sheer quantity or volume of service provided, although such simple workload totals—tons of garbage collected, number of arrests, gallons of water treated—tell us very little. If we create a ratio, however, we obtain more useful information: the number of cases cleared per number of arrests or the number of books circulated per 10,000 people. Most efficiency measures are also ratios: they relate the amount of service output to the input required to produce it. Efficiency measures often take the form of amount of output per worker-hour (the number of tons collected per worker-hour) or per dollar expended (the number of gallons per dollar). Efficiency measures are a useful way to compare performance over time or even between jurisdictions, where comparable information is available.

But efficiency measures do not indicate the extent to which the goals and objectives of a program are being met. For this we use effectiveness measures, or service quality/outcome measures, such as police call-response times or the frequency of preventive police patrols. These measures can also reflect the extent to which unintended adverse consequences occur or gauge the degree of public satisfaction with services.

Measures of productivity can also be used to assess service adequacy. Generally, productivity embraces both efficiency (number of tons of garbage collected per person-hour) and effectiveness (number of citizen complaints about refuse not collected). Productivity measures, then, are not distinct from efficiency and effectiveness measures—productivity indicators attempt to include measures of efficiency and effectiveness. An emphasis on productivity encourages the use of multiple measures, rather than a single indicator, to evaluate service quality.

In a flow chart, the measurement process might look like this:

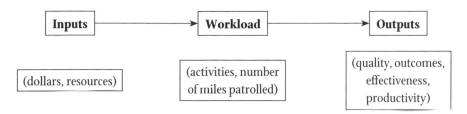

BENCHMARKING

Another method of establishing appropriate efficiency and effectiveness standards for municipal services involves comparison to practices in other cities. Whereas a great deal of attention is often given to "best practices," the ability to have a benchmark with which to compare your city's services to others can be an important tool in gauging performance.[4] Sometimes it is difficult to acquire comparative data on service performance in other cities, although survey research and online questionnaires have helped to increase the availability of such data. A common source of survey research information is *The Municipal Year Book*, published and augmented with datasets by the ICMA.[5] David Folz recommends that a city first establish a "quality of service framework for municipal services" and then select "best practice" cities, municipalities that have demonstrated exemplary performance, to serve as benchmarks of performance.[6] A new study of eleven services across forty-six cities recommends that comparison of service performance be carried out by means of "data envelopment analysis" (DEA), a method of efficiency measurement that is used to predict the most outputs that can be derived from the lowest level of inputs.[7] DEA has been used to study the practices of private firms and has recently been applied to analysis of service performance by governments.

PERFORMANCE MEASURES

Most authorities recommend that cities rely heavily on available information, at least in their initial effort to improve performance measuring and reporting. This practice has the obvious advantage of minimizing costs and the paperwork burden associated with information gathering, but it is unlikely that existing departmental records will be sufficient to provide the range of measures needed. In particular, indicators of quality, including citizen satisfaction, are not apt to be readily available. At the same time, it is important to recognize that performance measurement can become burdensome if we do not exercise some selectivity in choosing measures. Obviously, every aspect of a program cannot be measured, but more information may be available for measurement purposes than is generally recognized. The enduring research of scholar Harry Hatry [8] points to four sources of performance information:

1. *The inspection of physical features* may be used to supplement input measures or workload indicators. For example, in addition to calculating tons of waste collected, a city might evaluate street cleanliness. Washington, D.C., has tested procedures for doing so: trained observers inspect randomly selected streets and alleys within the city and then rate street cleanliness against a set of photographs depicting different degrees of cleanliness.

2. *Sample surveys* of community residents may used to gauge consumer satisfaction, the level of citizen participation, and public perception of employee courtesy. Although random-sample citizen surveys are the best methods for surveying residents, online surveys are becoming a common way to solicit opinion. Surveys can point out distortions in the picture that local officials may receive if they rely exclusively on complaint records or personal contact with interest groups or selected citizens. Surveys also can identify the proportion of service users and non-users, as well as the reasons for nonuse.

3. *Linking records* involves tracing governmental clients through one or more agencies to assess the effects of several related services. Hatry suggests, for example, that more data linkages among the police, the courts, and the correctional system would benefit all parties. Linked records were used to study the process by which cases involving neglected and dependent children in Nashville were adjudicated. The flow of children through the juvenile system was traced from the point of entry, through various short-term holding facilities, to the courts. The data were used to evaluate delay times as well as the apparent quality of care.

4. By *recategorizing* existing data in certain ways (by geographic subdivision, by economic class, by educational background), it may be possible to identify the impact of the program on selected neighborhoods or other clientele groups. This process allows the service agency to address more specifically the needs of targeted groups. Collecting service data by geographic area, for instance, is a must for efforts to improve equity.

USING MEASUREMENT DATA

Measuring the quality and effectiveness of municipal services can be useful in the following areas: program planning and budgeting, management operations, program analysis and evaluation, establishing performance targets, establishing employee incentive programs, and improving citizen feedback for governmental decision making. [9]

Program Budgeting

Effectiveness measures are indispensable to program budgeting, and this may be their principal application in cities that employ such budgeting systems. These measures can reveal which service areas are not meeting objectives and help to identify problem areas or areas that deserve high priority for resource allocation.

Service effectiveness data by themselves may not indicate why conditions are below expectations or what to do in those cases, but analysis of these data can point the way toward remedial action. In particular, citizens' ratings of various services—recreation, library, and transit, for example—may reveal that facilities are not being used because people are not aware of them. This information can prompt a city to consider ways to increase awareness.

Management Operations

Effectiveness data can be an important supplement to other information used by administrators for making decisions and allocating resources. These data must be collected more frequently when they are to be used for operational purposes rather than for annual program planning and budgeting. Where performance measures are available on a weekly or monthly basis, they may help to identify problems, modify priorities, or bring about reassignment of personnel. For example, street cleanliness ratings can be used to establish assignments of street-cleaning crews and equipment. Or, if daily water-supply tests reveal an excessive content of dangerous chemicals, personnel can be assigned to take immediate action. Where information is available by service district, the relative performance of district personnel can be monitored and changes made where necessary.

Program Analysis and Evaluation

Program analysis focuses on alternative courses of proposed governmental action; *program evaluation* concentrates on the effectiveness of current programs. For both processes, performance data are mandatory. We should observe, however, that regular effectiveness measurement does not replace the need for either of these activities. Instead, it is an essential ingredient in carrying out analysis and evaluation.

Establishing Performance Targets

One way to ensure that effectiveness measures make a difference in municipal operations is to establish performance targets, which allow management to monitor continuing progress toward specific objectives. These targets also give employees a goal, and they may even encourage innovation. Performance targets might be incorporated into a formal Management by Objectives (MBO) system, in which objectives are set and progress is determined by using a set of efficiency and effectiveness measures.

Establishing Employee Incentive Programs

Performance measures can become a significant part of employee incentive programs for managerial and nonmanagerial personnel. It is important that these measures be comprehensive so that employees are not encouraged to emphasize certain activities at the expense of others. For example, in some public schools, performance bonuses are provided to teachers and administrators if students achieve predetermined targets on state standardized tests or graduation rates. The New York City Department of Education implemented such a program in 2007–2008. Although the $3,000 incentive per employee proved to have little impact on student performance in the first year, the city chose to continue the incentive to assess its more long-term effects.[10]

Improving Citizen Feedback

Performance measures can stimulate more and better citizen feedback in two ways. First, the collection of certain qualitative information virtually requires citizen surveys. If collected properly, this information should be far more representative of community feelings than data on complaints or the limited personal observations of employees and officials. Second, the nature of the information is much clearer to the average citizen than are the commonly used workload measures. And an increased understanding of what government does could prompt more citizen involvement in local public affairs. This notion obviously assumes that performance indicators will be a featured part of any annual progress report made to the citizenry by city officials.

PROBLEMS IN USING PERFORMANCE MEASURES

Michael Lipsky's classic study of urban bureaucracy leads him to question the usefulness of performance measurements.[11] He argues, first, that job performance, especially that of street-level bureaucrats who exercise much discretion in their work, is extremely difficult to measure; objectives are ambiguous if not conflicting, and too many external influences affect performance. Second, he says, it is not even apparent that measured increases or decreases signal better or worse performance. Crime statistics illustrate this difficulty best: do increases in arrest rates represent improved police performance, or do they reflect deteriorating police performance in the face of increased criminal activity?

Third, Lipsky notes that bureaucrats change their behavior in response to what is being measured. This phenomenon was first highlighted by sociologist Peter Blau, who observed that employment counselors shifted their attention to the more easily employed at the expense of those more difficult to place—the practice is called "creaming"—when a system was implemented to evaluate their performance on the basis of placement rate. Lipsky insists that such behavior takes on the property of a general rule: Behavior in organizations tends to drift toward compatibility with the ways the organization is evaluated. Finally, he asserts that too many measures do not really reflect service quality.

In fact, he says, emphasis on quantity or even efficiency may have adverse consequences for service quality. Lack of concern for service quality can produce a "debasement of service," a situation that may infuriate the public if workers are given pay raises based on falsely credited productivity improvements.

If Lipsky's arguments are correct, should a city abandon all efforts to measure urban services? Probably not, but local officials certainly should keep these issues in mind as they consider whether and how to institute performance measurement. At the least, great care must be taken in fashioning a measurement program designed for municipal personnel whose positions allow great discretion and latitude in judgment.

IMPROVEMENTS IN EMPLOYEE PERFORMANCE

Enhancing productivity often focuses on improving employee performance, either by creating incentives that entice employees to put forth greater effort or by finding more efficient methods (technologies) of task performance. We examine the second strategy in the next section; here we look at the first, motivation.

What is the relationship between motivation and productivity? Daniel Yankelovich had been interested for some time in the changing work ethic in America. He points to a Gallup study done for the U.S. Chamber of Commerce, which concluded that large reservoirs of potential exist among workers and that managers can draw on these reservoirs to improve performance and increase worker productivity.[12] It seems that workers have the potential to be more productive, and—as many surveys show—they are willing to be more productive; yet most admit that they do not work as hard as they could. Why not?

According to Yankelovich, the fundamental answer is to be found in the existing reward system. Two factors seem to be involved here. First, there is the misdirection of financial rewards. Again, Yankelovich cites the Gallup survey: when workers were asked who they thought would benefit if their productivity were to improve, only 9 percent felt that they (the workers) would benefit; most assumed that consumers, managers, or even stockholders would reap the rewards. Clearly, then, one reason employees do not work harder or more effectively is that they see little chance of personal gain from the effort. The second factor is psychological—how workers are treated on the job. Again in the Gallup survey, when asked if they would work harder and do a better job if they were more involved in decisions relating to their work, 84 percent of the workers replied affirmatively. According to Yankelovich, the fundamental problem of productivity in our society lies "in the deeply flawed reward system, both psychological and financial, that now rules the American work place."[13] Therefore, our examination of motivational incentives must focus on two forms: monetary and nonmonetary.

Monetary Incentives

Money continues to have a powerful effect on human behavior, as it should. Public-sector employees should be rewarded for hard work. Thus we find a growing interest in using monetary incentives as a means of increasing motivation and stimulating greater output on the part of municipal workers.

Osborne and Gaebler argue fervently in *Reinventing Government* that individuals and, especially, groups of employees should receive personal bonuses based on their performance.[14] They also believe that public employees should be allowed to keep organizational productivity or budgetary savings for agency use. In Visalia, California, for example, employee groups get to keep 30 percent of productivity savings. The city's mechanics decided that they needed new tools, but no revenues were available to purchase them. After cutting energy consumption in the shop through various cost-saving activities, the mechanics were allowed to keep their percentage of the budgetary savings and use it to buy their new tools.

Nonmonetary Incentives

Programs involving nonmonetary incentives are designed to meet employees' needs for growth and development on the job or for more leisure time. A five-year study by Families and Work Institute, a New York–based nonprofit organization, adds to the growing evidence that workers are less willing to sacrifice for work and are putting more emphasis on their personal lives. "Workers are most willing to work hard and care about the success of their company [and the quality of their work] when they have good relationships with their supervisors, do not have to choose between work and their personal responsibilities and feel they have an opportunity to advance."[15] Employers can enhance productivity and loyalty, according to the research, by providing workers with flexibility, control, and a quality working environment. Such nonmonetary incentives can be structured in a variety of ways.

Job enrichment involves making work more interesting for workers and improving the quality of organizational life. Included in this category are *team participation*, to encourage cooperation and provide a more comprehensive view of the work process; *job redesign*, to give the employee greater control over how a task is done or responsibility for completing an entire piece of work rather than one segment of a task; and *job rotation*, to give the worker the broad experience that can increase understanding of the interrelatedness of various parts of the organization and to reduce boredom.[16]

The *quality circle* (QC) stresses employee involvement. It assumes that people will contribute useful suggestions for improving work methods and be more concerned about the quality of their work if they directly participate in decisions affecting their jobs. The QC concept, generally attributed to the Japanese, has become widespread in American industry as well as in the public sector. As we discuss in the next chapter, quality circles, or their equivalent, are an integral component of Total Quality Management (TQM), which, in the vernacular of reinventing government, allows organizations to be "customer-driven."

Flexible work schedules continue to be popular, but the use of this incentive may not be expanding as some had predicted. In the early 1990s, more than 20 percent of the total labor force was engaged in flextime or job-sharing.[17] But, according to a recent report by the Society for Human Resource Management (SHRM), fewer employers are now allowing flextime. The SHRM survey found that whereas "access to flex time soared from 29 percent to 43 percent between 1992 and 2002, . . . a survey of nearly 500 companies in 2005, however, showed a decline."[18] Flextime allows workers to set their own hours within a framework that meets the needs of the organization. Job-sharing allows an individual to work less than a normal (usually forty-hour) work week and share the position with another individual who also desires to work less than full-time. These two programs are particularly useful to individuals in meeting the needs of their dependents or in general to give workers more control of their lives and schedules. Research suggests that flextime has positive effects such as increasing morale and productivity and at the same time reducing absenteeism and tardiness.[19]

Performance targeting essentially means making explicit to workers, either individually or as a group, the type and level of performance expected from them over a specific time period.[20] Performance targeting is customarily incorporated into more comprehensive systems for directing and evaluating employee performance, such as MBO or TQM. Performance targeting helps to motivate employees to perform more efficiently or effectively by providing them with specific targets, objectives, or quotas to meet.

Dependent-related activities are growing in importance, in part because as many as two thirds of new entrants into the American workforce are women.[21] Discounted child-care programs, dependent-care accounts that set aside pretax dollars for child care, parental leave, and cafeteria-style benefits programs are important to members of both sexes, but especially to women. A mother who is divorced, for example, may choose additional days of paid leave instead of health insurance if her children are covered under their father's health care policy.[22]

TECHNOLOGICAL IMPROVEMENTS

Many authorities believe that substantial increases in municipal productivity are likely to come primarily from increased use of new technologies—which is how, historically, the great gains in output have been achieved in industry and agriculture. Municipalities represent fertile ground for the application of new technologies, because most city functions are labor-intensive. At the same time, many operations involve the use of hardware and equipment that lend themselves to change and innovation. For example, both GIS (Geographic Information Systems) and GPS (Global Positioning Systems) are technologies that have allowed municipalities to improve performance for locating, dispatching, and monitoring public employees and vehicles. And the data collected from these systems is used to analyze and model newer approaches to the organization of service delivery.[23]

Over the past several decades, a number of equipment improvements have been made in the areas of firefighting and solid-waste collection. Although these improvements often result in cost savings and productivity gains, they may also produce labor-management tension when workers perceive technological change as a threat to their jobs. A classic representative case is the city of Little Rock, Arkansas, where new labor-saving procedures and equipment were introduced without employee involvement or input.[24] Previously, a four-member crew had operated from each truck, picking up garbage at the rear of each house. Based on recommendations from outside consultants, however, management unilaterally adopted a new side-loading truck, the Shu-Pac, which could be operated by a single person, the driver. Sanitation workers, angry that this drastic change had been made without consulting them, refused to use the new trucks. Communications between labor and management virtually ceased, and the workers went out on strike. The dispute was eventually resolved, and sanitation department improvements resulted in annual savings of over $366,000. Still, city officials learned a valuable lesson in the politics of technological innovation.

Many cities have begun to develop what have been called "balanced measures systems" for performance.[25] Mayor Shirley Franklin of Atlanta set out to change the city's poor service performance when she was elected in 2002. Among the innovations that her administration advanced was the creation of a performance measurement system called the "Atlanta Dashboard."[26] This system is a scorecard of service efficiency and effectiveness that is linked to what citizens want—the outputs that they care about. So, for example, city officials are able to assess the quality of street cleaning by comparing citizen satisfaction survey results on street cleanliness to miles of streets cleaned by the city. A change in either result can be examined relative to the effect on the other measure.[27]

But efficiency measures and effectiveness studies are just two ways to evaluate service delivery. How well services are delivered according to the goals of equality and responsiveness is taken up in the sections that follow.

EQUITY OF SERVICES: A POLITICAL GOAL?

In a classic work on urban services, Frank Levy, Arnold Meltsner, and Aaron Wildavsky presented three ways of defining equity.[28] First there is *equal opportunity*, in which all citizens receive the same level of service. Second is *market equity*, in which citizens receive services roughly proportional to the amount of taxes they pay. A third approach is *equal results*, in which an agency allocates its resources so that people are in an equal condition after the money is spent. In terms of the street department, equal opportunity requires the agency to spend about the same amount of money to repair or resurface streets in all sections of the city, while market equity allocates street maintenance resources in accordance with the taxes paid by each neighborhood, and the equal results approach demands that areas of the community with substandard streets receive more attention until those streets are on a par with others in the city.

Levy, Meltsner, and Wildavsky suggest that these standards can be arrayed on a rough scale, on which each requires more resource redistribution than the previous one. Generally speaking, the most widely accepted approach today is the concept of equal opportunity. Market equity is a more conservative definition of equity, while equal results is more change-oriented, or liberal-progressive in nature. Unquestionably, the equity standard people adopt plays a crucial role in their judgment of agency performance.

In their analysis of schools, streets, and libraries in Oakland, California, these investigators found differing equity outcomes by service area. Partly because of federal aid, the schools had moved a bit beyond equal opportunity, toward some equality of results. The street department, in contrast, had not quite reached equal opportunity, leaning more in the direction of market equity. And the libraries tended even more toward market equity. Levy and his colleagues concluded that the more an agency relies on the Adam Smith rule—which states that the frequency of demand determines the level of services—the more the resource distribution process approaches market equity. In libraries, for example, the authors found that new funds were allocated to branches with the highest circulations. "The initiative lies with the customer, as library patrons 'vote' with their cards. The more books they take out, the more money their branch receives."[29]

Services are distributed in response to a number of influences, and some neighborhoods are likely to receive more than others. But is there evidence that low-income and minority groups are systematically deprived in the allocation of service resources? Findings are mixed. In a study of parks and fire protection in San Antonio, it was reported that the "underclass hypothesis" did not fare well—that is, parks and fire protection services were not systematically biased against the poor.[30] What about schools? Some studies suggest that public schools in black and low-income neighborhoods receive less money, employ less-qualified teachers, and have poorer facilities, but others have found that certain federally funded compensatory programs provide such schools with more resources than middle-class schools have. A similarly mixed situation has been reported regarding distribution of recreational facilities, which favor wealthy neighborhoods in some places, while, in others, the poor seem to benefit more.[31] In short, service delivery patterns produce what Robert Lineberry has labeled "unpatterned inequalities."[32]

Whether or not maldistribution of services is intentional, certain groups have gone to court in an effort to produce changes in service distribution. If it can be shown that discriminatory service provision is the result of racial discrimination, the courts may grant relief. In *Hawkins v. Town of Shaw* (1971), the Fifth Circuit Court of Appeals held that Shaw, Mississippi, had systematically deprived its black citizens of equal protection of the law by distributing unequally a number of urban services. Other similar suits have produced mixed results.[33] Service maldistribution apparently has to be quite severe for the courts to intervene, and in those cases, racial bias almost undoubtedly has to be proven.

How can a city investigate questions of service equity? The city of Savannah has developed a program to measure the equity of municipal services, as illustrated by the case study presented in box 7.2.

RESPONSIVENESS IN SERVICE DELIVERY

Responsiveness, the fourth goal in service delivery, reflects the degree to which citizens' preferences and demands are met. Determining such preferences can be difficult, since most citizens do not contact city agencies about service delivery. For example, a study conducted in the early 1970s in Milwaukee found that only a third of the whites and 6 percent of the blacks sampled had made contact with city government officials.[34] More than a decade later, political scientist Michael Hirlinger reported a contacting ratio of 64.2 percent in Oklahoma City. He noted, however, that "the overall contacting rate is considerably higher than most of the previous citizen contacting studies,"[35] which is usually in the range of 30 to 40 percent.

Are citizens satisfied with city services? Most survey data suggest that they are, although variations exist, by class and service area especially. A meta-analysis—a study that empirically examines a large number of quantitative studies—by Thomas Miller and Michelle Miller offers some details.[36] They analyzed 261 citizen surveys administered over a ten-year period across the country. They standardized the various survey results on a scale of 0 to 100—on which 0 stood for "very bad" and 25 for "bad"; 50 was "neutral" (neither good nor bad); 75 reflected "good" and 100, "very good." Over eight categories of community services, the average adjusted score was 67.2 percent, close to the 75 percent benchmark score of "good." For services evaluated by sixty or more jurisdictions, the three best-rated services were fire protection (81 percent), library (79 percent), and trash collection (78 percent). The three worst-rated services were animal control (60 percent), street repair (58 percent), and planning/zoning (57 percent).

Most city administrators would agree that people want more services but are reluctant to pay more taxes to fund them. One reason for this contradictory response is that many citizens feel they are not receiving real value for their tax dollars. A more general explanation has to do with the separation of payment of services from service delivery. As long as they do not pay directly for each service, most people prefer more services; but they still want lower taxes because the connection between taxes and services remains indirect. Some authorities contend that the use of service charges (user fees) or an even greater reliance on the private sector to deliver municipal services can help to illuminate the link between services and their cost.

Research suggests that, at least in big cities, service delivery varies in its responsiveness to public demands. Large-city service delivery has become quite regularized, dominated by bureaucratically determined decision rules. These rules can take several forms. Earlier, we mentioned the Adam Smith rule, by which the frequency of demand determines the level of certain services. In the same Oakland study that gave rise to this rule, it was found that

BOX 7.2   Policy and Practice

MEASURING SERVICE EQUITY

Recognizing that neighborhoods in Savannah differ considerably in living standards, city manager Arthur Mendonsa began a program to address variations. Called the Responsive Public Services Program, it had two purposes: to develop a set of measures reflecting important differences in the quality of life by neighborhood, and to make a systematic effort to close the gap between neighborhoods by providing more public services to those areas with unusual needs.

The city was divided into twenty-eight planning units or neighborhoods, and the following conditions were measured in each:

- Level of crime: the number of basic property and violent crimes (such as burglary, robbery, car theft) per 1,000 population
- Level of fires: the number of structure fires per 1,000 population
- Cleanliness: ratings of lots, streets, and alleys on a cleanliness scale ranging from 0 to 5
- Water service: leaks per mile and the number of developed properties without water service or with water-pressure problems
- Sewer service: sewage blockages per mile and the number of properties without sewer service;
- Housing: percentage of dwelling units classified as substandard
- Recreation services: facilities needed to bring the area into compliance with city standards
- Drainage conditions: the number of structures that had experienced flooding on a two-year and ten-year storm; frequency and the number of street segments closed on the same storm frequency
- Street conditions: miles of unpaved streets and the surface condition of streets measured on a scale from good to bad

Differences among neighborhoods on these measures were not minor, as shown by the following examples:

- The lowest neighborhood crime rate was 5.6 per 1,000 inhabitants; the highest was 320 per 1,000 inhabitants.
- The lowest neighborhood fire rating was 0; the highest was 7.47 per 1,000 inhabitants.
- The lowest water leak rate was 0.4 leak per mile; the highest was 22.7 per mile.

The objective of the program was to bring poorly rated neighborhoods up to an acceptable level compared to the city as a whole; neighborhoods would be surveyed every two years. To correct some of the deficiencies, the city has provided the following assistance for substandard neighborhoods:

- Cleanliness: increased the frequency of street sweepings and stepped up environmental code enforcement.
- Water service: instituted a program of replacing water-line laterals and begun planning for water system capital improvements to eliminate pressure and flow problems.
- Street conditions: initiated an ongoing street paving (or repaving) program.

(continued)

BOX 7.2   Policy and Practice (continued)

- Level of fires: instituted an intensive fire-prevention inspection program.
- Level of crime: set up crime-prevention programs, including a special patrol effort.

City manager Mendonsa admitted that in the quest for equity, "we may have to provide unequal levels of service in order to produce equal benefits from the services." For example, the city swept some streets once a week, others once every two weeks, others once every four weeks. The object, of course, was to produce equal levels of street cleanliness.

SOURCE: Adapted from Arthur A. Mendonsa, "Yardsticks for Measuring the Success of Service Programs in Savannah," *State and Local Government Review* 18 (spring 1986): 89–92.

---

professional norms and technical considerations also are important in shaping bureaucratic response in certain service areas. Another consideration affecting how municipal bureaucrats handle requests for service is how difficult the problem is: often, the simpler the problem, the more likely it is to be satisfactorily handled.[37]

An emphasis on customer service has certainly reshaped cities' approaches to service delivery and to the demands of citizens for better services. The Internet has enabled cities to deploy new tools that are potentially more responsive to citizen demands. E-government, especially the use of websites and e-mail to provide better service responses, is quite common in cities today. And, although these changes may in fact improve the efficiency and effectiveness of services, their primary objectives seem to focus on more responsive approaches to citizen needs and demands for services.[38]

Some cities have taken a novel approach to this issue by creating community benefits districts (CBDs). According to political scientists Susan Baer and Vincent Marando, these districts are typically enabled by state law that permits cities to create areas within their boundaries in which a supplemental tax assessment is permitted for purposes of funding additional services—such as security, economic development, or garbage collection.[39] The CBD allows a geographic subdistrict of a city to meet its residents' special demands for services by levying an additional level of taxation to support the additional activity. Baer and Marando's research shows that subdistricts that function like CBDs are found in at least twelve U.S. cities.[40]

One concern about CBDs is that they may exacerbate socioeconomic differences—that is, the poor and minorities may not be able to afford to live in a subdistrict where an additional tax levy pays for augmented services. This is a possibility that many cities with diverse populations cannot ignore because a fair amount of research has shown that satisfaction with services varies widely across racial, ethnic, and income groups. The differences in satisfaction with services across groups seem to be related to both perceived service quality and trust in government.[41]

Although bureaucrats are not oblivious to citizens' demands, they do not assess those demands in a very sophisticated fashion. They use what Robert Lineberry calls a *body count approach* to consumption measurement.[42] Ordinarily this practice involves the tabulation of gross totals—tons of garbage collected, number of dogs picked up, number of books circulated, and so on. These raw demand indicators, however, reveal very little about actual citizen preferences.

Lineberry goes on to argue that an even more important reason that bureaucracies are not very responsive is that they are monopolies. This point raises the issue of alternative service delivery arrangements. Are there alternative ways of providing urban services that might produce more competition in service delivery, and thus better services? Some say yes. For example, competitive government is one of the key themes in Osborne and Gaebler's *Reinventing Government*: "The issue is not public versus private. It is competition versus monopoly."[43]

ALTERNATIVE SERVICE DELIVERY

The rationale for developing alternatives to municipal service monopolies is simple: economists have long argued that monopolies are inefficient and unresponsive, while competition allegedly forces producers to operate as efficiently as possible in order to stay in business. The basic idea behind alternative service arrangements, then, is to stimulate greater productivity by introducing competition into the local public sector. Indeed, Osborne and Gaebler are convinced that a pivotal factor in the process of reinventing government is injecting competition into service delivery.[44]

Although E. S. Savas has identified as many as ten alternative delivery arrangements—including contracting to private and nonprofit organizations, intergovernmental contracting, franchises, subsidies, vouchers, voluntary service, and self-help[45]—a recent analysis of patterns in the use of these alternative service delivery approaches among cities and counties by the ICMA shows that only two options are used extensively across the full range of municipal services: contracting to the private sector (practiced by an average of 18 percent of local governments) and entering into intergovernmental agreements (practiced by an average of 16.5 percent).[46] Cities and counties use franchises infrequently, mostly for public utilities. Subsidies, also sparingly used, are more common for human services (such as programs for the elderly) and for cultural and arts activities. Nonprofit organizations are, on average, providing about 8 percent of the services that are contracted by cities and counties.[47] Local governments rely on volunteers somewhat more often than franchises and subsidies, mostly for public safety (fire suppression/control) and cultural programs. Given their widespread use, contracting and intergovernmental agreements are the alternative arrangements that we focus on here.

CONTRACTING OUT

Proponents claim many benefits for contracting out, or "outsourcing": foremost is controlling costs, and "external fiscal pressures" is a close second. Private-sector services may cost less because competition and the profit motive presumably bring operating efficiencies. For example, a large-scale study of contracting for local services in the Los Angeles area—from street maintenance to payroll processing—found that private firms could provide services cheaper than could municipal workforces, with no reduction in quality.[48] Contracting also allows a municipality to procure specialized services that are not otherwise available, to avoid large start-up costs, and to have greater flexibility in adjusting program size (without worrying about negotiating with recalcitrant municipal employees). There are disadvantages as well. Some argue that privatizing increases costs in the long run, since a profit is involved and the private contractor must pay taxes, too. Also, historically, the awarding of government contracts has been plagued by charges of kickbacks and corruption.

The process of deciding whether or not savings will be achieved by contracting out is not an easy task. Frequently, governments use line-item budgets, which concentrate on objects of expenditure rather than on activities performed by governmental units. If information about how much it costs to provide a particular public service is not available, a city cannot make accurate cost comparisons with private vendors. Also, before contracting, the full costs of outsourcing a public service should be determined, including indirect costs, contract administration costs, opportunity costs, and so forth.

Fortunately, help is available to city officials in determining these various kinds of costs for comparison. Public administration expert Lawrence Martin offers a five-step methodology for comparing the costs of government versus contract service delivery.[49] In brief, the model involves the following steps:

1. Determination of all costs associated with government service delivery
2. Identification of those costs that will be avoided by contracting out the service
3. Estimation of costs of delivering the service by contract, based on bids
4. Calculation of an "add on" to the contract bid—an amount determined by using the Office of Management and Budget's staffing formula for contract administration guidelines—to cover municipal contract administration
5. Comparison of the total costs of contract service delivery (identified in steps 3 and 4) with the government costs to be avoided by contracting out (determined in step 2)

If the costs to be avoided are greater than the costs to be incurred by contracting, then contracting out the service is, according to Martin, "reasonably valid and defensible, all things being equal."[50]

Next, local officials should develop a "request for information" (RFI) in which possible vendors could indicate their capacity and willingness to provide the service, if selected through a competitive proposal process (often called an RFP ["request for proposal"]). An RFI in a large metropolitan area may contain an abundance of firms that could undertake even fairly esoteric tasks, whereas in small communities, few if any vendors may be available, and the subsequent RFP process may, thus, be disappointing.

Drawing up contracts can be a tricky business as well; important details can easily be left out. If the specifications are not clear, the door is open to all kinds of mischief, including possible lawsuits. This step is critical for both parties. Most vendors want to do a good job, of course. But they need to know exactly what they are bidding on and what they must accomplish over the life of the contract. And the city must know precisely what it expects so that it can monitor the contract effectively. Indeed, careful contract monitoring is a must—service quality may depend on it. If the city does not work closely with the contractor, then it may have only itself to blame if something goes wrong.

Most studies identify two basic disadvantages or obstacles to contracting out. First, municipal employees may register strong opposition, fearing job losses and forfeiture of fringe benefits. Contractors often agree to hire laid-off city employees, but that assurance does not normally satisfy most municipal workers. Second, management itself sometimes fears the loss of direct control of a service.[51] The public rightly holds the city itself, not a private contractor, responsible for service performance. Consequently, some managers may want to exercise direct oversight of the work so that they can respond quickly in case of an emergency or change in circumstances.

Pros and cons aside, some services lend themselves more readily to contracting out than do others. In general, the services that appear to be the best prospects for contracting out are those with the following characteristics: (1) they are *new*, which avoids problems with city employees; (2) they have *easy-to-specify outputs* (such as solid-waste collection), which makes contract preparation and monitoring easier; (3) they require *specialized skills* (such as engineering or law) or *specialized equipment*, which smaller cities, in particular, cannot afford on a regular or permanent basis; or (4) they involve *large numbers of low-skill workers* (such as solid-waste collection and janitorial services), since these areas appear to hold the most promise of cost savings because of pay and benefit differentials between the public and private sector.

To minimize friction with employees, city officials should include in-house departments in discussions of outsourcing early in the process. Departments should be given the chance to make improvements to lower operating costs. If a contracting-out decision still seems desirable, managers should give serious consideration to allowing municipal departments to bid on the job (see the following section on competitive contracting).

One final point about contracting out or any other version of privatization: success may require a strong political champion, especially when the effort becomes controversial. The chief executive, of course, is the logical person to play that role; whether managers or mayors should take the lead in council-manager cities will depend on how the two work together and the leadership style of the mayor. Research by political scientist Anirudh Ruhil shows that city managers are the key catalysts in cities that have chosen to contract out for services.[52] A fifteen-year study of California cities' alternative service arrangements validates this finding with evidence that council-manager cities contracted out more than others, although most cities did not change service providers over this period of time.[53]

Solid-waste collection seems particularly well-suited to private contracting; fire protection does not. But contracting out firefighting services is not impossible. Since 1948, a private company, Rural-Metro, has been supplying fire protection service to residents of Scottsdale, Arizona, and several other communities in the Phoenix area.

Despite the widely acclaimed success of Rural-Metro in Scottsdale, the traditional municipal fire protection service has been extraordinarily resistant to privatization. Part of the reason is the success that firefighters have in convincing people that any change from the typical municipal operation might endanger life and property. They argue as well that homeowners may pay more for fire insurance if the community's fire-suppression capacity receives a lower rating from the national Insurance Services Office.

One final note on contracting. The main reason that cities choose to contract out services is cost—the expectation that it will be cheaper to contract with another party to provide services that would otherwise be provided by government. But there is an equally important consideration: trust. According to recent research by the ICMA, local officials' responses showed that the strongest predictor of outsourcing government services is the level of trust these officials have in the reputation and performance of contractors.[54]

COMPETITIVE CONTRACTING

Contracting out often means that a city expects to save money by handing over a service to a private firm. But urban managers are now learning that their own departments sometimes can operate more efficiently and can compete directly with private vendors. Again, the key is competition, not merely private delivery. So we see a rise in public-private competition, often called "competitive contracting."

The first well-known example of competitive contracting appeared in Phoenix, where, beginning in the late 1970s, city officials decided to allow municipal departments to engage in head-to-head competition against outside firms.[55] By 1982, the city auditor reported that out of twenty-two service contracts put out for bid over the previous few years, city employees had submitted the lowest bid ten times. Officials learned that outside vendors are more successful at winning jobs requiring unskilled or semiskilled workers; custodial service, for example, was the first job contracted out. Private companies apparently pay lower wages and provide fewer benefits. One of the special features of the Phoenix plan is the role of the city auditor, who must ensure that the city's bid is really comparable to that of private firms. Municipal bids, for example, must include all administrative costs, capital investments, and depreciation expenses. In fact, the city's bid goes in a sealed envelope, and the amount of the bid remains unknown to the department until the day bids are opened. Thereafter, if the city wins the contract, the city auditor provides continual monitoring of in-house performance.

Phoenix officials reported that the key to success is productivity improvement, which keeps city forces competitive. They work hard to involve employees in management decisions and to keep communication lines open. Officials point to two beneficial side effects of competitive contracting: because of the city's success, the process improves employees' morale and pride in their organization; and contracting has not only saved money on specific services but has had the long-term effect of holding down costs in areas where Phoenix does not contract. Mark Hughes comments: "It has led to more effective work methods throughout the city—mechanized refuse collection, modern street maintenance equipment, innovative equipment management, energy conservation."[56]

Other large cities have followed Phoenix's lead.[57] In the 1990s, Cleveland developed "Cleveland Competes," a program that includes, among other initiatives, competitive bidding between the city and private providers. In late summer 1995, Cleveland awarded contracts for downtown waste collection and local street resurfacing to city workers. The employees beat out private bidders after holding meetings to improve labor-management relations and reorganizing to become more efficient. Like many other cities in New Jersey, Newark has adopted a competitive contracting process with plain language that guides potential vendors through the process for submitting and winning a bid to deliver services to Newark.[58]

Indianapolis has been at the forefront of competitive contracting, calling its process "managed competition." It reports actual or expected savings of approximately $150 million as a result of competitive contracting. Before the process begins, the city may modify the service so that its workers will be better prepared for the competition. City departments have done well, winning about 80 percent of public-private competitions.

Under what circumstances does competitive contracting work best? Overall, most of the suggestions and admissions that apply to privatization generally also work for public-private competition. Lawrence Martin offers several recommendations.[59] He says that ancillary or support services—including housekeeping activities such as custodial services, billing, park or equipment maintenance, and even security services—are more suited to competitive contracting than are core services, such as police or fire protection. "Soft" services—which encompass activities that either allow significant discretion to contractors (such as legal, accounting, engineering, and architectural operations) or provide "helping" services (such as social and medical services)—are also more suitable for contracting than are core services.

Martin believes that stand-alone functions are more suitable for bidding than are interrelated services. Custodial operations, for example, are self-contained or stand-alone. Police communications, on the other hand, are interrelated with law enforcement actions; a failure or disruption in provision of this service would adversely affect the larger public-safety system. Finally, Martin recommends that cities use competitive contracting in the areas where private vendors are plentiful, because the availability of multiple providers should help to ensure a genuinely competitive process.

Local officials must also focus on certain internal organizational issues. In-house departments must be both willing and able to compete with external firms. Previously, we mentioned the importance of preparing city employees for competition. This step could range from close labor-management cooperation to reengineering (extensively modifying) a service to ensure more effective bidding by city workforces. Finally, political forces may affect the success of competitive contracting. Political opposition may arise for some of the same reasons that it does for any proposed privatization effort. Public employees, fearing job or benefit loss, may resist. Interest groups or elected officials, satisfied with the status quo, may prove obstructive. And even citizens may be skeptical if they fear that changes may adversely affect service levels.

Research on the long-term viability of competitive contracting is favorable. David Ammons and Debra Hill studied five large cities that had operated competitive systems for solid-waste collection for about a dozen years.[60] In their words, "There were no indications that the competitive systems failed to deliver as expected." Indeed, they reported that cost increases for garbage and trash service in these cities were below increases in national averages and below the level of inflation. The authors discovered a couple of other benefits as well: the city and private vendors learn from one another. In Oklahoma City, for example, when the city shifted from three-person to one-person crews operating side-loaders, the contract operation quickly followed suit. In addition, the competitive arrangement enabled several of these cities to avoid potential work stoppages.

Public-private competition is still rather new. Yet in critical ways it seems less likely than straight privatization to arouse political resistance. After all, city departments are given a chance to compete—and, with assurances of fair play, they may welcome the opportunity to show how good they are. Undoubtedly, we will see more competitive contracting in the future.

INTERGOVERNMENTAL AGREEMENTS

A second basic alternative to municipal monopoly is the intergovernmental agreement or contract. Certainly, there is nothing new about agreements or contracts between units of government; they have long been used as an important device to supply needed services. Some of the motivations for privatizing—potentially saving money, acquiring services needed only on a periodic basis, avoiding large initial cost outlays, and obtaining specialized services not otherwise available—also stimulate an interest in intergovernmental agreements. Many cities have followed the model of the agreements between cities and the county government in Los Angeles County, known as the Lakewood Plan. These service arrangements developed because many of the small suburbs were unable to afford the large initial investment needed to hire and equip a municipal workforce. The county, on the other hand, had built up the capacity to provide a range of urban services, so a natural symbiotic relationship evolved. Although legal and geographic considerations obviously limit the use of intergovernmental service agreements, many cities seem to be more and more interested in them. Recent reports confirm that municipal service provision by Los Angeles County is still growing and represents a significant share of the county's governmental activities.[61]

A survey of the experiences of California cities with alternative service provision in the 1980s and 1990s yielded some interesting findings. The researchers reported that, in general, cities were not wide adopters of alternative service delivery plans, but when they did change "it was less typical to contract out with the private sector and more common to engage another level of government, either through contracts with other public entities or by relinquishing the responsibility of service provision to independent government agencies such as special districts or counties."[62] And when the researchers looked at which services were contracted, they found that essential city services and those that represented larger shares of the city budget were more likely to be provided by intergovernmental contracting.[63]

Recent research by Mildred Warner and Amir Hefetz has compared the benefits of privatization to that of intergovernmental contracting. Their research suggests that alternative service delivery can be more efficient, but that contracting with another local government results in greater equity and voice for citizens than is provided in a private-sector service contract.[64]

Delivery by another government or public authority appears most frequently in health and human services, public works, transportation, and libraries. Some of these arrangements may not involve formal agreements among cooperating local communities. However, it is worth noting that the proportion of services provided through intergovernmental agreements actually dropped from 21 percent in 1992 to 17 percent in 2002.[65]

IMPLEMENTING AND EVALUATING URBAN PROGRAMS

The delivery of urban services or the implementation of urban programs is rarely a smooth, automatic, rational process. The best-laid plans of urban policymakers often are modified if not derailed by compromises, trade-offs, and power plays among those responsible for actual program performance. As we saw in chapter 4, good planning and good intentions are not enough; attention also must be paid to how services or programs actually are carried out. Periodic interviews with department heads and staff, periodic written reports, and, of course, complaints received all provide essential guidance on program or service effectiveness. But these traditional modes of monitoring and evaluating are sporadic and unsystematic. Especially when new programs have been initiated or in areas where costs have increased disproportionately, a more regularized approach to assessing performance is needed.

Basically, there are two kinds of evaluation: monitoring and program evaluation. The first of these, sometimes called *performance monitoring* or *process evaluation*, is concerned with regularly examining the general effectiveness of programs in major areas, such as public safety, health, and recreation. Monitoring attempts to identify general program-related changes, but it does not try to indicate what part specific governmental activities play in producing observed effects. In other words, monitoring does not separate program impacts from changes that may have resulted from nonprogram efforts, such as those by private groups.

Program evaluation goes further. It attempts to identify how the conditions of both the citizens and the community have changed as a result of a specific government program or set of activities. It seeks out both intended and unintended consequences, good and bad. A program evaluation proceeds through the following steps:

1. Determine the program objectives.
2. Translate the objectives into measurable indicators of achievement.
3. Collect data on the indicators for those who participated in the program (and for an equivalent group who did not participate).
4. Compare the data on participants and the equivalent nonparticipants.[66]

Once the data are in hand, managers can gauge program effectiveness and make knowledgeable recommendations concerning program continuation, modification, or even termination. Although the procedure seems simple, we see shortly that the whole process can be beset with a variety of unexpected problems. First, however, we should examine the different ways in which evaluation can be performed.

EVALUATION DESIGNS

Evaluation implies comparison. The major purpose of any program comparison is to identify changes that can be reasonably attributed to the program itself. Ideally, of course, we would like to compare what actually has happened with what would have happened had the program not been in effect. Since such controlled experimentation is impossible in the real world, however, the next-best procedure is to separate out the program's effects from other extraneous influences that might have produced some observable change.

Before we can discuss evaluation design, we must again consider program objectives and evaluation criteria. First, like program analysis and service delivery assessment, evaluation demands that objectives and criteria be put in measurable form. Second, evaluation criteria must focus on those conditions the program is intended to affect; workload measures, indicators of physical capacity, and number of clients served are insufficient if not inappropriate. Third, unintended consequences, especially negative side effects, must be considered explicitly. Fourth, more than one objective and more than one evaluation criterion should be specified. Finally, dollar costs always should be included as one criterion. With these requirements in mind, we can consider evaluation designs.[67]

Before-and-After Program Comparison

Measurement of program activity at two points—immediately before and at some appropriate time after program implementation—is the easiest, cheapest, most common, and most unreliable of the evaluation designs. No explicit provisions are made to control for outside influences. As Urban Institute researchers Harry Hatry, Richard Winnie, and Donald Fisk suggest, other plausible explanations for any observed change may exist, such as abnormal weather conditions, other public or private programs with coincidental objectives, and special traits of the target population not initially recognized. To the extent possible, a good evaluation design should take such potential factors into account; the before-and-after design cannot do so.

Despite its limitations, the before-and-after program comparison design may be the only practical approach when personnel and time are limited. For example, Washington, D.C., used a before-and-after design to evaluate Operation Clean Sweep, an intensive, one-time effort to remove litter and other solid waste in nine neighborhood service areas. Neighborhood cleanliness was assessed before and after the operation by trained observers using a series of photographs matched to a cleanliness rating scale. A before-and-after citizen survey was conducted to determine whether residents noticed any difference in cleanliness. City officials felt that no major external changes had affected the area under consideration, so the before-and-after design seemed a valid approach. Even though the city was disappointed by the lack of major improvements in street cleanliness—a decision was made not to continue the program—the evaluation itself was judged a success.

Time Trend Projection

Another evaluation design compares actual postprogram information with estimated projections based on preprogram observations made over a period of time. This approach uses statistical methods, including linear regression, to derive projected program values that are then contrasted with actual results.

> Crime or accident statistics, for example, may rise or fall for individual years, but when years are considered together a trend may be apparent. Comparison of data from one preprogram year with postprogram data may be influenced by extremes and thereby be misleading.[68]

Clearly, this design is superior to the single-point comparison of the before-and-after approach, but it still lacks the explicit control necessary to assess as accurately as possible the real impact of a given program.

Comparison with Other Jurisdictions or Populations

A third evaluation design identifies a comparable city or a comparable population within the same community in which the program is not operating. This approach was used by the State of Connecticut to assess the effects of a crackdown on highway speeding. Following the program's implementation, the automobile fatality rate in Connecticut was compared with fatality rates in neighboring states. The evaluation showed that some influence unique to Connecticut had caused a decline in fatality rates relative to those of neighboring states.

Although this design incorporates some controls for outside effects, it still falls short of the ideal approach—the controlled experiment. Also, finding comparable jurisdictions or populations is always a problem.

The Controlled Experiment

Hatry, Winnie, and Fisk refer to the controlled experiment as "the Cadillac of program evaluations." Undoubtedly it is the most powerful design of all; it is also expensive and difficult to perform. The essential feature of this approach is the selection of at least two groups: a control group and an experimental group. Members of the population (or probability samples thereof) are assigned randomly (that is, scientifically) to produce two groups that are as much alike as possible. The experimental group receives the program "treatment"; the control group does not. Postprogram performance is then measured and compared. This design is probably most effective where individuals undergo a specific treatment program in an area such as employment training, corrections, rehabilitation, health, or drug or alcohol abuse. Various quasi-experimental designs, in which true experimental conditions are approximated but not quite met, also can be used.[69] Why don't more cities undertake such controlled experiments? Because they are not easy to conduct, costs are usually high, and the necessary expertise is often not readily available. Even getting those involved to agree to a random assignment of population can present problems: practitioners often want to apply their professional knowledge and experience in assigning individuals to treatment groups, generally putting those who need the program services most into the experimental group rather than leaving the process to chance. This process of selection essentially defeats the purpose of the experiment.

Hatry, Winnie, and Fisk identify a fifth approach to evaluation: *comparison of planned and actual performance*. Although this procedure can hardly be called a design, they argue that it is a useful approach in the absence of any other evaluation method. Even so, they contend that comparisons of actual results with planned or targeted results are infrequently conducted.

Where the preferred experimental design—a controlled experiment—is not feasible, Hatry, Winnie, and Fisk recommend the use of the first three designs in some combination. They also advocate the regular and extensive use of the fifth approach—comparison of what was planned to what actually happened—as a supplement to the other evaluation designs.

EVALUATING PROGRAM EVALUATION

Good program evaluations require good research by analysts with good research skills. Not all cities have a research staff that can provide quality program evaluations. And most surprising, many of the reasons for poor program evaluations have not changed much over the years. Pamela Horst and her associates provide three key reasons why program evaluations are ineffective.[70] First, program implementers have great difficulty in stating clear, specific, measurable objectives. When asked for a statement of goals, they tend to answer in terms of services offered, number of people served, and so on. But to program evaluators, who want to know the intended *consequences* of a program, these are not valid program objectives.[71]

Second, serious difficulties arise in connecting program objectives to program effects and consequences. Different assumptions are made in different locales about what form program intervention can take and how it relates to the intended outcome. For example, the operating assumptions of one halfway house or therapeutic community may bear no resemblance to those of other institutions that go by the same name.

Finally, managers often feel that sound evaluation presents a clear and present danger—a threat to the comfortable status quo. Old ideas and timeworn practices die hard, and some managers hesitate to support evaluation if it appears likely to disrupt existing organizational arrangements.[72]

How can urban managers improve upon this? Horst and her colleagues recommend a "preassessment of evaluability." A determination should be made as to whether a major evaluation effort is warranted. In effect, the three root causes of ineffective evaluation should be raised in question form, as follows:

- Are the objectives, program activities, anticipated outcomes, and expected impact sufficiently well defined as to be measurable?
- Are the assumptions linking expenditure to implementation, outcome, and impact sufficiently logical to be tested?
- Does the person in charge of the program have sufficient capacity and motivation to act as a result of evaluation findings?[73]

Evaluation can make important contributions to the overall assessment of urban policy, but not all program evaluations provide useful results. As political scientist Janet Kelly concluded after examining services in fifty cities:

Perhaps the most serious challenge to researchers looking for empirical evidence of a relationship between public service performance and citizen satisfaction is the same that public managers face: finding performance measures that capture service outcomes. In the interim, we should take care not to confuse aspects of service quality and productivity that can be quantified with dimensions of service quality that matter to citizens.[74]

Figuring out what can be profitably evaluated remains the tough task of imaginative administrators.

CITIZEN SURVEYS

Community surveys can generate useful information about citizens' perceptions, preferences, and needs in regard to a variety of urban services. Responses to questions about service delivery and program effectiveness can be particularly valuable for policy analysis and program evaluation. Another basic reason for using surveys is to use citizen surveys in connection with the preparation of the municipal budget. Many cities have been using this process for years. Essentially, they ask citizens about their preferences for different areas and budgets for city services, using the responses to craft the final budget proposal. Douglas Watson, a city manager tells a similar story, describing the institutionalized use of citizen surveys in the budgetary and policymaking process in his city.[75] Research by the ICMA shows frequent use of surveys by cities and counties; over 60 percent of these local governments used at least one citizen survey in recent years.[76]

CONDUCTING THE SURVEYS

A prime consideration in conducting a survey is the degree of accuracy wanted. Survey consultants—whose expertise is likely to be necessary if a city has never undertaken a survey—can provide ready guidance on the degree of accuracy (based on sampling error) resulting from surveys of varying sizes. Sampling precision actually depends on two variables: sample size and the percentage of subjects responding to a particular question. For example, if 400 people were included in the sample, under the most demanding conditions, the sampling error would be plus or minus 5 percent, with a 95 percent confidence level. Thus, if half the respondents in a sample of 400 answered "yes" to a particular question, the real value in the larger population would be between 45 and 55 percent "yes" (95 times out of 100). Again, under the most statistically demanding conditions, a sample size of 800 would yield a sampling error of plus or minus 3.5 percent, with 95 percent confidence. Depending on the decision maker's need for accuracy, a sample of between 400 and 800 should be adequate for most communities, regardless of size.

Cost inevitably looms as a major consideration in conducting sample surveys. For this reason, cities should consider either a telephone survey or a mail questionnaire. Neither is likely to be as satisfactory as a personal interview, but both can be done less expensively. Most telephone surveys now utilize random digit dialing, a method that, done properly, with a relatively simple, short questionnaire, can yield good results.

The Internet has made the use of the survey tool quite easy—both for the local government and for the citizens being surveyed. Many city governments regularly place on-line survey questions on their websites and often promote the use of this tool by citizens through other means, such as e-mail. We can expect that the citizen survey will continue to grow in usage and popularity over time.

SURVEY LIMITATIONS

It is important to guard against several problems that can arise in conducting and using surveys. First, an opinion poll should not focus on complex issues about which citizens lack information. In one city, the small budget for tree management was eliminated after citizens ranked forestry lowest on a selected list of services. Windstorms later blew down a number of trees, and citizens were in an uproar when they discovered that forestry crews had been eliminated.

Second, the questionnaire should offer a range of possible alternatives or responses. In one survey, blacks were asked: "If there were no obstacles, financial or social, would you prefer to live in a black community or in a predominantly white suburb?" Those conducting the survey finally recognized that an important category was missing. When a follow-up survey included another choice—an integrated neighborhood—the results were enormously different: the large-majority preference for a black community in the first poll shifted to a smaller-majority preference for an integrated community in the second survey.

Third, the survey questionnaire should be designed and worded very carefully to minimize the chance that the poll will be misunderstood, or even abused. One community in the Southwest famously used a citizen survey to justify the construction of a nuclear power plant, yet the words *nuclear* and *atomic* did not appear in the questionnaire.[77] Even technically well-done surveys, though, can be deliberately misconstrued by those who want to use only part of the results to support their particular point of view.

Finally, those who will be deciding the issue should be committed to making use of the survey. Polls are of no value if official decision makers do not heed the results.

City officials must be cautious in the interpretation of surveys. It is important to know, for instance, whether citizens' views of services are affected by other issues, such as their trust in government, their sense of political efficacy (that is, does government care about me or my views?), or their experiences with government agencies. And, as shown in many different research projects, satisfaction with city services is determined in part by one's socioeconomic and demographic background.[78] Survey researchers and public officials must be able to isolate these factors in order to validly interpret the results of surveys.

Two final comments on citizen surveys seem warranted. Some research indicates that subjective service evaluations—that is, by citizens—do not correspond well with more objective measures of service quality.[79] Consequently, citizen surveys should not be used as substitutes for various objective indicators of municipal performance. And, as we saw earlier, studies show that attitudes toward services and taxes are generally contradictory: citizens often provide positive assessments of most services and want at least the present service level continued, but they don't want to pay more taxes. Because no one likes taxes, survey questions asking about service levels and tax rates must be very carefully drafted if the information is to be of much value. To the extent possible, the questionnaire design should force respondents to confront explicit trade-offs between services and taxes.

Overall, the potential advantages of using communitywide surveys seem to outweigh the risks. In no other way can public officials derive reasonably accurate, systematic information about how citizens think their city government is performing. In the absence of the market mechanisms of price and competition, democratic governments are under special obligation to make their operations as responsive as possible to the public will. And elections alone are not sufficient for that purpose.

SUMMARY

As this chapter has shown, goals for service delivery involve more than just improving efficiency and economy. For many years, a strong interest in equity has found its way onto the local agenda, and this consideration leads, in turn, to questions of responsiveness. Among other things, we are learning that the urban bureaucracy, through the operation of frequently unobtrusive decision rules, has a lot to do with how services are distributed and the extent to which delivery appears responsive to citizens' needs.

Many authorities are pessimistic about the capacity of the bureaucracy to modify its behavior in the absence of incentives of the sort normally associated with private enterprise. Predictably, therefore, an interest has developed in finding alternative delivery mechanisms, such as contracting to private firms, for certain services. Contracting out and public-private competition are on the increase as cities seek to save money by injecting more competition into the delivery process.

Still, cities continue to explore ways of producing quality services at lower costs. Many productivity programs rely on new strategies to enhance employee morale and motivation. As cities recognize the need to innovate and improve quality, employees may be given latitude to experiment, take risks, and become more entrepreneurial. The goal is to create a less hierarchical, more flexible, even team-based organization that can respond quickly to change.

How can urban managers determine whether programs are being implemented as planned? Improving service is impossible unless a municipality collects reasonably good information on the level and quality of services that are currently available. The key process is to intentionally determine if outcomes are being met. Most cities collect a variety of data, and data collection efforts have been enhanced by technology and online tools that provide instant feedback to municipal officials.

We know that, for a variety of reasons, employees do not always carry through as directed. Therefore, administrators often must undertake special efforts to monitor and evaluate program performance. Evaluation designs are of several sorts. The cheapest and easiest to perform, the before-and-after design, is also the least reliable; the best design, the controlled experiment, unfortunately is the most costly and difficult to undertake.

Citizen surveys increasingly have proved their worth in providing data about the public's perceptions of municipal services, although such surveys should not be substituted for objective service measures. And although these surveys are becoming easier to administer and to complete because of the Internet, these efforts are often costly and are sometimes misunderstood; and some experts even question the cognitive ability of citizens to assess service delivery accurately. Nevertheless, citizen surveys furnish information that public decision makers can obtain in no other way: "In a society committed to democratic norms, the views of the citizenry—no matter how (ill) conceived—are significant in themselves!"[80] Continual program monitoring, program evaluations, and citizen surveys can help a city government make more informed judgments about the quality and effectiveness of urban services.

SUGGESTED FOR FURTHER READING

Ammons, David N., ed. *Leading Performance Management in Local Government.* Washington, D.C.: ICMA, 2008.

Hatry, Harry P., Philip S. Schaenman, Donald M. Fisk, John R. Hall Jr., and Louise Snyder, *How Effective Are Your Community Services?* 3rd ed. Washington, D.C.: Urban Institute and ICMA, 2006.

Lyons, W. E., David Lowery, and Ruth H. DeHoog. *The Politics of Dissatisfaction: Citizens, Services, and Urban Institutions.* Armonk, N.Y.: M. E. Sharpe, 1992.

Miller, Thomas I., and Michelle Miller Kobayashi. *Citizen Surveys: How to Do Them, How to Use Them, What They Mean*. Washington, D.C.: ICMA, 2000.

National Performance Management Advisory Commission, *A Performance Management Framework for State and Local Government: From Measurement and Reporting to Management and Improving*, Chicago: NPMAC, 2010.

NOTES

1. David Greytak and Donald Phares, with Elaine Morley, *Municipal Output and Performance in New York City* (Lexington, Mass.: D.C. Heath, 1976), 11.

2. Ibid.

3. David N. Ammons, "Urban Services," in *Cities, Politics, and Policy: A Comparative Analysis*, ed. John P. Pelissero (Washington, D.C.: CQ Press, 2003), 254–255.

4. See David N. Ammons, *Municipal Benchmarks: Assessing Local Performance and Establishing Community Standards*, 2nd ed. (Thousand Oaks, Calif.: Sage, 2001).

5. *The Municipal Year Book* is published by the ICMA annually. The ICMA website (http://icma.org) provides datasets and research summaries on its surveys of city and county governments and practices.

6. David H. Folz, "Service Quality and Benchmarking Performance of Municipal Services," *Public Administration Review* 64 (March 2004): 209–220.

7. Adrian Moore, James Nolan, and Geoffrey F. Segal, "Putting Out the Trash. Measuring Municipal Service Efficiency in U.S. Cities," *Urban Affairs Review* 41 (November 2005): 237–259.

8. Harry Hatry, "Measuring the Quality of Public Services," in *Improving the Quality of Urban Management*, ed. Willis Hawley and David Rogers (Beverly Hills, Calif.: Sage, 1974), 50–54.

9. The following sections are adapted from an early collaborative monograph, *Measuring the Effectiveness of Basic Municipal Services* (Washington, D.C.: Urban Institute and ICMA, 1974), 9–15.

10. Matthew G. Springer and Marcus A. Winters, *New York City's School-Wide Bonus Pay Program: Early Evidence from a Randomized Trial, National Center on Performance Incentives*, Working Paper 2009–02 (April 2009).

11. Michael Lipsky, *Street Level Bureaucracy* (New York. Russell Sage Foundation, 1980), 48–51, 171.

12. Daniel Yankelovich, "The Work Ethic Is Underemployed," *Psychology Today*, May 1982, 5–8.

13. Ibid., 6.

14. David Osborne and Ted Gaebler, *Reinventing Government* (Reading, Mass.: Addison-Wesley, 1992), 117–124, 158.

15. Barbara Vobejda, "Survey Says Employees Less Willing to Sacrifice," *Washington Post*, September 3, 1993, A2.

16. *Employee Incentives to Improve State and Local Government Productivity* (Washington, D.C.: National Commission on Productivity and Work Quality, 1975).

17. Richard C. Kearney, *Labor Relations in the Public Sector*, 3rd ed. (New York: Marcel Dekker, 2001).

18. Jennifer Anderson, "Flex Time under Pressure in Tight Economy," *Ergoweb*, May 20, 2005, www.ergoweb.com/news/detail.cfm?id=1108.

19. Kearney, *Labor Relations in the Public Sector*.

20. This discussion is drawn from John M. Greiner et al., *Productivity and Motivation: A Review of State and Local Government Initiatives* (Washington, D.C.: Urban Institute Press, 1981), 119–120.

21. Norma M. Riccucci, "Affirmative Action in the Twenty-first Century: New Approaches and Developments," in *Public Personnel Management: Current Concerns—Future Challenges*, ed. Carolyn Ban and Norma M. Riccucci (New York: Longman, 1991), 91.

22. See Barbara Romzek, "Balancing Work and Nonwork Obligations," in *Public Personnel Management*.

23. See, for example, Cory Fleming, ed., *GIS Guide for Local Government Officials* (Washington, D.C.: ICMA Press, 2005).

24. This information comes from James F. Lynch, "The People Equation: Solution to the Solid Waste Problem in Little Rock," in *Public Technology: Key to Improved Government Productivity*, ed. James Mercer and Ronald Philips (New York: AMACOM, 1981), 201–209.

25. See National Partnership for Reinventing Government, "Balancing Measures: Best Practices in Performance Management, August 1999," at http://govinfo.library.unt.edu/npr/library/papers/bkgrd/balmeasure.html.

26. David Edwards and John Clayton Thomas, "Developing a Municipal Performance-Measurement System: Reflections on the Atlanta Dashboard," *Public Administration Review* 65 (May–June 2005): 369–376.

27. Ibid., 373.

28. Frank Levy, Arnold Meltsner, and Aaron Wildavsky, *Urban Outcomes: Schools, Streets, and Libraries* (Berkeley: University of California Press, 1974), 16–17.

29. Ibid., 233.

30. Robert L. Lineberry, "Equality, Public Policy and Public Services: The Under-Class Hypothesis and the Limits to Equality," *Policy and Politics* 4 (December 1975): 67–84.

31. George Antunes and Kenneth Mladenka, "The Politics of Local Services and Service Distribution," in *The New Urban Politics*, ed. Louis Masotti and Robert Lineberry (Cambridge, Mass.: Ballinger, 1976), 160.

32. Robert L. Lineberry, *Equality and Urban Policy: The Distribution of Municipal Public Services* (Beverly Hills, Calif.: Sage, 1977), 142; see also Kenneth R. Mladenka, "Citizen Demands and Urban Services: The Distribution of Bureaucratic Response in Chicago and Houston," *American Journal of Political Science* 25 (November 1981): 708.

33. See Daniel Fessler and Christopher May, "The Municipal Service Equalization Suit: A Case of Action in Quest of a Forum," in *Public Needs and Private Behavior in Metropolitan Areas*, ed. John E. Jackson (Cambridge, Mass.: Ballinger, 1975), 157–195.

34. Peter K. Eisinger, "The Pattern of Citizen Contacts with Urban Officials," in *People and Politics in Urban Society*, ed. Harlan Hahn (Beverly Hills, Calif.: Sage, 1972), 50.

35. Michael W. Hirlinger, "Citizen-Initiated Contacting of Local Government Officials: A Multivariate Explanation," *Journal of Politics* 54 (May 1992): 558.

36. This discussion is from Thomas I. Miller and Michelle A. Miller, "Standards of Excellence: U.S. Residents' Evaluations of Local Government Services," *Public Administration Review* 51 (November–December 1991): 503–513.

37. Mladenka, "Citizen Demands and Urban Services," 693–714.

38. See Alfred Tat-Kei Ho, "Reinventing Local Governments and the E-Government Initiative," *Public Administration Review* 62 (July–August 2002): 434–444.

39. Susan E. Baer and Vincent L. Marando, "The Subdistricting of Cities: Applying the Polycentric Model," *Urban Affairs Review* 36 (May 2001): 721–733.

40. Ibid., 723. The cities are Baltimore, Chicago, Cincinnati, Detroit, Great Falls, Houston, Louisville, Minneapolis, New York, Philadelphia, San Jose, and Seattle.

41. For a recent summary of this research and results of a new analysis, see Gregg G. Van Ryzin, Douglas Muzzio, and Stephen Immerwahr, "Explaining the Gap in Satisfaction with Urban Services," *Urban Affairs Review* 39 (May 2004): 613–632.

42. Lineberry, *Equality and Urban Policy*, 163.

43. Osborne and Gaebler, *Reinventing Government*, 76.

44. Ibid., chap. 3.

45. Originally discussed in E. S. Savas, *Privatization: The Key to Better Government* (Chatham, N.J.: Chatham House, 1987), 62; for a more recent treatment, see E. S. Savas, *Privatization in the City* (Washington, D.C.: CQ Press, 2005).

46. Mildred Warner and Amir Hefetz, "Pragmatism over Politics: Alternative Service Delivery in Local Government, 1992–2002," *2004 Municipal Year Book* (Washington, D.C.: ICMA, 2004), 8–16.

47. Ibid., 11.

48. Eileen Brettler Berenyi and Barbara J. Stevens, "Does Privatization Work? A Study of the Delivery of Eight Local Services," *State and Local Government Review* 20 (winter 1988): 11–20.

49. Lawrence L. Martin, "Proposed Methodology for Comparing the Costs of Government versus Contract Service Delivery," *1992 Municipal Year Book* (Washington, D.C.: ICMA, 1992), 12–15.

50. Ibid., 14.

51. See Sidney Sonenblum, John Kirlin, and John Ries, *How Cities Provide Services: An Evaluation of Alternative Delivery Structures* (Cambridge, Mass.: Ballinger, 1977), 33.

52. For an example of this research, see Anirudh V. S. Ruhil, Mark Schneider, Paul Teske, and Byung-Moon Ji, "Institutions and Reform: Reinventing Local Government," *Urban Affairs Review 34* (January 1999): 433–455.

53. Pascale Joassart-Marcelli and Juliet Musso, "Municipal Service Provision Choices within a Metropolitan Area," *Urban Affairs Review 40* (March 2005): 514.

54. Sergio Fernandez and Hal G. Rainey, "Local Government Contract Management and Performance Survey: A Report," *2005 Municipal Year Book* (Washington, D.C.: ICMA, 2005), 3–8.

55. This example comes from Mark Hughes, "Contracting Services in Phoenix," *Public Management*, October 1992, 2–4.

56. Ibid., 4.

57. The examples are found in *From Privatization to Innovation: A Study of 16 U.S. Cities* (Chicago: The Civic Federation, 1996), 13–21.

58. "Doing Business with the City [of Newark, New Jersey]." See www.ci.newark.nj.us.

59. Lawrence Martin, "Selecting Services for Public-Private Competition," *MIS Report* 18 (March 1996).

60. David N. Ammons and Debra J. Hill, "The Viability of Public-Private Competition as a Long-Term Service Delivery Strategy," *Public Productivity and Management Review* 19 (September 1995): 12–24.

61. Christopher Hoene, Mark Baldassare, and Michael Shires, "The Development of Counties as Municipal Governments: A Case Study of Los Angeles County in the Twenty-first Century," *Urban Affairs Review* 37 (March 2002): 575–591.

62. Joassart-Marcelli and Musso, "Municipal Service Provision Choices," 515.

63. Ibid.

64. Examples of the research of Mildred Warner and Amir Hefetz include "The Uneven Distribution of Market Solutions for Public Goods," *Journal of Urban Affairs* 24, no. 4 (2002): 445–459; and "Applying Market Solutions to Public Services: An Assessment of Efficiency, Equity, and Voice," *Urban Affairs Review* 38 (September 2002): 70–89. The specific findings mentioned are found in the latter article.

65. Warner and Hefetz, "Pragmatism over Politics," 11–12.

66. Carol Weiss, *Evaluation Research* (Englewood Cliffs, N.J.: Prentice Hall, 1972), 24–25.

67. The following sections draw on Harry Hatry, Richard Winnie, and Donald Fisk, *Practical Program Evaluation for State and Local Government Officials*, 2nd ed. (Washington, D.C.: Urban Institute, 1981), chap. 3 and appendix A.

68. Ibid., 31.

69. See Donald Campbell and Julian Stanley, *Experimental and Quasi-Experimental Designs for Research* (Chicago: Rand McNally, 1963).

70. Pamela Horst, Joe Ray, John Scanlon, and Joseph Wholey, "Program Management and the Federal Evaluator," *Public Administration Review* 34 (July–August 1974): 301.

71. Weiss, *Evaluation Research*, 26.

72. Ibid., 114.

73. Horst et al., "Program Management," 307.

74. Janet M. Kelly, "Citizen Satisfaction and Administrative Performance Measures: Is There Really a Link?" *Urban Affairs Review* 38 (July 2003): 863–864.

75. Douglas J. Watson, Robert J. Juster, and Gerald W. Johnson, "Institutionalized Use of Citizen Surveys in the Budgetary and Policy-Making Processes: A Small City Case Study," *Public Administration Review* 51 (May–June 1991): 232.

76. Thomas I. Miller and Michelle Miller Kobayashi, *Citizen Surveys: How to Do Them, How to Use Them, What They Mean* (Washington, D.C.: ICMA, 2000), 147.

77. Gregory Daneke and Patricia Klobus-Edwards, "Survey Research for Public Administrators," *Public Administration Review* 39 (September–October 1979): 421.

78. See, for example, Michael Licari, William McLean, and Tom W. Rice, "The Condition of Community Streets and Parks: A Comparison of Resident and Nonresident Evaluations," *Public Administration Review* 65 (May–June 2005): 360–368.

79. See, for example, Brian Stipak, "Citizen Satisfaction with Urban Services: Potential Misuse as a Performance Indicator," *Public Administration Review 39* (January–February 1979): 46–52. For an opposing view, see Jeffrey Brudney and Robert England, "Urban Policy Making and Subjective Service Evaluations: Are They Compatible?" *Public Administration Review 42* (March–April 1982): 127–135.

80. Brudney and England, "Urban Policy Making and Subjective Service Evaluations," 129.

CHAPTER 8   **THE MANAGEMENT PROCESS:**
THEORY AND PRACTICE

INTERNAL management consumes a good deal of urban managers' time and attention. Even in large cities, where external pressures and the need for policy leadership are constant, most managers, as noted in chapter 4, spend the bulk of their time administering the municipal organization.

Budgeting, planning, and managing human resources occupy a major portion of the day-to-day agenda, but internal management also involves motivating and leading those who bear the responsibility for providing vital city programs and services. Urban administrators must make key decisions regarding how well the municipal organization is performing. What can be done to encourage employees to do their best? Are there approaches and management strategies that will enable individual employees and the organization as a whole to perform more efficiently, effectively, responsively, and equitably? As identified in the previous chapter, these are the goals of municipal service delivery.

We begin this chapter with a discussion of organizations as open systems. This perspective allows us to understand the full range of influences on organizational performance, both internal and external. A special emphasis is placed on motivation and theories of human behavior, which help managers better understand why employees behave the way they do. Next we look at leadership. What do we know about effective organizational leadership? How does one become a "master manager?" A discussion of "managing for results" follows. In this section, we revisit and examine recent administrative reform efforts, but the main focus is on two management strategies—Management by Objectives (MBO) and Total Quality Management (TQM)—that facilitate the accomplishment of organizational goals and objectives. Finally, we discuss potential problems that might arise when management techniques that are new to a city are used. The entire chapter is placed in the context of organizational culture, an important concept in a period when all organizations, public and private alike, are asked to respond to change.

ORGANIZATIONS AS OPEN SYSTEMS

Organizations conceptualized as open systems actually consist of three parts.[1] First is the formal organization, defined by a host of characteristics such as the formal hierarchy, functional specialization, centralization/decentralization of authority, span of control, bureaucratic control, communication, line versus staff functions, and decision making. Within each formal organization exists an informal organization, defined as "groups that form outside or despite the formal organization."[2] Harold Gortner and his colleagues note that the informal organization "plays a significant part in determining the perceptions and attitudes of group members, as well as establishing the values and norms of behavior."[3] In terms of management, the presence of the informal organization requires that urban managers understand human behavior; they need to be organizational psychologists. Finally, as discussed previously, all organizations are surrounded by and respond to forces generated in their external environment. It is this pluralistic environment that distinguishes the *public* from the *private* organization. As keepers of the public trust, urban managers must respond to a host of diverse preferences, wants, and demands. Environmental contexts remain important predictors of organizational performance.

Recent research also emphasizes the importance of culture in the workings of all modern public organizations. This "predominant value system . . . helps to overcome the centrifugal tendencies of a large bureaucracy by instilling in its members a sense of unity and common purpose."[4] What motivates people to perform in public organizations? Based on survey data gathered from a large New York State agency, box 8.1 provides a case study of public service and motivation.

The discussion that follows explores in greater depth approaches to understanding human behavior and what implications these theories have for employee motivation and organizational leadership.

SCIENTIFIC MANAGEMENT

The scientific study of management, which dates back to the latter part of the nineteenth century, was given its most systematic exposition in the works of Frederick W. Taylor.[5] According to Taylor, careful analysis could uncover the single best way of performing any repetitive task. Jobs could be standardized and routinized, and then each employee could be selected and trained specifically to fit the needs of the job. Person and machine would work in glorious harmony at maximum output. Taylor recognized that workers would have to be motivated properly if this approach was to operate at its full potential. Simple enough. Using a theory of "economic man," Taylor assumed that people would work harder and more efficiently if they were rewarded in relation to their individual output. The more workers produced, the more money they made. Piecework was ideally suited to this philosophy of worker motivation.

We can argue about how scientific Taylor's approach was, but it did contribute significantly to improvements in the work methods and processes that made possible the mass production and assembly-line techniques of the modern corporation. And although it was not long before a reaction developed to the supposedly mechanistic, dehumanizing philosophy of scientific management, we can still identify certain management practices in use today that bear a strong resemblance to Taylor's approach. The current emphasis on

BOX 8.1   Policy and Practice

PUBLIC SERVICE AND MOTIVATION: MISSION DOES MATTER

In a recent *Public Administration Review* article entitled, "Public Service and Motivation: Does Mission Matter?" University of North Carolina at Charlotte political scientist Bradley E. Wright finds "[t]he importance of an organization's mission increases employee work motivation in the public sector by making the job more important, even after controlling for the effect of performance-related extrinsic rewards." Professor Wright employs the "goal theory of motivation" and a theoretical model comprised of seven factors to test certain assumptions about public service and motivation. These assumptions include the generally held beliefs that public sector organizations attract employees whose "values and needs are consistent with the public service mission of the organization" and public sector workers "place a lower value on financial rewards and a higher value on helping others (public service) than their private sector counterparts."

Wright's empirical analysis uses survey data from 807 self-identified managers and professionals in a New York state agency. He asked participants to respond to a series of perceptual questions about job characteristics, work environment, management practices, turnover intentions, and job alternatives on five- or six-point Likert scales.[1] Wright then created a scale for each of the seven factors in his conceptual model using multiple measures. For example, the dependent variable was labeled *work motivation*. The range of the scale was from 3–22 based on individuals' responses to four statements:

- I put forth my best effort to get my job done regardless of the difficulties.
- It has been hard for me to get very involved in my current job.
- I probably do not work as hard as others who do the same type of work.
- Time seems to drag while I am on the job.[2]

Wright asserts that six independent variables either directly or indirectly explain the dependent variable, *work motivation*. (1) *Mission valance* and (2) *extrinsic rewards* are assumed to have a positive impact on (3) *job importance*, which in turn has a direct impact on *work motivation*. (4) *Job difficulty* and (5) *job specificity* are both predicted to have a direct and positive impact on *work motivation* and to have indirect impacts as they filter through an intervening variable labeled (6) *self-efficacy*, which in turn is directly and positively related to *work motivation*. The goal theory of motivation suggests the impact of *job difficulty* on *self-efficacy* will be negative, while the relationship between *job specificity* and *self-efficacy* is positive.

Before turning to findings, we might quickly explain each of the six independent variables. *Mission valence* captures perceptions about the importance of the agency's organizational goals. One of the items used to measures these attitudes stated: "This division provides valuable public services." Others grant *extrinsic rewards* such as pay, promotion, and recognition in the organization; these rewards are not self-administered. Research shows that to be effective, employees must perceive a strong link between their performance and extrinsic rewards. One statement used in the study to gauge attitudes toward extrinsic rewards was: "Working hard is recognized by upper management." The variable *job importance* is hypothesized to be directly related

(continued)

---

[1] The five-point scale contained "almost never or never," "rarely," "sometimes," "often," and "almost always or always." The six-point scale was "strongly disagree," "generally disagree," "disagree," "agree," "generally agree," and "strongly agree."
[2] These statements are taken directly from the article. The 3–22 range for this variable using four measures is explained by the use of a five, and not six-point, Likert scale that is anchored at zero for one statement. For most of the seven measures, at least one item was coded in the reverse order.

in a positive way to *work motivation*. This job importance variable measures employees' beliefs that what they do is important. One statement used to gather attitudes about job importance was: "I feel that my work is important." Two of the remaining variables, *job difficulty* and *job specificity*, have direct influences on *work motivation* and indirect effects as they help define an employee's feeling of *self-efficacy*. *Self-efficacy*, in turn, directly impacts *work motivation*. In the words of Wright: "Higher levels of self-efficacy are often associated with better performance because employees are more likely to expend the necessary effort and persist in the face of obstacles if they feel that their efforts will eventually be successful." One indicator of the variable *job difficulty* was the statement: "My work is very challenging." *Job specificity* was measured by attitudes on two statements, one of which was "My supervisor clearly expresses work expectations to me." These two variables then influenced the *self-efficacy* scale, which was measured by three questions. An example of a question was: "I am confident that I can successfully perform any tasks assigned to me on my current job."

The statistical findings strongly support Wright's causal model. All path coefficients were in the hypothesized direction and all were statistically significant at the $p < .05$ level. The two job content variables, *job difficulty* and *job specificity*, significantly affected *work motivation* directly and indirectly through the intervening variable *self-efficacy*. The same holds true for the impact of *mission valence* and *extrinsic rewards*, indicators of job commitment, on *job importance*. In turn, *job importance* and *self-efficacy* showed significant and positive relationships with *work motivation*. The six variables collectively explained 69 percent of the variation in *work motivation*. This is a high level of explanatory power, especially when using attitudinal data.

Wright also highlights the impact of *mission valence* (organizational mission) on employees' attitudes toward the variable *job importance*. *Mission valence* showed the largest path coefficient ($\beta = .86$) of any variable in the model. In contrast, the other variable linked to *job importance*, *extrinsic rewards*, while significant, only showed a path coefficient of $\beta = .10$. The author notes, "Managers should . . . look at organizational mission as a motivational tool that can link performance to employee self-concept." Moreover, "managers must emphasize not only how the organization's values coincide with those of employees but also how employee performance contributes to the organization's ability to operationalize those values." Managers should clearly communicate to employees how their hard work "benefits society."

As the title of this box suggests, public sector organizational mission *does* matter. In fact, it matters a lot.

SOURCE: Bradley E. Wright, "Public Service and Motivation: Does Mission Matter?" *Public Administration Review* 67 (January–February, 2007): 54–64.

pay for performance is one. Productivity improvement is another: in some cities, management negotiates productivity contracts with groups of employees by tying supplemental increases in wages to increased levels of productivity.

HUMANISTIC MANAGEMENT

The Human Relations Approach

Building on the work of Elton Mayo and Fritz Roethlisberger at the Hawthorne Western Electric plant outside Chicago, a new approach to management evolved that came to be called human relations. "Human Relations dethroned Economic Man and installed Social Man in his place."[6] The human relations movement stressed the importance of the informal social structure within an organization and its effect on the behavior and motivation of workers. Moving beyond economic rewards, this approach emphasized other needs of employees, such as approval, belonging, and group membership, and claimed that meeting these human and social needs would create a more satisfied workforce. Although some advocates apparently saw this subjective improvement as virtually an end in itself, others believed that happier workers would be more productive. Undoubtedly, the human relations movement did much to improve working conditions, but research shows that happy, contented workers do not necessarily work harder or produce more. Also, the early human relations approach did little to motivate employees to search for higher-order needs, such as autonomy and self-actualization.

The Organizational Humanists

In the 1950s and 1960s, the early human relations theories began to be modified. Abraham Maslow, Douglas McGregor, Frederick Herzberg, and Chris Argyris offered views of human nature that took account of human needs in a more sophisticated way. Maslow, for example, suggested his now-famous hierarchy of needs, which he based on the assumption that needs are motivators of behavior only when they remain unsatisfied. Once the lower physiological needs (hunger, thirst, shelter) and security needs (both physical and economic) have been reasonably well satisfied, a higher level of needs is activated. Social needs (belonging and acceptance) occupy the next rung on the ladder; psychological or ego needs (status, recognition, esteem) emerge next; and, at the top, is what Maslow calls "self-actualization"—a state in which a person achieves his or her fullest potential as a human being.[7] Maslow's hierarchy implies that most employees are not motivated strictly by economic needs.

McGregor, building on Maslow's hierarchy, posited the existence of two polar opposite management approaches: Theory X and Theory Y. Theory X, the traditional view, holds that people are basically lazy and unambitious; they want to avoid work and responsibility. In trying to motivate employees based on the assumptions of Theory X, management must use a series of carrots and sticks. It can take a hard line, devising tight controls and pushing workers to produce more, or it can take a soft line, allowing employees greater participation. Both strategies have potential weaknesses: the hard-line approach may generate antagonism, resistance, even sabotage; the soft-line approach may reduce output. McGregor challenged this conventional management theory, suggesting that even though employees often seem to respond as though Theory X were valid, such behavior is not innate.

McGregor's Theory Y postulates that people do not inherently dislike work, but they do exercise self-direction and self-control in pursuit of goals they deem worthwhile. This approach implies that if employees are indifferent, lazy, intransigent, uncreative, uncooperative, and unwilling to take responsibility, management's methods of organization and control are at fault.[8] McGregor would have management create conditions under which members of an organization can achieve their own goals by directing their efforts toward the success of the enterprise. Under Theory Y, an organization can most effectively reach its own economic objectives by meeting the needs and goals of its members. Herzberg and Argyris also suggest that unless employees' needs for growth and development are met, they will be dissatisfied with their jobs.[9]

Maslow, McGregor, Herzberg, and Argyris have been called organizational humanists. They differed from the earlier human relations proponents in emphasizing the organization as well as the individual employee. Not only were these scholars concerned with providing greater opportunities for employees to gain a sense of recognition, accomplishment, and fulfillment from their work; they also recognized the organization's need to get the job done. They did not feel that these two goals were antithetical. In their view, managers and their subordinates can jointly set high performance goals and exercise responsible self-control in their achievement.[10]

The Humanistic Approach: An Appraisal

How accurately have organizational humanists captured reality? One serious flaw in motivational theories is their monolithic quality: they assume that all people have a common set of needs and that those needs are shared to the same degree. Critics argue that few people want the same things, at least to the same degree. Instead, employees want—and to some extent search for—jobs that are congruent with their individual preferences.[11] Other research findings suggest that many of the basic tenets of humanistic motivational theory do not apply to lower-level employees: "Evidence indicates a two-step hierarchy: Lower-level employees show more concern with material and security rewards, while higher-level employees place more emphasis on achievement and challenge."[12]

Research by Robert Rodgers and John Hunter supports a more optimistic appraisal of the link between job satisfaction and job performance. They find that job satisfaction does contribute to lowering absenteeism and employee turnover, which helps to boost productivity; also, these researchers say, such participatory management techniques as Management by Objectives can contribute to gains in employee output.[13] Similar thoughts are echoed by Soonhee Kim. Based on over 1,500 employee surveys collected in 1999 in Clark County, Nevada, he finds that a participative management style, employees' perceptions of the use of participative strategic management processes, and a participative management style that incorporates effective supervisory communication all lead to enhanced employee job satisfaction. Kim concludes, "Organizational leaders in the public sector should emphasize changing organizational culture from the traditional pattern of hierarchical structure to participative management and empowerment."[14]

Evan Berman, Jonathan West, and Maurice Richter hit the proverbial nail on the head when they comment that "one can espouse support for 'workplace humanism' and 'organizational effectiveness,' but in the end, it is what is done that matters."[15] As public organizations become more diverse (a topic we discuss in greater length in the next chapter), how can managers promote better organizational humanism both vertically and horizontally in city government? Based on a survey of senior managers in U.S. cities with populations over 50,000 (N = 222), Berman and his associates suggest that fostering workplace friendships—defined as "nonexclusive workplace relations that involve mutual trust, commitment, reciprocal liking and shared interests and values"—can provide large payoffs.[16] Very few managers in their survey disapprove of such friendships, and this finding holds true even when different genders are involved. Also, while some managers suggest that workplace friendships can increase the risk of office gossip and romances, and may create distractions from work, the positive benefits gained outweigh the costs, overall. The managers report, for example, the following effects:

- Managers' perceptions of employee productivity are significantly higher in organizations that also have a high level of perceived workplace friendship.
- Perceptions of high levels of workplace friendship increase the perceived willingness of employees to take risks by almost 50 percent, . . . the perceived willingness to be accountable increases 62 percent, . . . and perceptions of high employee motivation increase 31.0 percent.
- Organizations that attempt to foster a climate of openness and friendship in a majority of units reported significantly less employee stress . . . and lower employee absenteeism.
- Efforts to promote workplace friendship are negatively associated with a lack of professional norms and with playing favorites. This is further evidence that workplace friendship has positive organizational impacts.[17]

Berman and his associates conclude that "friendship can help employees to get their job done, provide a climate of openness and support, and increase cooperation and acceptance of change."[18] They also warn against the disingenuous use of "social engineering" to create friendships. Instead, the process should occur through managerial encouragement of friendships and by creating an environment characterized as open and honest—both laudable humanistic values.

Theory Z and REGO as Expressions of Organizational Humanism

Although much of the early work by the organizational humanists emerged in the 1950s and 1960s, two more recent books, one written in the early 1980s and one in the early 1990s, have given humanistic management a boost. Although both go beyond a concern for motivation to embrace a range of management ideas and principles, they offer insight into how effective organizations can accomplish more by emphasizing human values.

First, *Theory Z: How American Business Can Meet the Japanese Challenge* espouses the view that U.S. companies can improve quality and performance by adopting certain features of the Japanese approach to management. In some ways, Theory Z seems to be an extension of Theory Y—for example, its essence is trust and cooperation between labor and management. According to the author of the book, William Ouchi, Theory Z places a heavy emphasis on consensus decision making.[19] What sometimes is not understood is how far the Japanese carry the consensus process. For every important decision, "everyone who will feel its impact is involved in making it." The process can involve as many as sixty to eighty people and can drag on for days if not weeks. There is also a deliberate ambiguity about who is responsible for what decisions. The entire procedure is designed to promote mutual sharing and commitment to organizational objectives.

How applicable is Theory Z to the local public sector? One account of its use involves the New York City Sanitation Department's Bureau of Motor Equipment. As the bureau faced imminent collapse, its top management was forced to resign and a new team was brought in with a mandate to turn things around. Among other changes, the new leadership introduced collective decision making by creating a labor-management committee that gathered information and insights from the workforce on how to improve productivity and hold down costs. Within a few years, the bureau was "transformed from an organization deep in the red and unable to complete its assigned job to one which is operating so smoothly that it is actually beginning to generate an income."[20]

The second book with a prominent humanistic perspective is Osborne and Gaebler's *Reinventing Government*. Most frequently, REGO is discussed within the context of management techniques and processes such as MBO, broad-banding personnel systems, performance budgeting, or privatization. (We discuss some of these techniques and processes later, just as we examined privatization in the previous chapter.) But Osborne and Gaebler's prescription for what ails government includes many of the same "cures" that were advocated by organizational humanists fifty years ago. Thus, as we have noted several times, REGO "reforms" are nothing new. Instead, it is a restatement of what we have known for many years: that people and communities are important in governance. Three REGO reforms are particularly humanist in nature, calling for the empowerment of communities/neighborhoods, citizens, and government workers.[21]

Community-Owned Government

Reminiscent of the rhetoric associated with the community-control movement in the 1960s and early 1970s, community-owned government requires empowering residents, primarily at the neighborhood level. A basic premise is that services should be owned by the community, not by the bureaucracy. Examples are abundant, from community-oriented policing to job-training centers run in part by dislocated workers to neighborhood-based community development corporations and tenant cooperatives. Why community-owned service delivery instead of using professional service agents (that is, bureaucrats)? Osborne and Gaebler argue the following points: (1) that communities are more committed to their members than service agents are to their clients; (2) that communities understand their problems better than service professionals do; (3) that service agents deliver services, whereas communities solve problems and care about members; and (4) that communities are more flexible and innovative than large service bureaucracies because they are not bound by extensive rules and regulations. The logical conclusion of this argument is that citizens, neighborhoods, and/or communities should be empowered, both politically and administratively, and entrusted with ownership of local services. The case study presented in box 8.2 shows how former mayor Stephen Goldsmith incorporated community-owned government as part of his efforts to reform administrative processes in the city of Indianapolis.

Customer-Driven Government

In chapter 1, we noted that Osborne and Gaebler miss the target when they call citizens "customers," but the point is worth repeating. We understand their intention: to underscore that *citizens* should not be viewed as mere clients—that *citizens* are as important in government as customers are important in business. Government should meet the needs of the citizen-owner and not those of the bureaucracy. Big-name management thinkers from the late Peter Drucker to Tom Peters to Rosabeth Moss Kanter all tell of the importance of private-sector employees being in touch with their customers. In like manner, listening to the voices of citizens can be facilitated in the public sector by various mechanisms, including customer surveys (used in Los Angeles and Orlando), community surveys (used in Dallas, Dayton, and Fairfield, California), customer councils (used by housing authorities in Louisville), and complaint tracking systems (used in Phoenix). One management technique that can facilitate citizen-based government is TQM, which has been used for some time now in the private sector and has gained popularity in the public sector; we discuss this innovation later in this chapter.

Decentralized Government

Like the organizational humanists of the 1950s and 1960s, Osborne and Gaebler seek to empower workers and join Harlan Cleveland, former dean of the Humphrey Institute at the University of Minnesota, in calling for the "twilight of hierarchy." Osborne and Gaebler argue that public institutions should move from hierarchy to participation and teamwork, "to return control to those who work down where the rubber meets the road." Institutions can achieve decentralization through the use of participation management, labor-management committees, and no-layoff policies, and by flattening the organizational hierarchy. That last strategy is essential, because the "most serious resistance to teamwork and participatory management often comes from middle managers, not unions."

Teamwork can promote entrepreneurial government. For example, East Harlem schools are run by teams. Visalia, California, and St. Paul, Minnesota, use cross-departmental teams to develop new city projects. Teamwork brings the following advantages:

- Cross-departmental teams allow for more complete analysis of problems because employees from different departments will have different perspectives.
- Cross-departmental teams break down "turf" walls.
- Teams build bridges and networks throughout the city administration.

BOX 8.2   Policy and Practice

IDEOLOGY AND THE REVITALIZATION OF DISTRESSED NEIGHBORHOODS IN INDIANAPOLIS

If any one mayor in the United States captured the essence and spirit of administrative reform during the 1990s, it was Stephen Goldsmith. During his two-term tenure (1992–2000) as mayor, he helped to transform the city of Indianapolis into what a1995 issue of *Financial World* magazine termed "one of the best-managed cities in America." That same year, the Ford Foundation selected Indianapolis to receive its Innovation in American Government Award, and *Governing* magazine named Mayor Goldsmith as its Public Official of the Year.

In 2003, in a series of three articles in a single issue of the *Journal of Urban Affairs*, political scientist Stephen McGovern of Haverford College and former mayor Goldsmith, who joined Harvard's Kennedy School of Government after leaving public service, engage in an academic exercise in which McGovern provides an assessment of Goldsmith's performance as mayor of Indianapolis, then Goldsmith offers a "rejoinder," and finally, as the custom goes, McGovern makes a "response" to Goldsmith's rejoinder. At the heart of the debate between the two is not that Goldsmith used reforms advocated by New Public Management proponents to transform the city of Indianapolis—McGovern concedes that he did so: "Private business took over the city's microfilming, sewer-billing collections, and management of municipal golf courses. At the end of his two terms in office, Goldsmith asserted that the city had opened up over 80 services to competitive bidding, which he predicted would result in $450 million in savings through 2007" (4). Instead, the debate centers on how to label Goldsmith's ideological approach: McGovern favors "progressive," while Goldsmith, not surprisingly, prefers "a new active urban conservatism" or "compassionate conservatism" (27). It would be wrong to simply dismiss this disagreement as semantics, for, as we noted earlier, NPM reforms have deep neoconservative roots in public choice theory. Therefore, how his political ideology is *labeled* is important to Goldsmith.

At issue is Goldsmith's use of government power to aid seven targeted distressed neighborhoods around the downtown area of Indianapolis. At the time, the mayor noted, "We're saying that communities in the most difficult shape should have our highest priorities. We cannot write off 70,000 individuals, place them in hopelessness and hope to remain a humane city" (9). McGovern claims that the mayor was, therefore, a progressive: he aggressively used the power of the city in an effort to rebuild inner-city neighborhoods and his neighborhood programs had a redistributive thrust (9). The Goldsmith administration budgeted salary money for neighborhood coordinators in the seven targeted neighborhoods; discretionary funds were provided to the neighborhoods; and a $525,000 annual city commitment was used to leverage $712,000 in local and national foundations "enthusiastic about the concept of citizen empowerment" (8). The city also encouraged the revitalization efforts of local community development corporations (CDCs).

While McGovern praises Goldsmith's progressive actions, there is no hero worship in his assessment. For example, he notes the early success of the initiative and then documents how the efforts of private-sector investors, neighborhood leaders, and Mayor Goldsmith all fell short. Affordable housing production in the neighborhoods increased, leveled off, and then declined. The CDCs failed to meet expectations. In 1992, as part of the devolution of power from city hall to the neighborhoods, several dozen employees were dismissed

(continued)

BOX 8.2   Policy and Practice (continued)

from the Department of Metropolitan Development; the experience and institutional memory of some of the most experienced urban planners were thereby lost to neighborhood leaders (17). And while not "blaming the victim," McGovern suggests that the neighborhood leaders themselves were not aggressive enough in pursuit of public and private resources. He concludes: "Empowering people without supplying sufficient public resources and authority leads, at best, to modest expectations and outcomes in an environment that demands aggressive action from both the citizenry and the state" (23).

In his rejoinder, Goldsmith agrees with some of McGovern's points, noting that the "case study accurately captures my efforts to shrink city government" (30). He continues, "The conservative populist ideology based on empowerment described in the study is exactly what I meant to apply and to communicate to every stakeholder involved" (27). He even agrees with McGovern that despite his best efforts, his initiatives were not as successful as he had hoped they would be. What the ex-mayor does not agree with is McGovern's claim that his actions were progressive: "I plead guilty to the accusation of activism but innocent to McGovern's charge that my policies were inherently not conservative" (28).

SOURCES: *Journal of Urban Affairs* 25, no. 1 (2003): Stephen J. McGovern, Ideology, Consciousness, and Inner-City Redevelopment: The Case of Stephen Goldsmith's Indianapolis," 1–25; Stephen Goldsmith, "Rejoinder to Ideology and Inner City Redevelopment: Conservative Activism," 27–32; and Stephen J. McGovern, "Response to Goldsmith: Reflections on Government Activism and Community Development," 33–36.

- Teams often hold employees to higher standards of performance than do "bosses." Peer approval is an important evaluative reference point for most people in organizations.

Clearly, management approaches that accentuate the human potential of the workforce have come a long way since the early days of the human relations school. Today's emphasis on decentralization, participation, teamwork, creativity, and entrepreneurship comports well with the long-standing view that involved workers are the key to increased productivity. Nevertheless, the importance of leadership at all levels in government organizations is indisputable.

LEADERSHIP

Earlier we discussed the importance of community leadership by urban executives, particularly by popularly elected mayors. But leadership in city government has another dimension: the exercise of direction and supervision by management within the municipal organization itself. One observer comments that "leadership is the most important demand placed upon the urban administrator. The most saleable quality possessed by a city manager, county executive, or other similar official is his [or her] ability to coordinate, direct, and motivate others."[22] In fact, as public administration expert Robert D. Behn reminds us, "Leadership is not just a right of public managers. It is an obligation."[23]

Before we proceed further with our discussion of leadership, it is important to note that leadership is a slippery concept. There is no single accepted definition, no single accepted model of leadership. In fact, the literature on the topic is both voluminous and often contentious. Therefore, as we examine this vital aspect of management, remember the words of well-known management experts Paul Hersey and Kenneth Blanchard: "*A single type of leader behavior seems unrealistic.* . . . The primary reason why there is no 'one best way' of leadership is that leadership is basically situational, or contingent."[24] They also note that "*all* leadership theories. . . . have not been conclusively validated by scientific research."[25] Hersey and Blanchard assert that leadership approaches are not theories per se, but rather models or "sets of empirical generalizations," and they argue that this state of affairs accurately captures the essence of leadership, which demands that managers use different leadership styles day-to-day, or even minute-to-minute.

THE ELEMENTS OF LEADERSHIP

Most authorities believe that leadership in an organization involves a relationship among a *leader, follower,* and *situation*, or, to borrow Hersey and Blanchard's formula, L = f(1, f, s). Normally these elements interact in pursuit of some goal or objective. *Leadership*, then, is "the process of influencing the activities of an individual or a group in efforts toward goal achievement in a given situation."[26]

Leadership theory and practice have been influenced strongly by the approaches to human behavior discussed earlier. Scientific management emphasizes the job: the leader's role is to determine how best to accomplish a given task; the needs of the organization, not those of its individual members, are paramount. According to organizational humanists, the leader's task is to facilitate cooperation among *employees* while providing for their personal growth and development; individual needs, not the needs of the organization, are the principal concern.[27]

Contemporary thinking recognizes the importance of both *tasks* and *people*. Thus, leadership is concerned both with achieving some specific goal and with developing human potential and maintaining and strengthening the work group. But how is this to be done? Are there some people who, by virtue of their personal characteristics, turn out to be better leaders than others? Are certain styles or approaches to leadership more effective than others?

LEADERSHIP TRAITS

The idea that some people are born leaders has been popular throughout history. For many years, the study of leadership concentrated on identifying those traits that characterize natural leaders, but empirical research has failed to validate the leadership trait approach. This is not to say that a leader's personality is of no consequence—only that efforts to distinguish leaders from others on the basis of personality traits have been largely unsuccessful. The prevailing view is that leadership is largely *situation-specific*. One person may emerge as a leader in one case; another might rise to the top in a different context.

Still, a comprehensive review of the literature on leadership finds that certain characteristics seem to differentiate leaders from followers, effective leaders from ineffective ones, and higher-echelon leaders from lower-echelon ones. After citing a number of studies, distinguished researcher and longtime leadership expert Ralph Stogdill concludes:

> The leader is characterized by a strong drive for responsibility and task completion, vigor and persistence in pursuit of goals, venturesomeness and originality in problem solving, drive to exercise initiative in social situations, self-confidence and sense of personal identity, willingness to accept consequences of decision and action, readiness to absorb interpersonal stress, willingness to tolerate frustration and delay, ability to influence other persons' behavior, and capacity to structure social interaction to the purpose at hand.[28]

Stogdill insists that his findings do not represent a return to trait theory. Instead they reflect a movement away from the extreme situational approach that denies the importance of individual differences. He concludes that leadership consists of an interaction among members of a group in which the leader emerges by demonstrating his or her capacity for carrying a specific task through to completion.

LEADERSHIP STYLES

What about styles of leadership? Proponents of scientific management saw the need for hard-driving, authoritarian leaders— people concerned almost exclusively with getting the job done. Human relations advocates promoted more participative leadership styles, in which managers give maximum latitude to their subordinates. Current attempts to define leadership styles are more complex, but they still rely on the tasks-people dichotomy.

Tasks versus People

An often cited and classic model of leadership styles is shown in the continuum of leadership behavior in figure 8-1. Leaders who fall toward the more authoritarian end of the spectrum are likely to be task-oriented; those who are more democratic are inclined to be group-centered.

This bipolar theory has been expanded by management consultants Robert Blake and Jane Mouton into the form of a Managerial Grid, as shown in figure 8-2.[29] Concern for production is depicted on the horizontal axis; concern for people, on the vertical. A value

Figure 8-1   **A Continuum of Leadership Behavior**

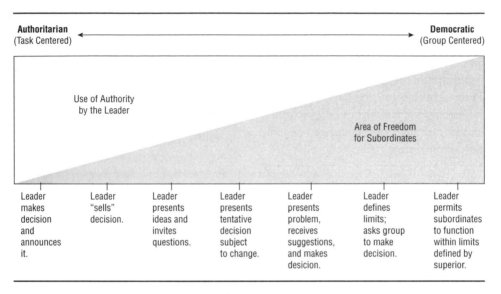

Authoritarian (Task Centered)						Democratic (Group Centered)
Leader makes decision and announces it.	Leader "sells" decision.	Leader presents ideas and invites questions.	Leader presents tentative decision subject to change.	Leader presents problem, receives suggestions, and makes desicion.	Leader defines limits; asks group to make decision.	Leader permits subordinates to function within limits defined by superior.

Use of Authority by the Leader

Area of Freedom for Subordinates

of 9 on either axis represents the maximum commitment to that orientation. The grid presents five basic positions:

- 1,1—Minimum effort toward the goal and toward sustaining the group
- 1,9—Maximum attention to group needs; little concern for output
- 9,1—Total interest in production; virtually none for the group
- 9,9—Maximum concern for both group and productivity
- 5,5—Average concern for both output and group needs

The 9,9 position encompasses not only goal-oriented behavior but also a desire to enhance organizational effectiveness through extensive employee involvement in problem solving.

The grid approach is more than a way of analyzing leadership style. The Managerial Grid—a phrase copyrighted by Blake and Mouton—has become a form of organizational development in which seminars and team-building exercises are used to effect a total change in the organization's work climate. The authors insist that evidence is available to show that 9,9-oriented managers—that is, those committed to team management—enjoy maximum career success.

Figure 8-2   **The Managerial Grid®**

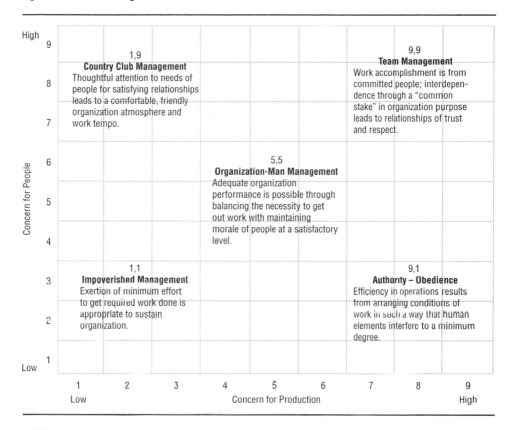

SITUATIONAL LEADERSHIP AND THE "MASTER MANAGER"

With the realization that leadership is a highly complex phenomenon came efforts to construct more sophisticated models of the process. Paul Hersey and Kenneth Blanchard offer an elaborate view of leadership that stresses its situational nature.[30] They identify four basic leadership styles—telling, selling, participating, and delegating—but insist that the appropriate style depends on the *readiness level* of the followers (that is, the extent to which a follower is able and willing to accomplish a specific task). Where followers' readiness is low-to-moderate, leaders should tell or sell; where it is moderate-to-high, leaders should encourage participation or even delegate. The idea is that employees with lower levels of readiness require strong, task-oriented direction. As workers became more ready or more responsible, leaders can place less emphasis on the requirements associated with a particular job and more on positive reinforcement and socio-emotional support (relationship behavior). The highest level of employee readiness calls for delegation, a style that encourages autonomy and reduces the need for both task direction and supportive relationships.

Blake and Mouton, originators of the Managerial Grid, take exception to Hersey and Blanchard's leadership theory.[31] They contend that, contrary to the assumptions of the situational model, there is only one best leadership style—their 9,9 approach. They discuss research in which a group of one hundred public and private managers were asked to choose between situational alternatives and 9,9-oriented alternatives to twelve hypothetical managerial problems involving different levels of employee maturity. For each level of maturity and for each of the twelve problems, the 9,9 responses were selected over the situational ones to a statistically significant degree.

Like Hersey and Blanchard, Robert E. Quinn would strongly disagree with Blake and Mouton's "one best way" position. And although he would support Hersey and Blanchard's "situational leadership," his theory is more dynamic and fluid. Drawing on the organizational change and culture literature, in his book, *Beyond Rational Management*, Quinn identifies positive and negative leadership zones.[32] These zones are based on four common organizational models or organizational cultures—human relations, open systems, rational goal, and internal process—and a vertical and horizontal axis. As shown in figure 8-3, the vertical axis ranges from chaos (too much responsiveness to the needs of workers and to environmental stimuli) to rigidity (too much control, order, and predictability). The horizontal axis ranges from belligerence and hostility (too much emphasis on external actors and on competition) to apathy and indifference (too much internal focus on system maintenance and coordination).

The outer, negative ring in figure 8-3 shows what happens when each of the four organizational values is carried to an extreme. The human relations model that focuses on relationship behavior becomes an "Irresponsible Country Club." Open-systems theory with an overemphasis on responsiveness, gathering external support, and political expediency becomes nothing more than a "Tumultuous Anarchy." When effort, productivity, efficiency, and authority (the rational goal model) are carried to an extreme, the organization becomes an "Oppressive Sweat Shop." Finally, too much control, procedural sterility, and following the rules (an internal process emphasis) can produce a "Frozen Bureaucracy."

In contrast, the inner, positive ring shows those characteristics of each organizational culture that can be used to foster caring, participative, responsive, innovative, productive, and stable organizations. The key to success, according to Quinn, is the ability of an organization to change continually and, as the negative inner circle warns, to clarify its values. No one model is correct for all situations. The more fully one set of positive values is pushed to the exclusion of another set, the greater the danger the organization faces. Quinn's *situational as well as dynamic* theory of leadership has important implications for management. It suggests, above all, that managers must constantly guard against pushing one approach to the extreme. By remaining sensitive to competing organizational values, a

Figure 8-3   **Robert Quinn's Positive and Negative Leadership Zones**

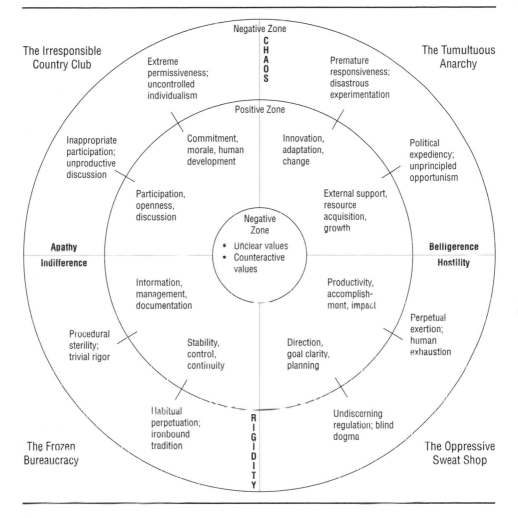

SOURCE: Robert E. Quinn, *Beyond Rational Management* (San Francisco: Jossey-Bass, 1988), 70. Reprinted with permission of John Wiley and Sons, Inc.

successful leader or manager—what Quinn calls a "master manager"—can learn to understand and adapt to constant organizational change.

In many ways, Quinn's model captures the real complexity of leadership and the situational or contingency approach to leadership as explained by James Owens about three decades ago. Owens notes that *effective* managers:

. . . expressed a virtual consensus that, based on their actual experience, each situation they handled demanded a different leadership style. No single style could suffice under the day-to-day, even minute-to-minute, varying conditions of different personalities and moods among their employees, routine process vs. changing or sudden deadlines, new and ever-changing government regulations and paperwork, ambiguous roles of workers, wide ranges in job complexity from simple to innovation-demanding, changes in organizational structures . . . and task technologies and so on. Contingency theory has come to mean, therefore, that the effective manager has, and knows how to use, many leadership styles as each is appropriate to a particular situation.[33]

MANAGING FOR RESULTS (MFR): MANAGEMENT BY OBJECTIVES (MBO) AND TOTAL QUALITY MANAGEMENT (TQM)

Clearly, leadership is important in public organizations. But city executives must also manage people, programs, budgets, information, technology, and a host of external constituencies in order to achieve politically defined goals and objectives (Appendix 8-A contains a list of 18 ICMA practices for effective local government.) Attaining peak organizational performance has always been a priority for local leaders, but in today's environment of high public expectations and fiscal scarcity, it is more important than ever. In chapter 1, we introduced two approaches to public management reform that emerged worldwide in the early 1990s—reinventing government (REGO) and the New Public Management (NPM). A principle thrust of the reforms advocated by both REGO and the NPM, along with individual and organizational accountability,[34] is to use administrative techniques (old and new) that emphasize *managing for results* (MFR). As Professors Brendan Burke and Bernadette Costello note: "Few have questioned the results orientation as an appropriate focus for public management's future; when the outcome orientation is combined with effective strategic planning in the MFR reform, top-down legitimacy is combined with bottom-up determination of programmatic performance, as well as a more motivated public work force."[35] Desired results might be gains in service delivery efficiency through the use of performance measurement, benchmarking, and/or privatization, or they might be more effective and higher quality service delivery by listening to citizens through a variety of available mechanisms. As the case study of Stephen Goldsmith in Indianapolis (box 8.2) showed, the desired results might be community/neighborhood empowerment resulting in greater service delivery equity. Results such as these, and many others, have been documented in cities that employ what Burke and Costello call a "holistic" approach to MFR implementation. Three such U.S. cities are Austin, Texas; Charlotte, North Carolina; and Phoenix, Arizona.[36]

Before we examine in detail two administrative strategies that have been successfully used since the 1950s to manage for results, we need to offer a final word about Osborne and Gaebler's ten-point prescription for reinventing government (see Appendix 8-B) and Hughes's thirteen-point New Public Management (see Appendix 8-C) as general reform programs.

Political science and public administration scholars have raised real and serious concerns about both management reforms. For example, as Norma Riccucci reminds us in a recent *Public Administration Review* article, Charles Goodsell, Linda deLeon and Robert B. Denhardt, H. George Fredrickson, Ronald Moe, and many others have detailed with great clarity and conviction the underlying problems associated with REGO and NPM.[37] Based on her own observations as well as the observations of others, Riccucci summarizes these issues as follows:

- REGO/NPM does not adequately explain or account for the role and purpose of government and how governmental, versus entrepreneurial, organizations developed in the United States.
- REGO/NPM lacks an understanding of the difference between government and governance: the former can be contracted out, while the latter cannot.
- Government in the United States is based on the rule of law, not the law of the marketplace.
- Citizens are not customers; they own public services.
- The American constitutional system is based on separation of powers and checks and balances, but REGO/NPM "front-loads" the executive branch with little regard for the role of citizens in the policymaking process or for the bargaining and compromise among various groups (that is, pluralism) and institutions that define American politics.
- REGO/NPM denigrates and diminishes the importance of public servants.

THE NEW PUBLIC SERVICE?

More recently, in their 2003 book *The New Public Service: Serving, Not Steering*, Janet V. Denhardt and Robert B. Denhardt offer a comprehensive and thoughtful critique of reinventing government and the New Public Management.[38] As the title of the book suggests, these public administration experts are neither strong advocates of Osborne and Gaebler's first principle of REGO—that government should steer more and row less—nor supporters of NPM's neoconservative economic premise that government should be run more like a business. In fact, they argue that "government shouldn't be run like a business; it should be run like a democracy."[39] Denhardt and Denhardt call for a New Public Service model: "a set of ideas about the proper role of public administration in the governance system that places public service, democratic governance, and civic engagement at the center."[40] Defining their New Public Service are seven tenets: (1) serve citizens, not customers; (2) seek the public interest; (3) value citizenship over entrepreneurship; (4) think strategically, act democratically; (5) recognize that accountability isn't simple; (6) serve rather than steer; and (7) value people, not just productivity.[41] In conclusion, they offer a ringing defense of their people-oriented model:

> The New Public Service is not just the latest management fad or technique. It is, instead, a definition of who we are and why we serve others. It is a fundamental reordering of values.

We don't embrace these values because they increase satisfaction, motivation, retention, effectiveness, and service and improve decision making (although we would argue they do). Rather, we simply act on them because we believe they are, and always have been, integral components of American democracy.[42]

In previous chapters, we have often referred to Owen Hughes's *Public Management and Administration*, which was one of the first and is still perhaps the best comprehensive book outlining the nature and meaning of the New Public Management model. Like Hughes's work, Denhardt and Denhardt's book is polemical, thoroughly grounded in the academic literature, and compelling. Moreover, on numerous occasions in preceding chapters, we have argued that there is no management or theoretical model that works for all places and at all times. Denhardt and Denhardt seem to understand this better than most, for, despite their strong advocacy of their New Public Service model, they leave room for "elements" of other perspectives:

> . . . the New Public Service clearly seems most consistent with the basic foundations of democracy in this country and, therefore, provides a framework *within which* [emphasis in original] other valuable techniques and values, including the best elements of the Old Public Administration and the New Public Management, might play out. The New Public Service provides a rallying point around which we might envision a public service based on and fully integrated with civic discourse and the public interest.[43]

In short, we think Denhardt and Denhardt got it right. Municipal leaders do not have to choose one perspective or the other; there is no "one best way." Instead, we believe that both REGO and NPM hold promise for urban managers as they incorporate into their overall management strategies those elements, techniques, and processes that "fit" their cities. As we have learned, environments and situational variables are powerful intervening factors that can and do influence leadership and management initiatives. *Successful* urban managers are equipped with a toolbox full of managerial strategies, some old and some new. Moreover, they have the cognitive capacity to know which strategies will work in their particular cities, and they also have the ability and confidence to correctly implement their management plans.

Now we turn to two management strategies that have been highly touted by public administrators—Management by Objectives (MBO) and Total Quality Management (TQM). Both are focused on managing for results, and both have been tried and proven effective. Neither is merely a "fad," as some variations of both techniques have been used for over five decades. In his popular public administration textbook, *Managing the Public Sector*, public administration expert Grover Starling says this about TQM:

> After years of experience, it is clear that TQM *can* [emphasis in original] be adapted to the public sector. . . . The number of states and localities involved in TQM is no longer in the dozens as it was a few years ago, but is in the hundreds. TQM's basics have been applied in

agencies and departments as disparate as mental health and motor vehicles. Cities, counties, and states nationwide now have official offices of quality, directors of quality services, and departments of excellence. . . . With the new public-management philosophy, poor workmanship and lax service have become unacceptable.[44]

Starling also touts the advantages of MBO if used effectively. Based on a 1991 meta-analysis of a large number of qualitative and quantitative MBO studies including private-sector and public-sector organizations by Robert Rodgers and John Hunter, he notes:

> On average, organizations that effectively use MBO are 44.6 percent more productive than organizations that do not. And in organizations where top management is committed to MBO—that is, where the objective setting begins at the top—the average increase in productivity is even higher: 56.5 percent. Overall, there is a 97 percent chance that organizations that use MBO will outperform those that do not use it.[45]

With these statements setting the context, let's examine MBO and TQM. Both management approaches hold the potential to facilitate "results-oriented government."

MANAGEMENT BY OBJECTIVES

Peter Drucker brought the phrase *Management by Objectives* (MBO) into common use in 1954.[46] One of its foremost proponents, George Odiorne, defined MBO as a "process whereby the superior and subordinate managers of an organization jointly identify its common goals, define each individual's major areas of responsibility in terms of the results expected of him, and use these measures as guides for operating the unit and assessing the contribution of each of its members."[47] Although, like many other management approaches, MBO originated in the private sector, Drucker insists that it is especially well-suited to governmental agencies, where objectives and results are critical. He contends that public service institutions are prone to the "deadly disease of 'bureaucracy'; that is, towards mistaking rules, regulations, and the smooth functioning of the machinery for accomplishment, and the self-interest of the agency for public service."[48]

MBO, in one form or another, has been widely accepted in local government. Based on a survey of all U.S. cities with populations between 25,000 and one million residents (N = 520), in 1995 Poister and Streib found that 47 percent of the responding cities indicated that they were currently using MBO.[49] The authors note that this finding runs contrary to the notion that MBO is "often discussed in the past tense, as a tool that has largely fallen into disuse."[50] In fact, of the cities then using MBO, 58 percent had had the system in place for less than five years. Findings also showed that among cities using the technique, 60 percent used MBO on a citywide basis, but only one-third of the MBO systems extended down to lower-level managers or employees at the operating level.

In terms of the use of MBO as a humanistic/participative management technique, more than 60 percent of the respondents using MBO reported that "objectives were negotiated on a fairly even basis between managers and their subordinates," and in another 15 percent of the systems, lower-level managers were provided "considerable autonomy to set their own objectives."[51] In terms of perceived effectiveness, only 4 percent of respondents rated MBO as ineffective; in most cities, the MBO system was rated as "very effective" (28 percent) or "somewhat effective" (about two-thirds). Effectiveness ratings were more likely to be higher if MBO was used citywide, if top managers were actively involved in the process, if the city reported that professional staff were assigned full-time responsibility for maintaining the MBO system, and if subordinate managers were granted more autonomy and employees perceived their input into the process as being on a even basis with that of management.[52]

Applying MBO

Although MBO can work in an autocratic setting or with "top-down goal setting,"[53] most descriptions of the process stress employee involvement—at least down to the small-group level. The heart of MBO, setting objectives, is normally a group activity. The following illustration, involving a police chief and the head of the police patrol division, shows how the system might work:

1. The chief and the division head, working separately, write out in detail their perceptions of the broad goals and responsibilities of the patrol division.
2. The two officials meet face-to-face and compare their written perceptions of the patrol division's goals. Then they reach collective agreement on each goal and its relative importance.
3. Again the chief and the patrol head work separately, spelling out a list of tentative objectives. Both take into account the agreed-on divisional goals and responsibilities as they establish specific objectives.
4. The two meet again and agree on the specific measurable objectives to which the division will be committed.
5. Finally, the chief and the division head specify completion dates for each objective. Dates can be precise (June 30) or flexible (eighteen to twenty-four months).[54]

After the patrol division's goals and objectives are set, the patrol commander initiates the MBO process with the various sections that make up the division. Thus, the process can be carried down even to the individual employee level. We might note that a fairly common distinction is made here between goals and objectives: goals specify the long-range state of affairs to which the organization aspires; objectives are the more immediate, specific targets that must be reached to accomplish the goals.

Once objectives and timetables have been established, the monitoring and feedback stages begin. Performance usually is assessed on a quarterly basis, at least at the departmental level. This timing is especially likely where the objectives are tied to a particular fiscal year; the city manager might be provided with either quarterly or semiannual reports from various departments. Table 8-1 depicts a way in which agreed-on objectives might be monitored, in this case for solid-waste collection.

Table 8-1   A Sample Format for Reporting Actual Versus Targeted Performance for MBO: Solid-Waste Collection

Performance measurement		Actual value previous year (FY 2004)	Target current year (FY 2005)	Quality performance			
				1st qtr.	2nd qtr.	3rd qtr.	4th qtr.
Percentage of blocks whose appearance is rated unsatisfactory (fairly dirty or very dirty—2.5 or worse on visual rating scale)	Target	18	13	16	14	12	10
	Actual						
Number of fires involving uncollected solid waste	Target	17	12	3	4	3	2
	Actual						
Percentage of households reporting 1 or more missed collections during a year	Target	17	12	a		12	
	Actual						
Percentage of households rating overall appearance of neighborhood as "usually dirty" or "very dirty"	Target	23	18	b		18	
	Actual						

SOURCE: Adapted from *Measuring the Effectiveness of Basic Municipal Services* Urban Institute and International City Management Association (Washington, D.C., 1974), 13. Reprinted by permission.
a. Citizen survey to be undertaken once—in third quarter.
b. Citizen survey.

The process seems orderly, but urban managers implementing MBO face several problems, not the least of which is setting workable objectives. We can identify four basic criteria by which decision makers can determine the workability of objective statements.[55] The first criterion is *significance*: everything that a city, division, or department does may not be of sufficient consequence to warrant inclusion in an MBO scheme; superiors and subordinates should be able to reach agreement on those items worthy of inclusion. Next is *attainability*: objectives must be realistic expressions of what a division or department can be expected to attain; if set too high or too low, objectives are of little value as a guide to organizational performance. Third is *measurability*: objectives should be quantified as much as possible; they must be expressed in such a way that someone can make an impartial judgment about progress or lack of it. Finally, the *understandability* of objectives is important: objectives must be clearly understood by both employees and outside groups that have an interest in what the department is doing; therefore, objectives must be stated in simple, nontechnical terms.

Assessing MBO

A number of years ago, Odiorne reported on a series of object lessons derived from an application of MBO in a western state. His warnings and suggestions remain relevant and seem just as appropriate at the municipal level.[56] First, decentralization, or the moving of important decisions to lower levels in the organization, is not a natural occurrence in political organizations; it meets resistance from those in the bureaucracy who stand to lose power. Second, the most important reason for the failure of MBO is the tendency to treat it as a paperwork system rather than a face-to-face management process.[57] "The logic of MBO alone won't carry it off if the system is depersonalized and mechanistic." Third, commitment is what makes MBO work, and its absence can cause it to fail; in particular, commitment *must* come from top-level city officials.[58] Finally, measuring objectives is not for purposes of punishing poor forecasters; objective setting should serve the positive function of providing management with vital signs and indications of the need for adjustment.

How well has MBO performed? On the positive side, several studies have found that when managers have an active role in designing and implementing MBO, it can have a significantly beneficial effect on the overall job satisfaction of participants. Of course, better morale is not MBO's major purpose—improved performance is. And as noted previously in this chapter, a recent assessment of MBO applications shows that "when there is high commitment from top management, MBO programs result in large productivity gain."[59] Local officials especially like the way MBO helps them in clarifying goals and assisting employees in defining the nature of their jobs.[60]

TOTAL QUALITY MANAGEMENT

Statistician W. Edwards Deming originated *Total Quality Management* (TQM).[61] As part of the effort to reconstruct the nation's manufacturing base, Deming was invited to Japan in 1950 to deliver management lectures. The Japanese embraced his ideas that quality is the common goal of all participants in an organization and that quality is a continuous, long-term process. By the early 1980s, Japan had emerged as a world economic leader, and so American companies began looking to TQM to raise their own declining rates of productivity and to enhance their competitiveness.

TQM can be defined as "the art of continuous improvement with customer satisfaction as the goal."[62] David Kearnes, former CEO of Xerox and later deputy secretary of education, characterizes TQM as "a race without a finish line."[63] It is important to understand that TQM, like MBO, is concerned with results. But where MBO is more concerned with measuring *outputs*, TQM focuses more on *quality* as the product of organizational effort. Traditional output methods such as MBO attempt to measure *individual* accomplishments and performance, while TQM stresses *teamwork* and collaborative efforts through such mechanisms as quality circles, cross-departmental/functional project teams, and matrix-like structures.

Applying TQM

According to John Larkin, "The success of TQM depends on a carefully thought-out, long-range strategic plan and meticulous monitoring of statistical data."[64] A local government management system should have five key characteristics before considering TQM.[65] First, the jurisdiction should have the ability to gather hard data on current service performance (usually measured as the level and cost of services) and customers' expectations. Second, an executive-level planning group is needed to set long-term strategic goals and objectives based on a careful analysis of current service performance. These goals and objectives should not be expressed in terms of outputs or line items; instead, targets for *service improvement* should be established. Third, a communication network should be established such that goals can be understood and acted on by all participants in the organization. Fourth, active management teams, both within and across departments, are needed. Finally, short-term, ad hoc teams and more permanent teams of employees, suppliers, and even customers use data to discover and implement service improvements.

Given these management abilities, a popular method for implementing TQM is the "cascading" or top-down process, in which top management members learn TQM methods and teamwork and then teach (or cascade) the principles to the next hierarchical level, and so on down the hierarchy.[66] Since cascading takes time, may not produce a consensual direction for improvement, and is long-term in orientation—often the antithesis of American management philosophy—frequently, TQM will require both a short-term and a long-term component.

A four-phase "Twin-Track" model for implementing TQM is shown in figure 8-4.[67] As the figure shows, the implementation effort begins with assessment and ends with institutionalizing the innovation. Assessment, which primarily requires determining the current levels of service quality using hard data, will probably involve citizen and employee surveys.

Figure 8-4   The "Twin-Track" TQM Implementation Model

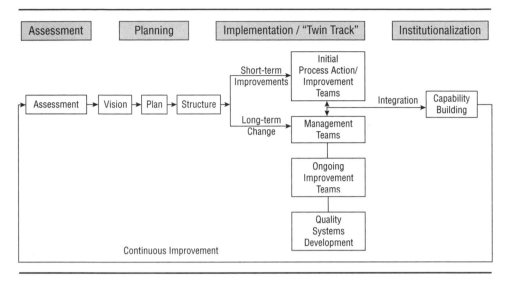

SOURCE: Adapted from Pat Keehley, "Total Quality Management: Getting Started." Reprinted with permission from the October 1992 issue of *Public Management* magazine, published by the International City/County Management Association (ICMA), Washington, D.C.

Planning requires development of a strategic plan for service-quality improvement; participants must analyze an array of statistical data to develop service-quality goals. Cascading TQM throughout the entire organization starts in the implementation phase. Pilot programs can be used to show quick gains, illustrating the power of the approach. TQM may also lead to new service delivery design methods and better methods for measuring service quality. As figure 8-4 indicates, the purpose of the "Twin-Track" approach is to show some short-term benefits and at the same time not lose sight of the long-term goal of continuous improvement. Finally, internal capacity in areas such as training, personnel, communication, and top-level commitment are put in place so as to institutionalize TQM as a way of thinking and not just another short-lived management exercise.

Assessing TQM

TQM or some similar type of quality initiative seems to have found a permanent place in American business. A number of the winners of the prestigious Baldridge National Quality Award—including Motorola, Westinghouse, Xerox, Cadillac (General Motors), Federal Express, and IBM—have embraced TQM and reaped the benefits of doing so.[68] Not surprisingly, however, TQM is not for everyone. Florida Power and Light, winner of Japan's Deming Award for quality management, slashed its programs after receiving complaints of too much paperwork. Despite winning a 1990 Malcolm Baldridge Award, the Wallace

Company, an oil supply company based in Houston, filed for Chapter 11 bankruptcy protection.[69] As we have said many times, environments and situational variables are important predictors of leadership and management success.

It also seems that TQM has found a home in government. Writing in *Governing* magazine, Jonathan Walters discusses how TQM is winning converts across the landscape of state and local government. He calls the movement "The Cult of Total Quality."[70] Governments such as those in New York City, Madison (Wis.), Fort Collins (Colo.), Dallas, Austin, Palm Beach County, Sacramento County Schools, Oregon State University, Gilbert High School (Ariz.), Arkansas, and North Dakota are into TQM. Sometimes the results have been spectacular. In the city garage in Madison, TQM resulted in a reduction of average turnaround from nine days to three days and a savings of $7.15 in downtime for every $1 in preventive maintenance—for a total annual savings of $700,000.[71] The quality-driven approach to city government may be costly, however. For a workforce of about 700 people, Wilmington, North Carolina, had an initial training outlay of about $75,000 for TQM and continues to pay about $30,000 a year.[72]

The case study presented in box 8.3 shows how TQM was used successfully to do more with less in the New York City Department of Parks and Recreation in response to a severe budget shortfall in the early 1990s.

In the *1994 Municipal Year Book*, Jonathan West, Evan Berman, and Mike Milakovich report on the use of TQM in local government.[73] Their study was based on a large-scale mail survey sent to all U.S. cities with 25,000 or more residents. Of the 1,211 cities surveyed, 431 usable responses were returned. Of these respondents, 237 (55 percent) were using TQM in at least one municipal service. Larger cities, cities in the South, and council-manager cities were more likely to be implementing TQM. Of all reporting cities, 24 percent had a central coordinating staff for quality and productivity initiatives, usually located in the personnel department. In terms of quality improvement (QI) activities across twenty-five municipal services, the five services most frequently identified for *service quality improvement* were police (35 percent), recreation (30 percent), personnel services (30 percent), parks (29 percent), and financial/budgeting reporting (29 percent). In terms of improving *customer service*, defined as "performance objectives that emphasize responsiveness to customers and customer satisfaction,"[74] as the QI, the top five services were police (59 percent), recreation (56 percent), parks (52 percent), streets (50 percent), and water/sewer(47 percent). Finally, for the *employee empowerment* QI, defined as a "formal or structured approach which enables individuals and teams to make important decisions about their own work and work environment,"[75] the top five services were police (41 percent), recreation (36 percent), parks (35 percent), personnel services (35 percent), and streets (33 percent).

On external and internal factors that spurred local officials to initiate TQM activities, the top three external reasons most frequently cited as "very important" by the respondents were citizen complaints (50 percent), voter demands (30 percent), and community

TQM COMES TO NEW YORK CITY

In response to the most severe budget cuts in New York City since the mid-1970s, TQM was brought into the City of New York's Department of Parks in the early 1990s. Commissioner Betsy Gotbaum became committed to TQM as part of a larger process to respond "to the rather severe pressure to do more with less." Commissioner Gotbaum, working with faculty members at Columbia University, decided that the TQM method would best be taught by putting it into practice. This "hands on" approach also insured that there would be some "quick victories." First, the faculty trained 25 managers in the parks department in TQM and project management. In the second phase of training, 120 employees learned TQM as they worked on the department's first twenty-four quality improvement projects. In the third phase, 50 additional managers and another 250 employees were trained by working on the next fifty improvement projects.

Steven Cohen and William Eimicke, faculty members at Columbia, report the overall results of ten randomly chosen quality improvement projects from the initial group of twenty-four projects; they also provide detailed case studies of three of these projects. For the ten projects reviewed, start-up costs equaled $223,000; ongoing savings for the ten projects totaled $711,500. Cohen and Eimicke estimate that the twenty-four projects would result in total savings of approximately $1.7 million in direct costs (not including indirect costs and long-term benefits). They also note that all of these savings actually would be "indirect early benefits," since the main purpose of the initial round of projects was to teach TQM, not to save money.

The three case studies reviewed in the study include quality initiatives in preventive vehicle maintenance, citywide timekeeping, and tree removal in Queens. The parks department operates five separate garages, one in each of the city's boroughs. The Randall's Island garage serves all parks department vehicles from Manhattan as well as vehicles used by parks department employees, whose duties take them across the city. Prior to the beginning of the quality initiative, the no-show rate for preventive maintenance inspection (PMI) was as high as 40 percent on any given day. The primary reason was the PMI process itself, which often resulted in retention of vehicles at the garage for no apparent reason for three to five days. After the implementation of TQM, the no-show rate fell below 5 percent. Quality initiative changes included reviewing maintenance schedules one month in advance to resolve scheduling conflicts, making a promise to return all vehicles the same day if delivered to the garage by 10:00 a.m., and prioritizing PMI over nonscheduled maintenance. After the quality initiative, over 95 percent of all vehicles were returned on time and the total annual savings associated with the project was estimated to be $106,550.

In the early 1990s, a centralized office replaced five separate borough offices for processing the approximately 3,300 timecards submitted weekly by parks employees. The total error rate in processing the timecards was about 1,000 per week, or about one out of every three cards processed. After the TQM team identified common errors and provided training on how to avoid and/or prevent such mistakes, the error rate dropped from 33 percent to 13 percent—about 660 fewer mistakes per week. Start-up costs for the quality initiative were about $4,000; savings were about 7,150 in personnel hours and about $97,030 in dollars each year.

The final quality improvement project involved the parks department in Queens, whose "climber and pruner" workers prune all trees along public streets and in parks and remove the dead trees. Prior to the

(continued)

BOX 8.3   Policy and Practice (continued)

establishment of the tree trimming/removal quality initiative, the parks department was discussing whether to contract out the service, but the quality improvement team in the parks department found a number of ways to improve service and save money. For example, in the past, one group of workers had cut dead trees, while another group cleaned up the debris at some later time and then another group removed stumps and backfilled. Sometimes these efforts were coordinated, but often not. After the quality initiative, teams of four workers were able to complete the entire process. Quality initiatives in this area saved the parks department about $115,000: "The Queens Forestry Project quality team was able to reduce the costs per tree [removal] to almost half of the contractor's costs."

Cohen and Eimicke believe that the TQM exercise proved the advantages of learning TQM by doing—since immediate improvements and savings tend to disarm critics, short-term gains can result in long-term commitment to the TQM system. They also like the quality initiatives' focus at the line level, since "worker participation and worker analysis of operations in the development of new organizational routines are at the heart of TQM."

SOURCE: Steven Cohen and William Eimicke, "Project-Focused Total Quality Management in the New York City Department of Parks and Recreation," *Public Administration Review* 54 (September–October 1994): 450–456.

---

planning activities (27 percent). The top three internal factors rated "very important" by survey participants were city manager's interest (59 percent), increasing employee productivity (47 percent), and budget pressures (45 percent). Respondents were asked which among twenty-one various strategies they had used to implement TQM in their cities. The top five strategies used to implement quality improvement were identifying customer needs (85 percent), increasing coordination (79 percent), monitoring internal performance (75 percent), monitoring citizen satisfaction (74 percent), and reformulating mission (71 percent). The top three strategies for ensuring employee participation in the process were involving employees (81 percent of the respondents said they had used this strategy), making decisions based on objective data (78 percent), and recognizing achievement (75 percent). Similarly, survey participants were asked to identify what strategies they had used to ensure political support for quality initiatives. The most frequently identified individuals or groups were city appointed officials—city manager/CAO (86 percent), senior managers (85 percent)—and then, elected officials—mayor (76 percent) and city council members (75 percent).

The respondents were also asked to identify the extent to which 22 potential barriers had impeded the QI initiative in their organization. At least 70 percent or more of the respondents listed ten barriers as important: demands on employee time (86 percent), employee resistance to change (83 percent), inadequate rewards for employees (81 percent), demands on leaders' time (80 percent), inadequate team building (78 percent), inadequate employee empowerment (78 percent), inadequate funds (76 percent), inadequate training funds (76 percent), traditional hierarchical structure (73 percent), and inadequate understanding (72 percent). Finally, survey participants were asked the extent to which they believed the TQM efforts had had a positive impact on several municipal performance indicators and processes. Not surprisingly, a large percentage of the city officials believed that the effort had had a positive impact on quality of service (89 percent), productivity (85 percent), increased communication (84 percent), customer satisfaction (83 percent), and amount of service to customer (82 percent)—all major promised outcomes of TQM.

In assessing the impact of TQM in government, we should note that political scientist James E. Swiss offers a strong argument that orthodox TQM will not work well in government.[76] He cites four primary impediments to the usefulness of traditional TQM. First, because TQM was originally designed for use with manufacturing operations, its focus is on products. In contrast, government primarily delivers services. Service delivery is more labor-intensive than manufacturing, and services are often produced and consumed at the same time; even if a service is being delivered with maximum efficiency, the behavior or appearance of the service agent can negate customer approval. In short, developing quality measures is harder to do in the public sector, and reducing variation in quality is difficult with street-level bureaucrats. Second, TQM is based on the idea of delighting the customer. Although this may be a laudable goal, defining the customer of a public agency is at best a tenuous job. Does the Food and Drug Administration serve patients with a particular disease who need a promising medicine approved, pharmaceutical interests, the health profession, or the general public? The literature in bureaucratic politics is replete with stories of how special interests have co-opted the long-term goals of agencies.

A third impediment is that orthodox Total Quality Management rejects the use of output-oriented techniques in favor of continuous improvement through changing inputs and work processes. Swiss argues that, in recent years, the public sector has made great strides in implementing such innovations as pay-for-performance, merit pay, program budgets, and MBO, and that effort should not stop. An emphasis on inputs and process may lead to goal displacement as bureaucrats look for more money and people (inputs), as legislators look at budget line items to see what their district gets (inputs), and as an elaborate system of rules and regulations—from hiring to procurement—is established to *control* the fourth branch of government. In the public sector, Swiss points out, an output orientation *can* lead us down the road of quality and toward a long-range vision. Finally, TQM demands an almost single-minded commitment to quality, best promoted by a very strong organizational culture. The task of fostering that essential culture resides with top leadership. But in public organizations, where upper-level executives (mayors and city managers) may not stay with the city for long, turnover at the top makes the job of creating and sustaining a strong, continuous organizational culture difficult, if not impossible.

Swiss concludes that "reformed TQM"—which "saves the orthodox principles of employee empowerment, continuous improvement, and quantitative tracking of product quality and of client reactions"—can be a useful tool for contemporary city management.[77] On the other hand, reformed TQM "jettisons orthodox TQM's hostility to output goals and measurements, de-emphasizes its demands for output uniformity and organizational culture continuity, and sensitizes managers to the dangers of satisfying just an immediate client."[78]

POTENTIAL PROBLEMS WITH MANAGEMENT TECHNIQUES NEW TO A CITY

Although efforts to change, improve, and reform public organizations should never cease, potential payoffs sometimes fall short of expectations. Public administration specialist Gerald Gabris identifies five dysfunctions that often arise from efforts to employ management techniques that are new to a city.[79]

First, because a number of changes in procedures and operations are required with each of these techniques, a *process burden* may be created—more paperwork, forms, data collection, and training sessions. Line managers tend to resent these extra chores, especially if they do not anticipate any beneficial changes as a result of the new technique.

Second, new management approaches may not take into account the unique setting of the department or organization. A department of public safety may have group norms, role relationships, reporting systems, and work outputs that are quite different from those of a public works department. Members of cross-functional teams associated with TQM may have different frames of reference. New management systems require *adaptation* and *close monitoring*.

Gabris identifies the lack of *internal capacity* as a third potential problem. "Too often, management techniques are recommended and adopted by public organizations that lack implementation capacity."[80] He goes on to describe a small city's frustrating experiences in trying to install a performance budgeting system. Most line managers had difficulty understanding the new system and did not see how it would improve effectiveness. Training sessions took longer than expected, and some supervisors felt that they were being required to take too much time away from more important responsibilities. In addition, the computer needs associated with the new budgeting procedures exceeded the city's in-house computing capacity. If put into place, the system would have required contracting out for additional computer time, at costs considerably over original estimates. So, once the outside experts who had recommended and designed the system departed, city officials decided to abandon performance budgeting—not because they opposed the idea, but because they realized that the city did not have the internal capacity to make it work.

Fourth, installing new procedures can produce *credibility anxiety*. Because employees as well as supervisors are often suspicious of new techniques, when failures occur, a ripple or spillover effect can be created, so that employees question the usefulness or credibility of changes that follow the failure.

The fifth potential problem, *unrealistic expectations*, is related to credibility anxiety. New management systems may be oversold in regard to both how much improvement can be expected and how much time changes will take. Even when local officials have been thoroughly briefed and have become convinced of a technique's value, they may expect quick results; if these results are slow in coming, the resulting disillusionment can lead to abandonment of the technique or to a reduced commitment from the top that dooms it to eventual failure.

To avoid some of these dysfunctional consequences, Gabris recommends such strategies as decentralizing and sharing the burden of implementing new techniques, providing incentives to eliminate burdensome procedures, engaging in substantial pre-implementation research, pre-testing, implementing only one technique at a time, and acknowledging and celebrating small successes. To this list of recommendations, one might also add that the "incentive package" that managers use in results-based management should be different from those used in traditional systems—at least this is the argument advanced by James Swiss in a 2005 *Public Administration Review* article.[81]

Swiss identifies four broad categories of incentives that are appropriate to results-based management: *intrinsic motivators* (such as desire to achieve or empowerment); nonmonetary *extrinsic rewards and sanctions* (such as praise or plaques); *personnel-based rewards* (such as promotions or individual and group bonuses); and *budget shares* (such as more or less budget for the agency based on results). Swiss argues that since "incentives in results-based management are tied to outcomes that may be slow to develop, difficult to produce, and politically charged," the first three types of incentives identified above—intrinsic, extrinsic nonmonetary, and personnel-based rewards may prove more productive.[82] Workers (managers and frontline employees) should be empowered and cross-trained, since job enlargement and the creation of cross-functional teams will facilitate the ability of workers to focus on organizational results "rather than narrow processes."[83] Extrinsic nonmonetary awards such as praise, plaques, titles, and increased autonomy should go to both individuals *and* groups. In addition, these awards should be focused on celebrating the small, short-term wins as well as long-term achievements. Finally, Swiss notes "results-based management systems would profit from lowering expectations for budget incentives while increasing their emphasis on innovative personnel-reward approaches."[84] He does suggest, however, that local government officials avoid extreme business model personnel system practices such as "fire at will."

SUMMARY

An organization should be viewed as an open system consisting of a formal structure, an informal structure, and an external environment. To neglect one part of the organization is to neglect the organization as a system. One of the basic issues in management theory is motivation: what motivates people to do the things asked of them on the job? Associated with different views of motivation are different theories of human behavior. Applied to management, these theories include the scientific management approach, the human relations approach, and organizational humanism. Some authorities contend that organizational humanists have overestimated the extent to which many workers, especially those in the blue-collar ranks, value job challenge and autonomy as opposed to material rewards. Still, the best-run companies here and in Japan continue to operate on the basic principle that involved workers are the most productive workers.

Leadership is another provocative, complicated topic. Although few deny its importance within the organization, research is again ambiguous regarding the leadership style that is most likely to be effective. The task to be done, the people involved, and the context in which it all occurs will determine the style of leadership that is needed. The consensus now seems to be that neither a democratic nor an autocratic leadership style can ensure increased productivity for all organizations at all points in time, although worker satisfaction does tend to be greater under more participatory leadership.

In recent years, results-based management has been advocated. Two older, proven management approaches that can be used in the drive toward results-based management are Management by Objectives (MBO) and Total Quality Management (TQM). Research in this chapter has shown that both management approaches are used extensively in local government today. Despite their being labeled "old" management strategies, in many cities the adoption of MBO and/or TQM has only occurred relatively recently.[85] The essence of MBO is the collaborative setting of measurable objectives and the use of these objectives to assess employee performance. Many see MBO as a way of bringing about greater decentralization, thus inculcating feelings of greater personal responsibility among employees. Meta-analysis research cited in this chapter suggests that MBO results in greater organizational productivity. More recently, TQM has been embraced by private-sector and public-sector organizations alike. Deming's approach to management calls for continuous improvement in the quality of products and services as defined by customers. Based on survey research, many local officials believe that these quality improvement initiatives are being met through TQM systems.

As public managers work diligently to apply leadership styles and management strategies to achieve peak organizational performance, it is important to realize that their job is arduous and that there is no "one best way" to follow. In some communities, elected and appointed leaders as well as the citizenry may be quite content to pattern the future based on the past—a caretaker approach to management is all that is required, or perhaps even tolerated. In these municipalities, one need not worry about results-based government. In most cities, however, urban leaders will continue to respond to the changes produced by their dynamic environments. This response will require that leadership styles and management techniques, both old and new, be used to meet the needs and demands of citizens in their specific communities.

SUGGESTED FOR FURTHER READING

Cohen, Steven, and Ronald Brand. *Total Quality Management in Government: A Practical Guide for the Real World*. San Francisco: Jossey-Bass, 1993.

Denhardt, Robert B., and Janet V. Denhardt. *Public Administration: An Action Orientation*. 5th ed. Belmont, Calif.: Thomson Wadsworth, 2006.

Fesler, James W., and Donald F. Kettl. *The Politics of the Administrative Process*. 4th ed. Washington, D.C.: CQ Press, 2009.

Quinn, Robert E. *Beyond Rational Management*. San Francisco: Jossey-Bass, 1988.

Starling, Grover. *Managing the Public Sector*. 8th ed. Belmont, Calif.: Thomson Wadsworth, 2008.

Total Quality Management magazine and *Total Quality Management* journal; both publications tend to focus on the private sector and global experiences with TQM, but articles on government applications of TQM are available.

Watson, Douglas J., and Wendy L. Hassett, eds. *Local Government Management: Current Issues and Best Practices*. Armonk, N.Y.: M.E. Sharpe, 2003.

APPENDIX 8-A

The *2005 Municipal Year Book* provides a listing of the eighteen International City/County Management Association (ICMA) practices for effective local government management first established in 1991. The inventory of "core content areas" is called the Applied Knowledge Assessment (AKA) and was operationalized by a group of faculty and staff from the Andrew Young School of Policy Studies at Georgia State University and staff members at ICMA in 1999. By October 2004, over 1,600 individuals had completed the AKA as a professional development exercise, as a means to improve their political and management competencies. The eighteen core areas are:

1. *Staff effectiveness*—coaching/mentoring, team leadership, empowerment, and delegating
2. *Policy facilitation*—including facilitative leadership, facilitating council effectiveness, and mediation and negotiation
3. *Functional and operational expertise and planning*—understanding the basic principles of service delivery and anticipating, organizing, and establishing timetables for the completion of projects
4. *Citizen service*—determining citizen needs and providing responsive and equitable services
5. *Quality assurance*—maintaining a high quality in staff, operational procedures, and service delivery
6. *Initiative, risk taking, vision, creativity, and innovation*—setting an example in these leadership areas and encouraging others in the city to do the same
7. *Technological literacy*—an understanding of information technology (IT)
8. *Democratic advocacy and citizen participation*—a commitment to democratic principles, respecting elected officials and community groups, educating citizens about local government, and recognizing the right of citizens to participate in local government decision making
9. *Diversity*—understanding and valuing differences among individuals
10. *Budgeting*—preparing and administering the budget
11. *Financial analysis*—understanding financial information to guide the cities' short- and long-term fiscal affairs

12. *Human resources management*—ensuring that employee policies and procedures are equitable, legal, and current and that human resources are adequate to meet programmatic objectives
13. *Strategic planning*—planning for the future of the organization and the community
14. *Advocacy and interpersonal communication*—facilitating the flow of ideas and information between and among organizational members
15. *Presentation skills*—conveying and presentation information and ideas
16. *Media relations*—communicating information to the media that educates and that builds a positive relation with the press
17. *Integrity*—personal, professional, and organizational integrity; and
18. *Personal development*—self-renewal and development.

For a more complete discussion of each of these eighteen core content areas see Gregory Streib, Mark Rivera, and Ignaci Navarro, "The State of the Practice: Performance on the ICMA Applied Knowledge Assessment," *2005 Municipal Year Book* (Washington, D.C.: ICMA, 2005), 33–40.

APPENDIX 8-B

Reinventing government (REGO) is based on ten principles of what government *should be*:

1. *A catalyst*—directing activities more than running programs, that is, it should "steer more and row less"
2. *Community-owned*—involving and empowering clients and citizens
3. *Competitive*—encouraging and promoting competition in service delivery
4. *Mission-driven*—stressing overall goals while minimizing rules and requirements
5. *Results-oriented*—concerned more with outcomes and less with inputs or resources used
6. *Customer-driven*—treating service recipients as valued customers
7. *Enterprising*—interested in earning as well as spending money
8. *Anticipatory*—preventing problems instead of merely curing them
9. *Decentralized*—flattening the organizational hierarchy to encourage more participation and teamwork among employees; and
10. *Market oriented*—leveraging change by using government incentives to affect market behavior.

For a more complete discussion of each point see David Osborne and Ted Gaebler, *Reinventing Government: How the Entrepreneurial Spirit Is Transforming the Public Sector* (Reading, Mass.: Addison-Wesley, 1992), and David Osborne and Peter Plastrik, *Banishing Bureaucracy: The Five Strategies for Reinventing Government* (New York: Plume, 1997), Appendix A.

APPENDIX 8-C

Owen Hughes's New Public Management, or "managerialism" as he calls it, is based on the following thirteen points:

1. *A strategic approach*—This feature emphasizes long-term planning and strategic management. As part of this approach, Hughes suggests that an organization must know how it fits into its environment, and the strengths, weaknesses, opportunities, and threats in that environment.

2. *Recognition that management is not administration*—In fact, Hughes devotes an entire chapter to this point, arguing that managers today are more political in nature, hired because they have track records and are responsible for achieving results. Being a manager is a skill in itself rather than an expanded role that a specialist "picks up" in moving from a function (engineer, accountant, attorney) into a management position.

3. *A focus on results*—This feature requires that an organization focus on outputs and outcomes, not on inputs.

4. *Improved financial management*—As Hughes explains, "The most important change in this area has been performance and programme budgeting systems to replace the older line-item budget and accounting systems."

5. *Flexibility in staffing*—A part of this feature is the trend away from position classification systems for senior-level managers, such as the Senior Executive Service in the U.S. federal government. Also, broad-banding systems make it easier to hire and move (promote or reassign) personnel, while changes in civil service rules make it easier to fire unproductive staff.

6. *Flexibility in organization*—One aspect of this feature is the disaggregation of large departments into different parts "by setting up agencies to deliver services for a smaller policy department." This process facilitates potential outsourcing.

7. *A shift to greater competition*—This feature requires competition "within and between public sector organizations and nongovernment competitors." In short, it is a call for greater privatization.

8. *The new contractualism*—This feature means that any government service can be provided by contract, either externally, by private or volunteer providers, or internally, by government agencies. These contracts require performance, which may be measured at various levels: for the individual frontline worker, for managers, or perhaps even for entire agencies or departments. Thus, regardless of who holds the contract—government or nonprofit agency or private-sector business—performance and accountability are required and measured under terms specified in a contract.

9. *A stress on private-sector styles of management practice*—This feature once again suggests greater flexibility in personnel and budgeting systems, such as merit pay, benchmarking performance, and performance budgeting.

10. *Relationships with politicians*—"Under the public management model the relationship between politician and manager is more fluid and is closer than before . . . The major skill needed for a public manager is how to be a bureaucratic *politician*" (emphasis in original).

11. *Relationships with the public*—This feature demands greater responsiveness to outside groups and individuals.

12. *Separation of purchaser and provider*—This feature echoes Osborne and Gaebler's injunction about separating steering from rowing. Or, as Hughes puts it: "Even if government is involved in any activity it does not need to be the final provider."

13. *Re-examining what government does*—"Advocates of the new public management, armed with theoretical insights from economics, have argued that there are some things government should not do." This has been especially true for public enterprises in Commonwealth nations.

See, Owen E. Hughes, *Public Management and Administration.* 3rd ed. (New York: Palgrave Macmillan, 2003), 54–60.

NOTES

1. This discussion draws largely from Michael E. Milakovich and George J. Gordon, *Public Administration in America*, 9th ed. (Belmont, Calif.: Thomson Wadsworth, 2007), chap. 4; Brian R. Fry, and Jos C. N. Raadschelders, *Mastering Public Administration: From Max Weber to Dwight Waldo*, 2nd ed. (Washington, D.C.: CQ Press, 2008), 1–16; Harold F. Gortner, Julianne Mahler, and Jeanne Bell Nicholson, *Organization Theory: A Public Perspective*, 2nd ed. (Fort Worth, Tex.: Harcourt Brace, 1997), chap. 3.

2. Gortner et al., *Organization Theory*, 67.

3. Ibid.

4. Grover Starling, *Managing the Public Sector*, 8th ed. (Belmont, Calif.: Thomson Wadsworth, 2008), 466.

5. For an excellent introduction to Frederick Taylor and the scientific management movement, see Fry and Raadschelders, *Mastering Public Administration*, chap. 2.

6. George Strauss, Raymond Miles, Charles Snow, and Arnold Tannenbaum, eds., "An Overview of the Field," in *Organizational Behavior: Research and Issues* (Madison, Wis.: Industrial Relations Research Association, 1974), 5.

7. Abraham H. Maslow, *Motivation and Personality* (New York: Harper & Row, 1954).

8. Douglas McGregor, *The Human Side of Enterprise* (New York: McGraw-Hill, 1960), 48.

9. Frederick Herzberg, *Work and the Nature of Man* (Cleveland: World, 1966); and Chris Argyris, *Integrating the Individual and the Organization* (New York: Wiley, 1964).

10. See Milakovich and Gordon, *Public Administration in America*, 168.

11. Ibid., 170.

12. Hal G. Rainey, *Understanding and Managing Public Organizations* (San Francisco: Jossey-Bass, 1991), 124.

13. Robert Rodgers and John E. Hunter, "A Foundation of Good Management Practice in Government: Management by Objectives," *Public Administration Review* 52 (January–February 1992): 27.

14. Soonhee Kim, "Participative Management and Job Satisfaction: Lessons for Management Leadership," *Public Administration Review* 62 (March–April 2002): 231.

15. Evan M. Berman, Jonathan P. West, and Maurice N. Richter Jr., "Workplace Relations: Friendship Patterns and Consequences (According to Managers)," *Public Administration Review* 62 (March–April 2002): 227.

16. Ibid., 218.

17. These are direct quotes and come from ibid., 225–226.

18. Ibid., 225.

19. William Ouchi, *Theory Z: How American Business Can Meet the Japanese Challenge* (New York: Avon Books, 1981), 15–36.

20. Ronald Contino and Robert Lorusso, "The Theory Z Turnaround of a Public Agency," *Public Administration Review* 42 (January–February 1982): 70.

21. This discussion is drawn from David Osborne and Ted Gaebler, *Reinventing Government* (Reading, Mass.: Addison-Wesley, 1992); chap. 2 discusses community-owned government, chap. 6 examines customer-driven government, and chap. 9 looks at decentralized government.

22. James Banovetz, David Beam, Robert Hollander, and Charles Zuzak, "Leadership Styles and Strategies," in *Managing the Modern City*, ed. James Banovetz (Washington, D.C.: ICMA, 1971), 133.

23. Robert D. Behn, "What Right Do Public Managers Have to Lead?" *Public Administration Review* 58 (May–June 1998): 209.

24. Paul Hersey and Kenneth Blanchard, *Management of Organizational Behavior: Utilizing Human Resources*. 6th ed. (Englewood Cliffs, N.J.: Prentice Hall, 1993), 110–112.

25. Ibid., 109.

26. Ibid., 94; the formula $L = f(1, f, s)$ also is found on this page.

27. Ibid., 96–97.

28. Ralph Stogdill, *Handbook of Leadership: A Survey of Theory and Research* (New York: Free Press, 1974), 81.

29. Robert R. Blake and Jane Srygley Mouton, *The New Managerial Grid* (Houston: Gulf, 1978).

30. Hersey and Blanchard, *Management of Organizational Behavior*, chap. 8.

31. Robert Blake and Jane S. Mouton, "Theory and Research for Developing a Science of Leadership," *Journal of Applied Behavioral Science* 18 (1982): 275–291.

32. Robert E. Quinn, *Beyond Rational Management* (San Francisco: Jossey-Bass, 1988). This discussion is primarily drawn from chapters 4 and 5.

33. James Owens, as quoted in Hersey and Blanchard, *Management of Organizational Behavior*, 113.

34. For example, REGO and NPM stress responsiveness in service delivery—that of government to citizens and to political elites, as well as that of managers to employees and of employees to managers. Such responsiveness holds the potential to bring about greater individual and organizational accountability.

35. Brendan F. Burke and Bernadette C. Costello, "The Human Side of Managing for Results," *American Review of Public Administration* 35 (September 2005): 271.

36. Ibid., 279–282.

37. Norma M. Riccucci, "The 'Old' Public Management versus the 'New' Public Management: Where Does Public Administration Fit In?" *Public Administration Review* 61 (March–April 2001): 172–175; Charles Goodsell, "Reinventing Government or Rediscovering It?" *Public Administration Review* 53 (January–February 1993): 85–86; Linda deLeon and Robert B. Denhardt, "The Political Theory of Reinvention," *Public Administration Review* 60 (March–April 2000): 89–97; H. George Fredrickson, "Comparing the Reinventing Government Movement with the New Public Administration," *Public Administration Review* 56 (May–June 1996): 263–270, and "Can Bureaucracy Be Beautiful?" *Public Administration Review* 60 (January–February 2000): 47–53; Ronald C. Moe, "The 'Reinventing Government' Exercise: Misinterpreting the Problem, Misjudging the Consequences," *Public Administration Review* 54 (March–April 1994): 111–122. The list of "others" is too numerous to cover here. However, for additional critiques of REGO/NPM, see Laurence Lynn, "The Myth of the Bureaucratic Paradigm: What Traditional Public Administration Really Stood For," *Public Administration Review* 61 (March–April 2001): 144–160; and David H. Rosenbloom, "History Lessons for Reinventors," *Public Administration Review* 61 (March–April 2001): 161–165. Finally, for a more global view of REGO/NPM, see Lois Recascino Wise, "Public Management Reform: Competing Drivers of Change," *Public Administration Review* 62 (September–October 2002): 555–567; and Mark Considine and Jenny M. Lewis, "Bureaucracy, Network, or Enterprise? Comparing Models of Governance in Australia, Britain, the Netherlands, and New Zealand," *Public Administration Review* 63 (March–April 2003): 131–140. Ichiro Noutomi and Makoto Nakanishi, "Net Results of the Japanese NPM Movement at Local Governments

since the Mid-1990s: Performance Budgeting, Total Quality Management and Target Based Budgeting," *International Journal of Public Administration* 30 (2007): 1393–1433.

38. Janet V. Denhardt and Robert B. Denhardt, *The New Public Service: Serving, Not Steering* (Armonk, N.Y.: M. E. Sharpe, 2003). Also see the expanded 2nd edition (2007) for a concluding chapter that provides examples of how the book's principles are being applied by governments in the United States and around the world.

39. Ibid., 3.

40. Ibid., 4.

41. Ibid., each tenet serves as a chapter title.

42. Ibid., 172.

43. Ibid., 172–173.

44. Starling, *Managing the Public Sector*, 411.

45. Ibid., 424.

46. Peter F. Drucker, *The Practice of Management* (New York: Harper & Row, 1954).

47. George S. Odiorne, *Management by Objectives* (New York: Pitman, 1965), 55–56.

48. Peter F. Drucker, "What Results Should You Expect? A User's Guide to MBO," *Public Administration Review* 36 (January–February 1976): 13.

49. Theodore H. Poister and Gregory Streib, "MBO in Municipal Government: Variations on a Traditional Management Tool," *Public Administration Review* 55 (January–February 1995): 50.

50. Ibid.

51. Ibid., 53.

52. Ibid., 54.

53. Odiorne, *Management by Objectives*, 140.

54. This illustration is similar to one found in Fred Pearson, "Managing by Objective," in *Developing the Municipal Organization*, ed. Stanley Powers, F. Gerald Brown, and David S. Arnold (Washington, D.C.: ICMA, 1974) 179.

55. Ibid., 180–182.

56. George Odiorne, "MBO in State Government," *Public Administration Review* 36 (January–February 1976): 28–33.

57. Starling makes the same argument in *Managing the Public Sector*, 424.

58. This statement applies to all levels of government and to all results-based management initiatives. For example, in his testimony before the Subcommittee on Government Efficiency, Financial Management and Intergovernmental Relations Committee on Government Reform, U.S. House of Representatives, J. Christopher Mihm, director of strategic issues in the Bush administration, told members of the committee: "One of the most important elements of successful management improvement initiatives is the demonstrated, sustained commitment of top leaders to change." J. Christopher Mihm, *Managing for Results: Next Steps to Improve the Federal Government's Management and Performance* (Washington, D.C.: General Accounting Office, February 15, 2002), 5.

59. Rodgers and Hunter, "Foundation of Good Management Practice in Government," 34.

60. Perry Moore and Ted Staton, "Management by Objectives in American Cities," *Public Personnel Management* 10 (summer 1981): 223–232.

61. The discussion in this paragraph is drawn from Warren H. Schmidt and Jerome P. Finnigan, *The Race without a Finish Line* (San Francisco: Jossey-Bass, 1992), chap. 1.

62. Ibid., xii.

63. As quoted in ibid.

64. John L. Larkin, "TQM Efforts Increase at All Levels of Government," *Public Administration Times*, June 1, 1991, 1.

65. Pat Keehley, "Total Quality Management: Getting Started," *Public Management*, October 1992, 10–11.

66. Ibid., 14.

67. Discussion of the model is drawn from ibid.

68. See Schmidt and Finnigan, *Race without a Finish Line*, chap. 13.

69. Jay Mathews with Peter Katel, "The Cost of Quality," *Newsweek*, September 7, 1992, 48–49.

70. Jonathan Walters, "The Cult of Total Quality," *Governing*, May 1992, 38–41.

71. Joseph Sensenbrenner, "Quality Comes to City Hall," *Harvard Business Review*, March–April 1991, 68.

72. Walters, "Cult of Total Quality," 41.

73. Jonathan P. West, Evan M. Berman, and Mike E. Milakovich, "Total Quality Management in Local Government," *1994 Municipal Year Book* (Washington, D.C.: ICMA, 1994), 14–25.

74. Ibid., 15.

75. Ibid.

76. James E. Swiss, "Adapting Total Quality Management (TQM) to Government," *Public Administration Review* 52 (July–August 1992): 356–362.

77. Ibid., 360.

78. Ibid.

79. Gerald T. Gabris, "Recognizing Management Technique Dysfunctions: How Management Tools Often Create More Problems than They Solve," *Public Productivity Review* 10 (winter 1986): 3–19.

80. Ibid., 10.

81. James E. Swiss, "A Framework for Assessing Incentives in Results-Based Management," *Public Administration Review* 65 (September–October 2005): 592–602.

82. Ibid., 594.

83. Ibid., 600.

84. Ibid.

85. Poister and Streib, "MBO in Municipal Government," 50, note that, of the cities that were currently using MBO in their survey, 58 percent had had the system in place less than five years. Similarly, Evan M. Berman and Jonathan P. West, "Municipal Commitment to Total Quality Management: A Survey of Recent Progress," *Public Administration Review* 55 (January–February 1995): 60, report that only 10 percent of the cities that were currently using TQM in their survey had been doing so for more than five years.

CHAPTER 9

MANAGING HUMAN RESOURCES

A SK ALMOST anyone involved with modern organizations—from executives to managers to supervisors to the workers on the line—and they will tell you straight out: *people define an organization*. While this sentiment may sound like a cliché, it is not. And it is particularly true when it comes to local government. The only contact many citizens ever have with city government is interacting with or just seeing public servants at work. Perceptions that citizens hold of street-level bureaucrats such as teachers, firefighters, sanitation crew members, police officers, social workers, and so on, often help to define their attitudes about the city in general. Thus, it behooves local leaders to make certain that they create an organizational culture and working environment that stresses the values of openness in communication and trust. Too much is at stake to treat city workers as simply cogs in the organizational machine. Human resources must be managed efficiently, effectively, responsively, and equitably; they must be handled with great care and concern.

Traditionally, personnel administration has been viewed as technical and specialized, and the major concern since the turn of the twentieth century has been the creation and maintenance of a *merit system* of employment. As discussed in chapter 3, the urban reformers wanted to take the politics out of city government, and the merit system was a principal means of achieving this objective. Today, city personnel departments are still concerned with a number of routine and customary tasks—recruitment, testing, selection, position classification, and compensation, to name a few. But recent developments and new tasks given to personnel departments have propelled them into major areas of controversy—areas where federal law and court decisions have mandated a variety of changes. For example, minorities and women are, increasingly, the new entrants into local bureaucracies. Local personnel departments face many new challenges as they manage diversity in the workplace. Concerns such as sexual harassment, comparable worth, and workplace violence are issues that the human resource manager must often help the organization to address. Americans with disabilities now have extended rights in the workplace. Managing for results requires greater, as well as better, use of productivity measures and performance appraisal. Municipal unions are still a strong and vocal force to be reckoned with in city politics, and rightly so. Local leaders are being forced to search for ways to accommodate all these pressures, and the human resources department usually plays a critical role in developing, implementing, and evaluating policies and procedures to address these personnel issues.

We begin this chapter by examining how public personnel administration should be organized. Second, human resource management functions such as staffing, classification, compensation, and performance appraisal are discussed. Third, we address many of the current issues associated with modern personnel systems, including questions about equal employment opportunity and affirmative action (EEO/AA); the Americans with Disabilities Act (ADA); the courts, EEO, and selection procedures; sexual harassment; comparable worth; and managing diversity in the workplace. Finally, we come to labor-management relations. How do public- and private-sector unions differ? Are their differences so pronounced as to warrant treating public-sector unions much differently from those in the private sector? Collective bargaining is the mainstay of labor relations—in both public and private sectors—in this country today. We outline the procedures, with particular emphasis on methods of resolving labor disputes, and then end the section with an examination of the controversy over strikes by public employees.

ORGANIZING THE PERSONNEL FUNCTION

STRUCTURE

When cities began to establish formal personnel policies and procedures, they logically followed the example set by the national government in 1883 with the creation of the Civil Service Commission after passage of the Pendleton Act. In most cases, this logic led to the creation of an independent civil service commission. These commissions, usually composed of three or five members, were concerned primarily with ridding the municipality of patronage politics by implementing competitive examinations for entry into city service. The commissions also attempted to protect the municipal workforce from political interference, by creating elaborate regulations and procedures to prevent employee dismissal for political or other reasons unrelated to work performance. But as the functional responsibility of city governments expanded, city employment grew, and new personnel issues and concerns developed, the concept of an independent civil service commission fell out of favor, or simply became outdated. Given the central role that personnel management played in the day-to-day operations of city affairs, it became clear that a personnel department should be added as a *staff-level agency*. Along with other staff departments—such as budgeting, legal, and policy development—the personnel department performed a support function to operating or line-level municipal agencies, such as police, fire, and parks and recreation.

The basic alternative to the civil service commission is the central (staff) human resources department, which is directly responsible to the chief executive. The rationale for making human resources part of the executive staff is the frequently cited "principle" that executive authority should be commensurate with responsibility. By 1962, the Municipal Manpower Commission had endorsed the concept of an executive-centered personnel system.[1] In 1970 the National Civil Service League took the same position.[2] An ICMA-sponsored survey of all cities with populations of 10,000 or greater conducted in the mid-1990s found that

49 percent of responding jurisdictions employed the central personnel board with no separate civil service commission.[3] A true independent commission with full powers was found in less than 2 percent of the cities.

PURPOSE

Regardless of the organizational structure employed, the fundamental purpose of most human resources departments, irrespective of the size of the city, is to create and maintain a merit system of employment. Of course, as Anne Freedman suggests in her provocative book, *Patronage: An American Tradition*, few cities would admit to having any other type of personnel system. Who favors patronage these days? And where it does exist, Freedman notes, it has largely "gone underground."[4] Later in this chapter we do consider, however, how the *concept* of merit has changed in response to challenges by minorities, women, and advocates of municipal administrative reform.

The evolution of the merit system in the United States is well documented by public administration scholar Patricia Wallace Ingraham.[5] A traditional merit system usually is based on the following principles:

- Recruiting, selecting, and advancing employees on the basis of their relative knowledge, skills, and abilities (KSAs)
- Providing equitable and adequate compensation
- Training employees, as needed, to ensure high-quality performance
- Retaining employees on the basis of the adequacy of their performance
- Ensuring fair treatment of applicants and employees . . . without regard to political affiliation, race, color, national origin, sex, or religious creed
- Ensuring that employees are protected against coercion for partisan political purposes and are prohibited from using their official authority for the purpose of interfering with or affecting the result of an election or a nomination for office.[6]

Although merit is the *fundamental* building block of modern American personnel systems for all levels of government (federal, state, and local), developing nations often experience a difficult time in reforming traditional systems based on patronage. Efforts to reform the Bangladesh civil service system is a case in point (see box 9.1).

Now we turn to a discussion of traditional personnel functions. For many years, the development and institutionalization of these functions occupied the lion's share of personnel specialists' time and attention.

HUMAN RESOURCE MANAGEMENT FUNCTIONS

Because personnel practices help to determine the nature of the municipal workforce, they indirectly affect everything a city does. Municipal human resource management decisions also have a potentially important impact on the local economy. Any significant cutback or slowdown in municipal employment affects minority job opportunities adversely

BOX 9.1   Policy and Practice

OLD WAYS VERSUS REFORM: ATTEMPTS TO MODERNIZE THE BANGLADESH CIVIL SERVICE SYSTEM

Bangladesh is a relatively small nation (about the size of the state of Iowa) located in South Asia surrounded largely by India, with the Bay of Bengal as much of the country's southern border. The nation gained its independence in 1971 and established a constitutional republic in 1991. Although small geographically, Bangladesh has a population of over 160 million inhabitants (the seventh most populated nation in the world). In comparison, the entire U.S. population is about 310 million. The nation employs a unitary form of political organization. As such, the central government, which is located in Dhaku, makes policies followed in districts and cities—including regulations defining the nation's civil service system.

In an article published in the *International Journal of Public Administration*, Professor Noore Alam Siddiquee, who served as Department Head of Political Science at the International Islamic University located in Kuala Lumpur, Malaysia, when the article was written, offers an in-depth analysis of efforts to reform the civil service system in Bangladesh the past two decades. He largely concludes that the effort in Bangladesh, like other developing countries, has been a failure. The "paradigm shift" has been difficult to make. "Though at times political leaders in ... [developing] countries have promised to modernize the management of public services, rhetoric has outpaced actions. Evidence shows that the changes brought about are rather marginal and that personnel functions in most case continue to be preformed by and large in the *old fashion*" (emphasis added). His analysis of the extent to which personnel functions such as recruitment, selection, training, promotion, compensation, and performance appraisal in Bangladesh reflect merit and support modern human resource management principles reveals that the nation continues to struggle to modernize its civil service system; personnel policies remain "deeply rooted in traditional policies and practices." Paramount among these *old ways* is the twin problems of corruption and patronage. As Professor Siddiquee notes, "Today corruption [in Bangladesh] is widespread at all levels of administration." Similarly, personnel activities such as transfers, rewards, advancements, and promotions "are determined more by personal contacts with and patronage of those at higher levels than by any other rational principles."

Specific constraints and contradictions with the current personnel system in Bangladesh include:

- The lack of human resource planning, with a "disconnect" between the needs of the public service and the labor supply educational institutions in Bangladesh provide. The public service needs skilled specialists while the universities "keep on flooding the market with generalists of whom the demand is extremely limited."
- Merit is not the guiding principle determining selection of employees. Instead, a quota system is used to fill 55 percent of government positions. The quotas are for women, districts, wards of freedom fighters, and tribal populations. According to Siddiquee, these candidates are "relatively inferior" and have not significantly advanced the concept of representative bureaucracy since unfilled quota positions are awarded to the larger and already well represented, in terms of quota groups, districts.
- Recruitment tests are "far from being objective, valid, and reliable in terms of assessing the candidates' qualities and potentials."

(continued)

BOX 9.1   Policy and Practice (continued)

- "Training methods . . . are mostly archaic and outdated."
- Seniority "has emerged as the sole determining factor" for promotions.
- Performance appraisals are inadequate and have become "an annual ritual of no practical significance."

In concluding, Professor Siddiquee asks the question: "Why is the Bangladesh civil service still characterized by traditional policies and practices?" He provides four explanations. First, political leaders in Bangladesh rely on senior bureaucrats for their specialized, technical knowledge in running the country. This dependence of politicians on bureaucrats is excessive; the withdrawal of top civil servant support for the regime in power could potentially destabilize the country. Second, most previous attempts to reform the civil service, according to Siddiquee, have been "cosmetic in nature" and undertaken to seek "external legitimacy and donor supports." As a very poor nation, Bangladesh depends heavily on the largess of institutions such as the World Bank, International Monetary Fund, and United Nations Development Program. These external actors have put pressure on government officials to initiate administrative reforms, especially in terms of transparency and accountability. Third, bureaucratic resistance to change has been stout. "Bureaucracy in Bangladesh has been a very powerful force, able to thwart any effort that seeks to dismantle the *status quo* and pose a challenge to its privileged position." Finally, as noted before, "corruption has become an important component of Bangladesh's administrative culture." Without a counterbalance to the power of the entrenched bureaucracy, those in power can ignore civil service rules.

In many instances, the civil service system in Bangladesh as described by Siddiquee in this article could have been a description of the American personnel system during the heyday of the urban machines (approximately 1850s to early 1900s) discussed in chapter 3. Federal government initiatives such as the Pendleton Act of 1883 and civil service reform groups that sprang up across American cities under the general rubric of the urban reform movement helped bring modern strategic human resource management to the *developing nation of America*. Like Bangladesh, the defining twin characteristics of America's urban machines were also *corruption* and *patronage*. It took significant political will, Progressive reforms, and an Industrial revolution to replace *old ways* with a modern civil service system in America.

SOURCE: Noore Alam Siddiquee, "Human Resource Management in Bangladesh Civil Service: Constraints and Contradictions," *International Journal of Public Administration* (No. 1, 2003): 35–60.

---

in inner cities. And because salaries loom so large in the overall city budget, personnel decisions—to add city employees, to grant pay increases—have serious consequences for revenue and tax policies (see chapter 10).

Personnel departments perform a host of activities.[7] Here we discuss the pivotal functions of staffing, position classification, compensation, and performance evaluation.

STAFFING

Historically, state and local governments simply have not been competitive with the private sector in attracting the "best and brightest." Because this failure was usually blamed on low municipal salaries, many cities (and state governments) felt compelled to offer competitive salaries and attractive fringe-benefit plans, including good retirement packages. Nevertheless, pay practices in local government have not kept pace with the private sector, especially for professionals. Writing in 1988, Elder Witt noted, "There is growing concern that public salaries, particularly at the highest levels of state and local government, have fallen too far behind, that good people are not entering or staying in government because of low pay."[8]

More recently, Lloyd G. Nigro, Felix A. Nigro, and J. Edward Kellough, three of the preeminent personnel scholars in the discipline, have argued that public-private pay disparities are not getting better. Their research suggests that although states and local governments pay more for lower-level jobs than does the private sector, private-sector employers pay more for white-collar jobs, especially at the higher levels of responsibility. Also, state and local governments' compensation for professional and administrative positions is significantly lower than that offered by private industry, while the pattern is mixed for technical, clerical, and blue-collar workers.[9]

Recruitment

Traditionally, most local public agencies adopted a largely passive approach to recruitment, a let-them-come-to-us philosophy. This practice produced a recruitment process based on having a friend or a relative who worked for the city. Remnants of this who-you-know strategy persist, but most authorities today urge public agencies to adopt a more aggressive recruiting posture.[10] In some municipalities, applications are received, candidates are examined, and appointments are made all in one visit to a public personnel agency, and open continuous examinations (with no closing dates) are common. In effect, the entire employment process has been sped up as a way of making public jobs more attractive and accessible.

The importance of recruitment to staffing efforts is likely to intensify in coming years. According to Gary Roberts, "The governmental labor force is considerably older than that in the private sector. Forty-four percent of governmental employees are 45 or older, versus 30 percent for private employers, and 27 percent of governmental employees are less than 30 years old versus 43 percent in the private sector."[11] Moreover, as Joseph Cayer notes, "The issue [of recruitment] will intensify as many [government] jurisdictions face losing as much as 50 percent of their workforces by 2010 due to retirement."[12] Increasingly, local human resources managers are going to find themselves competing with the private and nonprofit sectors for the best people to fill these positions.

Fortunately, many personnel departments saw the future some years ago and began to take efforts to enhance recruitment efforts. For example, based on a large sample of cities, a 1994 ICMA personnel survey showed that, in addition to posting public announcements of job openings, about 60 percent of reporting survey cities sent announcements to minority, female, and other special interest organizations, and 37 percent of those reporting sent them to unions and trade and professional associations.[13] More recently, Susan Mason and Lana

Stein note that to cast the recruitment net as widely as possible, contemporary practice in local government personnel administration includes sending job postings to "universities, minority newspapers, and community and neighborhood organizations."[14] They also note that given the increased skill levels required for employment in local government today, recruitment at America's colleges and universities is becoming more common.[15] Finally, a 2000 survey conducted by Jonathan West and Evan Berman that included 222 cities with populations greater than 50,000 demonstrates that local human resource departments are taking advantage of other, more innovative recruitment tools made possible by modern e-government.[16] They found that almost 70 percent of the cities use online recruitment in some form.[17] This finding is important since a 2004 ICMA survey that included over 3,000 cities and counties found that fully 91 percent of the governments had a website (up from 74 percent in 2002).[18] In jurisdictions with 25,000 or more residents, 98 percent of the governments report having a web portal. Clearly, the movement from traditional human resources management (HRM) to virtual HRM is in progress.

To a considerable extent, personnel recruitment today involves the extra effort to make the workforce more representative—an activity we consider in more detail in the next section.

Examination and Selection

Merit systems demand some objective measurement criteria by which to rank prospective employees. In most cities, this need translates into tests—either unassembled or written. An unassembled test (for which job candidates do not assemble in one place for an exam) might consist of the analysis by a personnel specialist of the job applicant's training and experience as demonstrated on various forms (resumes, transcripts, letters of reference, and so on); an oral interview might also be conducted. This form of testing has not stirred up controversy, as its written counterpart has.

The traditional assumption that written tests have the capacity to identify qualified workers has been under attack for a long time from a variety of quarters.[19] Much of the criticism has erupted over the issue of test validity. How well do employment test results correspond with job performance? This is the big question, and minority groups, women, and the disabled are the ones asking it—with good reason. As Nigro and his associates remind us, "Written tests are extensively used in the public sector to measure job knowledge or skills."[20] And this is particularly the case with local governments who rely heavily on them, despite the fact that many of these tests have not been properly validated. Moreover, a common practice is to use various components in the selection process sequentially, so that applicants who lose out at the written exam stage do not receive further consideration. And the fact remains that certain minority groups often do not fare as well on written tests as do members of the majority culture.

Why are written examinations so prevalent? Many public officials think these tests have advantages in addition to their presumed objectivity: they not only save a good deal of time (compared to oral exams); they also serve as a means of defense against hiring the obviously inept. In the words of Nigro, Nigro, and Kellough. "Despite problems associated with validity and adverse impact, written tests are likely to continue as the dominate way of rating applicants for a large variety of civil service positions. For personnel departments and agencies, they are administratively convenient and provide a quantitative and seemingly objective basis for ranking candidates."[21]

Yet the attacks on written tests and on the "rule of three" (requiring appointment of one of the three top scorers) have resulted in changes in traditional testing and certification practices; much innovation and reform is currently taking place. Public administration scholar Dennis Dresang provides a discussion of a number of these new policies and procedures, three of which we consider here.[22] The first, and most obvious, change is to increase the rule of three to some larger number—the rule of "n"—usually to 5, 7, or 10. This change is heavily favored by advocates of New Public Management reforms, since it provides managers with more flexibility and streamlines the hiring process.[23] A recent survey of members of the International Personnel Management Association and the Section on Personnel and Labor Relations of the American Society for Public Administration also suggests that the rule of three is growing less important to human resource managers.[24] In 1998, the personnel specialists ranked the rule of three as the tenth most important of fifteen staffing and selection techniques, and, looking forward to the year 2008, the survey respondents believe the technique will then rank in fourteenth place. The rule of three, along with paper and pencil exams and reductions-in-force, were the only three staffing and selection techniques to decline in significance of importance among the respondents.

Some jurisdictions have begun using a second procedural change called *category certification*. This approach acknowledges that tests are not absolutely precise measures and that all applicants who score within a certain range on a test should therefore be considered approximately equal.[25] This arrangement produces a much larger number of qualified candidates than does the usual rule of three, thus increasing the chances of a target group appointment (such as a woman or a member of a racial minority). As explained by Roberts, the categorical approach might group candidates into three groups—"satisfactory," "good," and "excellent"—and then certify anyone who falls in the "excellent" group. Maricopa County, Arizona, for example, groups candidates into three groups—"exceptional," "meets standards," and "meets minimum standards"—and submits the entire list for interviews.[26]

A third option for making hiring decisions is to decentralize the selection process to the line level, coupled with using methods other than written tests, such as probationary appointments or assessment centers. These civil service reforms are under way in a number of states and cities: "The states of California, Minnesota and Virginia and the cities of Baltimore, Dallas, Indianapolis and San Diego, for example, have decentralized their hiring systems and have dumped the rule of three. All but Baltimore and Dallas have also moved away from written tests to evaluate job candidates."[27]

The debate over the compatibility of merit and equal opportunity remains unsettled. Civil rights groups and advocates for administrative reforms continue to push for changes in the traditional practices that rely heavily on tests and credentials. And, as we discuss in a later section, the courts have played a major role in determining just how far institutions must go in modifying practices in order to ensure equal access to all groups.

CLASSIFICATION

Many authorities believe that *position classification*, which is based on rank-in-the-job, is the cornerstone or hub of modern personnel management.[28] If activities were not grouped together into positions requiring similar qualifications, duties, and responsibilities, not only would there be no accurate description of the workforce, but each individual would have to be treated separately. Obviously, this situation would create inconsistencies, especially in the area of pay. Indeed, perhaps the principal advantage of position classification has been the ability to standardize salaries.[29] The whole idea is to ensure equal pay for equal work—which, of course, is required by law.

To classify jobs in the city, job analysis is required. As an extension of Taylor's so-called scientific management (discussed in the previous chapter), job analysis "is a process of collecting information about the tasks a job requires to be performed and the knowledge, skills, and abilities necessary to perform those tasks."[30] This analysis must define the major activities associated with a job. This information is critical in order to validate selection techniques—that is, a selection device or devices (such as a written test, a performance test, interviews) used to choose an employee for a position must be demonstrably related to the tasks associated with the job. Jobs are then ranked based on required KSAs, necessary experience, and so on, and grouped into grades and classes. The compensation plan is integrated with the position classification plan so that employees are paid similar wages when they perform similar jobs.

Citing the advantages of classifying jobs is one thing; doing so accurately is another. Because class labels determine salary levels, classifications must be current. But cities seem to have a hard time keeping them up-to-date. Why? Departmental resistance is the primary reason. If classifications are to be valid, the personnel staff must investigate the nature of every job in the organization. And, in the eyes of many line agencies, such an investigation is an intrusion. Also, supervisors tend to overclassify employees, thereby rewarding their workers and enhancing the importance of their own jobs.

Many public-sector managers heavily criticize traditional position classification systems. Katherine C. Naff provides a list of ten frequently raised objections. Position classification often:

1. Creates narrow, rigid boundaries between jobs
2. Locks employees into functional silos
3. Accentuates hierarchy
4. Demands centralization and uniformity

5. Limits ability to offer competitive salaries
6. Assumes individuals' contribution to their job is static and never grows
7. Encourages playing havoc with the merit promotion process
8. Fails to keep up with changing technology
9. Impedes employee development
10. Creates conflict between managers and the classifiers who must "police" classification decisions[31]

Not surprisingly, contemporary administrative reform advocates are critical of position classification as it has developed over the past hundred years in the public sector. Clearly, many of the items on Naff's list are antithetical to the principles espoused by REGO and NPM enthusiasts who argue for the flattening of hierarchies, greater use of "teams" in service delivery, and providing managers with more tools with which to select, place, promote, and dismiss public employees. In *Reinventing Government*, Osborne and Gaebler call for several personnel reforms, including broad classifications and pay bands, performance-based pay systems, promotion and layoff policies based on performance instead of seniority or time-in-rank, aggressive recruitment of the "best" people to work in government, and paying public employees market-based salaries.[32]

While all of these reforms have captured much attention, almost all efforts to deal with problems posed by conventional position classification systems have concentrated on "(1) increasing their flexibility, (2) making it easier for supervisors to understand and use them, and (3) connecting them in supportive ways to the human resources management efforts of agencies."[33] One way to achieve such flexibility is through the *broadbanding* of positions. Naff comments: "Broadbanding can be seen as an extreme form of subtracting classifications. In this system, highly specific occupational series are replaced with much broader job titles, and broader pay ranges replace specific grade levels."[34] Broadbanding enhances managerial flexibility in many ways. Managers, for example, "can move employees horizontally and vertically among a wider range of work assignments without the need for a formal time-intensive promotion process."[35] Additionally, broadbanding classification and pay-grade structures also supports "efforts to administer pay in ways intended to meaningfully reward performance and recognize differences in skills and abilities."[36]

COMPENSATION AND PERFORMANCE APPRAISAL

Compensation

First and foremost, it is important to recognize that pay in the public sector represents a "political outcome."[37] That is, most city employees receive a salary that is legislatively appropriated from tax revenues, and city operating budgets must be balanced (see chapter 10). Moreover, as public administration experts Ronald D. Sylvia and C. Kenneth Meyer note, "Governments have no capacity for rewarding workers with stock."[38] Incentive pay is available in some cities, but it is not as widespread as in the private sector.

The compensation plan typically is tied to position classification. Several positions are assigned to a particular pay grade. Within each pay level there are steps, commonly five or six; the most frequent salary increment between steps is 5 percent.[39] How does an employee move up the pay ladder? Professor Joseph Cayer describes several ways, including across-the-board adjustments, merit or performance pay, gain sharing, and skills-based pay.[40] An *across-the-board adjustment* is perhaps the most recognizable method of pay adjustment among municipalities. Under this system, all employees get (or perhaps lose) a percentage of their base pay; usually, only those workers who receive satisfactory job performance appraisals are eligible for increased compensation. This approach is easy to administer, but it can play havoc with morale because it assumes that all employees are performing at the same level. High performers often lament the fact that their raise is the same as those whose contributions to the organization are judged as only satisfactory.

Over the last three decades or so there has been an increased interest in *merit/performance pay* and, to a lesser extent, *incentive pay* systems (such as gain sharing or skills-based pay). For example, in an ICMA-sponsored survey, Streib and Poister found that the use of performance monitoring and employee incentive programs increased dramatically in American cities between 1976 and 1988. The use of performance monitoring as a management technique grew by more than 30 percent over that period, at the end of which, 67 percent of survey cities were using the technique. Employee incentive programs almost doubled, growing by 48 percent (64 percent of survey cities used the technique).[41] Freyss found a slight decline in the use of municipal pay-for-performance and incentive pay programs between two large-scale ICMA surveys conducted in 1989–1990 and in 1994–1995. Nevertheless, over 50 percent of the responding cities in the later survey reported that they continued to tie pay increases to performance appraisals, and slightly more than 20 percent of the cities offered employees one-time bonuses or cash awards for superior performance.[42]

Some argue that pay for performance suffers from serious problems. For example, writing in 2010, well known public administration expert James Bowman in a biting critique entitled, "The Success of Failure: The Paradox of Performance Pay," suggests "that belief in performance pay is akin to an urban legend."[43] Similarly, Larry Lane, James Wolf, and Colleen Woodward claim that there is an "utter lack of empirical evidence, in the private and public sectors, that pay-for-performance has any positive effect on either morale or productivity,"[44] Such systems are not easy to develop and administer; performance monitoring systems take time, money, and human resources to create and are often a major concern to unions. Not surprisingly, union representatives want to help in defining what merit means, how it is measured, and how merit money is distributed. A pay-for-performance system carries with it real fiscal implications for the city, such as determining how many employees the city can afford to give permanent merit raises or one-time bonuses. Also, since supervisors and managers administer performance evaluations and since performance evaluations are linked to merit pay raises or bonuses, the discretionary power of supervisors and managers can lead to favoritism and inequity.

BOX 9.2　Policy and Practice

PAY-FOR-PERFORMANCE IN LOCAL GOVERNMENT

Babe Ruth understood pay-for-performance. In 1929, when someone pointed out that he was being paid twice as much money as President Hoover, the Babe's response was succinct: "I had a better year than he did."

Despite all the recent hype, holding government workers accountable through the use of pay-for-performance is not a new idea, as Elder Witt points out: "It has been discussed, defended, and criticized for the past decade. Those who do not like it continue to say it is both costly and disruptive to group morale. . . . [It] is, in fact, difficult, expensive, and controversial." The city manager of Aurora, Colorado, Jim Griesemer, notes, "It's not a panacea." Nevertheless, as a concept and practice, pay-for-performance is here to stay.

The real pioneers in the area of pay-for-performance are local governments. Scottsdale, Arizona, and its 1,060 city workers have been on the system since 1982. The 350-plus workers in Biloxi, Mississippi, have operated under this management tool since 1986. In 1989, Denver, Colorado, put its entire 8,000 workforce on performance pay. Biloxi finance and personnel director Steve Held notes: "I think pay-for-performance, in some form, is really the only way to go. It's a true merit system." The assistant city manager in Scottsdale, Richard A. Bowers, thinks pay-for-performance works well, but he also notes: "Even after years, the system needs constant review and tweaking and turning and asking people how they feel about it." A Denver personnel director, A. Fred Timmerman, asserts: "Where's the incentive to do anything more than meet expectations if I work outstandingly all year next to someone who's just meeting expectations and we get the same raise?"

The system is not self-executing. The city of Aurora, Colorado, is on its second try with performance pay. The first round failed because of inadequate training of supervisors. In Denver, the fear of favoritism in the evaluation process is a concern. Biloxi has three separate layers of evaluations. The former city manager of Scottsdale also notes that you can't sell the innovation on the grounds of efficiency: "If you try to promote pay-for-performance on the basis that you're going to spend less money on your people, you are bound to fail. . . . What you are doing is spending roughly the same amount smarter than under the old civil service system of across-the-board increases."

SOURCE: Elder Witt, "Sugarplums and Lumps of Coal," *Governing*, December 1989, 28–33.

Gain sharing is a type of pay-for-performance in which members of a group—say, employees in the municipal garage—receive a merit raise or bonus. Usually, the pay adjustment is based on increased productivity or savings resulting from the unit's work activities. Skills-based pay is a reward provided to an individual for acquiring specific skills that can benefit the city. For example, let's say a social worker at the municipal hospital goes back to the university and receives a Master of Social Work (MSW) degree. Since federal regulations allow the city hospital to charge back to the federal government higher Medicaid and/or Medicare rates for services rendered by a social worker who possesses a MSW, the city gains more revenue. The city, in turn, rewards the social worker by providing an adjustment in pay or perhaps helps to defray the individual's costs in earning the degree through a tuition reimbursement program—or perhaps does both.

GAIN SHARING

Since the late 1980s, the corporate sector has been looking to pay-incentive plans as a way to improve worker productivity. But unlike traditional incentive programs aimed at middle- and upper-level executives, interest today has shifted to introducing incentives for all employees. The term often used for these types of incentive plans is "gain sharing."

Gain sharing was developed in the 1930s by Joe Scanlon, a union leader. The conceptual base of this pay-incentive program is straightforward: when workers identify ways to reduce labor costs as a percentage of the cost of production, the reductions translate into increases in productivity, and workers share in the gains. As such, gain sharing plans provide an incentive for workers to focus on performance goals.

Payouts from gain sharing are typically modest—4–8 percent of base pay. According to Howard Risher, "Evidence to date confirms that gain sharing and other group incentives can have a significant positive impact on performance. Research supported by the American Compensation Association shows that employers can expect to gain three or four dollars for every dollar paid out to employees. Perhaps more important, gain sharing plans can have a positive impact on organization culture."

Such has been the case in Charlotte, North Carolina; College Station, Texas; and Baltimore County. The City of Charlotte, for example, started its gain sharing program in 1994. That program begins with the city manager setting a citywide savings goal. If the goal is met, half of the savings is set aside in an employee incentive pool, and the balance is returned to the general fund. Half of the money in the employee incentive pool is paid in equal shares to all city workers; the remaining half goes to specific city departments or units based on the achievement of specific goals.

In FY 95, the average payout was about $360 for each employee, compared to a possible $406 if all goals had been met. Charlotte city manager Pamela Syfert is pleased with the program. She notes that in a two-year period, the city returned $9.6 million to the general fund and provided city employees about $2.6 million in incentive pay. In addition, the "plan has had a noticeable impact on the attitudes of employees." Employees closely monitor targets and work as teams to achieve them.

Similar positive results associated with gain sharing are reported in College Station and Baltimore County. Risher concludes his assessment by noting that "gain sharing can be a powerful tool to realize improved performance. Excitement generated in these workplaces suggests that employees feel like winners. This is all too rare in today's public employment climate. It makes gain sharing worth considering."

SOURCE: Adapted from Howard Risher, "Can Gain Sharing Help to Reinvent Government?" *Public Management,* May 1998, 17–21.

Despite criticisms, pay-for-performance systems seems to have found a home in city government The two case studies in boxes 9.2 and 9.3 illustrate the concepts of pay-for-performance and gain sharing.

Performance Appraisal

Determining who gets merit pay or extra compensation for outstanding performance is not a simple matter. Personnel experts have struggled for years to devise acceptable systems for evaluating employee performance. If appraisal techniques do not measure performance, then performance pay becomes an empty process.

Most cities of any size now engage in formal employee evaluation. For example, in the 1994–1995 ICMA survey discussed earlier, Freyss reports that over 80 percent of cities responded that they had a performance appraisal system in place.[45] But the process varies somewhat between managerial employees and rank-and-file workers. Survey research reveals the following differences:

- About three-fifths (59 percent) of cities formally evaluate managerial employees. The comparable figure for nonmanagerial employees is 86 percent.
- Managerial appraisal is more frequently associated with the allocation of rewards, whereas nonmanagerial appraisal places greater emphasis on employee communication and development.
- Managerial employees are much more likely to be evaluated using a performance-based evaluation system such as Management by Objectives (MBO). In contrast, nonmanagerial employees are evaluated primarily using rating scales, a trait-based evaluation technique.[46]

Performance-based rating systems often rely on MBO or behaviorally anchored rating scales (BARS). These devices force the rater to select the phrase or statement that best describes how an employee might respond or behave under specific or general circumstances. Most experts agree that these approaches are superior to the more conventional rating scales, which ask a supervisor to rate a subordinate using a five- or seven-point scale over a group of generally desirable traits, such as efficiency, loyalty, promptness, or intelligence. Many observers consider these traditional scales as too subjective and often unrelated to job performance.

In an era in which administrative reforms promote teamwork, quality circles, and Total Quality Management (TQM), the customary performance appraisal process may have to be modified: "Traditional performance appraisals are bad simply because they tell too many people they are losers."[47] Charles Fox argues that formal appraisals should be "abolished or their use subverted."[48] He insists that TQM, mission-driven government, professionalism, and other factors make the technique a management dinosaur. Instead, he contends, groups can be evaluated according to mission or task completion, or employees can be rated as simply "satisfactory" or "unsatisfactory." Should a personnel controversy require adjudication, he argues, courts will accept the designations as long as they are used fairly and consistently.

Dennis Daley argues for a *360-degree* appraisal system if the primary focus of evaluation is on employee development. Feedback on performance is gathered from multiple raters (supervisor, subordinates, peers, and, typically, a self-rating). If job-related, information can also be gathered from those external to the organization (e.g., vendors, service users).[49] Daley notes that the 360-degree evaluation provides a more balanced and accurate form of appraisal since it is based on information from multiple perspectives, but the process is more complex and costly to administer than many other forms of evaluation.

ISSUES IN HUMAN RESOURCE MANAGEMENT

EQUAL EMPLOYMENT OPPORTUNITY AND AFFIRMATIVE ACTION

For some time now, cities have been truly committed to nondiscrimination in hiring. But this was not always the case in local government. In the early years of efforts to open the doors of municipal government and employ people of color and women—and later people with disabilities and alternative lifestyles—the battle to ensure equal employment opportunity (EEO) was often bitter and hard-fought. As late as the 1970s, protected groups hastened to point out that voluntary compliance and good-faith efforts had not changed the situation very much. This viewpoint was well articulated in 1973 by Herbert Hill, former national labor director of the NAACP:

> The record of thirty years of fair employment practice laws makes it absolutely clear that the concept of passive nondiscrimination is totally inadequate and obsolete. In practice a ritualistic policy of "nondiscrimination" or of "equal opportunity" usually means perpetuation of the traditional discriminatory patterns or, at best, tokenism. The law now requires the broad application of preferential hiring systems to eliminate the pervasive effects of racial discrimination in virtually every segment of the American economy.[50]

Hill's "preferential hiring" came in the form of affirmative action (AA) programs.

Since the 1970s, municipal human resource directors have attempted to develop and implement EEO and AA programs. As Cayer notes, both EEO and AA attempt "to make the public service representative of society as a whole"[51]—to make the public service more diverse. Diversity in the public sector is tied to the concept of representative bureaucracy: "the premise that all groups in society should be represented and will influence the public service in its actions."[52] Representational equity is often expressed as the ratio of the availability of a protected group in the municipal labor pool to its employment in city government in general or in various types of positions in the jurisdiction (such as firefighters, sanitation workers, and office assistants).

Today, as in the past, exactly what constitutes EEO and AA remains mired in a host of legal conflicts, at both the legislative and judicial levels. While most of the legal action takes place at the national level, the actual disputes arise from local conditions.

AFFIRMATIVE ACTION

EEO "requires that all groups have the same chance to compete for positions and are treated equally once employed . . . [It] requires neutrality on issues other than merit and ability in the personnel process."[53] The initial strategy for achieving equal employment opportunity was to concentrate on eliminating discriminatory personnel policies and practices, but limited achievements under this early effort led to the creation of affirmative action programs. AA mandates more than passive nondiscrimination; it requires action to redress employment imbalances for both racial and ethnic minorities and women. Above all, affirmative action focuses on results, not on promises and plans.

The concept of affirmative action was given the status of federal policy by executive order in the early 1960s. The approach officially reached state and local governments with the passage of the Equal Employment Opportunity Act in 1972. The act made local governments subject to Title VII of the Civil Rights Act of 1964, which prohibits employment discrimination. The 1972 act also established the Equal Employment Opportunity Commission (EEOC). Since passage of the 1978 Civil Service Reform Act, EEOC can investigate and bring suit against private and public employers for alleged violations of Title VII.

Preferential Hiring

Just how far employers must go in their nondiscrimination efforts is still being vigorously debated if not legally contested. Some agree with Herbert Hill that affirmative action mandates preferential hiring practices,[54] while others feel that preferential hiring smacks of reverse discrimination. Inevitably, the courts and Congress have been forced to decide the nature and scope of preferential hiring.

The Courts

Public administration expert John Nalbandian outlines the U.S. Supreme Court's position on affirmative action.[55] He argues that the Court has reached a consensus based on a two-part analytical approach. The first part examines the *justification* for taking race into consideration, concluding that "the more the impact the affirmative action has on non-whites, the more justification is required." The second part of the approach considers the *content* of the affirmative action activity, with particular attention to the consequences for nonminority employees: "The Court is concerned with limiting affirmative action tightly within the scope of the problem it is supposed to solve." In other words, "societal discrimination" may not be justification for affirmative action plans. And to the extent possible, AA plans should be tailored to bestow benefits on identifiable victims so as to mitigate the impact on innocent others. This approach seems to have been affirmed in the Court's ruling in 1995 in *Adarand v. Pena*. As Kellough explains, this decision requires that "any racial classifications incorporated into voluntary affirmative action programs by state, local, or federal employers must be shown to serve a compelling governmental interest in order to achieve Constitutional legitimacy ... Once a compelling government interest is identified, the method used to achieve the interest must be narrowly tailored."[56]

In the late 1980s, the Court decided three cases that "critics say have undermined the fairness of civil rights laws."[57] In *City of Richmond v. J. A. Croson Co.*, a 6–3 majority of the Court found that the minority business enterprise (MBE) set-aside program ordinance of the city of Richmond, Virginia, was unconstitutional.[58] Cities had designed such programs to ensure that minority businesses received a certain percentage of city contracts.

The second decision was in *Ward's Cove Packing Co. v. Antonio*, in which the Court ruled that showing racial discrimination by demonstrating adverse impact or disparate effect was no longer enough. This method had allowed employers to use statistical data to prove that women or minorities were underrepresented in a jurisdiction, job category, and so on, thus showing evidence of bias. Under the *Ward's Cove* ruling, litigants were required to tie specific employer practices to such underrepresentation, and even then, the employer could justify such practices by showing that they were based on reasonable and usual business practices.[59] This decision thus shifted the burden of proof from the employer to the plaintiff and made it easier for the employer to use standardized tests and diploma requirements even if they would have an adverse impact on protected groups.

The third case, *Martin v. Wilks*, came out of Birmingham, Alabama, where a group of white firefighters sued, claiming that the city's voluntary preferential hiring of blacks resulted in reverse discrimination. The Supreme Court agreed, paving the way for numerous reverse discrimination suits.[60]

Reactions to Court Decisions

In response to these actions and to President George H. W. Bush's veto of the 1990 Civil Rights Act, Congress passed the 1991 Civil Rights Act. Major provisions of the new legislation included the following steps:

- Overturning of the *Ward's Cove* decision by shifting back to the employer the burden of proof for statistical adverse impact. A "business justification" for racial imbalance once again requires "business necessity" and "job relatedness."
- Reversal of the *Martin v. Wilks* decision, thereby limiting the ability of whites to claim reverse discrimination in consent decrees.[61]

Affirmative Action Now and Tomorrow

After 40 years of history, what is the legacy of affirmative action? In a 2009 article published in the *Review of Public Personnel Administration*, Professor G. L. A. Harris offers her response to this question. The record is mixed, she argues. On the one hand:

Affirmative action has . . . been effective in improving the employment status of women and minorities, and without such programs, progress would have occurred at much slower rates, if at all. The results of affirmative action have been especially promising in the public sector, specifically in government where such programs are mandated, although nonprofit organizations have found ways to proactively install voluntary affirmative action programs.[62]

On the other hand, her analysis of a multitude of statistics from a number of governmental sources indicates:

Although there have been improvements, women and minorities are neither being advanced into positions nor are they afforded the same career opportunities at the same rates as White men. Women and minorities are further burdened, intentionally or unintentionally, by such barriers as gendered roles and concentration in given positions and/or occupations. Consequently, especially underrepresented minorities are found at the lowest rungs of the organizational ladder and secure lower earnings as well. In turn, the wage gaps between White men and women and between White men and minorities have undergone little change. Even in professional positions, especially minority women, are adversely impacted because of gender, race, and/or ethnicity. In academia, women have regressed on earlier gains made in faculty rank and salary. Women and minorities are further burdened by job segregation and are often clustered by groups in certain government agencies.[63]

Clearly, the legacy of affirmative action is best described as bitter-sweet.

While EEO is a permanent fixture in local government personnel practices, such may not be the fate of affirmative action programs. Just how long will AA extend into the twenty-first century? This question is hard to answer with accuracy, but AA programs are under intense scrutiny at all levels of government. For example, through the initiative process, voters have outlawed AA programs in California and Washington. With passage of the Civil Rights Act of 1991, Congress took a giant step forward in the protection of equal opportunity, but it appears likely that the Court will revert to a narrow interpretation of affirmative action policy guided by Nalbandian's two-part, justification/content test. Two Supreme Court decisions (heard at the same time) in 2003 seem to support this position. In *Grutter v. Bollinger* a majority of the Court found an affirmative action program at the University of Michigan Law School was narrowly tailored and therefore constitutional. In *Gratz v. Bollinger* (2003), the Court ruled that an undergraduate admissions program, also at the University of Michigan, that involved minority preferences was not narrowly focused and thus declared it unconstitutional.[64]

THE AMERICANS WITH DISABILITIES ACT OF 1990

Another major piece of legislation that has had a significant impact on personnel practices is the Americans with Disabilities Act (ADA) of 1990.[65] This legislation prohibits job discrimination by private and public employers in all employment areas (recruitment, benefits, testing, and so on) against people with disabilities. The law initially applied to employers with twenty-five or more employees; since July 26, 1994, it has applied to those with fifteen or more employees. The Equal Employment Opportunity Commission was given primary responsibility for implementation of the law.

The ADA was aimed at the more than 32 million working-age Americans who have a disability—14.9 million of whom have a severe disability.[66] Many of the issues associated with the law concern who is covered and what "reasonable accommodations" an employer needs to make for a disabled employee. In terms of disability, a person is covered if he or she (1) has a physical or mental impairment that substantially limits one or more major life activities, (2) has a record of such an impairment, or (3) is perceived as having such an impairment. While, in the law itself, Congress did not define physical or mental impairment or what the major life activities were, administrators have looked to previous legislation (the Rehabilitation Act of 1973) and EEOC guidelines for guidance. To ensure nondiscrimination based on disabilities, employers "cannot ask questions that would elicit information about physical or mental impairments before a job offer is made."[67] Also, a prospective employer cannot require a medical examination until after a job offer has been extended.

Finally, the ADA requires employers to make reasonable accommodations for workers unless doing so will create an "undue hardship." The following four criteria are used to help determine the nature or extent of such hardship:

- The nature and cost of accommodations needed
- The financial resources of the facility and the impact the accommodations would have on operations; also, the number of employees involved and the effect that providing the accommodations would have on expenses and resources
- The overall financial resources of the employer, employment agency, labor organization, or joint labor-management committee (the covered entity); the overall size of the business; and the number, type, and location of facilities
- The composition, structure, and functions of the workforce; the geographic autonomy of units; and the relationship between the facility where the employee would work and the covered entity[68]

Obviously, the meaning of the law must be determined as it is applied to individual cases, which results in numerous ADA cases being heard by the EEOC. In fact, between 1992 and 1999, ADA suits increased from 1.8 percent to 22 percent of the EEOC's workload.[69] But, if the EEOC does file a suit for an alleged violation of ADA provisions, beware: the agency wins over 90 percent of the approximately 24,000 ADA cases it litigates each year.[70]

THE COURTS, EEO, AND SELECTION PROCEDURES

As noted earlier, the Civil Rights Act of 1991 overturned the U.S. Supreme Court's decision in *Ward's Cove*. In doing so, it codified the Court's earlier decision in *Griggs v. Duke Power Company* (1971) and subsequent *Griggs*-type decisions. The *Griggs* doctrine sets forth several key testing and selection requirements necessary for an employer to avoid racial discrimination:

- Employment practices including tests are unlawful if they differentially affect persons by virtue of their race, sex, religion, or national origin.
- To be lawful, tests must be proved valid; that is, they must be shown to be job-related or predictive of performance on the job.
- Any employment practice, however fair and impartial, that tends to perpetuate the effect of prior discrimination violates the law.

The law prohibits actions that "on their face" treat protected classes (racial or minority groups, women, people with disabilities) unfairly. If the requirements of a job seem to disqualify women, for example, the employer must show that the standards are a "bona fide occupational qualification" (BFOQ); otherwise they will be struck down. For instance, a city cannot require that only a woman can handle a switchboard or that only a man can drive a garbage truck. Race itself is never a BFOQ.

Most municipalities do not tolerate discriminatory treatment, or disparate treatment, and have tried to eliminate it from their hiring practices (but see below). The more common issue now is *disparate effect* or *adverse impact*. Suppose the hiring or testing process for a position produces disproportionately few minority candidates. Is this discrimination? In these instances, the courts usually insist that the municipality show (validate) that the selection process and the test instrument are job-related; if the city fails to demonstrate test validity, the court then finds disparate effect and rules against the city. As a way of helping to establish the meaning of adverse impact, the EEOC, the Civil Service Commission, and the Departments of Justice and Labor jointly adopted an 80 percent rule: If the pass rate for minorities is not 80 percent of that for nonminority applicants, the examination procedure is considered on its face to have unequal impact. Under the 1989 *Ward's Cove* decision, the mere presence of statistical adverse impact was no longer considered enough ammunition for protected groups to go to court; under the Civil Rights Act of 1991, the old standard returned: the four-fifths rule once again is the litmus test for disparate impact. But, as Cayer notes, "The Supreme Court has demonstrated flexibility [with the rule], indicating that the overall employment record and the particular content of the employers' actions should be considered in deciding such cases."[71]

An example of a practice with discriminatory effect is the inclusion of minimum height and weight standards in the requirements for a position as a police officer. On the surface, these requirements—say, a height of 5 feet, 6 inches and weight of 140 pounds—may not seem discriminatory, but in practice they undoubtedly would disqualify far more women than men; thus their impact is disparate. If the city police department could show that the criteria were essential for performance on the job (job-related), the courts might accept them as legitimate. But, in fact, courts commonly reject height and weight requirements.[72]

How do local officials go about showing that selection procedures, most frequently tests, are job-related? Validation is required. Before discussing validation processes, let us return to the issue raised earlier concerning discriminatory or disparate treatment.

Title VII of the Civil Rights Act of 1964 as amended to include state and local governments prohibits both disparate treatment and disparate impact. In June 2009, the Supreme Court in *Ricci v. DeStefano* ruled that the City of New Haven, Connecticut, had discriminated against white and Hispanic firefighters when city officials refused to certify exam results that could have resulted in promotions for these firefighters.[73] City officials in New Haven made this decision after many meetings and in consultation with their legal department. Their reasoning was based on exam results, which statistically demonstrated disparate impact on minority candidates. They feared minorities could raise a serious claim of racial discrimination and sue the city. The city was taken to court by seventeen white and one Hispanic firefighter claiming disparate treatment. The Court agreed and held that "before an employer could engage in intentional discrimination for the asserted purpose of avoiding or remedying an unintentional disparate impact, the employer must have a strong-basis-in-evidence to believe that it would be subject to disparate-impact liability if it fails to take the race-conscious, discriminatory action."[74] According to Professor Shelly L. Peffer, the Court's vague definition of "strong-basis-in-evidence," is unsettling for human resource managers who are left with little guidance on how to avoid discrimination and must choose between being sued for disparate treatment or disparate impact discrimination. She concludes, "It appears that the real impact and meaning of *Ricci* is yet to be seen. The decision evokes more questions than answers, and there will definitely be more litigation on this issue."[75]

Test Validation

According to EEOC guidelines, tests, whether written or performance-based, can be validated in one of several ways.[76] The first is to prove *criterion-related validity* (either predictive or concurrent)—the city can prove that those who score higher on tests perform better on the job than those who score lower. In other words, a study would have to demonstrate that examination scores predict job success. This technique is based on statistical analysis and requires a large number of individuals in a job class or family; in essence, test scores are correlated with job performance scores. Obviously, this type of validation is expensive and in many cases simply not possible, so the EEOC allows two alternative types of validity to be used: *construct validity* and *content validity*. A test is said to have construct validity when it measures a specific theoretical construct or trait, such as clerical or mechanical aptitude, that is necessary for successful job performance. A content-valid test contains a representative sampling of tasks that closely resemble the duties to be performed on the job—a typing test for a job as a typist, for example. Both construct and content criteria, according to EEOC guidelines, must stem from a thorough job analysis.

COMPARABLE WORTH

The Equal Pay Act of 1963 prohibits pay differentials based on sex, thus ensuring equal pay for equal work. *Comparable worth* extends this concept considerably. At issue is whether the pay levels dictated by traditional market forces are fair to women—truck drivers and equipment operators, for example, almost always command more money than do typists and secretaries. Such historical practices rarely reflect whether the work requirements of the jobs really correspond with the levels of pay. Comparable worth mandates that jobs be evaluated and compensated primarily on the basis of what each demands in the way of education, training, experience, and skills. If work were evaluated in this manner, employers presumably would be forced to admit that women are underpaid for much of the work they perform.

A few statistics will help highlight gender and workplace issues.[77] In 2005 in the private sector, men and women were almost at parity in terms of percentage of the workforce, with men occupying 52 percent of the jobs and women 48 percent. In 1960, men held two-thirds of these positions. In the federal government in 2005, 43 percent of workers were women and females held 45 percent of the jobs in state and local governments. Women experience a high degree of job *segregation*, that is they work primarily with members of their own gender. For example, in 2005 across state and local governments, women held 86 percent of administrative support positions. In contrast, females represented 38 percent of officials/administrators, 24 percent of service/maintenance jobs, and 19 percent of protective service positions. Based on 2004 data, women who work in public administration earn 76 percent of what men earn. The comparable statistic for average salary differential between men and women across all occupations is 80 percent. This breadth of the wage differential develops over time. Based on 2007 Bureau of Labor Statistics data, for the age group 16 to 24, women, on average, earn close to what men earn—95 percent. For the 25 to 34 year age cohort, the average woman earns 88 percent of what the average man earns. By the time men and women reach their peak earning years, 45 to 54 years of age; women now earn 73.5 percent of what men earn. Wage differentials cannot be explained by the lack of education on the part of females. In 2004, 32.2 percent of male workers and 32.6 percent of female workers held a bachelor or graduate degree. In short, as Professors Mary E. Guy and Susan Spice note, "the workplace is not a level playing field."[78]

Comparable worth has been and remains a controversial issue. In 1981 the U.S. Supreme Court ruled "that the courts could not mandate comparable worth (equal pay for jobs of equal worth) but that legislation could do so."[79] In 1985 the U.S. Commission on Civil Rights rejected comparable worth, saying that it would lead to a "radical reordering of our economic system."[80] Opponents have also argued that objectively determining which jobs are comparable is an administrative nightmare, inviting discrimination, complaints, and abuse. Potentially high costs are cited as well, because female-dominated jobs would undoubtedly be evaluated upward, but there would be no corresponding lowering of pay for jobs held by males.

In 1981 San Jose, California, was one of the first local governments to address the issue of comparable worth, following a strike by American Federation of State, County, and Municipal Employees (AFSCME) Local 101.[81] One of the first major comparable worth victories at the state level occurred in the State of Washington (*AFSCME et al. v. Washington et al.*, 1983). A federal district court ordered the state "to pay thousands of women employees the salaries they were entitled to under the comparable worth plan originally adopted by the state."[82] The Ninth Circuit Court of Appeals reversed the decision in 1985. But, rather than have the case heard by the U. S. Supreme Court, Washington state officials "settled with the employee unions and a substantial amount of money was allocated for pay raises for individuals in jobs held primarily by women."[83]

SEXUAL HARASSMENT

Sexual harassment has been called an old problem but a new issue.[84] Both the prevalence and costs of sexual harassment in the public workplace have been well documented. For example, surveys conducted in 1981 and 1988 by the U.S. Merit Systems Protection Board found that, at both time points, about 42 percent of women and 15 percent of men had experienced some form of sexual harassment.[85] In 1980 the EEOC ruled that sexual harassment was a form of sex discrimination and thus a violation of Title VII of the Civil Rights Act of 1964, as amended to include state and local governments in 1972.

As such, during the 1980s, cities began to respond to concerns about sexual harassment. Research among a group of large communities showed that by the end of the decade most of the municipalities (84 percent) had formal sexual harassment policies, and about 70 percent also offered formal training programs.[86] Almost two-thirds of the cities reported filing one or more harassment complaints.

What comprises a model sexual harassment policy? Based on a review of extant literature, Laura Reese and Karen Lindenberg offer the following criteria:

- A clear statement of what sexual harassment is and that it will not be tolerated
- Strong commitment to and understanding of the policy by supervisors and top management
- Training programs for both employees and supervisors regarding the nature of sexual harassment to increase awareness of unacceptable behaviors
- Sensitivity training for supervisors to improve interaction with all parties involved
- Training for supervisors on the proper process for conducting investigations
- Clear procedures for dealing with sexual harassment complaints
- Clear lines for reporting sexual harassment that offer options yet avoid too many different actors
- Trained, neutral investigators to deal with sexual harassment complaints
- Investigatory teams composed of both genders
- Procedures that safeguard the confidentiality of both accused and claimant, including sanctions for breaches of confidentiality
- Timelines for various policy processes—interviews, investigations, findings, and reporting
- Specific procedures for reporting, to both the claimant and accused, the findings and outcomes of the investigation on at least some level
- Serious sanctions for inappropriate behaviors
- Incorporating attention to handling sexual harassment complaints in supervisory procedures[87]

MANAGING DIVERSITY IN MUNICIPAL GOVERNMENT

As public management expert Erica Gabrielle Foldy asserts, "Thinking and talking about diversity is ubiquitous in today's organizations."[88] She also notes that this observation is particularly true of public-sector organizations, which tend to have more diverse employee populations than their private-sector counterparts. As discussed previously in this chapter, diversity in city government is tied to the concept of representative bureaucracy. As applied to municipal government this concept means that the employee population of the city should roughly mirror the general population that it serves. This representational equity will in turn create a marketplace of perspectives and ideas tied to the presence of various population subgroups.[89] These subgroups include not only racial and ethnic minorities and women as the "major dimensions of diversity,"[90] but also younger and single parents, dual career couples, same-sex couples, workers who have both child-care and elder-care responsibilities (the so-called sandwich generation), people with disabilities, and workers of all ages who have their own generational needs, values, and expectations.

The management of diversity is not easy, but it is vitally important: managers "must figure out how to adjust organizational structures and cultures to capitalize on . . . diversity, thus ensuring both quality of work life and organizational effectiveness."[91] Sonia Ospina and James O'Sullivan detail how the San Diego city manager called for a training program focused on diversity. After review of public and private diversity programs, the city launched a citywide organizational culture change called "Diversity Commitment." To implement the program, a four-person "Diversity Team" from all levels in the organization was created as a steering committee. Using employee focus groups and action planning, short- and long-term strategies were developed. As a citywide initiative, the diversity effort attempted to "create an environment in which differences are valued and all employees participate in team service delivery."[92] Short-term diversity strategies included the creation of multicultural and bi-gender interview panels to enhance representation in the promotions and selection processes; the introduction of diversity modules as part of supervisory and management training programs; and the formation of task forces to address employees' priorities in areas such as career development, communications, and promotions.[93]

As a long-term initiative, city leaders began a sweeping employee communications effort, which includes monthly meetings of the Diversity Team with "employee associations, unions, informal city employee groups, representatives of police and fire department HR divisions, and a forum with managerial and union participation to discuss and resolve diversity issues as they arise."[94] According to Ospina and O'Sullivan, the diversity initiative is viewed as a true partnership among all employees of the City of San Diego. Moreover, the effort is the *shared responsibility of all the management in the city*, including HR managers, program managers, department heads, and the city manager.

In order to manage the impacts of diversity, Cayer suggests that traditional benefit programs may need modification. Foremost among the changes to be considered would be the introduction of *family-friendly* or *work-life benefits*, such as flexible working hours, job sharing, child care on site, telecommuting, and greater emphasis on career/professional development, domestic partner benefits, employee assistance programs, and financial planning. In addition, *cafeteria-style benefit plans*, which let employees choose benefits important to them, are usually required.[95]

LABOR-MANAGEMENT RELATIONS

Even though public employee unions appeared as early as the nineteenth century, their real growth came only after World War II. By the early 1970s, nearly two-thirds of all cities with populations over 25,000 were operating under at least one collective bargaining agreement with unions or local employee associations.[96] In 2008, total federal, state, and local union representation was 40.7 percent and membership was 36.8 percent.[97] In 1994, the peak year for government-sector unions, the comparable figures were 44.7 for representation and 38.7 percent for membership. Local governments have the highest representation rate at 46.1 percent; 42.2 percent of local government employees belong to a union. About thirty-five percent of state government workers are represented by unions, collectively 31.6 percent of all state government employees join unions. Private sector union representation has dropped from its 1954 peak of one-third of the nation's nonagricultural workforce to only 8.5 percent in 2008. The percentage is even lower for dues-paying union members—7.7 percent. Given the high rate of local government unionization, labor unions remain a significant force to be reckoned with in most American cities.

MUNICIPAL UNIONS

Workers join unions for a variety of reasons: economic, social, and psychological. The principal motive, especially for blue-collar workers, appears to be economic—the hope that a union will improve pay and working conditions through collective action. As public-sector union expert Richard Kearney notes:

> To a large extent public employees join unions for many of the same reasons as their counterparts in the private sector. They are dissatisfied with one or more important aspects of their jobs. Job-related conditions especially conducive to unionization include hazardous, physically demanding, or repetitive tasks; little input into job-related decisions; and perceptions of arbitrary and unfair management actions and decisions.[98]

Public- and private-sector unions differ, of course. Whether these differences are sufficient to warrant special treatment of those in the public sector continues to be debated.

Public-sector versus Private-sector Unions

How do public and private labor-management relations differ? Probably the key distinction is the lack of a profit motive on the part of public organizations. Some critics allege that in the absence of profit and price competition, city councils, for example, too easily give in to excessive employee demands. The monopolistic nature of most local public services means that elected officials can pass along the increased labor costs without fear of being priced out of business.

A second, related argument derives from the political context of municipal collective bargaining: because local employees can be a potent political force, a union has an undue advantage in dealing with a local public employer.[99] A corollary notion suggests that political pressure may force a city council to acquiesce in a labor dispute to avoid disrupting vital public services.[100] As Kearney says, "Unions may apply raw political power through real or threatened job actions, warnings of electoral defeats, and other intimidating behavior."[101] But, since unions are in the public spotlight, they "can always be blamed by public officials and the media for financial difficulties."[102]

A third point concerns the special nature of certain public services. Many analysts believe that police and fire protection must not be jeopardized by strikes; these services are too vital to be interrupted. Thus public-sector labor relations must be treated differently to ensure continuity of indispensable functions.

Some of these public-private distinctions appear more valid than others. On the matter of market incentives versus union power: if in fact public-sector unions have a special advantage over their private-sector counterparts, it should be reflected in proportionately higher wage gains for organized public employees. As public-sector unions gained rights, strength, and vitality in the 1960s and 1970s, emerging research on the financial impacts of these unions found that public employees who were organized realized greater economic gains than those who were not, but the differences were slight.[103] Moreover, a 1974 study found that the proportional gains by organized public-sector employees did not exceed those attained by union members in private firms.[104]

What has happened in the past thirty years or so? Have public-sector unions achieved wage and/or benefit increases that surpass those realized by private-sector unions? In general, Kearney says, the answer is no: "The empirical evidence is fairly conclusive that private sector unions are more successful than those in the public sector."[105] In his 2009 book, Kearney argues that, collectively, the fifty or so published articles studying public-sector unions and pay find that the impact of unions is slight to moderate.[106] He sums up:

> A review of the literature concludes that unions boost wage and benefits in government. The impact varies along dimensions of time, space, methodology, and function in response to numerous and highly variable social, economic, and political factors. The union compensation impact, which averages 5 to 6 percent for salaries and perhaps a bit more for the dollar cost of benefits, is far less than the impact attributed to private sector unions. [107]

The fear of excessive public-sector union power remains unsubstantiated.

Unions and Merit

Some fear that the growth in public unions bodes ill for the merit principle. Unions generally do support seniority as a basis for promotion, but not to the exclusion of merit. As Jerry Wurf, one-time head of AFSCME, notes, promotion should be awarded on the basis of merit and fitness, but "seniority must be the key determination for distinguishing between qualified applicants."[108] In actual practice, of course, seniority frequently is the primary basis for advancement, even in the best of merit systems. When it comes to compensation, unions have fought efforts by management to create pay differentials for similar jobs—except, of course, on the basis of seniority. Thus teacher organizations, for example, generally oppose compensation plans based on performance. Although public employee groups are relenting a bit on the pay-for-performance issue, unions in general are still wary of such schemes, arguing that they create tensions among employees and are subject to abuse by management.[109]

The general view today is that both collective bargaining and the merit principle are here to stay. Both management and labor, then, must get on with the task of ensuring their relative compatibility.

COLLECTIVE BARGAINING PROCEDURES

A 1999 large-scale, ICMA-sponsored survey of all 2,881 U.S. cities with populations equal to or greater than 10,000 shows that municipal unionization is widespread. Three out of four of the 1,401 responding cities reported the presence of unions and associations.[110] In 90 percent of the jurisdictions, local governments enter into contracts with the unions and associations; 94 percent of these cities bargain collectively with the organizations. The survey covered bargaining with five groups: police, fire, sanitation, public works, and others, which includes dispatchers, supervisors, and white-collar and administrative positions. Most (86 percent) of the jurisdictions use a "collective bargaining team." In smaller jurisdictions, teams are more likely to be comprised of full-time labor-relations professionals, consultants, and council members. In larger jurisdictions, the propensity is to use more managers and assistant managers on the teams. In smaller cities, the manager—city manager or chief administrative officer (CAO)—is likely to be the chief negotiating officer; in larger cities, a full-time labor-relations professional is more likely to serve as chief negotiator for the city. In all cities, the likelihood that a member of the collective bargaining team is a full-time labor-relations professional is 60 percent; an attorney retained by the city, 55 percent; a consultant, 44 percent; a member of the city council, 43 percent; an assistant manager, 30 percent; a department head, 25 percent; a personnel director, 23 percent; a manager/ CAO, 13 percent; and a mayor, 8 percent.

By far the most common practice among cities using collective bargaining is to grant unions *exclusive recognition*. This does not mean that all employees are required to join the union; exclusive recognition simply requires that once a bargaining agent has been properly selected, management must deal only with that employee group. Workers in these cities are not necessarily represented by just one union, however; bargaining units can be formed for a number of different components of the municipal workforce. On average, cities give exclusive recognition to five unions, but in some of the very largest cities, the number of bargaining units approaches the ridiculous—New York City, for example, has well over two hundred separate units. In most cities, there are separate organizations for police and firefighters, perhaps separate unions for sanitation and public works employees, and one or more unions representing the remaining line-level employees. In addition, there is a trend toward emulating the private sector by either excluding or constraining public-sector supervisors' bargaining rights.[111] For example, in the 1999 ICMA labor-management survey, only 27 percent of the cities provided exclusive representation for supervisory employee unions and associations.[112]

State legislation on collective bargaining tends to follow the requirements of the National Labor Relations Act in compelling good-faith bargaining. Just what this means is not always clear, although specific prohibitions sometimes are set forth in the enabling legislation. For example, an employer may be barred from interfering with the rights of employees. A city may be forbidden to discriminate or retaliate against employees for union activities. Employees, likewise, may be prohibited from interfering with or coercing other employees.[113]

Collective negotiations constitute much more than a rule-bound legal process. Bargaining at the municipal level can easily become a political contest. Employees, after all, represent a sizable voting bloc. They may seek to advance their interests not only at the bargaining table but also before the council directly, in the electoral arena, and even in the state legislature. In fact, a major concern of those who fear union power is this very potential for the extensive exercise of political influence by public employee organizations. As we have seen, local elections are notorious for their low turnout, so a well-organized bloc of employees may well be able to affect the outcome of any such contest. The assumption often follows that local politicians, eager for reelection, are especially sensitive to any action that might offend employee unions. As indicated previously, evidence over the past several decades shows that, on average, municipal union wage-and-benefit packages do not exceed those achieved by private-sector unions, but, as we also noted, this generalization does not hold true for all cities, for all occupations, and for all points in time. Therefore, the fear remains.

Undoubtedly, we must recognize the political environment in which local collective bargaining takes place, but the extent to which politics produces bargaining outcomes different from those that would otherwise be negotiated remains an open question. For example, in the 1999 ICMA labor-management survey, 91 percent of the cities reported the existence of a "management rights clause" in their contracts with labor. In 85 percent or more of these cities, the management rights clause allows the city to determine missions, policies, budget, and general operations; to determine the size and composition of the workforce; and to set standards and level of services.[114]

The political question aside, concern remains over possible union militancy. In fact, much of the literature on public-sector labor relations deals with various ways to minimize work stoppages.

Impasse Resolution

The purpose of collective bargaining is to arrive at a mutually acceptable agreement. When normal negotiation does not produce this outcome, labor disputes arise. Because most states prohibit strikes by public employees, some means other than striking must be found to resolve deadlocks. Over the years, three basic methods have evolved for dealing with labor-management impasses: mediation, fact finding, and arbitration. Mediation is the most common; arbitration, the least.[115]

Mediation brings in a neutral third party, acceptable to both union and management, to help the two parties to resolve the dispute themselves. If negotiations have broken down, the mediator's first task is to restore communication. A mediator ordinarily does not hold formal hearings, keep written transcripts, or release an opinion on the issues in contention. Mediation has been both popular and successful. The parties at issue are not reluctant to use the process because neither is obligated to accept the mediator's suggestions. A skilled mediator may be invaluable to parties that have had little negotiating experience.

When mediation is unsuccessful, *fact finding* is often the next step. This method also requires the use of a neutral third party to help resolve disputes, but in this case, the procedure is more formal, usually involving three stages: initiation of the process and selection of the fact finder, hearings to identify the issues, and submission of a report with recommendations. Although the fact finder makes written recommendations, they are not binding on either party. Again, consensus suggests that fact finding produces good results; still, some critics contend that if the method is too readily available, it reduces incentives for genuine bargaining at any earlier stage.

Arbitration is the most drastic and most controversial step in impasse resolution. Arbitration may take several forms. In *voluntary* arbitration, the two parties agree without compulsion to submit specific issues to a third party for a final, binding decision; most arbitration, however, is *compulsory*. This "binding arbitration" procedure is much the same as that used in fact finding: the disputants each select a representative, and the representatives in turn choose a neutral third party; hearings are held and transcripts kept; and a final recommendation is issued. Often, a decision is made that splits the difference between the union's last demand and the city's final offer, and, under compulsory arbitration, both parties are legally bound by the arbitrator's findings.

Controversy surrounds compulsory arbitration. Historically, management has resisted having the terms of a contract dictated by an outside group; unions, too, have had misgivings about what might be involved. Yet binding arbitration has become widespread in the private sector, often as a trade-off for a no-strike clause. Partly because of this growing acceptance in private business, binding arbitration has become more common in the public sector. Some observers feel that this resolution mechanism is also an effective deterrent to strikes. In many cities, its use is limited to public employee groups that provide indispensable services—police and fire departments, for example. Whether compulsory arbitration prevents strikes remains uncertain. Despite its growing popularity, one authority expressed reservations about its unrestricted application in the public sector some years ago. Myron Lieberman suggested that binding arbitration in public jurisdictions be limited to questions of fact; otherwise the practice deprives management of its legitimate right to make policy. For example, an employee fired for stealing public property might submit to arbitration the question of whether the theft had occurred but could not contest the form of punishment.[116]

An interesting twist to binding arbitration—"final offer arbitration" (FOA)—has appeared in recent years. Now used in fifteen states and several local governments, it was first employed by Eugene, Oregon, in 1971.[117] The approach requires the arbitrator to choose either management's or labor's last offer; there's no splitting the difference—it's winner-take-all. The procedure presumably forces both parties to make a final offer they can live with; otherwise, the arbitrator might select the other party's offer as a more reasonable settlement. Although FOA is an ingenious device to compel reasonable final offers, it does present several problems. First, it is inflexible: the arbitrator has no choice but to accept one or the other final offer. This may not be terribly serious with respect to wages, but it can prove troublesome in nonwage disputes. Early experience with FOA in Eugene suggests that the procedure seemed to work reasonably well, and that it does not seem to jeopardize the incentives to genuine bargaining—a fear many have concerning binding arbitration in any form.[118]

In the 1999 ICMA labor-management survey, about one thousand of the responding cities reported the presence of a labor-management grievance.[119] Not surprisingly, the most frequently cited type of grievance was "failure to abide by the contract" (72 percent). In terms of other specific actions taken by the city, grievances concerning "terminations" (33 percent) and "performance evaluations" (21 percent) were the most frequently cited cases. Most grievances were resolved in two weeks–to–one month (42 percent of the cases) or one-to-three months (38 percent of the cases). Mediation proved the most frequently used collective bargaining dispute resolution technique (used in 1,374 cases), followed by mandatory arbitration (1,325 cases), final offer arbitration, by issue (560 cases), fact finding (474 cases), voluntary arbitration (379 cases), and final offer arbitration, by package (180 cases).

Finally, cities sometimes create joint labor-management committees to avoid prolonged labor disputes, accelerate productivity, improve the work environment, and improve labor-management relations.[120] In 1978 Massachusetts became the first state to experiment with labor-management committees (LMCs).[121] A few years later, Jonathan Brock offered a description and assessment of the innovation. Under the plan, Massachusetts created a fourteen-member joint committee to oversee collective bargaining for the state's police and firefighters.[122] The committee included an equal number of representatives of labor and management (six members each), plus a neutral chair and vice-chair. The group was committed to settling disputes through direct bargaining by the affected parties whenever possible, and it had the legal authority to enter a dispute even before the parties declared an official impasse. The mechanism has worked well in the Bay State; the time taken to resolve the average labor-management dispute has been cut in half—from over six months to less than three. It is also cheaper, as fewer lawyers are involved for shorter periods of time.

Research in 2008 (thirty years after the committee was created), shows that Massachusetts' experience with its LMC continues to be successful, "with only a small proportion of cases going to arbitration."[123]

The Strike

"Approximately 90 percent of all strikes since 1960 have taken place at the local government level."[124] Traditionally, the law prohibits strikes by public employees, but this practice has not prevented strikes and work stoppages. Today, the total opposition to public-sector strikes is undergoing modification: as of 2008, ten states had legislatively granted at least some of their employees—usually those in nonessential work areas—a limited right to strike.[125] Still, strikes remain illegal for police and fire department employees and others who protect the safety and security of the public.

The strike issue is certainly the most controversial problem in public labor relations. Opponents tend to see a strike as defiance of public authority. Labor, in contrast, argues that there are no compelling differences between public and private employment, and, therefore, the strike should be considered a legitimate, useful weapon in all labor disputes. To some, the problem appears intractable because there is merit to both sides of the question. Many years ago, Sterling Spero and John Capozzola contended that the sovereignty issue was essentially bogus—"a convenient technique to avoid dealing with the merits of issues in disputes."[126] They argued, further, that "the public-private dichotomy fails to distinguish between necessity and convenience and takes no notice of the critical or noncritical character of the service."[127]

The Canadian government seems to have arrived at a unique solution to the issue of public sector strikes. Under Canadian law, after a union has been certified as a bargaining agent, it is required to specify one of two alternatives for impasse resolution: either referral to binding arbitration or mediation with the right to strike. If a union opts for compulsory arbitration, it cannot legally strike—and most national public unions in Canada have chosen compulsory arbitration. Variations on the Canadian federal experience are found in several provinces. Still, even if the strike option is elected, certain employees are prohibited from striking if "necessary in the interest of the safety or security of the public."[128]

Of course, the sticky question remains: How do we designate those employees whose jobs are essential to the safety of the public? If a distinction is made, it seems appropriate to give that group access to binding arbitration. Beyond that distinction, however, there would seem to be no compelling reason not to give other public employees the full rights of labor, including the right to strike. The Canadian approach or some variation thereof would seem to be a way out of the intractable strike situation.

MUNICIPAL UNIONS IN PERSPECTIVE

Public-sector labor relations have moved ever closer to the industrial model. Bilateral determination of wages and working conditions is now established procedure in most large cities, and municipal workforces are the most heavily unionized of all public employee groups. What does all this mean for traditional municipal personnel practice? First, in general, there is clear evidence that public-sector unions are not more successful than private-sector unions in achieving their economic goals. Second, public employee organizations are now affected in much the same ways as their private-sector counterparts by economic and social changes. With overall union membership declining and cities retrenching, the possibility of a strike seems less threatening. In the 1999 ICMA labor-management survey, for instance, "Only 17 authorized strikes were identified by city managers since 1988. . . . This reflects a general decline in public sector strike activity as reported in the industrial relations literature."[129] We have entered what John Capozzola has described as a period of "concessionary bargaining," which has stimulated considerable union interest in labor-management cooperation.[130]

Frank Swoboda makes a similar argument with respect to strikes: "The strike has become, in effect, the nuclear device in labor's arsenal of weapons, something to be used in total warfare."[131] Such strategic cooperation does not signal the end of collective bargaining, of course, but it does suggest that shrewd and realistic union leaders have recognized that tactical adjustments are necessary to cope with changing times. If management is also receptive, the new era of cooperation should mean more consultation with workers and greater involvement of employees in decision making in areas that generally have not been subject to mandatory bargaining. Capozzola also sees this as an opportune time for labor to do some soul-searching:

> The aim of negotiators to get more for the existing membership at the expense of the unemployed should be reexamined. Deep-rooted work rules reduce efficiency, hamper productivity and hinder foreign competition. In a similar vein, more introspection and study is needed to reconcile valid concepts of seniority and merit.[132]

SUMMARY

Traditional municipal human resource management practices have been considerably transformed in recent years. Organization is shifting from independent employment (civil service) commissions to executive-controlled personnel staffs. Whatever their organizational structure, cities overwhelmingly claim to use some form of merit system in their practices. Gains have been made in staffing and employee classification, but municipalities are still experimenting with pay-for-performance systems.

The equal employment quest by ethnic and minority groups, women, the aged, those with disabilities, and gay and lesbian groups has resulted in serious challenges to traditional personnel techniques and practices. In response to court decisions, federal pressure, and the recognition that it is simply the right thing to do, cities continue to modify personnel practices to ensure and manage diversity in the modern workplace. And while affirmative action seems to be in a period of decline, the courts continue to tailor remedies in response to perceived inequities. Other personnel procedures are undergoing change as well. The one-of-three rule is under attack; computer technology is being used to recruit and test candidates; factor evaluation classification systems are used to address comparable worth issues; federal courts mandate that examinations be validated; team-based management techniques are used to implement quality initiatives into the workplace; and broadband-ing classification schemes are finding a place in municipal governments as part of effort to provide city leaders more flexibility in managing human resources.

Other personnel issues have become salient in recent years. Workers with disabilities have secured new rights under the Americans with Disabilities Act of 1990. Congress dem-onstrated its dissatisfaction with Supreme Court decisions with passage of the Civil Rights Act of 1991. The old problem of sexual harassment has become a new issue—an issue that must be addressed by municipal executives to avoid the tremendous social and economic costs associated with this form of irresponsible human behavior.

Some fear that municipal unions will make the local bureaucracy too powerful; others insist that there is little difference between public and private employment and that public-sector unions should be dealt with accordingly. Certainly, municipal unions are here to stay, and cities must learn to accept and understand the key features of public-sector collective bargaining. Because most states still prohibit strikes by public employees, methods of impasse resolution—mediation, fact finding, and arbitration—are critical. Although no unanimity exists in this area, increasing attention has centered on binding arbitration and the use of limited strikes as ways to guarantee public employees the customary rights of labor while still ensuring the provision of vital public services. Although labor-management committees and partnerships are not yet standard fare in municipal administration, these practices represent a goal toward which we strive.

SUGGESTED FOR FURTHER READING

Condrey, Stephen E., ed. *Handbook of Human Resource Management in Government*. 3rd ed. San Francisco: Jossey-Bass, 2010.

Freedman, Anne. *Patronage: An American Tradition*. Chicago: Nelson-Hall, 1994.

Hays, Steven W., Richard C. Kearney, and Jerrell D. Coggburn, eds. *Public Personnel Administration: Problems and Prospects*. 5th ed. New York: Pearson, 2009.

Ingraham, Patricia Wallace. *The Foundation of Merit: Public Service in American Democracy*. Baltimore: Johns Hopkins University Press, 1995.

Kearney, Richard C., *Labor Relations in the Public Sector*. 4th ed. Boca Raton, Fla.: CRC Press, 2009.

Nigro, Lloyd, Felix Nigro, and J. Edward Kellough. *The New Public Personnel Administration*, 6th ed. Belmont, Calif.: Thomson Wadsworth, 2007.

NOTES

1. Municipal Manpower Commission, *Governmental Manpower for Tomorrow's Cities* (New York: McGraw-Hill, 1962).

2. *A Model Public Personnel Administration Law* (Washington, D.C.: National Civil Service League, 1970).

3. Siegrun Fox Freyss, "Continuity and Change in Local Personnel Policies and Practices," *1996 Municipal Year Book* (Washington, D.C.: ICMA, 1996), 13.

4. Anne Freedman, *Patronage: An American Tradition* (Chicago: Nelson-Hall, 1994), vii.

5. Patricia Wallace Ingraham, *The Foundation of Merit: Public Service in American Democracy* (Baltimore: Johns Hopkins University Press, 1995).

6. See Andrew H. Boesel, "Local Personnel Management: Organizational Problems and Operating Practices," *1974 Municipal Year Book* (Washington, D.C.: ICMA, 1974), 94; and Gregory Streib, "Personnel Management," in *Managing Small Cities and Counties: A Practical Guide*, ed. James M. Banovetz, Drew A. Dolan, and John W. Swain (Washington, D.C.: ICMA, 1994), 262.

7. Among the many excellent books that discuss these functions, three comprehensive personnel texts are N. Joseph Cayer, *Public Personnel Administration*, 4th ed. (Belmont, Calif.: Wadsworth, 2004); Ronald D. Sylvia and C. Kenneth Meyer, *Public Personnel Administration*, 2nd ed. (New York: Wadsworth Publishing, 2001); and Felix A. Nigro, Lloyd G. Nigro, and J. Edward Kellough, *The New Public Personnel Administration*, 6th ed. (Belmont, Calif.: Thomson Wadsworth, 2007).

8. Elder Witt, "Are Our Governments Paying What It Takes to Keep the Best and the Brightest?" *Governing*, December 1988, 30.

9. Nigro, Nigro, and Kellough, *New Public Personnel Administration*, 153.

10. See ibid., 85–96.

11. Gary E. Roberts, "Issues, Challenges, and Changes in Recruitment and Selection," in *Public Personnel Administration: Problems and Prospects*, 4th ed., ed. Steven W. Hays and Richard C. Kearney (Upper Saddle River, N.J.: Pearson, 2003), 107.

12. Cayer, *Public Personnel Administration*, 83.

13. Freyss, "Continuity and Change," 13–14.

14. Susan G. Mason and Lana Stein, "Local Government Personnel Administration: Heritage, Contemporary Practice, and Portents," in *Public Personnel Administration: Problems and Prospects*, 5th ed., ed. Steven W. Hays, Richard C. Kearney, and Jerrell D. Coggburn (New York: Pearson, 2009), 65.

15. Ibid.

16. Jonathan P. West and Evan M. Berman, "From Traditional to Virtual HR: Is the Transition Occurring in Local Government?" *Review of Public Personnel Administration* 21 (spring 2001): 38–64.

17. Ibid., 44.

18. David Coursey, "E-Government: Trends, Benefits, and Challenges," *2005 Municipal Year Book* (Washington, D.C.: ICMA, 2005), 14.

19. About thirty-five years ago, twenty-five objections to traditional testing for selection purposes were listed in Nesta M. Gallas, "The Selection Process," in *Local Government Personnel Administration*, ed. Winston Crouch (Washington, D.C.: ICMA, 1976), 134. Many of the objections remain valid today. Any recent public personnel text provides a discussion of potential issues and problems. See, for example, Nigro, Nigro, and Kellough, *New Public Personnel Administration*, 105–107; Sylvia and Meyer, *Public Personnel Administration*, 13–15; or Cayer, *Public Personnel Administration*, 85–90.

20. Nigro, Nigro, and Kellough, *New Public Personnel Administration*, 105.

21. Ibid.

22. Dennis L. Dresang, *Public Personnel Management and Public Policy*, 3rd ed. (New York: Longman, 1999), 222.

23. Owen E. Hughes, *Public Management and Administration*, 3rd ed. (New York: Palgrave Macmillan, 2003), 152–157.

24. Steven W. Hays and Richard C. Kearney, "Anticipated Changes in Human Resource Management: Views from the Field," *Public Administration Review* 61 (September–October 2001): 590.

25. See O. Glenn Stahl, *Public Personnel Administration*, 8th ed. (New York: Harper & Row, 1983), 131–132.

26. Roberts, "Issues, Challenges, and Changes," 117.

27. Jonathan Walters, "How Not to Reform Civil Service," *Governing*, November 1992, 33.

28. Position classification is also sometimes called job evaluation, see Nigro, Nigro, and Kellough, ibid 127, note 2.

29. See *New Public Personnel Administration*, 134–135.

30. Cayer, *Public Personnel Administration*, 60.

31. Katherine C. Naff, "Why Public Managers Hate Position Classification," in *Public Personnel Administration: Problems and Prospects*, 4th ed., ed. Steven W. Hays and Richard Kearney (Upper Saddle River, N.J.: Pearson, 2003), 126.

32. David Osborne and Ted Gaebler, *Reinventing Government* (Reading, Mass.: Addison-Wesley, 1992), 129.

33. Nigro, Nigro, and Kellough, *New Public Personnel Administration*, 144.

34. Naff, "Why Public Managers Hate Position Classification," 138.

35. Ibid.

36. Nigro, Nigro, and Kellough, *New Public Personnel Administration*, 145.

37. Ibid., 146.

38. Sylvia and Meyer, *Public Personnel Administration*, 198.

39. Jerome S. Sanderson, "Compensation," in *Crouch, Local Government Personnel Administration*, 196–197.

40. Cayer, *Public Personnel Administration*, 70–71.

41. Gregory Streib and Theodore H. Poister, "Established and Emerging Management Tools: A 12-Year Perspective," *1989 Municipal Year Book* (Washington, D.C.: ICMA, 1989), 46.

42. Freyss, "Continuity and Change," 14–15.

43. James S. Bowman, "The Success of Failure: The Paradox of Performance Pay," *Review of Public Personnel Administration* 30 (March 2010): 70.

44. Larry M. Lane, James F. Wolf, and Colleen Woodward, "Reassessing the Human Resource Crisis in the Public Service, 1987–2002," *American Review of Public Administration* 33 (June 2003): 138.

45. Freyss, "Continuity and Change," 15.

46. David Ammons and Arnold Rodriguez, "Performance Appraisal Practices for Upper Management in City Governments," *Public Administration Review* 46 (September–October 1986): 460–467; and Robert E. England and William M. Parle, "Nonmanagerial Performance Appraisal Practices in Large American Cities," *Public Administration Review* 47 (November–December 1987): 498–504.

47. Robert D. Behn, "Measuring Performance against the 80–30 Syndrome," *Governing*, June 1993, 70.

48. Charles J. Fox, "Employee Performance Appraisal: The Keystone Made of Clay," in *Public Personnel Management: Current Concerns, Future Challenges*, ed. Carolyn Ban and Norma M. Riccucci (New York: Longman, 1991), 67–68.

49. Dennis M. Daley, "The Trials and Tribulations of Performance Appraisal: Problems and Prospects in the Twenty-First Century, in *Public Personnel Administration: Problems and Prospects*, 5th ed., ed. Steven W. Hays, Richard C. Kearney, and Jerrell D. Coggburn (New York: Pearson, 2009), 110.

50. Herbert Hill, "Preferential Hiring: Correcting the Demerit System," *Social Policy* 4 (July–August 1973): 102.

51. Cayer, *Public Personnel Administration*, 174–175.

52. Ibid., 175.

53. Ibid., 177.

54. For an excellent discussion of this argument, see J. Edward Kellough, "Equal Employment Opportunity and Affirmative Action in the Public Sector," in *Public Personnel Administration: Problems and Prospects*, 4th ed., ed. Steven W. Hays and Richard C. Kearney (Upper Saddle River, N.J.: Pearson, 2003), 216–221.

55. John Nalbandian, "The U.S. Supreme Court's 'Consensus' on Affirmative Action," *Public Administration Review* 49 (January–February 1989): 39.

56. Kellough, "Equal Employment Opportunity and Affirmative Action," 221.

57. Charles Fried, "Restoring Balance to Civil Rights," *Washington Post National Weekly Edition*, June 3–9, 1989.

58. For a discussion, see Ann O'M. Bowman and Michael A. Pagano, "The State of American Federalism—1989–1990," *Publius* 20 (summer): 1–25; and Mitchell F. Rice, "Government Set-Asides, Minority Business Enterprises, and the Supreme Court," *Public Administration Review* 51 (March–April 1991): 114–122.

59. Julianne R. Ryder, "High Court Ruling Will Impact Affirmative Action," *Public Administration Times* 12 (June 23, 1989): 1, 11.

60. Ibid.

61. Sue Ann Nicely, "New Civil Rights Act to Adversely Impact Employers," *Oklahoma Cities & Towns*, February 14, 1992, 1, 3. See also Paul Gewirtz, "Discrimination Endgame," *New Republic*, August 12, 1991, 18–23; and Paul Gewirtz, "The Civil Rights Bill's Loopholes?" *New Republic*, November 18, 1991, 10–13.

62. G. L. A. Harris, "Revisiting Affirmative Action in Leveling the Playing Field: Who Have Been the True Beneficiaries Anyway?" *Review of Public Personnel Administration* 29 (December 2009), 359.

63. Ibid., 368.

64. J. Edward Kellough, "Affirmative Action and Diversity in the Public Sector," in *Public Personnel Administration: Problems and Prospects*, 5th ed., ed. Steven W. Hays, Richard C. Kearney, and Jerrell D. Coggburn (New York: Pearson, 2009), 232.

65. This discussion is drawn from U.S. Equal Employment Opportunity Commission, *The Americans with Disabilities Act: Your Responsibilities as an Employer* (Washington, D.C.: EEOC, 1991).

66. This discussion draws on Bonnie G. Mani, "Disabled or Not Disabled: How Does the Americans with Disabilities Act Affect Employment Policies?" in *Public Personnel Administration: Problems and Prospects*, 4th ed., ed. Steven W. Hays and Richard C. Kearney (Upper Saddle River, N.J.: Pearson, 2003), 271.

67. Ibid., 275.

68. Ibid., 276.

69. Sylvia and Meyer, *Public Personnel Administration*, 73.

70. Ibid.

71. Cayer, *Public Personnel Administration*, 87.

72. Nelson and Harding (attorneys), "An Introduction to Equal Employment Opportunity," *Current Municipal Problems* 9 (1982–1983): 84.

73. This discussion draws heavily from Shelly L. Peffer, "Title VII and Disparate-Treatment Discrimination Versus Disparate-Impact Discrimination: The Supreme Court's Decision in *Ricci v. DeStefano*, *Review of Public Personnel Administration* 29 (December 2009): 402–410.

74. Ibid., 402.

75. Ibid., 410.

76. See Cayer, *Public Personnel Administration*, 86–87; Nigro, Nigro, and Kellough, *New Public Personnel Administration*, 98–100.

77. Unless otherwise noted, these statistics come from Mary E. Guy and Susan Spice, "Gender and Workplace Issues," in *Public Personnel Administration: Problems and Prospects*, 5th ed., ed. Steven W. Hays, Richard C. Kearney, and Jerrell D. Coggburn (New York: Pearson, 2009), 236–252.

78. Ibid., 249.

79. Cayer, *Public Personnel Administration*, 72.

80. "Typist=Driver: Los Angeles Adjusts Its Salaries," *Time*, May 20, 1985, 23.

81. Richard C. Kearney, with David G. Carnevale, *Labor Relations in the Public Sector*, 3rd ed. (New York: Marcel Dekker, 2001), 152.

82. Nigro, Nigro, and Kellough, *New Public Personnel Administration*, 158.

83. Ibid.

84. Cynthia S. Ross and Robert E. England, "State Governments' Sexual Harassment Policy Initiatives," *Public Administration Review* 47 (May–June 1987): 259.

85. See U.S. Merit Systems Protection Board, Office of Merit Systems Review and Studies, *Sexual Harassment in the Federal Workplace: Is It a Problem?* (Washington, D.C.: Government Printing Office, March 1981), 2–14; and "Sexual Harassment Is Still a Problem in Government," *Wall Street Journal*, June 30, 1988, 10.

86. Connie Kirk-Westerman, David M. Billeaux, and Robert E. England, "Ending Sexual Harassment at City Hall: Policy Initiatives in Large American Cities," *State and Local Government Review* 21 (fall 1989): 100–105.

87. Laura A. Reese and Karen E. Lindenberg, "Assessing Local Government Sexual Harassment Policies," *American Review of Public Administration* 32 (September 2002): 296.

88. Erica Gabrielle Foldy, "Learning from Diversity: A Theoretical Exploration," *Public Administration Review* 64 (September–October 2004): 529.

89. Ibid.; also see Julie Dolan and David H. Rosenbloom, eds., *Representative Bureaucracy: Classic Readings and Continuing Controversies* (New York: M. E. Sharpe, 2003).

90. Cayer, *Public Personnel Administration*, 75.

91. Sonia Ospina and James F. O'Sullivan, "Working Together: Meeting the Challenges of Workforce Diversity," in *Public Personnel Administration: Problems and Prospects*, 4th ed., ed. Steven W. Hays and Richard C. Kearney (Upper Saddle River, N.J.: Pearson, 2003), 239.

92. Ibid.

93. Ibid., 240.

94. Ibid.

95. Cayer, *Public Personnel Administration*, 182.

96. Boesel, "Local Personnel Management," 87.

97. Unionization statistics come from Richard C. Kearney, "Public Sector Labor-Management Relations: Change or Status Quo?" *Review of Public Personnel Administration* 30 (March 2010): 94.

98. Kearney, *Labor Relations in the Public Sector*, 3rd ed., 21.

99. See Cayer, *Public Personnel Administration*, 152–154.

100. Jay F. Atwood, "Collective Bargaining's Challenge: Five Imperatives for Public Managers," *Public Personnel Management* 5 (January–February 1976): 24–32.

101. Richard C. Kearney, *Labor Relations in the Public Sector*, 4th ed. (Boca Raton, Fla.: CRC Press, 2009), 152.

102. Ibid., 148.

103. W. Clayton Hail and Bruce Vanderporten, "Unionization, Monopsony Power, and Police Salaries," *Industrial Relations* 16 (February 1977): 94–100.

104. James L. Freund, "Market and Union Influences on Municipal Employee Wages," *Industrial and Labor Relations Review* 27 (April 1974): 391–404.

105. Kearney, *Labor Relations in the Public Sector*, 4th ed., 161.

106. Ibid., 164.

107. Ibid., 167–168.

108. Jerry Wurf, "Merit: A Union View," *Public Administration Review* 34 (September–October 1974): 433.

109. For a review of unions and current administrative reform initiatives, see George T. Sulzner, "New Roles, New Strategies: Reinventing the Public Union," in *Public Personnel Management: Current Concerns, Future Challenges*, 2nd ed., ed. Carolyn Ban and Norma M. Riccucci (New York: Longman, 1997).

110. Robert Hebdon, "Labor-Management Relations in the United States, 1999," *2000 Municipal Year Book* (Washington, D.C.: ICMA, 2000), 23.

111. Joel M. Douglas, "Collective Bargaining and Public Sector Supervisors: A Trend toward Exclusion?" *Public Administration Review* 47 (November–December 1987): 492.

112. Hebdon, "Labor-Management Relations," 23–24.

113. See Kearney, *Labor Relations in the Public Sector*, 4th ed., 77–79.

114. Hebdon, "Labor-Management Relations," 25–26.

115. For a more detailed discussion of impasse resolution techniques, see Kearney, *Labor Relations in the Public Sector*, 4th ed., chap. 9; and Cayer, *Public Personnel Administration*, 160–163.

116. Myron Lieberman, *Public-Sector Bargaining* (Lexington, Mass.: D.C. Heath, 1980), 99–101.

117. Kearney, *Labor Relations in the Public Sector*, 4th ed., 278.

118. Peter Feuille and Gary Long, "The Public Administrator and Final Offer Arbitration," *Public Administration Review* 34 (November–December 1974): 575–583.

119. Hebdon, "Labor-Management Relations," 25–26.

120. See John R. Miler and Myron Olstein, "LMCs: Helping Government Function Effectively," *City & State*, October 23, 1989, 23.

121. Kearney, *Labor Relations in the Public Sector*, 4th ed., 281.

122. Jonathan Brock, "Labor-Management Conflict: Bargaining Beyond Impasse," *Washington Public Policy Notes* 12 (spring 1984): 4–5.

123. Kearney, *Labor Relations in the Public Sector*, 4th ed., 281.

124. Kearney, *Labor Relations in the Public Sector*, 3rd ed., 229.

125. Kearney, *Labor Relations in the Public Sector*, 4th ed., 232.

126. Sterling Spero and John Capozzola, *The Urban Community and Its Unionized Bureaucracies* (New York: Dunnellen, 1973), 313.

127. Ibid.

128. Eugene F. Berrodin, "Compulsory Arbitration in Personnel Management," *Public Management* 55 (July 1973): 13.

129. Hebdon, "Labor-Management Relations," 25.

130. John M. Capozzola, "Taking a Look at Unions: American Labor Confronts Major Problems," *National Civic Review* 75 (July–August 1986): 205–213.

131. Frank Swoboda, "Striking Out as a Weapon against Management," *Washington Post National Weekly Edition*, July 13–19, 1992, 20.

132. Capozzola, "Taking a Look at Unions," 213.

CHAPTER 10 FINANCE AND BUDGET

A CCORDING to local government officials, there are few problems that could not be solved, or at least made much easier to handle, if more money were available to local governments. In fact, no other issue dominates the agenda for a city as money does. Events of the past decade have made financial problems in cities worse. First, the effects of the September 11, 2001, attacks increased the obligations and costs to cities to provide public safety. Heightened concerns about domestic terrorism forced cities to spend significantly more in the areas of public safety and transportation services. The major recession that begun in 2008 also adversely affected cities, leading to reduced revenues, public employee layoffs, difficulties securing borrowed funds, and pension system deficits. And as we begin the second decade of the twenty-first century, the effects of the crises of the first decade of the new century have not subsided.

Cities engage in a never-ending quest for funds. The cost of programs and services imposes the greatest single constraint on local decision making. And, confronting the continuing demand for more and better services in the face of constantly increasing costs, cities must make tough decisions. Where does a city get its revenues? How does a city decide where to spend its funds? Which methods of budget control work best for the chief executive trying to run a city in a fiscally responsible fashion?

In the past thirty years, nearly every city in the nation has been forced to retrench—to practice cutback management—because of economic changes, especially those in the intergovernmental revenue system. Indeed, the rise of the reinventing government movement (REGO) and the application of theories of the New Public Management are direct responses to issues of money management in cities. In the twenty-first century, perhaps more than ever, virtually every significant policy decision must be considered in the light of available funds and the dynamics of the intergovernmental system that cities do not control.

This chapter begins by examining certain features of the municipal revenue-raising system, among them sources of funds, alternative revenue-raising options, and the political issues that arise when cities search for new sources of income. This is followed by a discussion of allocations and trends in city expenditures. Then we explore how funds are distributed among many competing needs—the process of budgeting in cities. Finally, we look at the overall process of financial management.

REVENUE RAISING

THE MUNICIPAL FINANCE SYSTEM

Most states require their municipalities to operate within a balanced budget. So, unlike the federal government, for example, deficit spending is not allowed. But a careful look at budget-making processes within cities show how challenging it is to balance the massive services cities must provide within the limitations on their revenue-raising structures.[1] Perhaps in no other country except Canada are local governments expected to do more. Yet the higher levels of government are inherently better tax collectors; the states and, especially, the national government not only have access to a broader range of wealth and income than do cities, but they also can achieve significant economies of scale in tax collection. The congenital imbalance between service responsibility and revenue-raising capacity has brought about the large-scale system of grants flowing from higher to lower levels of government. This elaborate grant system is another basic characteristic of municipal finance in this country.

Several other elements underlie the cities' revenue structure. State constitutional and statutory restrictions create severe constraints on municipal revenue-raising capacity, and federal guidelines and controls on grants-in-aid impose additional limitations. Also, the fragmentation inherent in local governments can divorce local resources from local needs, creating serious financial disparities within metropolitan areas. Finally, because of their limited geographic scope, cities are not adequately equipped to absorb "spillovers"—the significant costs of dealing with social problems that are not generated within their own borders. These spillovers can range from crime to poverty, and cities do not have good ways to recover the costs of public safety associated with visitors and tourists.

The drawbacks associated with cities' limited geographic territory could be alleviated partly by shifting the fiscal burden of urban services to higher levels. If greater responsibility for funding were assumed by national and state governments, at least three major defects of the present system would be eliminated: inadequate handling of spillovers, disparities in service and tax levels, and fiscal imbalance among levels of government.[2] Politically, however, greater fiscal centralization does not have much appeal. States are not enthusiastic about taking on more of the financial burdens of the central cities. Suburbs and smaller communities are largely indifferent to appeals to help the big-city poor; the prevailing commitment to a grassroots political philosophy—the fear of losing local control—remains a formidable barrier to sharing responsibility on a wider scale. Cities are not likely to have much success in shifting the financial burden upward unless the states provide more help.

REVENUE SOURCES

Historically, local governments have looked to the *property tax* as their primary means of raising revenue, because states traditionally have relegated this funding source to them. Its use remains prominent within local systems of finance, especially for schools and county governments. In recent years, however, cities have come to rely less on the property tax for financing current operations; intergovernmental transfers (grants-in-aid) have now displaced it as the principal source of municipal revenue.

Table 10-1 summarizes the sources of revenue for cities and shows how these sources changed during the past decade. Cities receive funds from two major sources: revenues that come from their own sources (74 percent) and intergovernmental funds provided by the federal or state governments (26 percent). This ratio between the two major sources has changed a bit from 2001. Cities are now relying more on their own sources of funds, a share of the revenues that grew by 43 percent. In contrast, during the same period (2001–2007), intergovernmental revenues grew at just 21 percent, with the states providing a smaller share of city funds than at the beginning of the decade.

Tax collection generated about 45 percent of municipal revenue in 2006–2007, up slightly from its share at the decade's onset. About half of all municipal tax receipts came from property taxes, followed by sales taxes and the more limited local income tax. Income and other taxes grew the most in the aggregate, increasing more than 63 percent over the period. Although other tax collections—such as payroll taxes and commuter taxes—increased, they still accounted for a very small portion (about 5 percent) of the total tax receipts. Charges, fees, and miscellaneous revenue accounted for about 28 percent of city revenues. But the growth in user charges slowed from 2001 to 2007 (+37 percent) compared to the 1990s when these nontax proceeds increased by over 63 percent.[3] Because

Table 10-1 **City Revenue Sources, 2001–2002 versus 2006–2007**

	2001–2002		2006–2007		2001–2002 to 2006–2007
	Total ($millions)	Share of Revenue (%)	Total ($millions)	Share of Revenue (%)	Change in Revenue (%)
General revenue	285,545		389,085		36.3
Own-source revenues	200,431	70.2	286,546	73.6	43.0
Taxes	119,995	42.0	176,497	45.4	47.1
Property	58,302	20.4	85,164	21.9	46.1
Sales	35,509	12.4	48,493	12.5	36.6
Income	15,160	5.3	24,759	6.4	63.3
Other	11,024	3.9	18,082	4.6	64.0
Charges and user fees	80,436	28.2	110,049	28.3	36.8
Intergovernmental revenues	85,114	29.8	102,539	26.4	20.5
From federal government	15,201	5.3	20,504	5.3	34.9
From state government	62,405	21.9	72,753	18.7	16.6
From other local governments	7,508	2.6	9,282	2.4	23.6

SOURCES: U.S. Census Bureau, *2002 Census of Governments*, vol. 4, no. 4; *Finances of Municipal and Township Governments: 2002* (Washington, D.C.: Government Printing Office, 2002), table 1, pp. 1–2; *2007 Census of Governments: Finance*, table 2; and *Local Government Finances by Type of Government and State: 2006–07*.

many tax rate increases require voter approval and support for them is low in many cities, municipal officials have continued to expand the use of charges and user fees in their budgets, as increases in these assessments do not require voter approval.

REVENUE-RAISING ALTERNATIVES

Cities vary considerably in the degree to which they rely on particular sources of revenue, primarily because of state laws and historical tendencies. For example, many older northeastern cities continue to rely heavily on the property tax, whereas western cities use it much less extensively. What are the pros and cons of the property tax?

The Property Tax

Although still a mainstay of local revenue-raising, the property tax is widely criticized by finance experts. First, it suffers from serious problems in administration. Large discrepancies in property evaluation inevitably result from the system of local assessment, producing problems of fairness and equity in the amount of property taxes paid within and across jurisdictions. Second, property tax systems are costly and inefficient for government to administer compared with other tax options. Third, the tax discourages property improvements and maintenance—why should an absentee landlord spend money to refurbish a building if the increased value simply brings higher taxes? Fourth, some authorities consider the property tax, as currently levied and administered, to be mildly regressive; the argument is that because the poor spend a larger share of their income for housing than other groups, they pay proportionately more than the well-to-do. Others argue that the property tax may not be any more regressive than most other sources of municipal revenue. And, indeed, some states and localities are reducing the tax's regressive effect by providing "circuit breakers"—tax breaks for the poor and the elderly. The real issue here is a comparative one: are the other revenue sources likely to be adopted in lieu of the property tax any less regressive? As we shall see, trading a reduction in property tax for an increase in another form of revenue may not benefit low- and moderate-income families.

The property tax remains controversial for other reasons as well. There is some question about the tax's elasticity—the degree to which it responds to changing economic conditions. Although property values have soared in the past quarter century, property tax collections have increased only half again as much. This lagging revenue yield can create an exceptional burden on older central cities, where this tax is heavily relied upon.

One other problem plagues the property tax: its visibility, which virtually guarantees universal unpopularity. Reports by the former Advisory Commission on Intergovernmental Relations (ACIR)—which routinely surveyed governments and citizens about taxes—showed that the local property tax was considered the "worst" or "least fair" tax, followed by the federal income tax.[4] Research continues to demonstrate that the property tax is widely disliked as a form of local revenue: "Public opinion polls reflect citizens' discontent with the property tax, as do ballot initiatives and campaigns in many parts of the country . . . to cap property tax increases."[5] But when all is said and done, the property tax is a mainstay of local government revenue policies, producing the largest share of taxes from municipalities' local residential and commercial property owners. Despite its unpopularity, voters have turned down several recent efforts to discard the property tax in favor of other forms of school financing. In fact, a study of Waterford, Connecticut, by Bill Simonsen and Mark D. Robbins shows that citizens are often supportive of increasing property taxes when they have favorable attitudes about the local government and the services it provides.[6] It is doubtful, then, that we will see the wholesale abandonment of the property tax, even as several states are struggling to rectify the gross inequities in school financing that result from the heavy dependence on this form of revenue.

Nonproperty Taxes

The sales tax is used by local governments in thirty-three states; some states restrict its use to only cities or counties, often prohibiting other local governments, such as special districts, from imposing sales taxes.[7] The sales tax has several potential strengths. Especially if the state collects the tax and rebates it to the city, administration is easy and efficient. The sales tax is also reasonably elastic. And people seem to favor it over other taxes, in part because it seems equitable—everyone pays on the same basis. In essence, however, the sales tax is regressive, as the poor pay a relatively larger share of their income for items normally subject to the tax. If certain exemptions are granted—say, on food and drugs— its regressive nature is blunted considerably. But even these exemptions are not without problems: they are costly; they create administrative difficulties; and they open the door to tax evasion.

The *local income tax* (including the payroll tax) is levied by cities in fifteen states,[8] but it is widely used in only three: Kentucky, Ohio, and Pennsylvania. Over 3,500 local jurisdictions (including counties and school districts) have adopted the tax; of these, fewer than 900 are outside the state of Pennsylvania. Several of the largest U.S. cities—including Detroit, New York City, Cincinnati, Cleveland, Columbus, Philadelphia, and Toledo—collect local income taxes. In Los Angeles, San Francisco, and Newark, taxes are imposed on an employer's total payroll.[9]

The local income tax is normally a flat rate—often 1 percent—on wages and salaries. Typically, the locality itself administers the tax, but in some places the state is authorized to do so. The administrative process raises several issues. First, there is the question of taxing nonlabor income. Most cities do not levy the tax on dividends, interest, and rental income, which gives a break to the wealthy, of course, but eases administrative problems.[10] The other major issue involves taxing nonresidents. Most cities would like to levy the tax on the income of nonresidents who work there; state law determines whether this is possible. If it is, what happens to a commuter who works in one tax-levying community and lives in another? Except in Philadelphia, such double taxation is precluded by law or court decision.

Where an income tax can be imposed, it has several advantages over the property tax. It certainly is less regressive, especially if nonlabor income is included. The income tax responds exceptionally well to changing economic conditions. And, the process of collecting income taxes may be more efficient that other taxes, such as the property tax that relies on cumbersome and outdated assessment processes. However, its low adoption rate in cities seems to be associated with a fear that a locally imposed income tax will deter development and steer businesses to other jurisdictions that do not assess such a tax.[11]

User Charges

Cities have been forced to shift to greater use of *fees and user charges* for services because of tax limits and intergovernmental aid cutbacks. Presumably, increased user charges contribute to greater economic efficiency by supplying services in response to community preferences. Also, many think such charges are more equitable than general taxes: people pay only for what they receive and, therefore, the direct user—not all taxpayers—will pay for the service.[12]

Some communities have pushed the limits of such pay-as-you-go government. As early as the mid-1980s, St. Paul, (Minn.), faced a serious budget shortfall but had little apparent chance of raising taxes.[13] For solutions to the problem, the city administration brought in the Rand Corporation, a California-based think tank. Rand's answer was simple: let city departments that are capable of earning money do so. A variety of options were presented. The city could charge for street lighting that exceeded a prescribed standard; residents or businesses requesting extra lights in front of their property would have to pay for them. Merchants who wanted turnover in parking in front of their stores would have to pay for painting the curb or installing parking meters. The library, according to Rand, should provide the customary book-lending service without charge, but a special fee might be required for such special services as videotape rental and bibliographic searches.

In the end, St. Paul did not adopt many of these proposals. However, the idea of such nontax revenue-raising, according to city finance director Peter Hames, is to make a profit where it can be done—logically, competitively, and without creating problems with citizens, unions, or other government bodies. David Osborne and Ted Gaebler agree: one of the ten principles of the REGO movement is to apply market-oriented thinking to government.[14] As the case study in box 10.1 highlights, collecting projected fees (and taxes) from residents, businesses, and property owners has also become more business-like with the help of technology.

Adopting new fees as an alternative to raising taxes is an approach that grows from the REGO movement. Under what conditions do city councils opt for a fee increase over a tax increase to fund city services? First, new research shows that city councils almost never reject a fee increase in favor of a tax hike.[15] Although the economic health of the city is a factor in the choice of fee increases over tax increases, institutional factors such as mayoral

BOX 10.1   Policy and Practice

CROSS CHECKING CITY REVENUES

Electronic improvements in Newport Beach, (Calif.), are a scofflaw's nemesis and a revenue official's dream. The city has developed a system that can connect all city department databases and compare city information to state business license and sales tax information.

The data comparisons can show, for instance, which businesses are operating without paying for a city business license. The result has been $890,000 in new business taxes—in addition to the $3 million a year that the city usually collects—since the program began in January 2004.

Funds also are coming in from residents who might formerly have failed to pay city fines and fees. In the past, one department could be processing a refund for overpayment on its service, while another department was canceling its service to the same resident for lack of payment. "We were sending refund checks to people who owed thousands of dollars," says Glen Everroad, city revenue manager.

Now, whenever residents request any service from the city—from a business registration to a dog license—city representatives check to see if they owe any money elsewhere in the system. If, say, they have unpaid parking tickets and are owed a refund on another service, the money will be transferred from the refund account to pay off the outstanding fine.

The new system sends residents one bill—a municipal services statement—instead of separate bills for different services. Newport Beachers can write one check to cover a water bill, a parking ticket, and a false-alarm fee. Or, they can navigate online to pay one or all of them using a credit card.

"Connecting all those dots has been a huge benefit for us in terms of customer service," Everroad says.

SOURCE: Based on Ellen Perlman, "Cross Checking," *Governing* 19 (July 2005): 52 Reprinted with permission of *Governing*.

power, city council professionalism, and state-imposed taxing limits are also important determinants in selecting user fee increases.[16]

Concern for the poor is one of at least two issues that can arise if a city moves heavily into user charges. Such fees and charges can be regressive in somewhat the same way as sales taxes can—penalizing the less-well-to-do, who usually pay proportionately more of their income for basic services. Research, in fact, shows that cities have been replacing federal funds by increasing user fees and charges for such services; as a result, "much of the cost has fallen on the poor."[17] To protect low-income residents, Rand suggests, the city might issue scrip or vouchers exchangeable for certain services to qualifying individuals—an approach not unlike the food stamp program.

Equity considerations aside, others fear that increased reliance on fees and charges may eventually undermine public support for the basic taxes on which core urban services depend.

THE POLITICS OF REVENUE RAISING

The first decade of the twenty-first century witnessed cities intensifying the search for alternative revenue sources not only because of the decline in federal aid but also in response to taxpayers' resistance to higher property taxes. Today we know that user fees and charges can do only so much; cities must consider other measures as well.

Intergovernmental funds are still critical to local government budgets. In response to the severe economic recession that began in 2008, the federal government created the American Recovery and Reinvestment Act of 2009, which distributed nearly $275 billion in grants and contracts to states. In many places, state governments provided a portion of these funds to local governments, often for infrastructure projects. Given the fiscal problems that confronted state governments because of the recession, the ARRA grants provided states with funds that could be passed on to cities that still depend on state funds for nearly 20 percent of overall revenues.

States are being asked to provide more help, not just in dollar form but more fundamentally by giving municipalities the legal authority to tap new revenue sources. In 2005, for example, local governments could impose a sales tax in only thirty-three states; in some states this authority is given only to counties, not to city governments.[18] Restrictions on income taxes are even more onerous. Given that most local taxes, except the property tax, require voter approval, it seems hard to justify such state-imposed limitations. And it would be unrealistic to expect a great deal of additional assistance from the states.

Cities, by and large, must continue to rely on their own initiative, which means that difficult decisions on whether or not to push for tax increases and which increases to opt for remain in the hands of local officials. Such decisions—especially when the pie is shrinking—can become quite controversial. How, then, should city leaders proceed? One of the few accounts of the politics of municipal revenue raising comes from Arnold Meltsner's observations of the efforts of city officials in Oakland, California, to obtain resources in what they believed to be a hostile environment.[19] Four operating or decision rules for local officials can be distilled from Meltsner's work.

First, hide the tax. One of the great arts of the tax game is to design revenue sources so that people do not know how much tax they pay. This tactic involves resorting to a variety of indirect revenue sources. Thus, cities often levy taxes on private utilities (which then pass them on to the consumer), on hotel rooms, on businesses or occupations, and on motor vehicles (often in lieu of a property tax); they impose charges for various municipal utilities and enterprises—sewer service charges, fees for tapping into the water system for new homes and businesses, or fees for cutting street curbs. Although many of these sources do not generate huge sums, their indirect nature may reduce political opposition.

A second and related rule is to minimize taxpayer resistance by using small, low-yield taxes instead of one large levy. Not only are low taxes less visible, but they also keep the taxpaying public fragmented. Most small taxes are salient only to small groups. With the exception of tax association representatives, those who care about taxes care only about specific taxes; hotel and motel owners, for example, care only about taxes that might hurt their business. A cigarette levy may be opposed only by cigarette retailers and wholesalers, and a fee for tapping into the water system or cutting curbs may draw attention only from builders and developers. Beyond these relatively small groups lies a quiescent majority that is largely unconcerned about such specialized taxes but can be mobilized if a tax issue becomes salient. The idea is to keep the attentive groups divided and the larger public quiet, if not satisfied.

A third rule concerns equity. Although city governments have given new consideration to issues of equality, including equity in service delivery, they have shown little concern for fiscal justice. City officials are often less interested in who *should* pay than in who *will* pay. "Local officials emphasize yields and leave the problem of income distribution to the federal government," says Meltsner. In effect, city officials are more interested that equity exists in service delivery rather than equality or fairness in who pays for the services.

According to the fourth rule, the city manager is the fiscal innovator. Finances are almost always at or near the top of the manager's agenda. In Oakland, for example, the city manager initiated an internal study to analyze each current source of revenue and to suggest new sources to meet a projected revenue-expenditure gap. The Oakland manager also assumed an educational role with other important groups: the council, community leaders, even city department heads. The city manager normally knows the nuts and bolts of taxes, follows relevant state legislation, and tries to keep up with what other cities are doing about finance. This superior tax knowledge puts the manager in the driver's seat; the result is that who pays is usually determined by the manager and the finance department staff. Council members tend not to be tax policy initiators, in any case. Their main concern seems to be holding down property taxes; as elected officials, they are especially sensitive to citizen concerns over this politically unpopular and relatively visible source of municipal revenue.

To generate support for new taxes, Meltsner offers a two-pronged strategy. Among community leaders, stress the specific connection between a proposed revenue source and community benefit. Instead of advocating a capital program that contains a shopping list of land, buildings, and improvements, officials should emphasize potential outcomes: less crime, better health, less flooding, fewer accidents, and more employment. With the larger public, Meltsner advises, stress only the benefits, leaving the tax-service nexus obscure. Local officials should not be squeamish, he argues, in consciously manipulating the benefit side of a proposal. A few years ago in Oklahoma City, for example, a temporary one-cent sales tax for a new jail was sold to the voters almost solely as an anticrime measure: "Vote yes and keep the criminals off the streets." Meltsner admits that building tax coalitions is not easy, but the effort should pay off in generating the support essential for success.

Is it political folly to consider new taxes? One might think so, given the recent history of tax revolts, beginning with the now-famous Proposition 13 approved by California voters in 1978. This property tax rollback measure was followed by a series of tax limitation efforts around the country. For example, Proposition 2 ½ in Massachusetts, which passed in 1980, prevents property taxes from exceeding 2.5 percent of the cash value of the local tax base. In response to perceived high tax rates among local governments, the Illinois General Assembly imposed a tax cap on its local governments in the 1990s, limiting tax rate increases to the lesser of 5 percent or the increase in the consumer price index. The low inflation rate of recent years meant that many local governments were able to raise their tax rates by less than 2 percent at a time when many expenses, especially labor contracts, were increasing at more than 5 percent per year. Yet despite some taxpayer rebellion, cities continue to win support for new tax levies.

EXPENDITURES

As mentioned earlier, cities continue to struggle to keep expenditures from outpacing revenues. The economic downturn that began in 2008 made this more challenging. Efforts persist to improve productivity, to identify new operating efficiencies, and to become more entrepreneurial. But cities spend most of their money on basic services. If we examine recent spending areas in cities, we see that, on average, cities have followed a fairly consistent level of spending on basic services in recent years.

Table 10-2 shows spending in millions of dollars by cities in 2006–2007 and comparable figures from 2001–2002. The functional area that consumes the largest share of the budget is public safety, which accounts for over 21 percent of cities' funding allocations; this area includes police and fire protection, local jails, and regulatory inspection services.

Table 10-2   **City Expenditures, 2001–2002 versus 2006–2007**

	2001–2002		2006–2007		2001–2002 to 2006–2007
	Total ($millions)	Share of Spending (%)	Total ($millions)	Share of Spending (%)	Change in Spending (%)
General expenditures	288,078		361,495		25.5
Public safety	60,315	20.9	77,684	21.5	28.8
Education & libraries	39,276	13.6	46,141	12.8	17.5
Transportation	32,858	11.4	40,182	11.1	22.3
Other	32,026	11.1	41,098	11.4	28.3
Environmental	29,351	10.2	38,920	10.8	32.6
Government administration	21,443	7.4	29,743	8.2	38.7
Interest on debt	15,784	5.5	18,946	5.2	20.0
Parks and recreation	15,606	5.4	20,002	5.5	28.2
Public welfare	12,904	4.5	11,352	3.1	−12.0
Housing and community development	12,563	4.4	16,638	4.6	32.4
Hospitals	10,012	3.5	12,953	3.6	29.4
Health	5,940	2.1	7,836	2.2	31.9

SOURCES: U.S. Census Bureau, *2002 Census of Governments*, vol. 4, no. 4, *Finances of Municipal and Township Governments: 2002* (Washington, D.C.: Government Printing Office, 2002), table 1, pp. 1–2; *2007 Census of Governments: Finance*, table 2; and *Local Government Finances by Type of Government and State: 2006-07*.

The next largest category is spending on education and libraries, but it is important to emphasize that most cities do not have the financial responsibility for public schools. In fact, education and some other services are usually provided by other local governments—for example, counties usually fund welfare; independent school districts handle local education; and special districts often run libraries, housing, and transportation. Thus, table 10-2 reflects the spending on these areas by a small number of large cities that run schools and social services, many in the Northeast.

Cities spend a significant portion of their budgets—on average about 22 percent—on the area often called "public works," which includes two key areas (1) transportation (local roads and highways, transit systems, and airports) and (2) environmental protection (sewerage, solid-waste disposal, and natural resources). It is instructive to see the growth in larger public services during this first decade. For instance, public safety grew by 29 percent, environmental services spending was up 33 percent, and parks and recreation was up 28 percent. Perhaps more surprising is that the cost of city government administration, which is about 8 percent of the budget, grew at a faster rate (up 39 percent) than any other area of spending. It leads one to question why it became so much more costly to manage government in the last decade.

Cities also must pay for debt service. Although interest payment on municipal debt is just 5 percent of the budget, over the decade the debt service payments grew at a large rate. From 2001 to 2007, interest on debt grew by 20 percent in city governments. Several other general observations can be made about city expenditures. First, as suggested earlier, some cities perform more services than others do. Those that are more functionally inclusive tend to spend more per capita, of course, than do those with a more limited scope of operations. A regional bias exists here: northeastern municipalities provide more services, on average, than do cities in the western states, where special districts or counties may perform more functions. Thus, when regional comparisons are made, northeastern cities may appear to be spendthrifts. However, although labor costs may be somewhat higher for cities in the more industrialized and unionized Northeast and North Central regions, the biggest difference in spending likely is tied to the more comprehensive scope of services often provided by cities in those areas. Levels of expenditure also tend to relate to city size: big cities spend more than smaller cities do on a per capita basis—again, because they generally perform more functions. In addition, large urban areas are likely to be called on to provide the more costly social services required for their proportionally larger dependent populations.

At the national level and especially among state governments, considerable revenue is dedicated to, or earmarked for, specific purposes, such as the gasoline tax for highway use. At the city level, considerably less earmarking occurs, except perhaps to repay revenue bonds financed from utility earnings. Most of the money for current municipal operations goes into a general fund, at which time it becomes available for spending on a variety of programs and activities. The city budget is the mechanism by which these funds are allocated.

BUDGETING

In simplest terms, a *budget* is a plan for resource allocation. In most municipalities, the chief executive prepares the budget and submits it for approval to the legislative body. Ordinarily, the budget contains a schedule of sources of city revenue by category as well as an indication of the categories or service areas for which funds will be spent. But budget making is far from a simple accounting exercise. Allocating financial resources among competing activities is an act of policymaking: the budget reflects the programs and policies the city intends to pursue. But resources are never sufficient to satisfy the demands of all interested groups, and conflict is inevitable. Because politics can be defined as conflict over public policy, budgeting obviously is a political process. But as we see later, budgeting is also a highly stable, predictable operation that remains considerably insulated from external forces and pressures. One of the continuing debates among students of local government budgeting focuses on the extent to which budgeting responds to external influences such as demands by citizens, interest groups, unions, and other demand-makers and environmental conditions in the political system.

THE BUDGET PROCESS

Generally, budget making is a three-stage process: departmental request; executive review, modification, and consolidation; and legislative review, amendment, and enactment. The actual budget cycle is likely to be initiated, in larger cities at least, by the budget office acting on behalf of the chief executive. Initiation of the process usually encompasses giving some guidelines to department heads concerning program emphasis or limits on requests for increases.

As part of either the executive or legislative reviews, citizen participation may be solicited for the budget proposals. The effectiveness of citizen participation in shaping budget outcomes is not clear. But research does suggest that inclusion of citizens can be a useful step in developing a budget that has wider support among the taxpayers. In a study of budget processes in Topeka, (Kan.), and Burlington, (Iowa), Aimee Franklin and Carol Ebdon tested a model of citizen participation and found that a variety of factors—ranging from city structure to participation mechanisms—shape the effectiveness of citizen roles in the budget processes.[20]

The Role of Department Head

It is commonly accepted that department heads always ask for more than they received last year. As one of the leading scholars on public budgets, Aaron Wildavsky, remarked, "Padding in the expectation of cuts is part of playing the game."[21] One might assume, in this age of REGO, that padding budgets is no longer an acceptable practice, but research suggests that this is not the case. One survey revealed that about 65 percent of local officials continue to pad budgets.[22] Just as departments always ask for more, chief executives invariably cut, so department heads often are merely adopting the counter-strategy of submitting budget figures that can be cut. Lewis Friedman characterizes department heads as advocates—their job is to push hard for their programs. They mark up their requests by the amount they expect will be eliminated, trying to neutralize the adverse effects of the cutting process and so end up with the amount they wanted initially.[23]

Preparing budget requests tends to be a highly incremental process that is dominated by well-developed practices and routines. Common features of this process at the city level include the following strategies:

- Spend all your appropriation. Failure to use up an appropriation indicates that the full amount was unnecessary in the first place, which in turn implies that your budget should be cut next year.
- Never request a sum less than your current appropriation. It is easier to find ways to spend up to current appropriation levels than to explain why you want a reduction.
- Put top-priority programs into the basic budget. Chief executives and city councils seldom challenge programs that appear to be part of existing operations.
- Make increases appear small, and describe them as though they grew out of existing operations.
- Give the chief executive and the council something to cut. This excess padding enables them to "save" money and justify their claim to promoting "economy" in government. Giving them something to cut also diverts attention from the basic budget and its vital programs.[24]

The Executive Role

Budgeting at the municipal level is generally an executive-centered process. Particularly in large cities, the municipal budget is the mayor's budget—the mayor's priorities dominate the department totals and citywide tax and wage policies.[25] This is also true in many medium-sized cities. The mayor "is the key figure in making most of the decisions. . . . He guides the city council in its considerations. He feels it is his budget. And he uses it to make his influence felt throughout city government."[26]

The chief executive—mayor or manager—charged with the responsibility for the budget almost always compiles the separate departmental requests into a single comprehensive document. In the process, cuts are inevitable, because the executive's role is to bring efficiency and economy to the process. The cutting process stems from two factors: the belief that most departments pad their requests, and the legal requirement that municipal budgets be balanced. In larger cities, the budget officer and staff play a significant part in analyzing requests for new funds. Here program analysis, productivity measurement, or program evaluation may come into play. Frequently, the budget officer reaches a compromise with various departments on proposed increases before the draft budget reaches the executive. In the end, the manager must judge the merits of expenditure requests. This is where the executive exerts maximum influence and puts his or her stamp on the recommended budget.

The Role of the City Council

City councils retain the final legal authority to approve the budget. Legislative bodies are widely assumed to lack the time, expertise, and staff to do much more than make minor modifications to an executive's budget. But governing boards may not be as passive as is often thought.

First, councils may feel compelled to make overall reductions in an executive's recommended budget, although, usually, the percentage is small. Second, when asked, council members indicate that they are not just rubber stamps for executive proposals. They apparently examine the budget with considerable care, ask a great many questions, and require the executive to justify a number of budget choices. Through council committee hearings and floor debate, the executive budget is amended so that it bears an element of the council's policy priorities, too. That is, in adopting the budget, the council exercises legislative oversight and tries to enact a budget that reflects its own agenda as well as that of the executive.

Considerable research has been conducted on the impact of form of city government—mayors, managers, and councils—on city budgeting. Are cities any more efficient in their budget policies when they are organized as council-manager rather than mayor-council systems? Similarly, do mayors or managers or even city councils perform better as budget managers than do others in city government? Nearly forty years of research has produced conflicting results.

The classic work of Robert Lineberry and Edmund Fowler suggested that reform governments—those with council-manager form, at-large representation, and nonpartisan elections—taxed and spent at lower levels than did unreformed governments, particularly those organized as mayor-council systems.[27] Other researchers showed that this may not be true. For example, one must account for the budgeting effects of the varying scope of responsibilities among cities. Where city governments operate public schools or deliver local welfare services, budgets will be higher, regardless of how thoroughly reformed the government may be.[28] Research by David R. Morgan and John P. Pelissero showed that, over time, changing to a reform-style government had no significant impact on the revenue or spending side of city budgets. In fact, changing to a less reform-style structure also had no impact on the overall budget.[29] Further confirming these findings in a recent historical study, political scientist Anirudh Ruhil showed that in cities that changed to a council-manager form, per capita spending decreased occasionally, but not permanently.[30] However, other research has shown that city managers may be better at keeping property taxes lower and spending increases smaller than are strong mayors.[31] And recent research by Barbara McCabe and Richard Feiock validates the importance of the type of governance system to keeping tax and spending decisions of city governments in alignment with citizen preferences.[32]

THE TRADITIONAL APPROACH: LINE-ITEM BUDGETING

Traditionally, budgeting has been an incremental process. This year's budget, with a slight change in available resources, is basically the same as last year's. In one analyst's words, "the budget is a slowly changing thing, consisting of a series of marginal changes from previous budgets."[33]

Budgeting by *line item* virtually ensures incrementalism, and most governments at all levels still employ a line-item budget. The format specifies dollar amounts by department for a host of detailed expenditures, often grouped under three basic categories: personal services, operating expenses, and capital outlay. Line-item budgeting was a natural outgrowth of the Progressive reformers' early efforts to make governments more fiscally accountable. Presumably, where line items of expenditures were detailed, auditors or external critics could more easily ascertain that the city government did not overspend. Line-item budgeting, then, stems from the desire to control governmental spending, not from an interest in developing effective services and programs.

Incremental budgeting would seem to leave little room for the influence of outside forces. Most political scientists see budgeting as a political act; the budget has even been described as the "prime expression of political decision."[34] This perception implies extensive negotiation, bargaining, and even conflict among contending groups. But empirical research casts doubt on the extensiveness of external group participation in the municipal budgeting process. Finding little evidence of external political influence in the budget-making process, one researcher asserted that "budgets in municipal governments are reasonably abstracted documents, bearing little direct relationship to specific community pressures."[35]

Finally, we should note that most city budgets are annual in nature but must be revised during the course of the year. This process, called "rebudgeting," is quite common but little studied. Research on the topic finds that revising and updating the officially adopted budget during the fiscal year is a less visible and more technical process that further enhances the power of administrators.[36]

BUDGETARY REFORM

For years, academics and practitioners have called for alternatives to the traditional line-item budget, whose principal limitation is the inability to show any connection between resource allocations (human and fiscal) and program outputs (activities). The presumptive cure is to devise a budgeting format that focuses on performance or program activities. Municipal budget reform has taken several approaches over the past half century, among them, performance budgeting, planning-programming-budgeting (PPB) systems, and zero-base budgeting (ZBB). However, despite some newer reforms in budgeting, such as the expenditure control budgeting (ECB) system, little has changed in city budgets. A strong reliance on (or comfort with) line item budgeting continues to exist. In this section, we briefly examine the older budget reforms.

Performance Budgeting

Performance budgeting was a product of the New Deal. Concomitant with the rise of the national government in the 1930s was the perceived need to focus more on the management of public programs. Performance budgeting differs from the previous control orientation of the line-item budget in two important ways. First, it maximizes the value of effective management; the budget is a way to manage programs, not simply to control expenditures. Second, performance budgeting is concerned with what happens with resources after they are allocated. Designating objects of expenditure is not enough—instead, the budget should be redesigned so that each agency identifies activities performed, develops performance measures (projected cost of each activity), and prepares performance reports that compare goals and projected costs with accomplishments and actual costs.[37]

Beginning in the 1960s, performance budgeting gave way to PPB and then, in the 1970s, to ZBB. In actuality, PPB and ZBB are no more than sophisticated extensions of performance budgeting; the former maximizes the value of planning in budgeting, and the latter maximizes the value of decision making in budgeting.[38]

Planning-Programming-Budgeting System

The PPB approach is based on the rational-comprehensive model of decision making. Under PPB, expenditures are organized into program categories. Budget decisions are then made by analyzing alternative spending proposals, both within and among program categories. This analysis takes into account both cost and program performance.[39] PPB also incorporates long-range planning, often over a five-year period. PPB, in short, embraces three components: budgeting by program category, analysis, and planning.

PPB, which is often referred to simply as program budgeting, remains in use in some cities today. Figure 10-1 provides an example of a program budget for the fire-suppression division of a city fire department, including goals, objectives, and output measures in addition to the dollar amount requested for each of the various program elements. It would be possible, of course, to add a line-item budget to this format rather easily by listing the costs by year for personnel, maintenance and operations, contractual items, and even capital purchases. A program budget provides quite a bit more detail than does a simple line-item budget.

By increasing the level of information and grouping activities along functional lines, PPB is supposed to contribute to more rational decision making. But implementing this new approach is not easy. Budgeting officials in Ann Arbor, Michigan, learned several lessons when they implemented a PPB system.[40] First, it is not wise to introduce a drastic new system during the normal budget period. Second, more data can easily be produced than decision makers can readily assimilate. Third, generating better program data is a two-edged sword, at least for departments—it can highlight weaknesses as well as justifying program expansion. Fourth, the total conversion process takes a long time— perhaps three or four years. And, finally, the program budget should not be converted to a line-item budget.

Figure 10-1   **Example of a Program Budget for Fire Department, Suppression Division**

Department: Fire   **Division:** Fire Suppression

Goal: To minimize harm or damage to persons and property caused by fires and explosions.

Objectives:
1. To reduce average dollar property loss for residential fires by 3 percent.
2. To reduce average dollar property loss for commercial fires by 2 percent.
3. To reduce fire deaths by 10 percent.
4. To reduce overall mean response time from 5.3 to 5.2 minutes.

Program Output Measures

	Actual 2011	Estimate 2012	Target 2013
1. Average dollar property loss—residential	$21,564	$22,013	$21,353
2. Average dollar property loss—commercial	$69,724	$70,112	$68,710
3. Fire deaths per 100,000 population	5.2	5.1	4.6
4. Mean response time (min.)	5.4	5.3	5.2

Program Costs

Program Element	2011 Actual	2012 Appropriated	2012 Expended	2013 Proposed
Administration	$ 1,100,000	$ 1,144,100	$ 1,142,200	$ 1,184,400
Communications	1,283,500	1,334,800	1,332,600	1,381,800
Fire response	14,987,800	15,586,700	15,568,700	16,134,400
Training	366,700	381,400	380,700	394,800
Operation and maintenance	550,000	572,000	503,000	592,200
Contractual	47,000	50,000	49,800	52,400
Totals	$18,335,000	$19,069,000	$19,037,000	$19,740,000

Because of the difficulties involved in implementing PPB, several elements appear to be crucial for success: strong, continuing support from top management; a well-trained staff to direct and coordinate the program; a period of three-to-five years for full implementation; and methods for dealing with considerable resistance from some, if not most, operating departments. Irene S. Rubin and Lana Stein's case study of budget reform in St. Louis, for example, found that the city's new program and performance budget was the result of improved technology (computerization), a professional staff, and strong executive (mayoral) leadership.[41]

Implementation problems are not the only grounds on which PPB has been criticized.[42] The approach contains a strong centralizing bias that many do not like; generally speaking, PPB is a top-down process. Critics also object to the tendency of PPB proponents to minimize or ignore the political context within which budgeting takes place. Most of the objections are virtually identical with those aimed at all forms of systems analysis: the difficulty in quantifying intangibles, too much reliance on economic cost-benefit criteria, and so on.

Zero-Base Budgeting

According to Peter Pyhrr, its originator, zero-base budgeting involves two basic steps: developing and ranking decision packages.[43] Developing a decision package involves specifying a program activity, its cost, the service provided, and the level of effort required to achieve each prescribed target increase or decrease. Department heads then rank the decision packages according to priorities established at higher levels. The process of ranking the decision packages continues up the line, as each management level reviews, compares, consolidates, and establishes program priorities. The chief executive prepares the final list of decision-package rankings, which is then forwarded to the city council.

According to a survey of budget directors who use ZBB, it is most helpful in reallocating resources from lower- to higher-priority projects and in making more rational budget cuts. The main complaints center on the time and paperwork required and the reluctance of department heads to offer decision packages at a funding level lower than their present appropriation. Budget directors also note the tendency of some departments to manipulate priority listings by ranking popular activities lower than activities with little chance of being funded.[44]

An Assessment of Past Budget Reform

Budgeting in American cities has changed tremendously over the past several decades. However, while various budgeting reforms have been institutionalized, most cities cling to the line-item budget. Program budgeting in one form or another has grown more popular, especially among larger communities and those in western states; as many as 45 percent of cities have reported using this approach, although usually in combination with a line-item format.[45] Not surprisingly, cities that have adopted efficiency-focused reform structures such as the council-manager plan of government are likely to adopt budget reforms more quickly than are other cities.[46] Few cities—only about 7 percent—have relied on a full-blown PPB system. Zero-base budgeting has never been widely adopted at the municipal level, and interest in ZBB has waned in recent years. In the survey mentioned earlier, fewer than 12 percent of the cities reported employing ZBB, even in combination with other budgeting approaches.

Budget expert Allen Schick best summarizes the views on budgetary reform:

> There is little interest these days in big reforms of the sort that animated performance budgeting, planning-programming-budgeting (PPB), and zero-base budgeting (ZBB) in earlier decades. ... It is now part of the lore of budgeting that PPB and ZBB promised more improvement than they produced. These actual or perceived failures taught a generation of budget practitioners and scholars that comprehensive change is costly and disruptive, has uncertain prospects, and produces unintended side effects.[47]

This is not to suggest that all efforts to reform municipal budgeting have been unsuccessful, or that all have been entirely discarded. Stanley Botner notes that "a professional budgetary system might well include features of performance budgeting in addition to the object and program approaches."[48] In short, the contemporary municipal budget is a hybrid—line-item in format, but exhibiting performance and program budgeting characteristics. And there is a new budgeting reform on the rise, most frequently called expenditure control budgeting.

REINVENTING BUDGETING

Expenditure control budgeting (ECB) is part of a new thrust of budgetary reform called "entrepreneurial budgeting."[49] Included in this wave of reform are mission-driven budgeting and budgeting for results. Perhaps the principal advocates of entrepreneurial budgeting are David Osborne and Ted Gaebler, who argue that the process of "reinventing government" must include freeing managers from the line-item budget.[50] They insist that traditional line-item budgeting encourages waste, because agency officials must spend money or lose it, and stifles initiative, because managers have little discretion in spending. Instead, they propose that budgeting should be "mission-driven" and aimed at results. Mission-driven budgeting and budgeting for results, however, are simply recycled versions of performance/program budgeting—they focus on program goals, outputs, outcomes, and employee performance. Expenditure control budgeting, in contrast, offers a new approach to municipal budgeting. It encompasses a *process* that can be used to budget for results and implement mission-driven budgeting.

ECB is the creation of Oscar Reyes, an assistant finance director in Fairfield, California. B. Gale Wilson, the nationally honored and recognized long-time (now retired) city manager of Fairfield, installed the innovation in 1979 in response to the impact of Proposition 13 on city finances. Six months later, then–city manager Ted Gaebler brought the budgeting reform to Visalia, California. "To date, the application of ECB is limited,"[51] but it can be found in a dozen or so jurisdictions.

ECB has been defined as "a comprehensive budgetary system that uses retained savings to promote managerial innovation."[52] In Fairfield, where the innovation originated, ECB basically produced three results: it eliminated line items, it allowed departments to keep what they did not spend, and it turned the city council budget into a two-page document that set expenditure limits.[53] In essence, department heads now are given block grants and plenty of discretion. Retained savings accrue and carry over from one year to the next, and they must be used to fund new programs, projects, or maintain existing services in a period of retrenchment.

An expenditure control budget includes these general operating features:

- Each department receives a base budget that is annually adjusted for population growth and the cost of living (inflation).
- The base budget assumes existing service levels. The chief executive and council must approve service-level changes, and the chief executive can adjust base budgets to correct minor imbalances.

- Department heads are responsible for future costs of programs and must pay for service expansions from retained savings.
- A proportion of all savings generated from productivity is carried over to the next year.

In operation, ECB is very different from previous budgetary reforms. It starts out as a top-down process but ends up giving more autonomy to operating departments. The council monitors performance and demands accountability for results.

One problem associated with ECB is overcoming bureaucratic inertia. Departments that enjoy favored status may fear losing their position of privilege, and departments that are not favored may feel that they deserve a higher base budget to compensate for past actions. Another problem is the unwillingness of elected officials to decentralize power to agency personnel. The legacy of political control through the line-item budget is hard to overcome.[54]

The benefits of ECB are improved efficiency and innovation. Fairfield officials contend that they saved about $5 million in an eight-year period. In one year, Chandler, Arizona, saved over $2 million.[55] Perhaps just as important, ECB fosters trust between those who rule and those who are responsible for the delivery of public services.

We must not forget that the budget is a political document. Regardless of format, the budgetary process involves considerable interaction and consultation, if not negotiation, among a relatively limited set of internal actors. Values and beliefs certainly come into play when the budget pie is cut, as various individuals and departments pursue their objectives and protect their turf. Moreover, cities cannot control the forces that will affect the flow of revenues, and they cannot always adjust their demands for spending to changes taking place in the system. As the case study presented in box 10.2 shows, even when the local economic system is thriving, the city budget can experience significant distress related to the tax system and demands for services.

CAPITAL IMPROVEMENT PLANNING AND BUDGETING

In addition to an annual operating budget, most cities of any size prepare a capital improvement budget. Cities need to anticipate and plan for the construction and financing of large-scale public improvements. A capital facilities plan is supposed to ensure that these projects are carried out according to a well-prepared program that reflects the city's needs and ability to pay. Because major capital improvements substantially affect city taxes, capital planning can reduce tax-rate fluctuation by systematically staggering projects.[56]

Capital budgeting is usually a lengthy process that begins with capital planning. It begins with the preparation of a comprehensive city plan, or master plan. This planning document may project in broad outline form the capital requirements over a period of, say, twenty-five years. The next step is preparation of the capital improvement program or schedule, which has a much shorter time horizon—perhaps five to eight years. This document sets forth a year-by-year list of projects and facilities to be constructed or renovated. Finally, a capital budget makes specific provisions for the first year of the improvement program, and it is then revised annually to reflect completion of projects and necessary modifications.[57]

Figuring out how to pay for capital needs is a major concern of capital planning and budgeting. In most cities nowadays, making large-scale capital improvements means going into debt. Where debt financing is required, cities usually have two options: general obligation (GO) bonds or revenue bonds. GO bonds require a vote of the people because their repayment is guaranteed by the full taxing power of the issuing government; usually, the debt is serviced by increasing the property tax. Revenue bonds, however, often can be issued without a popular vote; ordinarily, the city simply pledges to use a certain portion of the revenue from some municipal revenue-producing facility for debt retirement. Improvements to the water and sewer systems frequently are accomplished by means of revenue bonds; the city council (or utility authority) may then raise the utility rates to pay off the bonds. Because revenue bonds are not backed by the "full faith and credit" of the city, they generally bear an interest rate that is 1 percent or so above that of GO bonds. Thus, the city pays more in debt service to issue revenue bonds.

Because most cities use debt financing for capital improvement, the capital budget may have little or no connection with the operating budget. Partly for this reason and partly because of the uncertainties in funding, capital programming and budgeting undergo frequent change. Projects are modified, postponed, or in some cases accelerated, depending on circumstances. Certainly, the availability of federal or state grant money affects the process. Capital planning and budgeting, then, are not as orderly as many would like. There are no automatic neat linkages flowing from the comprehensive plan to the capital improvement program, to the capital budget, and on to the operating budget.[58]

WHITHER CITY BUDGETING?

Cities have been urged for years to reform their budget making. PPB, ZBB, and ECB have captured the support of reformers, but most cities have resisted giving up line-item budgeting completely. To wrap up our consideration of municipal budgeting, we should reexamine the provocative advice of Meltsner and Wildavsky, found in the classic piece, "Leave City Budgeting Alone!"[59] They contend that municipal budgeting is not just a way of allocating resources. Its real purpose is control—to permit officials to hold down costs so that expenditures do not exceed income and necessitate new taxes. The city's budget-cutters lack the information, time, and staff to explore programmatic changes in any detail during budget time. These authors argue that no proposal to change city budgeting is acceptable if it makes the budget appreciably less useful for control and cutting purposes, calls for a large increase in personnel, requires a high level of analytic talent, or depends on the existence of, or the likelihood of obtaining, good data relevant to actual decisions. In short, they believe that strong political leadership and the intelligent but modest use of program analysis can help cities more than drastic budgetary reform. Apparently, a lot of city officials agree.

BOX 10.2   Policy and Practice

BIG CITY BUDGET WOES AMID ECONOMIC EXPANSION

In recent years, the city of Pittsburgh (Penn.), has been confronting an unusual economic situation. The city seems to have overcome its turbulent economic fortunes of the 1980s, and there is cause for hope in the economy. Today, the city is experiencing an economic surge in the medical, educational, and financial sectors, and job growth is climbing. However, even in the face of economic improvements, the city government finds itself in extreme danger due to its immense budgetary problems.

The situation in Pittsburgh, dubbed the "Pittsburgh paradox," demonstrates that a burgeoning economy does not necessarily coincide with good fortune for city government. The government's economy has been characterized as "near collapse," and it has posted a structural budget deficit every year since the mid-1990s. In recent years, the problems have grown worse, and between 2002 and 2004, Pittsburgh's budget collapsed entirely.

As a result of its extreme economic weakness, the city has been forced to drastically reduce services. In 2003 all city pools and recreation centers were closed, and the already high parking tax was increased by 50 percent. Furthermore, Pittsburgh has had to lay off large numbers of city workers, leading to a scenario that was described by city controller Tom Flaherty as "Pittsburgh's Waterloo." To address a situation that had clearly gotten out of control, the State of Pennsylvania sent in two state oversight boards, which issued a plan for economic recovery that called for even harsher budget cuts and drastic tax increases amounting to $40 million. While this plan was opposed by most in Pittsburgh, the city had run out of options, and severe measures were perceived as necessary.

How could this happen? A city facing economic improvement is not often seen in the dire situation that Pittsburgh faces, so what explains this development? In the case of Pittsburgh, much of the problem lies in the tax structure and the demographic shifting of the metropolitan area population. For example, Pittsburgh is losing large amounts of money in income and property taxes. In the mid–twentieth century, nearly everyone who worked in the city lived there, but today 300,000 workers live outside the Pittsburgh city limits, taking away much-needed tax money. The city currently has the second highest ratio of city jobs to city population in the nation, thus requiring a strong revenue stream to pay the hefty city payroll. Furthermore, an outdated tax system ensures that 45 percent of Pittsburgh's companies are not required to pay business taxes. In addition to these tax exemptions, Pittsburgh loses out further as industries other than steel continue to grow; the city receives less money from property taxes due to the fact that these companies require less property than do the steel plants. Finally, Pittsburgh has a significant nonprofit sector, and the city cannot collect property taxes from these tax-exempt businesses.

Therefore, although two of the growing sectors—education and medicine—continue to construct new buildings, the city gains nothing. Its tax structure ensures that even as businesses continue to flourish, Pittsburgh cannot take advantage of this economic growth, leading to a "mismatch between its economy and its fiscal health."

This mismatch amounts to an ugly economic situation in a city where the citizens already pay high taxes, including a 3 percent income tax to the city and school districts. Still, the city is in a constant search for new taxes, but most of the likely sources are prohibited by the state, so the result has been deeper service cuts. Pittsburgh's spending is traditionally high, which has led to a level of debt that will be hard to surmount. As a

(continued)

result, Pittsburgh has been forced to institute both large budget cuts in service areas and some new taxes, such as the replacement of the business tax with a payroll tax that requires all businesses to pay a certain amount per employee. Additionally, to address the problem of large numbers of workers living outside the city, the occupational privilege tax (OPT), a personal tax levied by municipal governments on people who work in the city, will increase from $10 to $120 per year.

Whether these changes in the budget and revenue stream will work remains to be seen. But this budgetary reform is clearly only one step of many that will be needed to revive a city characterized by one city council member as "broke and on the brink of disaster." The Pittsburgh paradox shows that even as the economies of large cities have rebounded, municipal taxes, fees, and spending plans may still leave some cities suffering budget woes.

SOURCE: Adapted from Anya Sostek, "The Well That Dried Up," *Governing* 18 (October 2004): 36–38, 40–41.

MANAGING MUNICIPAL FINANCES

Although budgeting is certainly at the heart of municipal financial management, that process incorporates a series of interrelated basic functions of which budgeting is only one part. Figure 10-2 shows five of these functions and identifies the linkages among them.

FORMING GOALS AND OBJECTIVES

The degree to which municipalities formally define their goals varies considerably. To the extent that they are written out, larger objectives are most likely to appear in the city budget, perhaps separately for each department. Whatever the degree of formality, top management and department heads presumably engage in an ongoing process of identifying the community problems and needs toward which city programs should be directed. Likewise, municipal managers—if not continuously, at least at budget time—enter into a process of reviewing past performance in addressing those issues and concerns. Perhaps by the use of performance evaluation or MBO, program managers may decide to shift priorities to the areas showing the greatest need. Or, the city council or city manager, responding to community pressures, may force a reordering of the agency agenda. This sort of needs assessment and analysis, even if it is largely a muddling-through process, occurs in cities of all sizes.

PLANNING AND BUDGETING

The next step is to incorporate community needs and objectives in the formal document that allocates financial resources—the city budget. Whatever the budget format, it should incorporate multiyear financial planning, which is not an easy matter. In noting the rarity of long-term financial planning in the public sector, Jacob Ukeles observes that "politicians in general, out of long and bitter experience, are notoriously uninterested in being pinned down with regard to decisions they may take affecting the next several months, let alone

Figure 10-2   Integrated Municipal Financial Information System

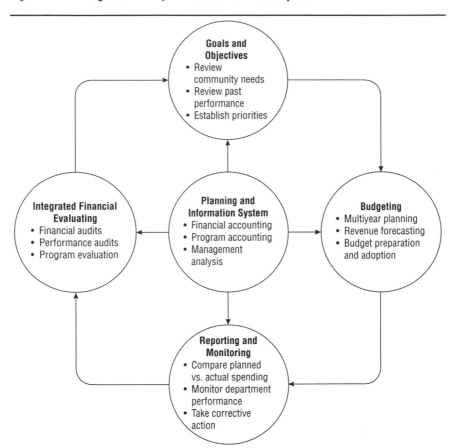

Goals and Objectives
- Review community needs
- Review past performance
- Establish priorities

Integrated Financial Evaluating
- Financial audits
- Performance audits
- Program evaluation

Planning and Information System
- Financial accounting
- Program accounting
- Management analysis

Budgeting
- Multiyear planning
- Revenue forecasting
- Budget preparation and adoption

Reporting and Monitoring
- Compare planned vs. actual spending
- Monitor department performance
- Take corrective action

SOURCE: Adapted from *Program Measurement Handbook*, Office of the Mayor, City and County of San Francisco, February 1980, as reproduced in *Linkages: Improving Financial Management in Local Government*, by F.O'R. Hayes et al. (Washington, D.C.: Urban Institute, 1982), 6.

two, three, or four years in the future."[60] But he goes on to compare cities and states with large corporations, insisting that public entities, like those corporations, must look ahead to manage effectively. What does advance planning do? It facilitates cash-flow management, focuses attention on infrastructure maintenance needs, and removes the element of surprise, should revenue receipts diverge from past trends.

How can a city plan over a multiyear period? As a start, it should prepare a written revenue projection plan to accompany the municipal budget. The plan should list specific revenue sources, assumptions used, and comparisons of budget-year projections to current-year estimates and prior-year receipts. A projection is only as good as the assumptions on which it is based, so full disclosure of all assumptions is critical. This three-year prospective provides city management and the city council with a means for judging how well the city has estimated revenue in the past.[61]

REPORTING AND MONITORING

Several issues arise in reporting and monitoring the financial developments in city government. First, measurable objectives and targets should be part of the budget, to facilitate both the monitoring process and accountability.[62] In the terminology of REGO, this is managing for results. In addition to the use of program performance measures, financial monitoring also demands regular reporting.

Small- and even medium-sized cities may experience considerable difficulty in developing the capacity to monitor financial trends. To assist these cities, the ICMA issues a series of handbooks for evaluating a city's financial condition, containing information on collecting data, charting trends, and interpreting the results of financial indicators.[63] These indicators include uncollected property taxes, user charge coverage, revenue shortfalls, operating deficits, enterprise losses, long-term and short-term debts, pension liability, and level of capital outlay. The approach asks the city to construct these indicators from existing data over a five-year period and to observe how they change. The indicators are then updated each year to enable the city to identify financial problems and plan corrective action.

EVALUATING

Another facet of REGO is evaluation of financial practices and program implementation and outcomes. The ICMA has been a leader in advancing the practice of evaluating financial conditions in cities.[64] Evaluating the financial system demands auditing in one form or another. In the past, this process usually involved a once-a-year financial audit, perhaps by an outside auditing firm, to determine whether the city's financial practices conformed to accepted standards and legal requirements. This is still common practice, but some cities are taking a closer look at program results as well. Research from a team at the Urban Institute demonstrates that the program results audit is really a form of program evaluation.[65] As with any such evaluation, an effort is made to determine how well the program is working, whether it is meeting its objectives, and how much the program itself has contributed to observable changes. The Urban Institute reports that program audit findings are a basis for terminating marginal programs and for changing others.

THE INTEGRATED FINANCIAL INFORMATION SYSTEM

Linking the basic components of the financial management system is the primary emphasis of Frederick Hayes and his colleagues. A fully integrated system is built on a unified database that includes both financial and program information. The authors admit that there are no prescribed steps that can be followed by every city to create essential linkages. They suggest, however, that often the first step toward integration is to tie together the basic accounting and budgeting functions. They also discuss the potential usefulness of a financial management improvement committee.[66] This group would consist of the mayor or city manager, the chair of the council's finance committee (if one exists), the finance director, the budget director, and the chief internal auditor; heads of some operating agencies might be included as well. The committee would develop basic policies and strategies, identify priorities, review projects, and assess progress periodically. The committee, as such, would not have managerial responsibility because most specific financial functions would be carried out by the separate agencies represented on the committee. Hayes and his colleagues acknowledge that few local governments can develop a fully integrated, comprehensive financial management system without help from outside consultants and contractors.

SUMMARY

In the twenty-first century, U.S. cities still must raise most of their revenue within their own borders. Yet the most efficient revenue-raising machinery and the most productive tax sources belong to the federal and state governments. This intrinsic fiscal imbalance creates considerable pressure for cities to seek federal and state aid. But as the economic downturn of the first decade showed, states had less means to help cities, and the temporary source of new federal funding was the American Recovery and Reinvestment Act. As intergovernmental revenue to local governments dwindled, cities have been forced to turn inward to cut spending or to rely on their own resources for new revenue. Many cities' experiences with REGO initiatives have paved the way for new approaches to revenues and budgeting.

We still hear calls for cities to move away from heavy reliance on the property tax. Sales and income taxes are becoming more popular in many places. A case also can be made for greater reliance on user charges—charges that place a larger burden on those who are especially heavy users of certain services and facilities. REGO certainly promoted fees over taxes in many places. As cities try to pull themselves up by their bootstraps, figuring out how to pry more dollars out of the local citizenry becomes a high priority.

The budgetary process of allocating city funds to programs represents a significant political act by which scarce resources are apportioned among competing needs. But research also shows that municipal budgeting is a highly incremental process that, to a considerable extent, remains isolated from external influences. Incrementalism apparently results in part from the widespread practice of line-item budgeting. Because of the many alleged shortcomings of this budget format, reformers have urged its replacement: PPB, ZBB, and, more recently, ECB are lauded as substitutes. But do these approaches to municipal budgeting meet the needs of city officials? Do they allow the budget to serve its vital control and cost-cutting functions? Their limited acceptance suggests that many city officials do not think so and continue to allocate funds in a line-item format.

Most authorities now recognize that budgeting is only one step in the process of managing the city's finances. An integrated financial management system includes several related elements—goal setting, long-range planning and budgeting, reporting and monitoring, and evaluating—and the integrated information system that links them together. Whatever approach the city takes in its revenue-raising, spending, and budgeting activities, the continuing shortage of resources demands that today's urban managers monitor financial practices more closely than ever before. And the political system has only become more complex and more conflictual—making the budget process all the more challenging for chief executives in the twenty-first-century city.

SUGGESTED FOR FURTHER READING

Aronson, J. Richard, and Eli Schwartz, eds. *Management Policies in Local Government Finance.* 5th ed. Washington, D.C.: ICMA, 2004.

Bland, Robert L. *A Budgeting Guide for Local Government.* 2nd ed. Washington, D.C.: ICMA, 2007.

Fuchs, Esther. *Mayors and Money: Fiscal Policy in New York and Chicago.* Chicago: University of Chicago Press, 1992.

Kelly, Janet M. and William C. Rivenbark. *Performance Budgeting for State and Local Government.* 2nd ed. Armonk, N.Y.: M.E. Sharpe, 2010.

Rubin, Irene S. *The Politics of Public Budgeting: Getting and Spending, Borrowing and Balancing.* 6th ed. Washington, D.C.: CQ Press, 2009.

Stein, Robert. "The Politics of Revenue and Spending Policies." In *Cities, Politics, and Policy: A Comparative Analysis,* ed. John P. Pelissero, 217–236. Washington, D.C.: CQ Press, 2003.

NOTES

1. This observation, still relevant today, was made over thirty five years ago by Dick Netzer, in *Economics and Urban Problems,* 2nd ed. (New York: Basic Books, 1974), 65.

2. Ibid., 231.

3. U.S. Census Bureau, *2002 Census of Governments,* vol. 4, no. 4; *Finances of Municipal and Township Governments: 2002* (Washington, D.C.: Government Printing Office, 2002), table 1, pp. 1–2.

4. For example, see ACIR, *Changing Public Attitudes on Governments and Taxes, 1991* (Washington, D.C.: Government Printing Office, 1991), 1.

5. David R. Berman, "State-Local Relations: Partnerships, Conflict, and Autonomy," *2005 Municipal Year Book* (Washington, D.C.: ICMA, 2005), 52. See also Richard Cole and John Kincaid, "Public Opinion and American Federalism: Perspectives on Taxes, Spending and Trust—An ACIR Update," *Publius* 30 (winter 2000): 189–201.

6. Bill Simonsen and Mark D. Robbins, "Reasonableness, Satisfaction, and Willingness to Pay Property Taxes," *Urban Affairs Review* 38 (November 2003): 831–854.

7. Berman, "State-Local Relations," 53.

8. Ibid.

9. ACIR, *Significant Features of Fiscal Federalism: Budget Processes and Tax Systems—1992* (Washington, D.C.: Government Printing Office, 1992), 1:73–75.

10. See John L. Mikesell, "General Sales, Income, and Other Nonproperty Taxes," *Management Policies in Local Government Finance,* 5th, ed. J. Richard Aronson and Eli Schwartz (Washington, D.C.: ICMA, 2004), 289–314.

11. David Brunori, *Local Tax Policy: A Federalist Perspective* (Washington, D.C.: Urban Institute Press, 2003).

12. Berman, "State-Local Relations."

13. Gale Tollin, "City Paying Its Own Way," *Norman Transcript,* March 17, 1983.

14. See David Osborne and Ted Gaebler, *Reinventing Government* (Reading, Mass.: Addison-Wesley, 1992), chap. 10.

15. Timothy B. Krebs and John P. Pelissero, "What Influences City Council Adoption and Support for Reinventing Government? Environmental or Institutional Factors?" *Public Administration Review* 70 (March–April 2010): 261.

16. Ibid., 265.

17. John Forrester and Charles J. Spindler, "Assessing the Impact on Municipal Revenues of the Elimination of General Revenue Sharing," *State and Local Government Review* 22 (spring 1990): 82.

18. Berman, "State-Local Relations."

19. This section draws on the classic work of Arnold J. Meltsner, *The Politics of City Revenue* (Berkeley: University of California Press, 1971).

20. Aimee L. Franklin and Carol Ebdon, "Are We All Touching the Same Camel?: Exploring a Model of Participation in Budgeting," *The American Review of Public Administration* 35 (2005): 168–185.

21. Aaron Wildavsky, *The New Politics of the Budgetary Process* (Glenview, Ill.: Scott, Foresman/Little, Brown, 1988), 235.

22. Len Wood, "Budget Tactics: Insights from the Trenches," *Public Management* (October 1993), 16.

23. Lewis Friedman, *Budgeting Municipal Expenditures* (New York: Praeger, 1975), 62.

24. Thomas J. Anton, *The Politics of State Expenditures in Illinois* (Urbana: University of Illinois Press, 1966), 49–52, as adapted in Thomas R. Dye, *Understanding Public Policy*, 2nd ed. (Englewood Cliffs, N.J.: Prentice Hall, 1975), 226.

25. John Crecine, *Governmental Problem-Solving: A Computer Simulation of Municipal Budgeting* (Chicago: Rand McNally, 1969), 38.

26. Arnold Meltsner and Aaron Wildavsky, "Leave City Budgeting Alone! A Survey, Case Study, and Recommendations for Reform," in *Financing the Metropolis*, ed. John Crecine (Beverly Hills, Calif.: Sage, 1970), 344.

27. Robert L. Lineberry and Edmund P. Fowler, "Reformism and Public Policies in American Cities," *American Political Science Review* 61 (September 1967): 701–716.

28. Roland J. Liebert, "Municipal Functions, Structures, and Expenditures: A Reanalysis of Recent Research," *Social Science Quarterly* 54 (March 1974): 765–783.

29. David R. Morgan and John P. Pelissero, "Urban Policy: Does Political Structure Matter?" *American Political Science Review* 74 (December 1980): 999–1006.

30. Anirudh V. S. Ruhil, "Structural Change and Fiscal Flows: A Framework for Analyzing the Effects of Urban Events," *Urban Affairs Review* 38 (January 2003): 396–416.

31. Theodore J. Strumm and Matthew T. Corrigan, "City Managers: Do They Promote Fiscal Efficiency?" *Journal of Urban Affairs* 20, no. 3 (1998): 343–351.

32. Barbara Coyle McCabe and Richard C. Feiock, "Nested Levels of Institutions: State Rules and City Property Taxes," *Urban Affairs Review* 40 (May 2005): 634–654.

33. Crecine, *Governmental Problem-Solving*, 41.

34. Kenneth Boulding, *The Parameters of Politics* (Urbana: University of Illinois Press, 1966), 10.

35. Crecine, *Governmental Problem-Solving*, 192.

36. John Forrester and Daniel R. Mullins, "Rebudgeting: The Serial Nature of Municipal Budgetary Processes," *Public Administration Review* 52 (September–October 1992): 467.

37. For more on the use of performance in cities, see Janet M. Kelly and William C. Rivenbark, *Performance Budgeting for State and Local Government*, 2nd ed. (Armonk, N.Y.: M.E. Sharpe, 2010).

38. George J. Gordon, *Public Administration in America*, 4th ed. (New York: St. Martin's, 1992), 357.

39. Bryan Downes and Lewis Friedman, "Local Level Decision-Making and Public Policy Outcomes: A Theoretical Perspective," in *People and Politics in Urban Society*, ed. Harlan Hahn (Beverly Hills, Calif.: Sage, 1972), 323.

40. This discussion is drawn from Donald J. Borut, "Implementing PPBS: A Practitioner's Viewpoint," in Crecine, *Financing the Metropolis*, 304.

41. Irene S. Rubin and Lana Stein, "Budget Reform in St. Louis: Why Does Budgeting Change?" *Public Administration Review* 50 (July–August 1990): 426.

42. See Michael Babunakis, *Budgets: An Analytical and Procedural Handbook for Government and Non-profit Organizations* (Westport, Conn.: Greenwood, 1976), chap. 5.

43. Peter A. Pyhrr, *Zero-Base Budgeting* (New York: Wiley, 1973), xii, 5–18.

44. Perry Moore, "Zero-Base Budgeting in American Cities," *Public Administration Review* 40 (May–June 1980): 253–258.

45. Glen H. Cope, "Municipal Budgetary Practices," *Baseline Data Report* 18 (May–June 1986): 5–7.

46. Irene S. Rubin, "Budget Reform and Political Reform: Conclusions from Six Cities," *Public Administration Review* 52 (September–October 1992): 454.

47. Allen Schick, "Micro-Budgetary Adaptations to Fiscal Stress in Industrialized Democracies," *Public Administration Review* 48 (January–February 1988): 532.

48. Stanley B. Botner, "Trends and Developments in Budgeting and Financial Management in Large Cities in the United States," *Public Budgeting and Finance* 9 (autumn 1989): 39.

49. Dan A. Cothran, "Entrepreneurial Budgeting: An Emerging Reform?" *Public Administration Review* 53 (September–October 1993): 445.

50. See Osborne and Gaebler, *Reinventing Government.*

51. Ibid., 4.

52. Eric B. Herzik, "Improving Budgetary Management and Fostering Innovation: Expenditure Control Budgeting," *Public Productivity and Management Review* 14 (spring 1991): 239.

53. Cothran, "Entrepreneurial Budgeting," 446.

54. Herzik, "Improving Budgetary Management," 243.

55. Cothran, "Entrepreneurial Budgeting," 446–447.

56. Bruce E. Benway, *Introduction to Modern Municipal Budgeting* (Orono: Bureau of Public Administration, University of Maine, 1973), 5.

57. For more on budgeting for capital purposes, see Paul L. Solano, "Budgeting," in *Management Policies in Local Government Finance*, 5th ed., ed. J. Richard Aronson and Eli Schwartz (Washington, D.C.: ICMA, 2004), 155–205.

58. Ibid., 358.

59. Meltsner and Wildavsky, "Leave City Budgeting Alone!" 348.

60. Jacob B. Ukeles, *Doing More with Less* (New York: AMACOM, 1982), 87.

61. Daron K. Butler, "Revenue Forecasting and Management," *Public Management*, June 1979, 10–11.

62. Frederick O'R. Hayes, David Grossman, Jerry Mechling, John Thomas, and Steven Rosenbloom, *Linkages: Improving Financial Management in Local Government* (Washington, D.C.: Urban Institute, 1982), chap. 7.

63. The latest array of tools and publications is available at the ICMA website: http://icma.org.

64. See Karl Nollenberger, *Evaluating Financial Condition: A Handbook for Local Government*, 4th ed. (Washington, D.C.: ICMA, 2003).

65. Hayes et al., *Linkages*, 154–155.

66. Ibid., 161–162.

M ANAGING urban America has never been easy. To the many women and men who hold political and administrative positions in cities today, the job must at times seem almost impossible. A host of competing interest groups clamor for their "fair share" of government goods and services. The local tax base in many places is simply inadequate, and both federal and state aid continues to decline. Local taxpayers demand more and better services in return for their hard-earned tax dollars. Many people believe that government is too big and wasteful and needs to be reformed to achieve gains in efficiency and productivity. On the other hand, citizens still look to government to fulfill not only their day-to-day service needs, but also their dreams. According to a recent National League of Cities report entitled *The American Dream in 2004: A Survey of the American People*, "Nearly three-quarters (72 percent) [of the respondents] believe that the government should actively help Americans achieve the 'American Dream'— including 48 percent who believe this strongly."[1] Citizens do expect much from their local leaders. Therefore, the pressures on urban managers have never been greater to provide local services efficiently and effectively while still meeting the political criteria of equity and responsiveness in service delivery.

What does the future hold for our cities and their leaders? Obviously, we cannot know for certain, but there is no doubt that municipal executives will be required to manage and lead. The day-to-day administration of the city necessitates the management of people, programs, money, information, technology—and political conflict. For help in managing the city, city leaders can draw upon their academic and work experiences, as well as a plethora of management strategies, models, programs, leadership styles, and analytic techniques. But, as discussed in chapter 8, today's manager must also manage these management tools. Fads, fancies, and "one best ways" rarely solve the complex human and technical problems that managers face today.

Management skills alone, however, are not enough. City executives must also be leaders. They must envision a future and then offer plans to achieve their visions. They must lead by example, and they must be held accountable for their actions and the actions of other city employees. Moreover, they must provide this management and leadership in an era of scarce fiscal resources. The local manager must also manage *politics and ensure ethical behavior*. Managing urban America requires the formulation, implementation, and evaluation of local policies. These policies allocate values—the very definition of politics.

Also, the local manager must lead without fear or favor when it comes to instilling and promoting ethical behavior in the city. Finally, the modern city executive must manage uncertainty. Today, perhaps more so than at any time in American history, local leaders must be ready to cope with the effects of man-made and natural disasters. Managing the at-risk city requires disaster management knowledge and expertise.

This final chapter serves not as a summary of the previous chapters, although key themes and concepts discussed throughout the book are revisited here. Instead, we offer some final thoughts about managing the urban future in the three critical management areas identified earlier. First, we discuss issues associated with management and leadership, such as managing the politics of scarcity, the job of the urban manager, leadership within the municipal organization, and managing the management process. Next, we examine the politics of managing urban America and discuss administrative ethics. Finally, we look at issues and dilemmas associated with managing disasters.

MANAGEMENT AND LEADERSHIP IN AN AGE OF PERMANENT FISCAL CRISIS

The "politics of scarcity" is hardly a thing of the past. Cities have been through a long period of fiscal austerity, a time of revenue reduction and "belt-tightening" in many places. Although their financial circumstances improved briefly in the mid-1990s, by the beginning of the twenty-first century the cities' fiscal woes had returned. Then in December 2007 the bottom, so to speak, "fell out" and the national economy experienced the worst downturn since the Great Depression. How are cities coping? An article in the *2010 Municipal Year Book* provides some answers.

Based on survey data from the ICMA's State of the Profession 2009 survey, Gerald Miller from Arizona State University outlines the impact of the recession on American cities with populations of 2,500 and more residents and county governments that use an appointed manager.[2] Miller summarizes survey findings thusly: "Sixty-six percent of managers believe that the measures they have taken to mitigate the fiscal crisis—including increased use of fee-supported services and contracting out, reshaped employee benefits and pension systems, limited pay increases, tightened financial management procedures, and reinvigorated economic development efforts—represent a new way of doing business that will continue beyond the fiscal crisis."[3]

This précis seems to answer the question poised by Miller in the title of his article, "Weathering the Local Government Fiscal Crisis: Short-term Measures or Permanent Change?" Perhaps David Osborne and Peter Hutchinson's book published in 2004 entitled *The Price of Government: Getting the Results We Need in an Age of Permanent Fiscal Crisis* was a harbinger of things to come. Osborne and Hutchinson argue that in terms of government we have entered an "age of permanent fiscal crisis."[4]

The local managers responding to the 2009 survey discussed above seem to agree with Osborne and Hutchinson. According to Miller, city executives believe that the "dire fiscal problems" they face "point to permanent, structural budget imbalances."[5] The combination of the post–September 11, 2001, public safety concerns and costs and the major economic recession near the end of the decade pushed municipalities toward a seemingly permanent state of fiscal crisis.

Turbulent times demand creative and innovative solutions. How does one get by with less when the problems are more pressing and complex than ever? According to San Francisco's former mayor, Dianne Feinstein (now a U.S. senator from California), today's urban leaders face problems that their predecessors never dreamed of. America's busiest executives are no longer in the private sector; they are modern mayors, city managers, and other top-level urban officials who are beleaguered by a seemingly infinite variety of issues, problems, and complaints. In Feinstein's words, "Mayors who once worried about clean streets now have to worry about clean air, toxic wastes, controlling development, job training, teenage pregnancy, narcotics, labor relations and, of course, the economic viability of their cities."[6] To this list of worries, we must add disaster response and management, which includes domestic and international terrorism.

What knowledge, skills, and abilities must the top executive possess in order to lead the organization forward in these changing times? It seems important to take a closer look at what the job of the urban manager demands in these days of limited resources, rapid change, and increasing complexity.

THE JOB OF THE URBAN MANAGER

Before examining some of the more specific requirements of the municipal manager's job, we should consider briefly the more general issue of what makes a good executive. In a seminal article published in the *Harvard Business Review* in 1955, Robert Katz argued that effective administrative performance depends on fundamental skills rather than on personality traits.[7] In particular, he states, effective administration rests on the development of three kinds of skills: technical, human, and conceptual. *Technical skill* comprises an understanding of and proficiency in a specific activity involving methods, processes, procedures, or techniques—specialized knowledge, in other words. *Human skill* is the "executive's ability to work effectively as a group member and to build a cooperative effort within the team he [or she] leads." This skill involves not only communicating with others but also setting an example through one's own behavior. Katz also mentions the necessity of creating an atmosphere of approval and security in which subordinates feel free to express themselves, to participate, and to carry out activities without constant supervision. Finally, *conceptual skill* is the ability to see the enterprise as a whole and to understand how it relates to other organizations and to the larger community. Because, in a way, conceptual skill encompasses both technical and human skills, it becomes increasingly critical at the top level of administration. Even if a leader has good technical and human skills, weak conceptual skills may jeopardize the success of the whole organization.

More recently, other ways of perceiving the nature of executive leadership have appeared. One of the best efforts to synthesize empirical studies on leadership comes from

George Barbour Jr. and George A. Sipel, who see effective leadership as growing out of four behaviors: "visioning," communicating the vision, acting on the vision, and caring about people and the organization.

"Vision is based on the beliefs and values that constitute the leader's motivating force for action."[8] Having a vision is one thing; getting employees to share your vision is another. How do executives get employees to internalize shared beliefs? They communicate the beliefs constantly, not only by word but by example. According to Michael Walsh, former CEO of Tenneco Inc. (one of the nation's top diversified industrial companies) and once U.S. attorney for the Southern District of California, visionary leadership requires "communicating [organizational goals] and the need to change to people at all levels of an organization."[9] For example, when Walsh was CEO of Southern Pacific Railroad, he conducted a series of "town meetings" over two months that included virtually every one of the company's approximately 30,000 employees. His talks focused on the company's need to change.

The third behavior, acting on the vision, requires creating conditions under which subordinates are encouraged to work to their full potential. As Roy Pederson, former city manager of Scottsdale, Arizona, comments: "Insist on some values—absolutely and unswervingly. And then get out of the way. Give people a challenge and leeway to move. Let them breathe. Don't get in their way vicariously either by loading the organization down with lots of formal rules and regulations."[10]

The fourth and final behavior of effective leadership, according to Barbour and Sipel, is caring about people and the organization. Caring about people means treating both employees *and* citizens with respect. Employees should be treated in a humane way and not simply as cogs in the organizational machinery. They should be provided a safe work environment and paid a decent wage. They should be empowered and included in the decision-making process. Excellent leaders believe in and take pride in the organization; "they believe that what they and the people who work with them accomplish makes a difference."[11]

LEADERSHIP WITHIN THE MUNICIPAL ORGANIZATION

Is formulating a set of core values—that is, creating a vision—more difficult for a public organization than for a private firm? Some years ago, Kenneth Gold studied ten highly successful organizations, five public and five private.[12] Two noteworthy general characteristics were found to be common to all ten organizations: first, organizational objectives were extremely well articulated and clearly communicated to all levels; and, second, employees believed that their organization was special in some way and were generally proud to be a part of it. Not surprisingly, Gold observed that public agencies had more trouble than private firms in stating a clear and consistent mission. He noted that several federal agencies—for instance, the U.S. Forest Service and the Customs Service—possessed a higher degree of mission awareness than is found in the typical public organization, primarily because their scope of service was relatively narrow. The more diverse the mission, the harder it is to develop and promulgate a sense of shared commitment.

Are there other unusual or special conditions that may influence the role of today's urban manager? As municipalities are forced to become more independent (both programmatically and fiscally) and entrepreneurial, local administrators must become more effective in mobilizing community resources—public, private, and community groups—to solve communitywide problems.[13] The separation of public and private at the local level is breaking down; the operative word now is *interdependence*, a quality that emphasizes the necessity of a collaborative approach to problem solving. City managers must identify strategic partners and learn to form alliances and joint ventures that extend beyond conventional public-private partnerships. The process of negotiating and collaborating with policy actors and concerned citizens outside city hall can take several forms. An increasingly frequent development is some form of service sharing or interlocal agreement, as in the following examples:

- In Wilmington, North Carolina, a public housing authority provides the facilities, while the city provides the staff; they share the cost of providing a recreation program.
- The construction and operation of a fiber-optic communications network was financed through a nonprofit organization created by the City of Austin, the Austin Independent School District, the State of Texas, the University of Texas, and Austin Community College.
- Winnetka, Illinois, shares an attorney with a neighboring city.
- Thornton, Colorado, and nearby Adams County share the cost of an emergency dispatch center.[14]

Shared alliances and joint ventures demand unusual public leadership and entrepreneurial skills.

Who should provide the real leadership that everyone thinks is so crucial in the modern city—the professional manager or the elected official? As we noted in earlier chapters, in the idealized council-manager plan, political and policy leadership resides in the hands of the elected city council members. The manager provides policy advice, of course, but he or she operates behind the scenes so as not to steal the political spotlight from elected officials. Is this concept completely outmoded today? Probably so. Svara's "complementarity model," discussed in chapter 4, posits that policymaking is best conceptualized as a shared activity between elected officials (mayors and council members) and administrators (city managers and local bureaucrats).[15]

Before we leave this discussion of management and leadership in the modern city, we should respond to an important question about the management process itself. Given the wide variety of management and leadership techniques, models, and strategies available, how should local elected and appointed city employees go about choosing which management tools to use?

Public and private managers alike are bombarded with prescriptions about how to solve issues, problems, and concerns if they will only do this or that. They are told that the ills of the city can be cured if they "re"-something—reform, reinvent, reengineer, realign, and/ or rediscover. Once again, as Robert Quinn reminded us in chapter 8, becoming a "master manager" requires the ability to adapt constantly to a fast and ever-changing political environment using *all* of the management and leadership techniques, models, and strategies at our disposal. Once again, let us reiterate, there is no *"one best way" that fits all times, places, and occasions*. Be cautious of those selling a single tool (let us call it "the universal management ratchet") that magically fixes all problems.

MANAGING POLITICS

Some observers have concluded that public administration may be an "occupation, an activity, an applied art—but it is most certainly not a true profession."[16] A former city manager, William Donaldson, prefers to think of the job as a craft heavily steeped in politics, and he contends that the first problem in improving municipal management is to make managers better *politicians*.[17] John Isaacson, who spent decades head-hunting top executives for state and local governments, agrees: "Too much of an emphasis on public policy study and not enough on political survival means that schools have been pumping out a generation of administrators unprepared for life in the big city."[18] He argues that a degree in public administration should include "some combat training" in the meaning and nature of politics. After all, a key task for the local manager is to manage political conflict in the political environment of the local system.

How do we impart the necessary but intangible political skills to future urban administrators? Is it possible to provide post-entry—much less pre-entry—training that can help urban managers to become more successful executive leaders? Astrid Merget, dean of the School of Public and Environmental Affairs at Indiana University, argues for more practitioner-teachers. Many observers urge greater use of internships and practica, where students work on real problems with real public administrators. Sabbaticals for city executives, similar to those available to federal-level members of the Senior Executive Service, might prove useful. Some "flagship" schools, such as Harvard, Berkeley, Michigan, and Princeton, are moving back to a more practical orientation in their public affairs/administration programs.[19] Harvard's use of the case-analysis method for teaching administrative and political skills is well known.

Traditionally, political skills have been learned through experience—in the school of hard knocks. According to former manager Donaldson, political skills can be improved or even developed by taking part in political campaigns.[20] For city managers, this experience might be gained through involvement in school-board or special-district elections, or in state legislative battles; even running for some allegedly nonpolitical office in a church or other organization might approximate Donaldson's recommended firsthand experience of the give-and-take of politics. In some communities, of course, too much active politicking on the part of a city manager would raise eyebrows, so he or she would have to operate with considerable caution and would be well-advised to secure the approval of the city council before plunging into a school-board or legislative election.

Although the value of direct political participation is hard to dispute, it may be possible nonetheless to sketch out some guidelines and suggestions from which even novice administrators might profit. We do know something about political behavior and political institutions, after all. We know, for example, that power is vital to effective political leadership; that bureaucracies in modern society are the depositories of expertise; and that the urban manager who does not understand the importance of external influences on city affairs and does not understand the nature and meaning of politics is doomed to failure.

Administrators must exercise power to implement, defend, and improve controversial programs. Even for programs that are less visible and less controversial, the use of power may be required to ensure success.[21] The skillful use of power greatly enhances an executive's capacity to get things done. Political scientist Norton Long put it in more dramatic terms: "The lifeblood of administration is power."[22]

The politics of urban management may involve power relationships between the local chief executive and three principal constituencies: the city council, the bureaucracy, and a myriad of external groups. In chapter 4, we considered the relationship between the city manager and the city council. Now we examine how the manager can influence the other two constituencies—the bureaucracy and external groups.

We can identify two basic ways to produce bureaucratic change. The first is organization development (OD), whereby outside consultants are brought in and training programs initiated—all to make the workforce more forthright, trusting, and cooperative. The assumption, of course, is that this effort will enable the organization and its individual members to grow, to become more effective in and more adaptable to a rapidly changing environment. In a less formal way, creative leaders can undertake a variety of additional steps, as we saw in chapter 8; they can encourage employee involvement in hopes of producing a more committed and productive workforce.

Another approach to organizational change takes a different tack. It is based on the "theory of economic man": that people do not change their behavior unless it pays them to do so. Articulating this approach in his book, *Inside Bureaucracy*, Anthony Downs assumes that all participants—officials, politicians, citizens, bureau clients—are *utility maximizers*. That is, each person implicitly assigns certain values, preferences, or utilities to various options or courses of action. Each individual then compares utilities and chooses the act or combination of acts that produces the highest total utility.[23] Thus, organizations (and their individual members) are unlikely to change unless the perceived benefits of some new behavior outweigh the costs of the change.[24] Considerable inertia is built into any large organization; existing practices represent a considerable sunk cost—years of effort, thousands of previous decisions, and a wide variety of experiences. Change becomes harder to effectuate in the following circumstances: (1) the deeper the reduction in elements of value to bureaucrats (such as personal or organizational power, prestige, income, and security); (2) the larger the degree of change required; (3) the greater the number of officials affected by the change; and (4) the larger the organization.

Forces that favor bureaucratic change include the following factors:

- *The desire to do a good job.* Bureaucrats who are ambitious or strong advocates of the agency's goals can become dissatisfied with the status quo and propose new ideas and methods.
- *The desire for aggrandizement.* Personal ambition breeds innovation. Bureaucratic expansion may produce gains in power, income, and prestige for individual officials.
- *Self-defense.* Change in an organization is often defensive, a reaction to external pressure.

Despite these forces for change, Downs argues that inertia usually wins out. His major point is that producing change within the organization can be difficult and time consuming. The key to modifying existing behavior, then, is to be sure that individual employees perceive a personal payoff from any proposed change. If people can be *persuaded* that the benefits of a proposed action outweigh its costs, the opportunities for change improve greatly. Indeed, the exercise of influence here would seem to depend on the power of persuasion.

Finally, as systems analysts remind us, the external environment has a significant impact on organizational activities. Debate continues over the extent to which an appointed administrator can openly solicit political support. Yet a classic study of managers in the San Francisco Bay Area revealed that a slight majority of the officials there endorse the idea of advocating policies even when important parts of the community are hostile.[25] Assuming that external support is essential for the success of such policies, how does one go about creating it?

The answer is interpersonal techniques, a battery of methods often used by politically successful strong mayors. The heads of executive-centered coalitions rarely command—instead, they negotiate, bargain, and persuade. They must be the key managers of conflict in their local political system. And today's urban administrators must have the resources to do the same.

First, tremendous political support can be garnered from running a city government effectively. Even the best politicians recognize this fact: the late mayor of Chicago, Richard J. Daley, always insisted that good government was good politics. A second source of support, especially with the city council, is a reputation as a reliable source of information. Credibility is an administrator's stock-in-trade. Policy leadership would be impossible if elected officials and other interested parties could not rely on the manager as a prime source of timely, dependable information. Thus, urban administrators must know their business and their city—knowledge is, indeed, power.

Practitioners Rapp and Patitucci provide some guidelines and suggestions for executives who want to enhance their political influence.[26] The authors acknowledge that, in the last analysis, this skill is best learned by doing. Still, they contend that useful information can be derived from the experience of others, and their advice for getting results when working with various groups includes the following precepts:

1. *Understand the status quo.* It is important—indeed, imperative—to understand the reasons for and the beneficiaries of the existing conditions you are trying to change. Although the benefits are not always obvious on the surface, some person or group profits from the policies, programs, and procedures that now exist and may well resist changing them. Figure out who benefits and why, in order to anticipate opposition.

2. *Recognize power where it exists.* If the change is large, invariably more than one person, group, or institution will be affected. Thus, achieving a desired change will likely depend on putting together the proper coalition. Who has the power to bring others in? Who might have the power to veto a proposed course of action? Following this guideline requires open-mindedness.

3. *Create a sense of due process.* No matter how good an idea is, implementation may be severely undermined if those affected do not perceive the process by which the decision was made as fair. At the least, affected parties must be given a genuine opportunity to be heard; such groups must also believe that their ideas are being received with an open mind.

4. *Understand the importance of timing.* According to Rapp and Patitucci, "Knowing when to push for a decision and when to pull back is a skill that characterizes managers who are consistently able to achieve good performance."[27] Often, of course, it is difficult to persuade people (such as elected officials) to act when no crisis is at hand; this predisposition is reflected in the common saying, "If it ain't broke, don't fix it." Yet there may be times when the manager must try to persuade others that the appropriate time to move on a project is before a crisis hits. How does one know when to push? Experience and judgment are about all that will help here.

5. *Know when to compromise.* Rapp and Patitucci insist that "one of the most oversold and least understood concepts in politics and public management is the notion that getting things done is the art of compromise."[28] They argue that some decisions involve compromise; others do not. Even more problematic, sometimes it may not be clear when or how much compromise is necessary. The authors are surely correct in insisting, however, that compromise should not be the strategy of first resort.

Finally, Rapp and Patitucci maintain that creating external support requires spreading the credit for success, recognizing that change takes time, and understanding the necessity for follow-up (because public decisions are rarely final).

Obviously, initiating and guiding urban change is no easy task. Enacting a policy proposal and seeing it through to a successful conclusion require an enormous talent for making diverse interests work together—a skill that is essential to produce both internal and external change.

One final cautionary note: There are still those who think city managers are not ideally situated to function as community change agents—after all, they are only "hired hands." The community is not really theirs; it belongs to the people, who elect their representatives to provide the basic tone and direction of city government. Remember, too, that many if not most council members still cling to the politics-administration dichotomy. Wise managers move cautiously, avoid the public eye, and give all the credit to the elected political leadership.

ENSURING ETHICAL BEHAVIOR

On taking office, every public servant, elected or appointed, enters into a covenant with the people: that the officeholder will not use her or his position for personal gain. Additionally, public officials must ensure that policymaking and service delivery occur without favoritism or discrimination.

Ethics is hard to define, and some say that, like politics, it is impossible to teach. How, then, are we to proceed? Public administration expert Grover Starling provides some answers. Ethical behavior normally involves a commitment to high moral principles or high standards of professional conduct. Even though there are no absolute standards of right or wrong, Starling insists that ethical behavior can be taught. In fact, he says that learning more about value systems and ethical conduct can have these practical payoffs for the public administrator:

- The study of ethics can *facilitate decision making*. Having wrestled with the value conflicts underlying previous decisions, officials can more readily identify and resolve pending ethical questions.
- A knowledge of ethics can help to *promote greater consistency in decision making*. Reliance on a coherent set of principles engenders respect from employees who see the administrator as fair.
- By studying ethics we can *understand the value dimensions of a decision* that might otherwise appear value-free.
- Grappling with ethical issues comes with the territory of working in the public sector and for the public: *it is the right thing to do.*
- The study of ethics can help public servants to make more reflective decisions.[29]

Finally, an ethical code might operate as another means of ensuring bureaucratic accountability. We can identify various external forces that govern the actions of administrative officials: public opinion, group pressures, professional standards, and, of course, legislative oversight. But an individual's internal norms may play a powerful role as well.

A basic grasp of right and wrong coupled with a firm commitment to the public interest can help to keep public officials on the right track. The ICMA has developed an "ethical climate survey" for local government, including a process for analyzing and acting on the results.[30]

MANAGING THE TWENTY-FIRST CENTURY AT-RISK CITY

Contemporary cities face disasters, both man-made and natural: In 1993 six people died and more than a thousand were injured by an al Qaeda–backed terrorist attack on the World Trade Center in New York City. Two years later, Timothy McVeigh, an American terrorist, bombed the Murrah Federal Building in Oklahoma City, claiming the lives of 168 men, women, and children. In 1996 a pipe bomb exploded in Atlanta's Centennial Park during the Summer Olympics, killing Alice Hawthorne and injuring 100 others. On Tuesday, September 11, 2001, more than 3,000 people, including 343 firefighters and 60 police officers, perished in New York City when terrorists flew hijacked airliners into the World Trade Center towers, and 189 people died as a plane carrying 64 passengers crashed into the Pentagon in Arlington, Virginia. In order to thwart terrorist plans to fly a fourth hijacked plane into the U.S. Capitol, passengers on that flight overtook the terrorists, but their plane, carrying 44 passengers and crew members, crashed in a field in Shanksville, Pennsylvania. In New Haven, Connecticut, a bomb exploded on May 21, 2003, at the Yale Law School; no injuries were reported.[31]

On July 31, 1976, a flash flood killed 139 people in the Big Thompson Canyon in Colorado.[32] The Mount St. Helens volcano eruption in 1980 killed 57 people in the initial explosion. In 1994, 57 people died and property losses of $20 billion—the highest from an earthquake in U.S. history—resulted from the Northridge Earthquake, north of Los Angeles. In August 2005, Hurricane Katrina, a Category 5 hurricane with winds as high as 175 miles per hour, hit the Bahamas, Cuba, South Florida, Mississippi, Alabama, the Florida Panhandle, and greater New Orleans. The devastation was tremendous: an estimated $75 billion in damages (double the cost of Hurricane Andrew in 1992) made Katrina the most expense natural disaster in U.S. history. More important, it caused the deaths of more than 1,800 people in four states. Coupled with the floods resulting from collapsed levees, Hurricane Katrina seemed likely to result eventually, in the words of a *New York Times* editorial, in "the death of an American city"—New Orleans.[33]

As the memories of each of these sad events suggest, the task of managing modern American cities has changed. It is no longer enough to plan for roads, sewers, and convention centers. It is even not enough to plan for natural disasters such as the fires, floods, and tornadoes that have always put the American city at risk. Today, city leaders must also plan for man-made disasters, including the domestic and international terrorism that threatens the health, safety, and security of local residents. And it is important to recognize that all such disasters—both natural and man-made—must be managed as events. As geographer David Alexander reminds us, disasters tend to be repetitive events, forming a cycle that, for purposes of management, can be divided into four phases: mitigation, preparation, response, and recovery (including reconstruction).[34]

As explained by Alexander, the first two phases of emergency management—mitigation and preparation—take place before disaster strikes. *Mitigation* "comprises all actions designed to reduce the impact of future disasters."[35] Conceived and carried out in a quiescent period before a potential disaster looms, mitigation activities include both structural measures that require engineering solutions to promote safety and nonstructural measures such as legislation, insurance, land-use planning, and evacuation plans. *Preparation* "refers to actions taken to reduce the impact of disasters when they are forecast or imminent."[36] Examples of this activity include actual evacuation of vulnerable populations (the poor, the elderly, patients in hospitals and nursing homes), putting in place transportation networks and security, and sandbagging levees as floodwaters rise. Planning for evacuation is mitigation; making sure that the plan is executed and that people get out of harm's way is preparation, or "preparedness."

The next two phases of disaster management—response and recovery—take place during and after a catastrophe hits. *Response* "refers to emergency actions taken during both the impact of a disaster and the short aftermath."[37] The primary goals here are human-related: to save and protect people, to rescue victims, and provide care. *Recovery* is "the process of repairing damage, restoring services, and reconstructing facilities after disaster has stuck."[38] Often, as will be the case in New Orleans, recovery is a long and arduous process. All four phases of disaster management are important. Clearly, one would assume that "responding" to the needs of victims is most important, and, of course, providing for the health and safety of survivors of disaster is paramount. But, if mitigation plans are put in place and executed during the preparedness phase, response efforts will be more successful. There simply is no substitute for careful planning in disaster management.

How well are local managers preparing their cities to manage throughout a disaster? In 2005 the ICMA conducted a survey of city and county managers.[39] The results of this survey of nearly 2,800 local government managers show that over 80 percent of cities have conducted homeland security risk assessments since 9/11. Over 60 percent have developed or amended their comprehensive emergency management plans and over half of these cities conduct emergency drills and train non-first-responders (such as administrative personnel) in disaster preparedness. These managers attach great importance to this type of preparation; indeed, 89 percent of the managers said that a terrorist threat to government buildings was their greatest potential threat.

Disasters represent a real and significant environmental factor that local officials must manage in twenty-first-century cities. Urban scholars John J. Harrigan and Ronald K. Vogel capture the essence of this threat well when they speak of "vulnerable cities."[40] Donald Kettl relays the same sense of urgency and anxiety in the title of his recent book, *System under Stress: Homeland Security and American Politics*.[41] From a systems perspective, effective homeland security requires intergovernmental cooperation and coordination. Or, as the title of a recent General Accountability Office report on homeland security suggests, *Effective Intergovernmental Coordination Is Key to Success*.[42] In a 2005 article in *Governing* magazine, Jonathan Walters and Donald Kettl argue that in the case of Hurricane Katrina, effective coordination and communication between levels of government was lacking: "As Katrina so powerfully illustrated, a fragmented intergovernmental response can be disastrous."[43] In terms of urban management, it is important to remember this rule: "The first step in homeland security [and disaster management in general] . . . is to help civilians who find themselves under attack. This is primarily a job for local governments."[44]

A CALL TO SERVICE

In the final analysis, the real impediment to superior leadership at the local level may be that the very best qualified candidates may eschew public service. Alan Altshuler argues that the real crisis in governance is the inability of governments to lure top people to public-sector jobs, given the low salaries and the loss of privacy they must endure in today's high-profile political arena. "The question is, how do you get first-rate people to put up with this? The amazing thing, really, is that you still see so many terrific people for whom the call of public service is so strong."[45]

No more challenging job exists in today's complex society than that of the urban manager. Only those with a genuine commitment to making the urban world a better place to live need apply.

SUGGESTED FOR FURTHER READING

Box, Richard C. *Citizen Governance: Leading American Communities into the 21st Century*. Thousand Oaks, Calif.: Sage, 1998.
Chrislip, David D., and Carl E. Larson. *Collaborative Leadership: How Citizens and Civic Leaders Can Make a Difference*. San Francisco: Jossey-Bass, 1994.
Denhardt, Janet V., and Robert B. Denhardt. *The New Public Service: Serving, Not Steering*. Expanded edition. Armonk, N.Y.: M. E. Sharpe, 2007.
Schachter, Hindy Lauer. *Reinventing Government or Reinventing Ourselves*. Albany: SUNY Press, 1997.
Vale, Lawrence J., and Thomas J. Campanella. *The Resilient City: How Modern Cities Recover from Disaster*. Oxford: Oxford University Press, 2005.

NOTES

1. National League of Cities, *The American Dream in 2004: A Survey of the American People* (Washington, D.C.: National League of Cities, 2004), 19.

2. N= 8,548. In total, 22 percent of the city and county officials responded.

3. Gerald J. Miller, "Weathering the Local Government Fiscal Crisis: Short-Term Measures or Permanent Change?" *2010 Municipal Year Book* (Washington, D.C.: ICMA, 2010), 33.

4. See David Osborne and Peter Hutchinson, *The Price of Government: Getting the Results We Need in an Age of Permanent Fiscal Crisis* (New York: Basic Books, 2004).

5. Miller, "Weathering the Local Government Fiscal Crisis," 36.

6. Dianne Feinstein, "Who Are the Nation's Busiest Execs? Mayors," *City and State*, November 1987, 12.

7. Robert L. Katz, "Skills of an Effective Administrator," *Harvard Business Review* 33 (January–February 1955): 33–42.

8. George Barbour Jr. and George A. Sipel, "Excellence in Leadership: Public Sector Model," *Public Management* (August 1986): 3–5.

9. Jonathan Walters, "Reinventing Government: Managing the Politics of Change," *Governing*, December 1992, 32.

10. Roy R. Pederson, "Solving the Management Equation," *Public Management*, August 1986, 9.

11. Barbour and Sipel, "Excellence in Leadership," 5.

12. Kenneth A. Gold, "Managing for Success: A Comparison of the Private and Public Sectors," *Public Administration Review* 42 (November–December 1982): 568–575.

13. Jeff S. Luke, "Finishing the Decade: Local Government to 1990," *State and Local Government Review* 18 (fall 1986): 132–137.

14. Penelope Lemov, "In Hard Times, Even Governments Must Share," *Governing*, September 1993, 26.

15. James H. Svara, "The Myth of the Dichotomy: Complementarity of Politics and Administration in the Past and Future of Public Administration," *Public Administration Review* 61 (March–April 2001): 176–183.

16. Richard L. Schott, "Public Administration as a Profession: Problems and Prospects," *Public Administration Review* 36 (May–June 1976): 256.

17. William V. Donaldson, "Continuing Education for City Managers," *Public Administration Review* 33 (November–December 1973): 504–508.

18. Quoted in Jonathan Walters, "Combat Training for the Impossible Job?" *Governing*, July 1993, 56.

19. Jonathan Walters, "Can Innovation Be Taught?" *Governing*, November 1993, 56.

20. Donaldson, "Continuing Education for City Managers," 507.

21. Robert C. Fried, *Performance in American Bureaucracy* (Boston: Little, Brown, 1976), 193.

22. Norton Long, "Power and Administration," *Public Administration Review* 9 (winter 1949): 257.

23. Anthony Downs, *Inside Bureaucracy* (Boston: Little, Brown, 1967), 81.

24. This discussion comes from ibid., chapter 16.

25. Ronald O. Loveridge, *City Managers in Legislative Politics* (Indianapolis: Bobbs-Merrill, 1971), 49.

26. Brian Rapp and Frank Patitucci, *Managing Local Government for Improved Performance* (Boulder, Colo.: Westview, 1977), 336–344.

27. Ibid., 340.

28. Ibid., 341.

29. Grover Starling, *Managing the Public Sector*, 7th ed. (Belmont, Calif.: Wadsworth, 2005), 192–193.

30. ICMA, "Take the Ethical Climate Survey," *Public Management* 81 (May 1999): 23–25.

31. This information is taken from Donald F. Kettl, *System under Stress: Homeland Security and American Politics* (Washington, D.C.: CQ Press, 2004), chapter 1; CNN Interactive, "Blast Victim's Family Asks for Privacy," July 28, 1996, at www.cnn.com/US/9607/28/blast.victim/index.html; CNN Interactive, "Let the World Not Forget," July 27, 1997, at www.cnn.com/US/9707/27/olympic.bombing/index.html; CNN.com, "Bomb Explodes at Yale Law School," May 22, 2003, at www.cnn.com/2003/US/Northeast/05/21/yale.explosion.

32. Unless otherwise noted, incident information comes from case studies reported in William L. Waugh Jr., *Living with Hazards, Dealing with Disasters: An Introduction to Emergency Management* (Armonk, N.Y.: M. E. Sharpe, 2000), chapters 3 and 4.

33. "Death of an American City," *New York Times*, December 11, 2005, A22.

34. David Alexander, *Principles of Emergency Planning and Management* (Oxford: Oxford University Press, 2002), 5.

35. Ibid.

36. Ibid.

37. Ibid.

38. Ibid.

39. ICMA, "Homeland Security 2005," http://icma.org/upload/bc/attach/{5F901D0C-9C2F-486C-8F15-EB7E844DA8F1}homelandsecurity2005web.pdf.

40. John J. Harrigan and Ronald K. Vogel, *Political Change in the Metropolis*, 7th ed. (New York: Longman, 2003), 3.

41. Kettl, *System under Stress*.

42. Patricia A. Dalton, *Effective Intergovernmental Coordination Is Key to Success* (Washington, D.C.: United States General Accounting Office, August 20, 2002).

43. Jonathan Walters and Donald Kettl, "The Katrina Breakdown," *Governing*, December 2005, 25.

44. See Kettl, *System under Stress*, 10; and Donald F. Kettl, "Connecting the Dots," *Governing*, October 2002, 14.

45. Walters, "Reinventing Government," 40.

INDEX